SAVING GERMANY

McGill-Queen's Studies in the History of Religion
Volumes in this series have been supported by the Jackman Foundation of Toronto.

Series One: G.A. Rawlyk, Editor

Series Two In memory of George Rawlyk
Donald Harman Akenson, Editor

SAVING GERMANY

North American Protestants and Christian Mission
to West Germany, 1945–1974

James C. Enns

McGill-Queen's University Press
Montreal & Kingston | London | Chicago

© McGill-Queen's University Press 2017

ISBN 978-0-7735-4912-8 (cloth)
ISBN 978-0-7735-4913-5 (paper)
ISBN 978-0-7735-4914-2 (ePDF)
ISBN 978-0-7735-4915-9 (ePUB)

Legal deposit first quarter 2017
Bibliothèque nationale du Québec

Printed in Canada on acid-free paper that is 100% ancient forest free
(100% post-consumer recycled), processed chlorine free

McGill-Queen's University Press acknowledges the support of the
Canada Council for the Arts for our publishing program. We also
acknowledge the financial support of the Government of Canada
through the Canada Book Fund for our publishing activities.

LIBRARY AND ARCHIVES CANADA CATALOGUING IN PUBLICATION

Enns, James, 1959–, author
Saving Germany : North American Protestants and Christian mission
to West Germany, 1945–1974 / James C. Enns.

(McGill-Queen's studies in the history of religion. Series two ; 77)
Includes bibliographical references and index.
Issued in print and electronic formats.
ISBN 978-0-7735-4912-8 (cloth). – ISBN 978-0-7735-4913-5 (paper). –
ISBN 978-0-7735-4914-2 (ePDF). – ISBN 978-0-7735-4915-9 (ePUB)

1. Protestant churches – Missions – Germany (West) – History – 20th
century.   2. Protestants – Germany (West) – History –20th century.
3. Evangelicalism – Germany (West) – History – 20th century.
4. Missions, Canadian – Germany (West) – History – 20th century.
5. Missions, American – Germany (West) – History – 20th century.
I. Title.   II. Series: McGill-Queen's studies in the history of religion.
Series two ; 77

BV2440.E46 2017   266'.443   C2016-906400-X
                                   C2016-906401-8

Set in 10.5/13.5 Minion Pro with Gill Sans Nova Condensed
Book design & typesetting by Garet Markvoort, zijn digital

In loving memory of and dedicated to my dad and mom,

Cornie and Kay Enns

CONTENTS

ACKNOWLEDGMENTS

In bringing such a project to completion I am humbled by the many people who have supported and, in a variety of ways, assisted me during the researching, writing, and editing of this book. At the risk of overlooking some, I want to express my deep appreciation and gratitude to a number of people who were especially helpful to me during this decade-long undertaking. It is appropriate to begin with the person who "discipled" me through the dissertation phase of my research and writing of the book, my long-suffering supervisor, Brian Stanley. Brian's scholarly insight, patient advising, meticulous editing, gracious critique, and generous and timely encouragement all served to bring my ideas and arguments to fruition when I was writing this initially as a doctoral dissertation. He taught me what it means to be a dedicated scholar and master of one's craft. Beyond his faithfulness and skill as my academic supervisor, it was through his kindness and hospitality that he became a caring mentor and a friend.

In making the transition from dissertation to publishable monograph, my editor at McGill-Queen's University Press, Kyla Madden, has been a great encourager, timely advisor, and loyal advocate in shepherding this neophyte writer through the process of getting the manuscript presentable for publication. Thank you, Kyla, for believing in the project and encouraging me along each step of the way. Thanks also to two of my students, Nicolle and Zachery, who proofread early drafts of the manuscript.

A whole host of librarians, archivists, and mission-office staff gave generously of their time and expertise in directing me to the right resources. These include Bob Shuster and his staff at the Billy Graham Center Archives; Taffey Hall and Bill Summers at the Southern Baptist

Historical Library and Archives; Betty Layton and Deborah Bingham Van Broekhoven at the American Baptist Historical Society and Archives (in Valley Forge at the time); Dennis Stoeze at the Mennonite Church USA Historical Committee and Archives; Martha Smalley at the Yale Divinity School Library; and Werner Beyer at the Deutsche Evangelische Allianz-haus in Bad Blankenburg. Janine van Vliet worked as my proxy at the Presbyterian Historical Library in Philadelphia for several days in order to find and photocopy material on the Church World Service. Andreas Sigrist provided the same service for me on short notice at the United Church of Canada Archives in Toronto. Key missionary staff who gener-ously made their office files available to me include Jack Stenekes and Bob Janz of Janz Team Ministries (now TeachBeyond), and Bill Sundstrom at the European headquarters of Campus for Christ. Without their expertise and attention I would never have discovered the quality resources that made this project feasible.

Important financial support for travel and research came from grants from St Edmund's College, Cambridge; the Southern Baptist Historical Society; and Teach Beyond. I am grateful to my employer, Prairie College, for granting me a full-year sabbatical and two years of study leave in order carry out my research at Cambridge University, and then in creating the necessary flexibility in my teaching schedule to make numerous research trips to Germany thereafter.

I am deeply grateful for the friendship and support of folks I got to know while at Cambridge. Special thanks to Stephen, Fiona, and Pat for their support, and to the members of that elite graduate student histor-ical society, the Venerable Bedeian Tearoom Gang: Todd, Michael, Phil, Ethan, and David.

Closer to home, many thanks to my colleagues – current and past – at Prairie College who were especially supportive and helpful. Special thanks to Myron Penner, for first encouraging me to go down this road; Michael Pahl, for being a caring fellow pilgrim on the dissertation trail; Jan van Vliet, whose steady support kept me from discouragement; Doug-las Lewis, who helped me keep the end in view; and Mark Maxwell and Glenn Loewen for acting as head cheerleaders down the home stretch. The librarians of the T.S. Rendall Library, Veronica Lewis and Bill Nyman, de-serve medals for their faithfulness in tracking down and securing obscure sources from distant institutions through inter-library loan. Their service was invaluable. Also a special thanks to the congregation at St Barnabas

Anglican Church for their support and encouragement during my years in the dissertation wilderness as well as when entering the "promised land" of publication. As fellow members of the Circle, Phil, Ron, and Vance helpfully reminded me that there is more to life than scholarly pursuit.

Special thanks go to two people who launched and then helped sustain this project: first to Ernie Hodges, whose friendship and generous financial support turned this venture from being mere wishful thinking into a reality. His gracious investment in my research provided me the privilege of studying under a world-class scholar at one of the world's leading universities. And to George Durance, whose words of encouragement and whose belief in the value of my research helped me through some of the most difficult periods.

Finally, I could never have considered undertaking such a demanding project – with long periods of time spent away from home – without the faithful and selfless support of my family, both from the living and recently deceased. My siblings David and Carol, my recently deceased brother Lauren, and parents Cornie and Kay deserve particular thanks for cheering me on. My daughters Kathryn (and son-in-law Aaron), Simone, and Camille deserve special honour and gratitude for allowing their dad to go off to England to study for two years. The highest honour, of course, goes to Anne, my wife, whose constancy, critical insight, and patient love were indispensable both in completing my doctoral studies and bringing this manuscript to publication. Words can only begin to express my gratitude and love for you.

Cartographers who are called on to map out previously uncharted territory provide a set of landmarks and reference points that make the terrain navigable for those who follow. While in the main their notations make future journeys safe and successful for others, it can turn out that some of the finer byways and later discovered points-of-interest were either overlooked or not as clearly demarcated as later travellers would have wanted. Such is the case in venturing into new historiographic terrain. In spite of the fact that this effort is necessarily selective and not comprehensive in telling the story of missionary efforts in Cold War Germany, I trust that my initial map will prove to be a fair, accurate, and helpful guide for others who wish to explore the terrain for themselves.

James C. Enns
June 2016

ABBREVIATIONS

AB	*Allianz Brief*
ABHSA	American Baptist Historical Society and Archives
ABFMS	American Baptist Foreign Mission Society
ABR	American Baptist Relief
ADEA	Archives of the Deutsche Evangelische Allianz
ALA	Angus Library Archives
AMG	American Military Government
BGCA	Billy Graham Center Archives
BGEA	Billy Graham Evangelistic Association
BWA	Baptist World Alliance
BWA-RC	Baptist World Alliance Records Collection
CC	*Christian Century*
CfC	Campus Crusade for Christ
CM	Crusade Manual (Billy Graham crusades – ADEA)
CCM	*Canadian Churchman*
CRALOG	Council of Relief Agencies Licensed for Operations in Germany
CWS	Church World Service
DCO-CfCE	Records of the Communications Director's Office, Campus Crusade for Christ, Europe
DEA	Deutsche Evangelische Allianz
DEk	Deutsche Evangelistenkonferenz
DMF	*Der Menschenfischer*
DP	displaced person

EA	Evangelische Allianz (Swiss)
EAB	*Evangelisches Allianzblatt*
EBF	European Baptist Federation
EKD	*Evangelische Kirche in Deutschland*
EMBS	European Mennonite Bible School
ERN	European Relief Notes
FCC	Federal Council of Churches
HICOG	High Commissioner's Office for Germany
IBTS	International Baptist Theological Seminary
ICOWE	International Congress on World Evangelization (Lausanne 1974)
JTM	Janz Team Ministries
JTMW	Janz Team Ministries, Winnipeg office
JTMRR	Janz Team Ministries Records Room (Kandern, Germany)
LWR	Lutheran World Relief
MCC	Mennonite Central Committee
MCCAC, AMC	Mennonite Central Committee Archives Collection, Archives of the Mennonite Church – USA
NCC-CWS, PHS	National Council of Churches – Church World Service, Presbyterian Historical Society
RAS	Religious Affairs Section
SBHLA	Southern Baptist Historical Library and Archives
SBC-FMB	Southern Baptist Convention – Foreign Mission Board
UCO	*United Church Observer*
UEA	*United Evangelical Action*
USNA	United States National Archives
WCC	World Council of Churches
WRS	War Relief Service (Roman Catholic)
YFC	Youth for Christ
YFCM	*Youth for Christ Magazine*

SAVING GERMANY

Saving Germany: Not Your Typical Mission Field

In 1942, as the tide of the Second World War began to turn against the Axis powers, Rev. Adolf Keller, a professor on the faculty of the University of Geneva and an active promoter of the emerging World Council of Churches (WCC), began looking ahead to the postwar needs of Western Europe.[1] As a Swiss citizen and resident, he could see the devastation of the war without being caught up in it. He also had travelled extensively in the United States, preaching to congregations on behalf of the Federal Council of Churches (FCC), and had sensed the growing missionary interest in Europe by American Christians.[2] From this dual vantage point he anticipated the profound needs of postwar Europe and at the same time recognized that America possessed the material resources and spiritual zeal to address those needs. Writing with prophetic insight three years before the end of the war, he described the carnage that would remain once the guns were silenced: a displaced army of refugees made up of widows, orphans, and the unemployed would cover Europe like a plague of locusts. "The heart of Europe will be … burnt out, swept empty, and filled with a nostalgia for a new content. It will take years to clean up the ruins of a broken culture."[3] He went on to note that restoring provisional economic and political order would be relatively simple. The task of restoring the moral fabric and healing the spiritual wounds of Europe would be much more daunting. "But who will comfort the bitter and despairing souls and heal them? Who will be able to minister to the affliction and moral sickness of a Continent filled with broken hearts and nations? Who will re-educate a young generation which has thrown away former values and sits in a dark vacuum?"[4]

He then turned his attention on the United States, a country he saw as the source of postwar material aid, but also as possessing the Christian vitality and missionary vision to offer spiritual aid. Keller was at once hopeful and wary, as he envisioned two possible results of such an American missionary enterprise: "Must we expect a mission from powerful Churches trying to save and deliver the Continental soul from its European sickness, and to heal it with a new vigorous and inspiring gospel of their own? Or will Europe have to face a cultural and educational campaign bringing the 'American Century' to the European centuries, educating them for the new democracy?"[5]

In laying out these alternatives, Keller understood the two divergent currents in American Protestantism and its modern missionary expression. The first alternative, and definitely the preferable one, in his judgment, was an American missionary witness that worked within the larger context of an emerging Protestant ecumenism, with its cultural excesses tempered by international influences. The latter option was a form of revivalist Christianity associated with American fundamentalism and married to a set of socio-political ideals peculiar to the American cultural experience. Keller was concerned that this kind of missionary expression of Manifest Destiny might very well do more harm than good if it became the dominant posture of American Protestants toward Europe after the war.

While accurately predicting the rise of the North American missionary involvement in postwar Europe, Keller erred in casting it as an either/or option. The history of Protestant missions from North America to Europe after the Second World War, and to Germany in particular, saw both the ecumenical and evangelical impulses at work in the dual tasks of offering humanitarian relief and spiritual renewal. The range of these Protestant missionary responses to postwar Germany from across the Atlantic is the subject of this book.

At first glance, such a response appeared neither new nor surprising. The transnational flow of Christian revivalists and church workers between anglophone and German communities dated back to the previous century.[6] After the Second World War, however, the reason for such traffic, especially from North America to Germany, changed significantly. Up until the rise of the Third Reich – the relational strains created by the First

World War notwithstanding – transatlantic denominational ties, as well as more informal networks created by shared concern for mission work and spiritual renewal, allowed Protestants in Germany and North America to view each other as partners in a common cause. While Germany could claim historical primacy as the birthplace and traditional heartland of the Reformation, Protestants on both sides of the ocean saw each other as allies in the task of spreading the Christian message in their respective homelands as well as in "missionary lands."[7] By 1945, however, the views of North American Protestants toward Germany had been coloured by Nazi atrocities and Germany's role as instigator of another world war.

Once the guns fell silent and the wretched state of Germany's postwar condition began to emerge, North American Protestant churches were quick to adopt Keller's perspective and respond to both the spiritual and material needs of the German people, alongside those of the European peoples who had been victims of Nazi aggression. As Keller's musings implied, Protestants were not of one mind when defining the nature and scope of the mission to save Germany, and their responses varied widely, based on their perceptions of what sort of nation Germany had become in the wake of Nazi totalitarian rule: was Nazism an aberration that only a revived German Protestant church could address in order to restore Germany to her place in Christendom; or was the religious legacy of Nazism such that postwar Germany was in actuality a post-Christian nation in need of re-evangelizing with the help of missionaries from abroad? As will be evident in the following chapters, North American Protestants who favoured the first approach supported the Christian internationalist vision of the emerging ecumenical movement. These Protestants, such as Keller himself, tended to be members of churches whose roots lay in the magisterial Reformation and/or that supported the ecumenism of the newly formed World Council of Churches. Supporters for the latter approach tended to come from the ranks of conservative evangelicals associated with the fundamentalist movement, and from those who belonged to denominations descended from the Radical Reformation.

The missionary response of North American Protestants to Germany's plight was also intertwined with the new geopolitical face of postwar Europe. As the barrier between Western democratic countries and those under the domination of the USSR became more sharply defined, the mission to Germany included an ideological dimension that frequently conflated spiritual goals with saving the country from the clutches of

Communism. Thus the Protestant mission was caught up in the ideological battles that defined Cold War relations between the United States and the USSR.

This book analyzes and assesses the role of North American Protestant churches, as well as relief and mission agencies that participated in the reconstruction and spiritual rehabilitation of West Germany, with particular emphasis on the period from 1945 to 1974. While the records from the above agencies are often fragmentary and episodic, a coherent narrative emerges whose wider significance can be assessed when seen in the context of major political and religious developments in both Germany and North America during the early decades of the Cold War up to 1974.[8] The selection of this year as the termination point for this study is twofold: first, 1974 was the year of a landmark missionary conference, the International Congress on World Evangelization held in Lausanne, Switzerland. The congress was significant for Protestant missions in general because it signalled that even conservatives were beginning to abandon the traditional Western missionary view of the globe. This traditional view divided the world into two categories: countries that were part of Christendom and countries that were "missionary lands."[9] At Lausanne, congress delegates affirmed that "the dominant role of western missions is fast disappearing," and that the missionary task was now a global one, thus making the division anachronistic.[10] This affirmation acted as a vindication for North American missionaries working in Germany during the postwar period whose very presence in that country illustrated the changing paradigm. Therefore, 1974 represents a watershed for North American Protestant missions in the Cold War era, both in Germany and more generally.

Second, the mid-1970s also marked a period in which the value of both the American and Canadian dollar went into sharp decline vis-à-vis the Deutschmark, resulting in a significant retrenchment of resources and personnel by North American mission agencies operating in Germany. While missionary activity in Germany did not cease after 1974, mission agencies, as will be shown in chapter 6, were forced to adjust to the new operating realities, which frequently included a reduction of personnel. The postwar decades up to 1974 therefore are the period during which the major missionary themes that defined the Cold War era were most prominent. Nevertheless, the book's sixth chapter will pay some attention to the period from 1974 to 1989, in which these themes reached their denouement.

The Significance of the Mission to Germany: Four Historiographical Contexts

The narrative of North American Protestant humanitarian and missionary involvement in West Germany during the Cold War is a complex story that straddles four overlapping historiographical fields of research: (1) the field of North American Christian missionary and humanitarian work during the postwar period, specifically in Germany; (2) the field of international relations in Cold War Europe; (3) the history of postwar German Protestantism; and (4) the history of Western Europe's shifting religious identity as it continued its transition from the lingering notion of Christendom to some form of post-Christian society. In order to understand the wide-reaching significance of the North American missionary work in Germany, it is important to see how it connects to each of these fields, and in doing so breaks new historiographical ground in each one.

North American Christian Missionary and Humanitarian Work in Postwar Germany

The largest body of literature on early American humanitarian and religious involvement in Germany has been written by military-diplomatic historians. In their accounts, most of these scholars have acknowledged the efforts of the American Military Government (AMG) to address the religious needs of the German people through the establishment of its Educational and Religious Affairs Branch. Others have dealt with the humanitarian challenges of handling the massive influx of refugees from Eastern Europe, but none of these historians has paid attention to the role of American religious agencies in addressing these challenges.[11] German historians have also contributed an indigenous perspective on American humanitarian work, but here again, the specifically religious dimension of that work is overlooked.[12] Cultural historians such as Richard Pells, Alexander Stephen, and Mary Nolan have written insightfully on the themes of Americanization and anti-Americanism in Germany from the early postwar period through the later Cold War decades, and although their work addresses a wide range of cultural issues, they have ignored questions related to religion and the role of religious institutions and agencies as part of this cross-cultural interaction.[13]

The most informative historical accounts of North American Protestant involvement in the German relief effort have chronicled the work of specific denominational agencies. Richard Pierard and Dana Albaugh have researched the work of American Baptists under the auspices of the Baptist World Alliance (BWA).[14] In the same vein, Mennonite, Lutheran, and Quaker historians have also produced accounts of their respective denominational relief organizations, as has the World Council of Churches.[15] While a number of these accounts are carefully researched, in each case little context is provided as to the wider activity of Protestant relief and mission work taking place in Germany at the time.

Historians of the North American mainline churches have also written about the missionary work of these churches, as it relates to Europe. William Hutchison, and to a lesser degree, Grant Wacker, have written critically and candidly about the trajectory of mainline missionary work in the twentieth century.[16] While Germany never became a mission field for the mainline churches in the way it would for conservative evangelicals, both Hutchison and Wacker give passing reference to the cooperation of American churches with their European counterparts through the WCC.[17]

Accounts that document the work of conservative evangelical transdenominational mission agencies are not so much concerned with critical historical analysis and reflection as they are with informing and inspiring an already supportive readership. Little mention is made of humanitarian and relief aspects of addressing Germany's needs, as these mission agencies focused primarily on evangelism and church work.[18] A second characteristic of these accounts is a tendency to treat missionary activity in Germany as a regional variation of missionary work in Europe as a whole. For these North American writers, Europe is a collective mission field in need of evangelizing, and as such is treated as a multilingual, yet uniformly spiritually needy entity.[19]

From this overview it is evident that in the historiography of North American involvement in postwar relief and reconstruction work in Germany, as well as its spiritual rehabilitation, little attention has been paid to the role of mission agencies in these efforts. One of the purposes of this book is to address this omission by describing and explaining the role played by Protestant mission agencies in relief and reconstruction in Germany after the Second World War. In doing so it will be evident that this investment in relief and reconstruction would go on to become a central missional characteristic of an emerging ecumenical Protestant internationalism.

By examining an array of mission agencies that represent a fuller and more complete picture of Protestant missionary activity in postwar

Germany, this description moves beyond existing celebratory and single mission agency treatments. Such an approach also reveals a critical shift that occurred in Protestant missionary thinking as a result of the mission to Germany. Missionary participation in spiritual rehabilitation, humanitarian relief, and Christian education in the wider context of Germany's reconstruction led to a shift in the way in which some sections of the American church understood the missionary enterprise more generally. The mission to Germany brought to the surface a growing rift that had been developing in Protestant missionary circles for much of the interwar period.[20] Protestants who supported the new ecumenical expression of Christianity represented by the formation of the World Council of Churches increasingly moved away from the traditional twin missionary priorities of "evangelizing and civilizing" that had dominated their work to this point. The new priority for supporters of ecumenical Protestantism was a form of Christian internationalism based on respect for indigenous cultures, including their religious practices. Thus the key task of missions was no longer to convert people to a form of Christianity in which evangelizing and civilizing went hand-in-hand. Instead the new priority for ecumenical Protestants was assisting needy Christians in foreign lands toward self-help, leaving the specific task of Christian proclamation to indigenous believers. Their participation in the massive reconstruction effort to supposedly civilized Germany was instrumental in causing ecumenical Protestants to alter their traditional belief that Christian mission was inextricably linked to the cultural trappings of Western civilization. Germany, and to a lesser degree the rest of Western Europe, became a primary object of North American missionary endeavour, and as a result of their mission to "civilized" Germany, North American missions associated with ecumenical Protestantism largely abandoned the vocabulary of evangelism and civilization for the more malleable and broadly humanitarian concept of self-help.[21]

In making this argument I am suggesting that the humanitarian emphasis of some North American missions to postwar Germany foreshadowed wider trends in Protestant ecumenical internationalism. I also argue that the ongoing relationship between North American missions and German Protestants during the Cold War reflected the more general bifurcation taking place in Christian internationalism. North American churches and mission agencies committed to the ecumenical movement saw their task in Germany as finished by the mid-1950s, once the *Wirtschaftswunder* was well under way.[22] In contrast, conservative evangelical North American missionaries whose agenda was principally to convert Germans to an evangelical understanding of Christianity, remained active well into the 1970s, by which decade Christian internationalism was seriously divided between the advocates of Third World humanitarian development, or liberation, and the apostles of global conversion.

Thus, the mission to Germany acted as a kind of missiological laboratory for ecumenical Protestants, as it represented an initial experiment in the shift away from the traditional understanding of missions toward a new vision of Christian internationalism. In doing so, this book not only brings to light a relatively unexplored narrative in Protestant missions – the mission to Germany – but also shows that this event was a watershed in North American Protestant missionary theory and practice.

International Relations in Cold War Europe

The role of Christian mission in the ideological struggle against Communism in Western Europe has been little explored by historians. Current historiography has shown the importance of religious rhetoric in American foreign policy in advancing its ideological goals during the Cold War. Mark Silk, Jonathan P. Herzog, and Robert Jewett, among others, have produced insightful works on the relationship between the revivalist rhetoric of American Christianity and the anti-Communist rhetoric of American foreign policy during the Cold War.[23] Walter Russell Mead and Walter McDougall have shown that this syncretism of missionary zeal with the goal of making the world "safe for democracy" has characterized American foreign policy since Woodrow Wilson's presidency.[24]

More recently, Axel Schäfer and Andrew Preston have shown that conservative evangelicals who served in the US government during the Cold War decades were influential in developing American foreign policy along lines compatible with their theological understanding of the world.[25] Their focus has not been on the role of American missionaries abroad so much as it has been on conservative evangelicals who worked in political institutions at home. Gerhard Besier and Konrad Jarausch have provided a German perspective on the ideological and sociological dynamics at work in early postwar Germany that were significant in shaping the efforts of American ecumenical Protestants to promote democracy as a deterrent to Communism.[26] While not dealing directly with Protestant missionaries, all three of these works provide a helpful political and ideological context for examining the role played by North American missionaries who ventured to "save Germany" from the ideological threat of Communism.

This book examines this relatively unexplored aspect of America's Cold War activity by assessing the degree to which North American missionaries carried this same, tightly culturally bound package of political ideology and Christian gospel with them as they worked in West Germany, which had now become the vulnerable eastern edge of democratic Europe during the Cold War. Among the nations of Western Europe, Germany in particular was a flashpoint for ideological tensions between the two Cold War superpowers. Not only was the political division of Germany a constant reminder of these ideological differences, but the ubiquitous presence of NATO troops also indicated that West Germany was an endangered area, under imminent threat of Communist encroachment should the guardians of Western democracy cease to be vigilant. John Foster Dulles, American secretary of state under President Eisenhower, elevated his country's foreign policy of containing Communism and promoting the spread of democratic liberalism to a divinely ordained mandate of a Christian nation.[27] It was a policy that he described in religious language, thereby making America's international role synonymous with Christian mission.[28]

It is important to clarify that the understanding of Communism among Protestant missionaries was not uniform. While Dulles, whose ecclesial roots were in the Protestant mainline, espoused a hard-line position in confronting Communism in Europe, ecumenical missionaries from the same ecclesial camp took an increasingly divergent view. Ecumenical missionaries were not opposed to the socialist economic practices of Communism but rather to its threat to political and religious freedom.[29] Consequently their missionary efforts in Germany, as will be seen in chapter 1, emphasized democracy as the best way to combat any reversion to political tyranny – be it in the form of Nazism or Communism. At the same time they championed a more conciliatory stance toward the Communist governments of Soviet-dominated Eastern Bloc countries, believing that such a dual strategy – promoting democracy in a recovering West Germany while seeking rapprochement with Communist Soviet Bloc governments – was the best way of practising an internationalism that realistically promoted long-term peace and security and simultaneously supported religious freedom of those in Communist lands.[30]

For conservative evangelical missionaries, Communism was seen as an enemy to Christianity on a number of levels, but primarily because it was a rival religion of state-enforced atheism. This view was widely popularized in conservative Protestant circles by Fred Schwarz in the 1960s, but, as will be evident in chapter 3, was already being articulated by missionaries early in the postwar period.[31] From this flowed a derivative set of evils: Darwinian evolution and the loss of personnel freedoms that formed the core values of democratic capitalism, which for many conservative evangelicals was the political system most compatible with Christian beliefs. Thus for them, Communism was a rival religion that needed to be engaged not solely on spiritual terms but also on political-ideological ones.

Among denominational missionary organizations there was no clear single approach. Baptists tended to steer more closely to the conservative evangelical view, but at the same time, in an effort to support their denominational kindred in the countries of Communist Europe, they were also in sympathy with the internationalist approach of ecumenical Protestants. Mennonites, whose wariness about government intrusion of any sort into religious life, were more inclined to adopt a similar view toward Communism as their ecumenical counterparts. Communism tended to be a threat to the religious freedom of private individuals; its socialist economic ideals, however, actually resonated strongly with traditional Mennonite communitarian practices and were thus not seen as conflicting with democratic freedom.

In examining the ways in which missionaries promoted democratic freedoms, I argue that during the early postwar period North American Protestant missionaries were in fact integral to the task of rescuing Western Europe from the variously perceived threats of Communism.

By the 1960s and 1970s German public attitudes toward America became increasingly critical. This change was due in large part to the American Cold War strategy to check the spread of Communism through ongoing nuclear weapons production and an escalating military presence in Vietnam. During these decades, whenever American Christian missions were unable to separate their Christian witness from their country's foreign policies, the effectiveness of their missionary efforts was clearly limited. Conversely, whenever Protestant missionaries were able to translate their warnings about the Communist threat into a broader concern about an increasingly visible secularism, they were able to forge constructive working partnerships with like-minded German Christians, thus making their message seem less ideologically American. In doing so, they also received a more receptive hearing from the German populace who continued to be attracted to missionary activities that borrowed heavily from elements of American popular culture to which Germans were attracted. Analyzed in this light, my work adds a new dimension to the historiography of American international relations in Cold War Europe.

The German Protestant Church in the Postwar Decades

Before proceeding, it is important to address the issue of terminology when writing about German Protestant churches. Historians of German Protestantism tend to use the terms *Landeskirche, Volkskirche,* or *Evangelische Kirche in Deutschland* (EKD) interchangeably when referring to the established, state-church in Germany.[32] For the sake of simplicity and consistency, I have opted to use only the two terms, *Landeskirchen* and EKD – the former when referring to the historic Protestant church in each of the German Länder, and the latter when referencing the postwar national church as a whole.

The historiographical record of German Protestantism falls into two broad institutional categories: accounts of the *Landeskirchen,* which dominate the scholarly landscape, and those of the *Freikirchen,* the much smaller group of independent churches that existed outside of the EKD orbit (see below for a further description of these churches). By analyzing and assessing the role of North American missionaries across the spectrum of German Protestant church life, a fuller picture emerges as the nature and extent of missionary involvement. This can be seen by looking at North American missionary work in three broad areas: (1) the scope and significance of the mission to the *Landeskirchen;* (2) the scope and impact of the mission work among the *Freikirchen;* and (3) the important role played by North American missionaries in developing and nurturing a new trans-denominational identity among German Protestants, known as the *Evangelikaler* movement, which helped build bridges between the two ecclesial camps.

While much has been written about the history of the *Landeskirchen* under the Nazi regime, scholarly work on the postwar recovery of the churches has received noticeably less attention. Most of the studies in this smaller body of material have coalesced around three dominant themes: (1) the process of church reconstruction and institutional rebuilding;

(2) the development of early postwar relationships by the EKD with both the AMG and the WCC; and (3) the efforts of the *Landeskirchen* to address issues of war-guilt and anti-Semitism.[33] Historians largely have treated these themes singly in their analyses of the postwar recovery of German Protestantism, with North Americans appearing on the margins as supporting players. None have shown how the involvement of North American Protestants simultaneously in all three areas can be seen as part of a concerted missionary response to the needs of the *Landeskirchen*. By viewing the work of North American Protestants through such a wide-angle lens, which examines all facets their interactions with members of the *Landeskirchen*, this book moves beyond the siloed thematic approach of the historiography to give a more complete understanding of the role played by North Americans in the recovery and reintegration of the *Landeskirchen* into the international community of ecumenical Protestantism.

My examining lens becomes even wider by considering the impact of North American missionaries on the *Freikirchen*. Little historical research has been done on the work and influence of North American Protestants among the smaller German church groups known as the *Freikirchen*, which were the independent denominations of German Protestantism.[34] Two scholars who have examined the role of these smaller groups operating on the margins of the German Protestant spectrum are Erich Geldbach and Jörg Ohlemacher. However, similar to their *Landeskirchen* counterparts, they make little or no mention of the role of North American Protestants in the reconstruction and recovery of these churches in the postwar period. As such, the material presented in this book adds an as yet unexplored dimension to the story of German Protestantism during a significant period of re-formation and recovery after the destructiveness of Nazism.

North American churches and mission agencies had a significant influence among the *Freikirchen*, primarily through the tasks of postwar rehabilitation and reconstruction of church life. The largest missionary effort to the *Friekirchen* came from two North American denominational families, Baptists and Mennonites. Both were active in the massive relief effort to postwar Germany, but in so doing, were especially concerned for giving aid and support to their denominational kindred in that country. These denominational groups in Germany were members of the minority *Freikirchen* and had a history of being discriminated against by the larger *Landeskirchen*.[35] In the midst of extensive physical devastation and demographic upheaval, missionaries from these North American denominations saw an important opportunity to give aid to their German kindred. Through their work in relief and reconstruction, North American missionaries helped their denominational counterparts in the *Freikirchen* move from a place of marginalization to one of greater credibility and legitimacy in German Protestant life. As a historically marginalized religious community, members of the *Freikirchen* found that the work of their denominational missionary kindred from North America helped to establish them as a credible and respectable ecclesiastical option in German Protestant life. Conversely, by focusing on the German churches whose roots were in the Radical Reformation, these denominational mission agencies believed they were helping to complete the work of the sixteenth-century Reformation by further challenging the religious hegemony of the *Landeskirchen*. In doing so, the significance of the North American mission for German Protestantism can be seen in the achievement of a greater measure of denominational pluralism within a Protestantism that had historically privileged the established *Landeskirchen*.

In highlighting the contribution of North American missionaries to the previously marginalized *Freikirchen*, and not just the established churches of the EKD, this book brings greater breadth and nuance to the topic of the German church's postwar recovery.

The third area in which North American missionaries played a crucial role was in the emergence of the trans-denominational *Evangelikaler* movement as part of the landscape of German Protestantism from the 1960s onward. This movement has received some attention from German scholars who have traced its growth and resultant place on the spectrum of German Christianity. In seeking to clarify the movement's identity, Erich Geldbach makes the helpful distinction between the terms *evangelisch* and *Evangelikal*. Historically, for Germans the term *evangelisch* was simply a synonym for "Protestant." Beginning in the 1960s, those German Protestants who began to identify themselves as *Evangelikal* had much in common with North American conservative Protestants who already saw themselves as part of the transnational and trans-denominational evangelical movement rooted in the Wesleyan revivals of the eighteenth century. Geldbach goes on to state that by coining this neologism, *Evangelikaler* Protestants deliberately linked themselves with transnational evangelical groups as a way of affirming their identity apart from being merely *evangelisch*. However, he does not explore the history of the movement beyond this introductory description, nor does he make any effort to trace links between American and German evangelicals, particularly through North American missionary initiatives.[36]

German church historians who come the closest to doing this include Jörg Ohlemacher, Fritz Laubach, Friedhelm Jung, and Stephan Holthaus.[37] While these authors acknowledge the contribution of American evangelist Billy Graham, most of their attention is given to explaining the particular character of *Evangelikaler* identity and its affinities with Anglo-American evangelicalism more broadly.

My work adds a missing piece to the history of the German Protestantism by bringing to light the role of transatlantic missionaries in nurturing the *Evangelikaler* movement in the later decades of the Cold War. North American missionaries did so primarily by establishing working partnerships with the German trans-denominational Deutsche Evangelische Allianz (DEA). These partnerships were initiated mostly by conservative evangelical mission agencies who found common ground with the DEA in their shared missionary agenda of evangelism, revival, and conversion. Mission agencies such as Janz Team Ministries and the Billy Graham Evangelistic Association (BGEA) played a key role in defining and nurturing the identity of a new *Evangelikaler* movement among German Protestants. The *Evangelikaler* shared not only the same conservative theology as Anglo-American evangelicals, but also a similar commitment to evangelizing their fellow countrymen and women. This evangelistic message was directed not only at those outside the church, but also to nominal Christians in the German churches.

As mentioned at the beginning of this historiographical discussion, much of the story of the recovery of German Protestantism in the postwar period has been dominated by accounts of the *Landeskirchen*. While the established churches under the newly configured EKD continued to be numerically far larger than the minority *Freikirchen* population, in the chapters that follow it will be apparent that important developments in German postwar Protestantism occurred beyond the boundaries of the visibly dominant *Landeskirchen*. This book will show how North American missionaries played a key role in aiding and shaping these developments.

Western Europe's Shifting Religious Identity

Europe's changing religious identity is a relatively recent subject of academic interest.[38] But several decades ahead of this scholarly interest, conservative evangelical missionary practitioners and missiologists were well aware that the label of "Christendom" no longer applied to Europe. For them, the rise of National Socialism resulting in the Second World War simply confirmed what they had suspected since the turn of the century: the spiritual geography of Europe had changed to the extent that it had become a post-Christian mission field.[39] Church pastors and mission society leaders began mobilizing the faithful to participate in the revival, or re-evangelization, of Europe.[40] Christian decline has been the dominant interpretive paradigm of these studies, but the writings of W.A. Visser 't Hooft and Grace Davie suggest that the decline in support for religious institutions, such as churches, need not be equated with the demise of religious interest, or even practice. Both have argued that religious interest among modern Europeans during the latter half of the twentieth century remained strong, but that it was channelled toward alternatives outside traditional institutional structures.[41]

More recently, Philip Jenkins has pointed out that secularism in Europe was already being undermined in the later decades of the Cold War by the influx of immigrants from Christian communities of countries in the Global South.[42] This perspective is shared by Gerrie ter Haar and Roswith Gerloff, who have traced the growth of African diaspora communities in Western European cities. These diaspora groups included significant numbers of Christians who, once settled in Europe, founded their own churches and began evangelizing their fellow-immigrant and European neighbours.[43] This body of research is part of the relatively new, but fast-growing field known as "World Christianity." As evident from the above authors, the attention has been directed toward the re-Christian-izing of Europe through new church communities founded by migrant peoples from countries of the Global South.[44] One purpose of this book is to show how the work of North American missionaries is an integral part of the emerging story of World Christianity.

It was in fact these missionaries in German-speaking Europe who, during the early decades of the Cold War, anticipated Europe's shifting religious identity toward secularism well before Christian diaspora communities from the Global South began to promote Europe as a new mission field. More particularly, conservative evangelical missionaries from North America to Germany were among the first to see and act upon Western Europe's changing spiritual condition.

Well before the Second World War, North American conservative evangelicals had seen the Roman Catholic countries of Europe as mission fields: after the war, that perception broadened to include Protestant countries, such as Germany.[45] After 1945 the heartland of the Reformation was no longer recognized as Christendom but increasingly as a post-Christian society. While ecumenical Protestants sought to harmonize Christianity and secularism by exploring possible "theologies of the secular," conservative evangelicals responded quite differently. For them, secularism represented a continued drift by Germany away from its Christian heritage. It will be suggested that conservative evangelicals, committed to missionary activism, brought a mixture of new and traditional ways of communicating the Christian message to secular Europeans.

This changing perception of Europe fatally undermined the concept of Christendom as a specific geographical demarcation. It represented an initial but very significant step toward the decentring of Christianity and thus anticipated the rise of World Christianity, and its new operational credo of Christian mission being "from everywhere to everywhere."[46] The emergence of World Christianity has so far been understood to have its genesis in the rapid growth of Christianity in the Global South, especially since the 1970s. This book makes the argument that the decentring of Christendom was already clearly signalled in the years after 1945 when North American Protestants sounded the missionary call to save Germany.

Such a decentralizing of Europe in the geography of Christianity is significant in that it foreshadowed the growing doubts of North American Christians about the identity of Canada and the United States as Christian countries. In pointing out this connection, this book adds another dimension to the literature on the decline of Christianity in the modern West, while at the same time pointing ahead to new branches of Christian vitality that have grown into what is now known as a decentralized World Christianity.

A Word about Methodology and Structure

The methodological approach used in developing the above arguments draws on the field of transnational historical studies, on two levels.[47] On the first level, following the lead of Ian Tyrell and Akira Iriye, this book tracks and examines the work and influence of a selected group of volunteer mission agencies as they move from their home nation/cultural territory into a foreign one.[48] These mission agencies did not represent the governments in their home countries in any direct official way, yet they exercised a significant influence on religious institutions – some of which were official civic institutions – and ideological thinking of the people in the host country. In doing so, their influence can be examined through the twin lenses of intercultural relations and international relations. The first lens brings into focus the impact of missionaries on private citizens and organizations, and the second their influence on civic institutions and political thought. However, where Iriye understood international relations as flowing into intercultural relations, my approach reverses this causal order, particularly when considering Cold War ideological issues.[49] There is already a substantive body of research on the intercultural influence of the United States generally in Europe, and in Germany in particular, during the Cold War period, but these studies pay little or no attention to religious organizations and to the movement and impact of religious ideas across national borders.[50] The story of Protestant missions to Germany shows that private religious organizations have a significant place in the transnational matrix of global interaction.

Transnationalism also works on a second level, in that this study includes mission organizations and personnel from Canada and the Unite States. There are notable differences in the Christian subcultures of both countries, but at the same time, there were (and still are) significant cross-border links between Protestants in both countries. This was particularly true for missionary organizations and practices during the Cold War. In the three categories of mission agencies active in Germany introduced below, Canadian and American missionary personnel were present. While American missionaries were in the majority in mission agencies, such as the conservative evangelical Youth for Christ, and the denominationally based Baptist missions, Canadians made up a significant percentage of Mennonite Central Committee personnel in Germany, and Canadian Baptists also supported relief efforts in Europe undertaken by the Baptist World Alliance.[51] The largest conservative evangelical mission in Germany during the Cold War years was Janz Team Ministries, a Canadian mission that later included a growing number of American personnel. In the case of mainline Protestants who were largely committed to the ecumenical missionary approach of the World Council of Churches, the vast majority of personnel committed to Germany were American, but Canadian Lutherans were also substantial contributors to the ecumenical early postwar mission to Germany through Canadian Lutheran World Relief.[52] Such an overlap of shared missionary concern toward Germany, and the integration of American and Canadian personnel in a number of participating missionary agencies, indicate that the mission to Germany already had its roots in an informal but visible transnational outlook. In acknowledging this dimension in the mission to Germany, this book explores the transnational dynamics at work not only between the missionaries and the host country where they worked, but also among the missionaries themselves. This will be particularly evident in chapter 3 when examining the work of conservative evangelical mission agencies.

The range of Protestant missionary responses to postwar Germany can be organized into three categories: ecumenical missionaries, denominational missionaries, and conservative evangelical missionaries.[53] These categories are based on a combination of commitments to specific ecclesial and/or missionary institutions and the attendant philosophies of mission that flow from those institutional models. While the categories can be seen to overlap in some areas (for instance, Southern Baptist missionaries are classified under denominational missions, but also had much in common with conservative evangelical missionaries, as will be clarified below), these three categories are an effective and credible way of analyzing and explaining the varied institutional approaches and philosophies of North American missionaries.

The first category is ecumenical mission agencies. The three most prominent expressions of the ecumenical mission came through the Religious Affairs Section (RAS) of the American Military Government in Germany, the World Council of Churches, and the Church World Service (CWS). Although the staff of the RAS were officially government employees, they were also Protestant churchmen drawn from the ranks of denominations that supported the WCC and its internationalist ecumenical vision. Thus these military officers served as the first wave of missionaries sympathetic to the values and aims of the wider ecumenical mission. Alongside these military missionaries were Americans who worked in Germany directly under the aegis of the WCC. Like RAS personnel, these missionaries came mostly from church denominations that were members of the Federal Council of Churches (FCC), such as Presbyterians, Episcopalians, Methodists, and Lutherans. The CWS was formed in 1946 by the FCC churches primarily to gather and send relief supplies to postwar Europe. As such, the CWS served as the chief coordinator in the United States for the WCC's mission to Germany. In Germany itself, the CWS provided a combination of humanitarian aid and resources for spiritual renewal. Its personnel worked alongside WCC representatives in liaising with German relief agencies and clergy to distribute material aid and provide resources for church reconstruction.

Chapter 1 examines the role and impact of the ecumenical mission through the work of the RAS, WCC, and CWS.[54] Their mission was defined by the priorities of helping the German EKD rebuild itself through offering assistance in humanitarian relief and church reconstruction, and of democratizing German society by promoting democratic principles in German church life. In the former, ecumenical missionaries advocated a vision of Christian internationalism that had its genesis in the decades of the interwar period and made aid toward self-help one of its chief goals, thereby steering sharply away from the more traditional missionary practice of evangelism.[55] In the latter case, American missionaries worked to instil democratic ideals in German clergy and church leaders. Once it became evident that the EKD had recovered from the war to a point of economic self-sufficiency, and that its operational protocols reflected a commitment to democratic principles, the ecumenical mission was essentially completed.

Denominational mission agencies comprised a second type of missionary response. Unlike their ecumenical counterparts, denominational missionaries went to Germany as representatives of a particular church denomination, or family of denominations. These included missionaries from denominations such as the Salvation Army and the Quakers; however, the two denominational families with the largest and most sustained mission to Germany were the Baptists and the Mennonites. During the early postwar period, Baptist groups in North America coordinated their missionary efforts in Germany through the Baptist World Alliance (BWA). In addition to supporting the BWA, Southern Baptists in the United States carried out their own mission of training European Baptist pastors by founding a seminary in Switzerland shortly after the war. North American Mennonites carried out mission work in Germany primarily through the Mennonite Central Committee (MCC), a humanitarian aid agency that sought to bring relief to the most needy Germans, but also specifically to aid Mennonite communities in Germany. In a fashion similar to that of the Southern Baptists, the MCC went on to build a school for theological education in Switzerland that served Mennonite churches in German-speaking Europe.

Chapter 2 examines the range and impact of the denominational mission by analyzing the work of the Baptist and Mennonite mission agencies introduced above.[56]

As with the ecumenical mission, a chief concern of denominational missionaries was to promote democratic principles in Germany. Thus the denominational mission was defined by a theme in common with its ecumenical counterpart. However, instead of working with the *Landeskirchen* of the EKD, Baptists and Mennonites used their own denominational church groups in Germany, which belonged to the smaller, marginalized *Freikirchen*. As such, in addition to promoting democracy, a second key theme in the denominational mission was the impact of its work on German Protestant church life. In helping their respective denominations, and by extension all member groups of the *Freikirchen*, find a place of greater credibility as legitimate expressions of German Protestantism and not a foreign transplant, denominational missionaries made a significant contribution to German church life.

Conservative evangelical mission agencies make up the third category of missionary responses to Germany. Missionaries in this category were members of independent mission agencies whose personnel were drawn from a range of denominations and church groups but were unified by a common theology, usually summarized in a "doctrinal statement." Missionary candidates were required to demonstrate their agreement with the mission's doctrinal statement, as well as affirm their willingness to abide by its operational principles, as prerequisites for serving with the mission.[57] Most of these independent mission agencies were founded by theologically and socially conservative evangelicals, who, during the first half of the twentieth century, adopted the label of "fundamentalist" to distinguish themselves from Protestants whom they accused of abandoning the "old-time religion" for the more "liberal" theological teachings of modern scholarship. They also continued their conservative stand in opposition to forms of worldly entertainment, such as cinema and popular music, as well as decrying the vices of tobacco and alcohol.[58] By the early 1940s a like-minded group of leaders within the American fundamentalist movement sought to distance themselves from the label. In their perception, the movement's increasingly militant rhetoric and its ongoing tendency to define itself by what it opposed – typified by the proclamations of fundamentalist Carl A. McIntire – ultimately led to theological and cultural dead ends. As a means of separating themselves from this increasingly pejorative "branding," they reclaimed the label of "evangelical" to describe what they believed to be a more positive affirmation of a Christian revivalist message while still retaining a strong socially conservative stance. Led by men such as Harold J. Ockenga and Charles E. Fuller, they founded the National Association of Evangelicals in 1943 as a rallying point for like-minded churches, mission organizations, and individuals.[59] During the Cold War decades, evangelist Billy Graham became its most visible representative.

Realizing that the term *evangelical* can still represent a broader spectrum of Protestants in their stance on social issues, particularly in entertainment and personal vices, I have opted for *conservative evangelical* as a term that best captures the theological and social commitments of this stream of Protestant missions during the Cold War years.

The conservative evangelical mission was characterized by emphasis on the traditional missionary activities of evangelism and revivalism. In this regard it differed markedly from the humanitarian and self-help priorities of the ecumenical mission. To the degree that conservative evangelical mission focused on working with like-minded Germans in trans-denominational coalitions that included representatives from both the *Landeskirchen* and the *Freikirchen,* it was also distinct from the chief concern of the denominational mission. Conservative evangelicals sought to present a simple Christian message that appealed to individuals to "come to Christ." Their intention was to work alongside churches in the task of evangelism, and not to compete with them by starting alternative church groups.

To give a representative picture of the conservative evangelical mission to Germany, I selected four mission agencies, based on the size and significance of their respective works in Germany. Youth for Christ (YFC) was the first conservative evangelical mission to gain access to postwar Germany. Its initial mission through military personnel and travelling evangelists from North America was important, not only in establishing links with like-minded German Protestants, but also in motivating other mission agencies to become involved in Europe. One such organization was the Canadian mission Janz Team Ministries (JTM), which went on to become the largest North American mission in West Germany during the Cold War years.[60]

YFC and JTM are the subjects of chapter 3. In examining the work of these conservative evangelical missions, two themes are prominent: the role of these missionaries as agents of democracy, and their importance in nurturing a trans-denominational community of German Protestants who would eventually carve out a new identity in German Protestantism as *Evangelikaler*.[61]

Chapter 4 focuses exclusively on a third important conservative evangelical missionary: Billy Graham.[62] As the most widely recognized American Protestant of his day, and, from an attendance perspective, the most successful mass evangelist of his day, Graham's activity in Germany deserves particular consideration. Richard Pierard points out that outside of the United States and Great Britain, Germany was the country that Graham visited most frequently for preaching missions during the Cold War.[63] In addition to the BGEA and DEA records, Graham's preaching missions to Germany attracted widespread attention in German Protestant circles and generated tremendous publicity in the secular German press. Thus, the magnitude of Graham's impact on German Protestantism is well documented, and, given the large scale on which his evangelistic work took place, his role and impact as a missionary to Germany merits special consideration. The two themes that come out in Graham's work are his role as a promoter of democracy and outspoken critic of Communism, and his ability to forge and give leadership to the emerging *Evangelikaler* movement by connecting German adherents of the movement to the wider international evangelical movement.

Although 1974 is the terminal date of the central research narrative of this book, chapter 5 offers a postscript to the narrative by outlining key developments and changes in the American mission to Germany between 1974 and 1989, the date conventionally taken to mark the end of the Cold War. The source material available from denominational and conservative evangelical mission agencies proved less substantial for this period, in part because commitments in personnel and finances by these agencies were scaled back. As a result, missionary developments could not be traced in the same depth as in the earlier period. Nevertheless, enough data were available to trace the lines of an appropriate postscript to address the key themes of the Protestant mission work during the twilight years of the Cold War.

Two developments in this period are of particular significance: first, the response of denominational and conservative evangelical missions to a more visible secularism; and second, the increasing devolution of control of mission work to German nationals. In both cases the theme of

Germany as a post-Christian mission field comes to the forefront. While the existence of North American missionaries in Cold War Germany implied such an understanding, this changed spiritual status of Germany from the centre of European Christendom to a secular, post-Christian mission field was now openly discussed, not only by the missionaries, but by German Protestants themselves. As a result, mission work continued, but altered economic conditions and key socio-cultural shifts on both sides of the Atlantic, and caused North American missionaries to adjust their missionary strategies and reassess their relationships with German supporters. The result was an increased emphasis on cultural contextualization of the Christian message, and greater indigenization of missionary personnel. Thus, chapter 6 presents a fitting denouement and conclusion to the key events and themes that defined the mission until 1974.

The conclusion offers a summative overview of the previous chapters, and then engages in a final discussion of the significance of the main arguments advanced in the previous chapters for each of the four historiographical areas. In doing so, I suggest possible avenues for future investigation and reaffirm the importance of the Protestant mission to Germany for themes that extend well beyond the narrower confines of conventional religious history. The conclusion also looks at the respective internal assessments of the mission to Germany made by the three main groups of ecumenical, denominational, and conservative evangelical missions, before attempting a scholarly assessment of the significance of this chapter in the modern history of Christian missionary enterprise.

Ecumenical Protestants and the Reconstruction of Germany, 1945–1974: Mainline Protestants Offer Relief and Rehabilitation

The State of Postwar Germany: A New Kind of Mission Field?

The horrible heritage which the war left for Germany is pressing mostly about those who were not responsible for the war and who had to suffer, as the helpless and defenseless, all its horrors. They are the people who need our help more than any other.

An endless stream of refugees is coming into these parts of the country looking for food and shelter, clothing and work. Families are split up: parents looking for their children, boys and girls [searching for] their parents …

It is the Church towards which all hopes are directed now … People set their hopes on Christians within and without [Germany]. It is a tremendous alternative put before us: either Europe will see the starvation and death of millions of people; trouble and even strife and inner revolution will be the dreadful by-product of this development; Nihilism and chaos will be the end – or the German people will realize once again that there is something, after all, in Christian love and forgiveness, and that they are not mistaken if they turn from the idols of nationalism and false racial doctrines to the Church of Jesus Christ who taught the world charity and mercy. The will realize that they do not hope in vain …

Come over and help us![1]

This tragic state of affairs and ominous prognosis was offered by Hans Lilje, Lutheran bishop of Hanover, as he surveyed the carnage visited on his own country by the Allied armies. Hitler's expansionist aspirations, combined with his brutal policies of ethnic cleansing, had exacted a horrendous retribution on his own people. As reports from German civilians, occupational military personnel, and North American humanitarian observers began to find their way into North American media, the magnitude of Germany's destruction and the suffering of its civilian population struck an increasingly sympathetic chord with Protestant Christians. While the United States and Canada had experienced the suffering of war through the loss of their soldiers' lives, their homes and workplaces had remained undamaged. When confronted with stories of unremitting suffering and pictures of unimaginable destruction, the sheer magnitude of Germany's plight could no longer be rationalized in political policies of vengeance or moral demands of retribution.[2]

The destruction inflicted by Allied armies was most noticeable in urban areas, especially those that housed industries believed vital to the German war effort. In 1939 Germany had a reported 15.7 million habitable residential units. Eighteen months after the war there were only 8 million.[3] The numbers were even more disheartening at the local level. Dr Hans Thimme, a Lutheran pastor in the province of Westphalia itemized the destruction in his diocese: 330 of 610 churches, 236 of 249 parish buildings, 28 of 35 hospitals, 85 out of 118 pre-school buildings, and 363 of 692 vicarages all completely destroyed or seriously damaged. The death toll was equally devastating: fifty-one pastors, sixty-eight assistant pastors, twenty-six probationer pastors, and fifteen theological students all killed, with another sixteen pastors and eighteen assistants listed as missing. Bombing raids had killed 28,065 people; and in the Westphalia diocese alone parishes mourned 96,732 war dead and another 185,686 missing.[4]

Similar devastation was reported by American aid workers during their early tours of postwar Germany. After visiting cities such as Stuttgart, Pforzheim, Frankfurt, and Berlin, Sylvester Michelfelder, a Lutheran pastor, noted that he was overcome by what he had witnessed: "Pompeii is in a better state of preservation than these cities ... Even the ruins are ruined."[5] US General Lucius Clay described Berlin in 1945 as a "city of the dead." From the air the bombed-out cities looked like a moonscape with people living more like moles amidst the mounds of rubble.[6]

The extensive destruction had left an estimated 7.5 million Germans homeless, but the humanitarian crisis was further exacerbated by the influx of an additional 12 million refugees of *Volksdeutsch*, displaced Germans from Eastern Europe evicted from their homes in territories that had been ceded to Germany's eastern neighbours as part of the peace settlement. The terms of surrender reached by Stalin, Roosevelt, and Atlee at the Potsdam Conference in August 1945 included the westward shift of Germany's eastern border to the Oder-Neisse Line, to be followed by the "orderly and humane" migration of German citizens from territories now belonging to Poland and the Soviet Union, as well as from other prewar German enclaves in territory now belonging to Romania, Hungary, Czechoslovakia, and Yugoslavia.[7] The reality worked out quite differently. Already the Soviet army had unleashed a wave of massacre, rape, and plunder in its invasion and occupation of eastern Germany using Stalin's justification that "nothing in Germany is guiltless, neither the living nor yet the unborn."[8]

In enforcing the Potsdam Agreement, a second wave, almost as devastating as the first, was now visited on German expellees by their Eastern European evictors. One eyewitness account described the process in a region of Poland:

The Germans in the towns and throughout the countryside received orders to leave their homes on very short notice. Their baggage was not to weigh more than 10 pound. Polish militia and military police hurried the people along with riding whips and kicks. Houses were often closed within 15 or 20 minutes after the occupants received evacuation orders. Plundering and willful destruction began immediately. The seriously ill and aged had to be left behind without any medical help or care ... There were daily robberies ... [Evacuees] were stripped of baggage, suitcases, beds, shoes, provisions. Many women were raped. At Frankfort-on-the-Oder, men arrived without shoes and trousers, wearing only underclothing. Some of the women had their clothes literally torn from them. The accompanying soldiers used whips and fists on the people ... The smallest children died for lack of milk ... Mostly the dead lay in roadside ditches. After a while old people broke down completely and begged the younger ones to go on without them ...

Homeless, uprooted from their native soil, the people wander along the highways. Sick, exhausted, covered with vermin, they somehow press forward toward one goal, a new home. But wherever

they go, they are turned away, ordered on, misdirected, brought
back for new instructions, and then ordered on again.[9]

In spite of high-profile voices of protest, such as Eleanor Roosevelt, who
spoke out against the atrocities of the expulsion before the United Nations General Assembly, the violence meted out on German expellees by
those who had suffered at Nazi hands had popular – if unrepentant – support among these country's leaders. A Czechoslovak official responded to
Roosevelt's speech by stating, "We in Europe have a right to look at things
in our own way. We have suffered more than many delegates in this room
can imagine."[10]

What the Allied Control Council anticipated as the relatively orderly
flow of three million Germans into the four zones (see map) of the newly
reconfigured Germany turned into a chaotic torrent of over twelve million expellees overrunning an already desolated and shrunken country.
It is estimated another two million expellees died in transit. On reaching
the Eastern Zone of Germany controlled by the Soviet army, most expellees pressed further westward, opting to settle in regions governed by the
Western Allies.[11] Two years after VE day, the territory comprising what
shortly would become officially West Germany was the unwilling recipient
of eight million expellees. They were joined by additional refugees from
Soviet-controlled eastern Germany seeking to escape Communist rule. It
made the total postwar forced migration of fourteen million people the
largest people migration in history.[12]

This unexpected, dramatic influx of displaced persons (DPs) into the
bombed-out rubble of the Western Zones raised the already acute problems of homelessness and starvation to catastrophic levels. As Winston
Churchill wryly observed, "Refugees bring their mouths with them."[13]
Instead of being welcomed by their compatriots in the western zones as
fellow sufferers in a common cause, they were seen as competitors for
scarce resources, interlopers whose presence would further reduce their
own chances of survival. Thus DPs found themselves abused and unwanted on all sides.

This added burden on the people living in the western occupational
zones did little to soften the initial policies of Allied governments toward
them. Initially the Allies had opted for the policy of a "hard peace" toward
Germany, insisting that all outside aid be directed first toward the countries that had been the victims of Nazi aggression. Only after their needs

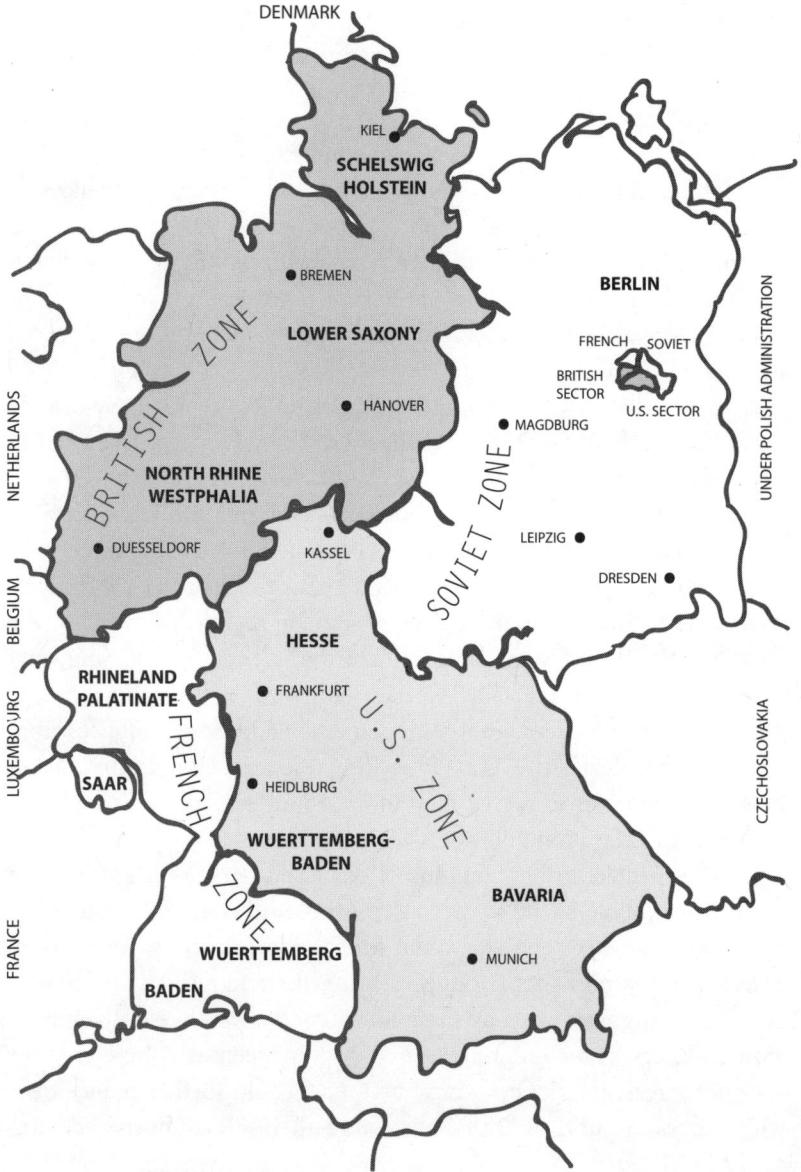

Occupied areas of Germany, 1946

had been met were the Germans to be considered eligible to receive outside aid. At the same time the American Military Government (AMG) in Germany insisted they had the necessary resources and ration distribution system that would provide each German resident 1,550 calories of food a day. There were two problems immediately evident with this policy: the first was that such a caloric benchmark was at best still only a starvation-level diet; and second, with the sudden unexpected influx of refugees, most regions were not able to meet even this minimal calorie requirement. As word of these conditions began to be publicized in the American media, the magnitude of the humanitarian disaster quickly became apparent and, as will be evident in the following pages, galvanized relief agencies into action.[14] Quaker humanitarian activist Hertha Kraus's observations after one of her visits to Germany foreshadowed the missionary vision and will for Germany taking shape among Christians back in the American homeland: "Defeat has closed down on Germany, and the penalties fall on the innocent and guilty alike." And while the AMG and other occupational governments were doing their best in the "stupendous task" of addressing the needs of the Germany people, "all their best efforts are crippled unless they receive much stronger support from their home communities. Only then would [the AMG] be able to turn from mere restrictions and security controls toward a more positive and cooperative policy geared toward reconstruction and rehabilitation."[15]

For North American Protestants there was another dimension to Germany's plight that fuelled the sense of mission already evident from the great material needs of her people: the spiritual dimension. Bishop Lilje's "Macedonian call" for help from overseas was an appeal based just as strongly on his people's spiritual needs as on their material ones. The German church was the only national institution that had managed to survive the war intact, but as Lilje reminded his North American readers, its state was precarious and its needs immense. At the same time its opportunities to bring spiritual renewal and moral reorientation never seemed greater; the German church needed help before this opportune moment was lost. Lilje's analysis was echoed by American church leaders such as Samuel McCrea Cavert, who, from his early postwar visits to Germany, sensed a weary cynicism among Germans and deep frustration and hopelessness.

The real danger in Germany at the time was not a new upsurge of militarism, but the growth of this nihilistic spirit. "The Germany of today could almost be described as a spiritual vacuum ... the basic problem is to fill that spiritual vacuum with a positive faith. Unless this is done, it is difficult to see how hopeful objectives in the economic and the political realms can be achieved."[16]

It was this combination of material and spiritual need that confronted Protestant Christians when they first arrived to begin their missionary endeavours to save Germany.

Who Are the Ecumenical Protestants?

The first North American Protestant missionaries to gain access to postwar Germany were those from the US mainline denominations committed to ecumenical cooperation. This cooperation found its most tangible expression through two ecumenical bodies: the Federal Council of Churches in Christ (FCC) in the United States, and the international World Council of Churches (WCC).[17] The FCC, established in 1908 in an effort to give a more visible unity to Protestantism in the United States, had an original membership of over thirty denominations. But well over half of its constituency, and an overwhelming majority of its leaders, were drawn from seven denominations that made up an unofficial, yet recognizable, Protestant establishment in American Christianity in the first half of the twentieth century. These seven denominations also became known as the Protestant mainline churches and consisted of the Episcopalians, Presbyterians, Congregationalists, Lutherans, the white divisions of the Methodists and Baptists, and the Disciples of Christ.[18]

With the exception of the Baptists (see chapter 3), the missionary contribution of the above denominations to "saving Germany" came through the Church World Service, a relief agency created by the FCC in response to the needs of postwar Europe. The work of North American Lutherans could also be seen as another exception because, like the Baptists, they had their own denominational relief agency. In 1945 they founded Lutheran World Relief (LWR) as an agency through which to channel funds for relief and reconstruction to postwar Germany. Right from the outset, however, the decision was made by LWR's leadership to cooperate closely with the WCC's work in Germany, and wherever possible, to use the same distribution channels for humanitarian relief and spiritual aid.[19] As such, the Lutheran mission was synchronic with the work of the WCC, and thus is better understood as part of the ecumenical missionary effort.[20]

The second key agency in the ecumenical mission was the World Council of Churches. Although the WCC was not officially launched until its 1948 assembly in Amsterdam, its Department of Reconstruction and Inter-Church Aid had been in place since 1942. Two American members of this department, Samuel McCrea Cavert, general secretary of the FCC, and Sylvester Michelfelder, a Lutheran pastor from Ohio, were instrumental in channelling humanitarian and spiritual aid from the United States to needy churches in postwar Germany.[21]

The mission of ecumenical Protestants to Germany thus encompassed the activity of American mainline denominations, mediated primarily through the CWS and the WCC. Through the remainder of this chapter the terms *ecumenical Protestants* and *mainline Protestants* will be used interchangeably when referring to members of the above cluster of denominations, but excluding Baptists, who preferred to use their own denominational channels in responding to the needs of postwar Germany.

Defining the Ecumenical Mission: Promoting Democracy and Facilitating Self-help

Mainline Protestants saw their missionary mandate as two-fold: first, to assist the established Protestant *Landeskirchen* in making the transition from working under the totalitarian restrictions of National Socialism to functioning in a democratic society, which championed religious freedom and civic responsibility; and second, to enable German Protestant churches to meet the material and spiritual needs of their fellow citizens as the country rebuilt itself out of the ruins of the war.

In the case of the former, American missionaries found themselves promoting democratic church governance and the wider civic and ideological tenets characteristic of American democracy. In the early period of postwar recovery, mainline Protestants functioned as agents of democracy by supporting the denazification of the German *Landeskirchen*, by encouraging the development of democratic structures in the established German church, and by paving the way for the EKD to be accepted back into the fold of ecumenical international Protestantism. Once the initial postwar crisis had passed, the democratic nature of the ecumenical mission also included supporting the German churches as they sought to check the spread of Communism in their country. By acknowledging the importance of instilling a democratic mindset in German Christians, ecumenical Protestants signalled their belief that Christian mission involved a necessary political dimension, that of advocating civic and religious freedom.

The cultivation of democratic ideals, both as a detoxification against a defeated, yet latent Nazism, and as an inoculation against a virulent, highly contagious Communism was seen as important, but not as the sole dimension of the mission. Thus the second goal of enabling the German *Landeskirchen* to help their own citizens by providing material and spiritual aid was seen as a necessary catalyst for the first one. North American ecumenical Protestants believed that democracy as a socio-political ideology could take root successfully in German soil only if the "Christian presuppositions of democracy [had] been re-established in the German soul."[22]

But who would see to this re-establishment? Traditional missionary thinking assumed that such a task could be most effectively undertaken by sending missionary personnel from "Christian lands" to evangelize and win converts among the native population of "heathen lands." Germany, however, was not only newly perceived as a mission field, but also had been a recent enemy in a brutal global war during the last five years. The *Christian Century*, the principal ecumenical media voice of the American mainline, quoted Cyril Garbett, archbishop of York, in summarizing the approach of the ecumenical mission: "It is easy to say we must reconvert Germany, but in practice it will be very difficult. It is ludicrous to think that the victors can send to Germany missionaries to undertake the task. It must be done by the Germans themselves."[23] The editor of the *Christian Century*, therefore, called for a new kind of missionary approach, one that began with establishing links of cooperation and fellowship between North American Protestant leaders and faithful Christians in Germany.

> The establishment of such [ecumenical] cooperation and fellowship with the faithful Christians of Germany is the most urgent of the innumerable tasks which the war has laid at the door of the ecumenical church. It is a missionary task of the first order, and a new kind. Such a mission would not address itself evangelistically to the German people ... Instead its essential purpose would be to identify itself with them in their sufferings and their faithfulness and to reinforce their weakness with spiritual and practical help as they bear their own unique witness to Christ among a people which has been coerced into forgetting him.[24]

Writing just months after the war's end, the editor of the *Christian Century* proved prophetic as ecumenical Protestants adopted a mission of enablement toward self-help when reaching out to the German church during the early postwar years. In doing so, mainline Protestants showed a willingness to rethink the whole concept of Christian missions more generally, moving away from their previous emphasis on evangelizing and civilizing, toward the tasks of humanitarian aid and assistance toward self-help as more astute ways of reaching people with the gospel. By adopting a different set of missionary priorities for their work in Germany, ecumenical Protestants widened a rift that had been developing in North American Protestant circles since the early 1930s.[25] In contrast to their conservative evangelical counterparts, who held to the traditional approach of resident missionaries seeking conversion through evangelistic proclamation, ecumenical Protestants signalled their determination to chart an altered course in missionary work toward self-help, thereby enabling indigenous Christians to minister to the spiritual and material needs of their own people.[26]

This shift in Protestant internationalism was not limited to American mainline churches, but was also supported by their Canadian ecumenical counterparts. The two largest Canadian mainline churches, the United Church of Canada and the Anglican Church of Canada, ran articles in their respective denominational journals, the *United Church Observer* and the *Canadian Churchman*, which endorsed the WCC mission of self-help for the German churches, and at the same time called for resistance to the threat of Communism in Europe.[27]

The ecumenical mission to Germany was carried out on two levels simultaneously: the first was the level of government, in which representatives of the mainline churches, along with Roman Catholic and Jewish delegates, were invited to work under the postwar American Military Government of occupied Germany, as members of, or reporting to, the Department of Educational and Religious Affairs. In their role as public servants, ecumenical Protestants functioned as liaisons between the executive office of the AMG and the leaders of the German Protestant churches. At the same time they worked on a second level of private, voluntary ecumenical relief agencies: the American-based Church World Service, and the WCC's Department of Reconstruction and Inter-Church Aid.

A decade after the end of the war, ecumenical Protestants viewed their mission to Germany as completed. The rapid economic recovery of West

Germany as a democratic state, alongside the recovery of the German *Landeskirchen* and their successful integration in the WCC, were indicators that the goals of the US mainline Protestants had been achieved. After 1955, ecumenical Protestants remained interested in and concerned for the welfare of Germany, particularly in light of escalating Cold War tensions. Their ongoing relationship with German Protestants, however, was that of as an equal ecumenical partner in the global mission of the WCC.

The remainder of this chapter will be devoted to analyzing and assessing the Protestant ecumenical mission as it developed at these two levels of service. In both cases I will explicate these two themes of the mission: as an agent of democracy, and the shift in missionary vision of ecumenical Protestants away from direct evangelism to enabling indigenous churches in the tasks of humanitarian and spiritual self-help.

Public Servants as Missionaries: Ecumenical Protestants in the AMG, 1945–1955

Democratizing the German Church

The first US Protestants formally to be given the task of helping the German church after the war were a handful of mainline churchmen working through the Religious Affairs Section (RAS), a small branch of the AMG administration. The RAS had the responsibility of dealing with church leaders on matters pertaining to religious life in Germany. The chief of the RAS was Marshall Knappen, a former Congregational minister turned academic historian.[28] Knappen was one of several churchmen connected to the RAS who came out of mainline church denominations, and whose work with the German churches reflected the interests and concerns of US ecumenical Protestantism. As such they represented a first, if unofficial, wave of American Protestant missionary endeavour to postwar Germany.

Given the political context of their relationship with German church leaders, the general mandate of the RAS was to promote the development of democratic thinking and values in the postwar German church.[29] Within these restrictive parameters, and the operational realities of a minimal staff and meagre budget, Knappen and his fellow RAS officers knew their influence on German church life would be extremely limited.[30] Nevertheless, they sought to work in conjunction with German clergy to rebuild and rehabilitate church life.

The efforts of the RAS staff were further challenged by the overwhelming humanitarian needs created by the influx of roughly twelve million

Volksdeutsch and other DPs from Eastern Europe, and, more immediately, by the ambivalent attitude of senior policy-makers in the AMG toward the German clergy.[31] With the collapse of the country's political-economic structures, the German *Landeskirchen* was the only national institution to come through the war still intact. As such, officers of the AMG viewed German church leaders as both an asset and a threat: as an asset because their status as civil servants of the only national institution to survive the war intact made them key players in rebuilding Germany's regional and national government bodies; as a threat because the ties of the *Landeskirchen* to the Nazi regime made them a potential obstacle in promoting democracy among the German people.[32]

This ambivalence led to a rather confusing, if not contradictory, approach by the AMG when dealing with German church leaders during the early postwar period. Initially the American military officers tasked with rebuilding local government structures worked closely with German clergy in doing so. As the AMG organized itself into a more complex and formal structure, its higher-echelon officers adopted an increasingly suspicious and patronizing posture toward the churches, viewing them as potential breeding grounds of radical nationalism in need of denazification. This latter view was fuelled by the pro-nationalist comments made in a newspaper interview by Martin Niemöller, the Lutheran pastor and anti-Nazi hero shortly after his release from a Nazi labour camp.[33] Such competing viewpoints made it difficult for RAS staff to relate to German church leaders with a measure of consistency and reliability.[34]

Given the American credo of "separation of church and state," AMG policy-makers had little desire to involve themselves in the internal organization and theological orientation of German church life. Their concern was essentially political, so for them it was important that churches be conduits of democratic thinking and not resistant cells of an autocratic nationalism.[35]

In the face of these challenges from senior AMG leaders, Knappen and his staff drew up a set of objectives and strategies that reflected their own limitations, while remaining faithful to the broad objectives of the occupational government, summarized in the four *D*s: demilitarization, democratization, denazification, and decartelization.[36] All four of these really became variations of the one primary *D*: promoting democratic principles in the reconstruction of German religious life and institutions. Insofar as their resources would allow, the RAS staff were committed to the following program in working with the churches:

1 Denazification of church leaders and the dissolution of all Nazi
   organizations related to church governance
2 Democratization of congregations by assisting church groups
   in educating their parishioners about the social and political
   responsibilities of the individual citizen
3 Demilitarization by emphasizing moral re-education that
   reflected the values of peace and democracy
4 Decartelization of religion as much as possible by promoting
   "freedom of worship and respect for all religious institutions"[37]

In regard to the purgative goal of denazification, the RAS experienced
more frustration than success. Knappen realized early that taking an
interventionist role in the process would only make martyrs out of many
clergy in the eyes of fellow Germans and feed a growing alienation among
the German population toward the AMG.[38] Even if the AMG had given
the resources to Knappen and his staff to carry out a more thorough
housecleaning of pro-Nazi clergy, it is unlikely they would have been any
more effective than the reluctant efforts made by the German Protestant
churches in carrying out the task. General Lucius Clay, military governor
of the US zone, wryly observed that when it came to denazification he
had never seen so many contradictory opinions put forward by so many
experts claiming to know the "German mind."[39] Sensitive to the deteriorating nature of German–American relationships early in the occupation
period, Knappen wisely opted to keep the RAS to the more restricted role
of monitoring the German churches as they carried out an internal cleansing of their clerical ranks of Nazi collaborators.[40] Initially Knappen's data
on the German clergy's complicity with the Nazis led him to estimate that
as many as 4,000 pastors and priests had been compromised by their collaboration with Hitler. But by August 1946 when denazification hearings
were abandoned, the result was the removal of only 321 from 19,134 clergy
across the American zone.[41]

The staff of the RAS saw more favourable responses from German Protestant clergy in their efforts to promote democracy by more constructive means. One of these was to facilitate contact and interaction between
German clergy and church leaders from democratic countries. The RAS
assisted in setting up one of the Bad Boll conferences in July 1948. Here, for
the first time since the war's end, American and German Lutheran theologians came together on an equal footing to discuss mutual theological

concerns.[42] By 1949 the RAS reported that it had arranged and sponsored trips to the United States for sixty-one lay and clerical religious leaders to familiarize them with democratically informed approaches to religious education and mass media. The initial responses from German participants had been positive: a certain *Pfarrer* Geisendoefer and a Dr Buschman had returned to Germany, enthusiastic over the things they had learned during their trip. "Advance reports indicate that [all the participants to date] will use their influential positions – all are in key spots – to help shape policies and programs in the direction of democratic principles."[43]

In 1948 the RAS had also arranged for ten American religious education specialists to come to Germany and share their expertise with their German peers.[44] In this instance Americans with experience in radio and print journalism instructed German religious leaders on how to use these media to teach Christian morality within a democratic context. This instructional visit played a direct role in the formation of Evangelischer Pressedienst, a Protestant news service, for the dissemination of democratic thinking among the wider German public.[45]

RAS members believed that one of the best ways to rehabilitate the Protestant church along democratic lines would be by arranging contacts between leaders of the *Landeskirchen* and of the international ecumenical movement. In addition to inviting German observers to attend the inaugural assembly of the WCC in Amsterdam in 1948, RAS staff also prepared for German churchmen to receive visits from European leaders representing the WCC to give advice on interfaith relations, social action, and inter-church relations. In 1949 twelve ecumenical study conferences were held in centres throughout the US Zone, involving 360 church leaders from across Germany. The following year a similar set of international consultations was arranged by the RAS in cooperation with the WCC on the issue of social action. The grateful responses that the RAS received from German clergy indicated such programs were having the desired effect of building trust and confidence between the RAS and the newly constituted Evangelische Kirche Deutschland (EKD), and, more importantly, of bringing German Protestantism into the fold of a democratically oriented ecumenical Christianity.[46] In all of this, members of the RAS sought to promote democracy in the German church through a non-coercive "reorientation" to a way of religious life based on democratic ideals.

Another way by which the RAS sought to promote a democratic spirit within the German church was to sponsor initiatives internal to German church life that fostered religious freedom and individual choice by promoting a measure of cooperation with dis-established Protestant *Freikirchen* groups. In his early conversations with the leading German bishops of the EKD, which now united the postwar *Landeskirchen*, Knappen had been encouraged by the strong opposition these men had toward Communism. However, he was equally concerned over their nationalistic sentiments, reminiscent of old-order Prussian monarchism, coupled with their suspicion of liberal democracy as totally alien to the German mind.[47] Knappen and the RAS realized that any effort to reform the *Landeskirchen* along disestablishment lines was a practical impossibility and would create a public relations nightmare both in Germany and in the United States. The cases of Sweden and England showed that an established church could in fact be compatible with a democratic political order.[48] As a result, a more realistic strategy for dealing with the EKD was to ameliorate the traditional nationalist and exclusivist leanings of its current leadership by promoting greater ecumenical cooperation between the EKD and the *Freikirchen* groups, as well as inter-confessional dialogue with German Catholic and Jewish groups. In so doing, the RAS hoped to produce a greater acceptance of religious freedom and choice among the German people more generally, and within the EKD in particular. To that end the RAS assisted German Protestants in establishing the Arbeitsgemeinschaft Christlicher Kirchen in Deutschland and in arranging interfaith councils within Germany, which brought Protestants, Catholics, and Jews together to meet regularly.[49]

After early setbacks, arising from an approach that focused on the forceful extermination of Nazism, Knappen and his staff quickly shifted to an approach of friendly persuasion in which they played the role of facilitator and bridge-builder in cultivating democracy in German church life. They sought to use indirect ways to connect German church leaders with ecumenical Protestant leaders from democratic countries who would then offer their advice as clerical peers, not as paternalistic conquerors.[50] By using a more winsome approach, which invited German Protestant leaders to incorporate democratic principles and methods into church life, RAS staff were able to see a measure of success.

In the summer of 1949, when the AMG began handing over political power to the West German government, the RAS continued its activities under the newly created US High Commissioner's Office for Germany (HICOG) until 1955, when it was officially terminated. In its new reduced role as a mere external advisory agency of the State Department to the German government, the RAS continued to offer its services to the German churches in order to promote "freedom of religion, inter-faith understanding and cooperation, and international religious relations."[51] At the same time the RAS commissioned two leaders of American ecumenical Protestantism to assess their work to date and advise them of future plans under HICOG. The two men were Dr Roswell P. Barnes, associate general secretary of the FCC, and Dr Paul C. Empie, executive director of the Lutheran National Council. While their report pointed out ongoing concerns relating to authoritarian leadership in German church life, Barnes and Empie gave the RAS staff high marks for winning the confidence and respect of German church leaders. The report recommended that the RAS continue in its goal of assisting and encouraging German churches toward democracy primarily by facilitating ongoing contact with church groups and other international Christian agencies. In so doing, the RAS would help German Protestants overcome fifteen years of spiritual and cultural isolation imposed on them by Nazism and would "further stimulate the German people to participate in the spirit of brotherhood and good will in the world community of nations."[52]

In spite of small staff and limited financial resources, the RAS continued to offer programs that would "assist and encourage" the practice of democracy in German churches. As per Barnes and Empie's recommendation, these programs were designed to expose German church leaders to the democratic thinking and practice of their American counterparts. In doing so, the RAS staff saw themselves as bringing moral and spiritual reorientation to German church life so that churches could be the religious midwife to a more thoroughly democratic, just, and humanitarian society.[53]

Helping German Churches to Help Themselves

The second missionary priority of ecumenical Protestants – that of enablement toward self-help – also found expression in the RAS mandate of working with the German churches during its ten-year existence. Although democratizing the church had been their primary concern, RAS staff members gave timely assistance to German Protestant church leaders as they sought to bring spiritual and humanitarian relief to their own people. As they understood this aspect of their mission, "In all [our] undertakings, emphasis falls on helping the German people, by drawing on their moral and spiritual resources, to reorientate themselves. Military Government assistance can only be regarded as a beginning or as a continuing incentive. The main job, however, must be done by the German churches themselves."[54]

Such an approach characterized the mainline Protestant shift in missionary thinking away from direct evangelism towards an emphasis on cooperative assistance with indigenous churches. This perspective was also notable for what it chose to exclude from its missionary mandate, namely prescribing a specific theological agenda for the objects of its mission. Here too, RAS policy toward the *Landeskirchen* was in line with the spirit of ecumenical missions. From the very outset the RAS avoided any involvement in the actual theological deliberations and direction of the *Landeskirchen*.[55] In doing so they were not only recognizing the limitations of their influence on German church life, but were also being consistent with American mainline ecumenical Protestantism, which adopted a necessary latitudinarian stance on confessional differences between denominations.[56]

The mission of enabling German self-help took shape in three ways: securing travel permissions and passage for German clergy; supplying material goods necessary for church life and worship; and securing funding for German programs aimed at spiritual rehabilitation. For the first of these, Knappen and the RAS staff often found themselves acting as travel agents and convoy escorts by arranging transportation permits and then accompanying German clergy across zonal boundaries so they could meet together to plan a new national church structure. The devastation of Germany's transportation infrastructure, the scarcity of fuel and motor vehicles, the priority given to AMG personnel over German civilians for train travel, and the bureaucratic red tape involved for Germans to cross zonal boundaries made arranging even the smallest gathering of church leaders from across the country a major logistical challenge. German church leaders appealed to the RAS staff for help in making the necessary travel arrangements so that these meetings could take place. Knappen and his staff played a particularly crucial role in convening the 1945 conference at Treysa, which laid the groundwork for the restructuring of the *Landeskirchen* in the form of the EKD.[57]

Second, RAS officers also helped EKD clergy to access the material resources necessary for worship and church life. The range of resources the

RAS helped the EKD procure can be seen in one of the 1947 reports the RAS filed with AMG headquarters. In September they helped churches find sacramental wine and candles; delivered German Bibles donated by the British and Foreign and American Bible Societies; provided printing presses to publish religious education materials; and facilitated return of church property appropriated by the Nazis back to the EKD.[58] By carrying out these services RAS staff were giving German clergy the necessary materials to rebuild church life out of the rubble of the war.

The third method of facilitating self-help was through direct funding of church programs. The AMG was particularly willing to fund church youth programs, as it believed they were vital for promoting democratic thinking among future leaders of the country. In the immediate aftermath of the war, it was the Roman Catholic and EKD churches that alone possessed the organizational structure to provide young people – many of them homeless – with some form of recreational and educational alternative to the defunct Hitler Youth programs. When the Americans discovered that 43 per cent of the 2.3 million young people in their zone were attending church-sponsored youth programs, the RAS found that their AMG superiors were quick to approve special assistance to these churches, particularly funding for church youth workers to attend workshops and seminars on youth leadership.[59]

Along with reorienting the EKD toward democratic thinking and practice, RAS members believed that enabling German churches to reach out to their own people constituted the first vital steps in Germany's longer journey toward spiritual and moral rehabilitation. In the spirit of ecumenical mission, the Protestant churchmen in the RAS sought to encourage and assist the *Landeskirchen* in taking these initial, if tottering steps to that end.

Ecumenical Mission through Private Voluntary Agencies: The Work of the CWS and the WCC

The most concerted ecumenical missionary thrust from North America came through the Church World Service (CWS), and through US representatives in the WCC. As stated above, the CWS was an ecumenical Protestant relief agency founded in May 1946 by the denominations that comprised the Federal Council of Churches in Christ (FCC), in response to the immense humanitarian needs resulting from the war. Besides operating in Germany, the CWS also delivered humanitarian relief to other countries in Europe and Asia. Germany was the single largest recipient of CWS aid until 1952, when India surpassed it.[60] As mentioned at the outset of the chapter, other Protestant denominations committed to the ecumenical movement, most notably the Lutherans, also participated in the rehabilitation of Germany through their own denominational channels; however, these denominational relief programs were deliberately integrated in the WCC's distribution network in Germany. As such they were one more expression of the ecumenical mission.[61] For North American Protestants who supported the WCC expression of ecumenism, the most significant result of the mission to Germany was the shift in missionary priorities that it represented: the traditional priority of evangelism increasingly was taking a back seat to the task of enablement toward indigenous self-help. Before turning to that theme, it is important to recognize the emphasis on teaching democracy, which also figured prominently in the mission of these voluntary agencies.

Ecumenical Protestants as Advocates and Activists in Promoting Democracy

As already indicated, the Protestant mainline churches expressed great concern for Germany's political recovery along democratic lines. They believed that such a goal could best be realized if voluntary aid agencies, such as churches, were allowed to participate in the country's material and spiritual rehabilitation. Articles in the *Christian Century* pointed out that American access to Germany meant not only the chance to offer material aid, but also the opportunity to extend the hand of Christian fellowship to the German churches and to encourage them in practising political responsibility. Such an approach would do much to stamp out the vestiges of the "chauvinistic nationalism" among Germans, allow them to see an example of genuine democracy in action, and draw them into the wider international family of democratic nations.[62] For ecumenical Protestants, the building of a democratic German community was far too important and large a task to be entrusted to any one group. "Not even military government holding supreme powers under a temporary mandate should attempt to carry out that task by itself. It needs to be supplemented by voluntary leadership from many groups, by humble and devoted personal service."[63]

This same call was echoed by Canadian ecumenical Protestants in their denominational journals. The *United Church Observer* recommended that

AMG "replace the soldier by the missionary" as the most effective way of cultivating a Christian civic consciousness. This approach, instead of the ongoing presence of military occupation, would provide an opportunity for democracy to prove its moral superiority. Voluntary aid offered out of Christian charity could overcome German suspicion and reticence toward democratic freedoms.[64] In addition the *United Church Observer*, along with the *Canadian Churchman* featured articles warning readers more generally about the perils of Communism, and in the case of the latter, urged its readers to support a policy of self-help for Western European countries as a means of checking its spread.[65]

When it came to actual implementation ecumenical Protestants practised a two-fold missionary strategy in their efforts to cultivate democracy in Germany: they adopted a posture of political advocacy, influencing American foreign policy toward Germany through political lobbying and media pressure; and they were among the leaders in promoting ecumenical internationalism by helping the newly established EKD enter the international ecumenical fold of the WCC.

In their role as political advocates, ecumenical Protestants practised a broader understanding of Christian mission than was demonstrated by their conservative evangelical and denominationally focused counterparts. Mainline Protestants shared with other Protestant groups the desire to bring humanitarian and spiritual aid, and promote democratic freedoms, but, to a much greater extent than the latter two groups, they were committed to carrying out that mission through direct political engagement with government policy-makers and by mobilizing public opinion through their print media. While other Protestant mission and voluntary service organizations may have wished for direct access to American foreign-policy-makers, for the most part they did not have the connections to the corridors of power in Washington that the ecumenical mainline denominations did.[66]

Shortly after the war, the leaders of the FCC were some of the first North American Protestant churchmen to gain access to Germany. They were able to do so through the political connections of Stewart Herman, a young American Lutheran minister, who had pastored a church in Berlin for Anglo-American expatriates until the United States entered the war in 1941, and subsequently worked for American military intelligence, the Religious Affairs Section of the AMG, and the WCC. The FCC delegation included Franklin Fry, president of the United Lutheran Church, Methodist Bishop G. Bromley Oxnam, and Episcopal Bishop Henry Knox Sherill.

The result of their first-hand exposure to the staggering needs of the German people caused FCC leaders to reverse their earlier endorsement of the US government's claim that Germany's material needs were being met adequately by the AMG.[67]

In January 1946, Oxnam and Fry were part of an FCC delegation who obtained a meeting with President Truman in the hope of influencing him to change AMG policy, which prohibited outside voluntary agencies from carrying out relief work in Germany. When Fry produced a letter from the British Army on the Rhine, sanctioning the shipping of American church-based aid to German churches in the British Zone, Truman promised the FCC delegates that Americans would not be upstaged by the British. He went on to assure them that the American Zone would soon be open to aid from American churches, and two months later such a policy was in place.[68] The incident showed that FCC leaders could advance the goals of the ecumenical mission to Germany through a political sphere of influence not readily accessible to smaller Protestant agencies.[69]

Alongside their efforts to work through high-level political channels, ecumenical Protestants used print media to generate a groundswell of public support to pressure the US government into changing its punitive policy toward Germany and to allow church-based groups to participate in Germany's moral and material rehabilitation.[70] The call for an open-door policy for international voluntary aid went hand-in-hand with promoting democracy; civilian charity from democratic countries was seen as the most effective way of rehabilitating the Germans from Nazism, and inoculating them against the rising threat of Communism.[71] While ecumenical leaders, such as Fry, supplied press releases for pastors to use in denominational and local newspapers, the *Christian Century* became the national voice of ecumenical advocacy on behalf of Germany.[72] From 1945 to 1947, the *Christian Century* released a steady stream of articles proclaiming the need for a less punitive foreign policy toward Germany as the best means of cultivating democratic freedoms and meeting the material and spiritual needs of the nation.[73]

There were two significant differences between the way in which the mainline's key ecumenical journal discussed the concerns of postwar Germany and the approach adopted by denominational and conservative evangelical ones. The first was the nature with which both groups engaged these issues. Whereas denominational and conservative evangelical print media tended to spiritualize foreign policy issues for their readers, the *Christian Century* adopted more of a this-worldly context and evaluation of international events. Thus attentiveness to aspects of state-craft and geopolitical analysis were the primary focus in its coverage of Germany, instead of the evangelical proclivity of looking for prophetic significance in these events.[74] Second, whereas conservative evangelical and denominational missionary publications ran articles by pastors, Bible teachers, and career missionaries, the *Christian Century* recruited leading experts in foreign policy, social welfare, and European ecclesiastical affairs to write its articles. Such experts included Max Rheinstein, a law professor at the University of Chicago and an expert on Germany, and European ecumenical leader Adolf Keller, who wrote on the rehabilitation of the German *Landeskirchen*.[75] The weighty opinions of such recognized authorities were reinforced by the editorials of the *Christian Century*'s own staff writers with provocative titles as "What Is Mass Starvation?" and "For a Democratic Offensive."[76]

By using media exposure and direct lobbying, ecumenical leaders deliberately sought to mobilize public opinion and influence government legislators to adopt a less punitive approach to instilling democratic values in Germany. By May 1946, the *Christian Century* reported that their advocacy was beginning to pay off. That month the US government lifted its ban on private aid, and supplies from the newly formed umbrella agency, the Council of Relief Agencies Licensed for Operation in Germany (CRALOG), began to flow into Germany.[77] In July 1947 the editorial page of the *Christian Century* claimed a moral victory when it announced the Truman administration's renunciation of its initial "vindictive plan," designed by Secretary of State Henry Morgenthau. The change was seen not only as "a confession of failure," but a "confession of sin." The new policy of helping to rebuild German industry was in line with "Christian teaching as to the treatment of one's enemies."[78]

The second strategy that mainline Protestants adopted to cultivate democracy in Germany, especially in the *Landeskirchen*, was to provide a way for them to rejoin the international ecumenical community. By doing so, the American ecumenical mission moved beyond advocacy to activism. This activism was not solely an American initiative, but was undertaken in a wider context of international ecumenism represented by the WCC, and was concerned not only with Germany, but with a broader agenda of reconciliation and recovery for all the churches of war-torn Europe.[79] In the minds of Anglo-American ecumenists, however, Germany remained the key nation for any kind of lasting and fruitful postwar ecumenical movement in Europe.[80] It was not enough merely to rid the German churches of the pernicious infection of Nazism; it was also necessary to help them see their responsibility to help shape the civic moral character in general. American ecumenists saw the best hope for achieving this shift in the leaders of the Confessing Church movement. Although not without its own internal divisions and disputes, this movement was perceived by American Protestants as best representing that segment of German Protestantism that had not been seduced by Nazism's attempt to undermine the Christian churches through the creation of the Protestant Reich's Church. At the end of the war it was also the leaders of the two main factions within the Confessing Church who were at the forefront of designing the *Landeskirche*'s provisional national administrative structure at the Treysa Conference in 1945.[81] Among this group were notable clerical leaders, such as Martin Niemoeller, and Bishops Theophil Wurm and Otto Dibelius, who had strongly and consistently resisted the Nazi regime during the war. For the editors of the *Christian Century* this was a hopeful sign that "passive acceptance of the sovereign authority of the state," which characterized traditional Lutheranism, was giving way to a theology that "insisted upon the sovereignty of Jesus Christ over the whole range of secular society, including the state."[82] With the war finally over, American ecumenists, along with other WCC leaders, saw this as an opportune moment to nurture this emerging sense of social responsibility in the German *Landeskirchen*. Reintegrating the German churches into the international ecumenical community was seen as the most effective way of ensuring that the *Landeskirchen* would not be seduced again by the siren song of jingoistic nationalism.[83]

The defining event of this part of the mission took place in October 1945 in Stuttgart, when the first official meeting of the council for the newly organized Evangelische Kirche Deutschland took place. As a first step in re-establishing relations between the international ecumenical movement and the German churches, Willem Visser 't Hooft, the general secretary of the WCC, had secured an invitation from Pastor Martin Niemöller of the EKD council, to bring a WCC delegation to Stuttgart for an informal exploratory conversation on how this could be achieved. Two American ecumenical leaders, Samuel McCrea Cavert and Sylvester Michelfelder, were members of the delegation who met with EKD council members.[84] The key challenge for the WCC delegation was how to broach the issue of war guilt without sounding punitive and judgmental. Recent revelations to the wider world about the Nazi death camps had given Protestants in North America cause to suspect that the German *Landeskirchen* had been complicit with the Reich in its genocidal program. Although the EKD was under the leadership of pastors who had been at the forefront of the Confessing Church, the most noticeable voice of protest against the Nazi regime's efforts to enforce their policy of *Gleichschaltung* in the *Landeskirchen*, they had not so far made any public statement that addressed the German church's responsibility for the atrocities carried out in the cause of German racial superiority.[85] Cavert and Michelfelder sensed that the public mood in their own church constituencies back in the United States would not support reconciliation with a reconstituted national Protestant church without some sign of penitence. At the same time, the WCC delegates realized that for church leaders from the Allied and neutral nations openly to demand such a statement from the German churches ran the risk of driving them back into nationalist isolation, thus leaving the fledgling WCC bereft of a member church deemed essential to its success.[86]

In their initial meeting with the EKD council, the WCC delegation agreed to begin the conversation by saying, "We have come [to Stuttgart] to ask you to help us to help you."[87] Although the rest of the initial discussion between the WCC delegation and EKD council was warm, if not emotional, in seeking a way toward reconciliation and renewal of fellowship, it was clear that the EKD needed to make some public statement about its complicity with the legacy of the Nazi regime. On 19 October the EKD leaders released what became known as the Stuttgart Declaration. In it they described their own church as sharing in the responsibility for Germany's military aggression: "With great anguish we state: through us endless suffering [has] been brought to many peoples and countries ... We have for many years struggled in the name of Jesus Christ against the spirit which found its terrible expression in the National Socialist regime of tyranny, but we accuse ourselves for not witnessing more courageously, for not praying more faithfully, for not believing more joyously, and not for loving more ardently."[88]

The declaration went on to express the renewed commitment of the German church to repentance, spiritual renewal, and the desire for joining the ecumenical fellowship offered by the WCC. Reporting on the meeting in the *Christian Century*, Cavert was guardedly optimistic. He quoted from the Stuttgart Declaration at length, commending the EKD council members for producing a forthright statement that recognized "the moral responsibility of the German people for the evil policies of the National Socialist regime and the failure of the church to oppose the policies with sufficient vigor." In his judgment, "the leadership of German Protestantism [was] now in the hands of men whom we can fully trust and who deserve our wholehearted cooperation."[89] Cavert was hesitant about believing that the Stuttgart Declaration actually represented the view of the rank-and-file of the German church, but even if this were not the case, the fact that the new EKD had elected men to leadership who did hold such views was a strong indicator that German Protestant leaders were in harmony with the spirit of the ecumenical movement.[90]

The Stuttgart Declaration paved the way for the EKD's entry into the WCC. The significance of the presence of German delegates at the WCC's inaugural assembly in Amsterdam in August 1948 played out on several levels. Before the assembly, Wilhelm Mann, a pastor in the EKD, wrote about the hopes and uncertainties that German delegates carried with them to Amsterdam. On the one hand there was an overwhelming sense of shock as German leaders emerged from their protracted isolation of the war years to hear the reports of their own country's atrocities. The reports "opened our eyes to the abyss which separated Germany from the rest of the world, to the lies which we had lived, to the horrors with which Germany's name had been stained, to the total political, cultural and spiritual isolation into which we had fallen."[91] On the other hand, Mann also wrote of letters of empathy, forgiveness, and fellowship sent to him and his colleagues, which helped them feel accepted into the ecumenical community.

On another level this sense of forgiveness and restoration took a more tangible and dramatic expression during the conference itself when German delegates were billeted in Dutch homes. Many of these delegates later admitted their fear and apprehension as they entered Holland; but when they were treated as honoured guests, their initial fears were replaced by deep gratitude and a sense of having been reconciled with their enemies.[92]

Another way in which ecumenists from the United States used their influence in the EKD to promote a democratic spirit among the German churches was through the distribution of American material relief supplies. The initial stance of the Allied occupational powers called for a hard peace. Among the Western Allies it was US policy-makers who advocated most strongly for such a position. In April 1945 an American government directive for the US Occupational forces, JCS 1067, outlined in broad strokes what such a peace would look like. Germany was "not to be occupied for the purpose of liberation but as an enemy nation." Germany did not qualify for any UN aid, which would go only to those European countries that had been victims of German aggression. Fraternization between personnel of the occupying powers and the Germans was strongly discouraged.[93] The directive went on to stipulate that the German people would have to rely largely on their own meagre resources and would have to form their own relief agencies and networks for distributing whatever aid the Allied governments chose to make available to them.[94]

Much of the content of JCS 1067 found its way into the Potsdam Agreement and thus formed the initial approach of occupational governments taken by all four Allied powers, not just the Americans. For American voluntary relief agencies particularly, this punitive stance was exacerbated by other policies such as the Trading with the Enemy Act under which Germany was still classified during the early months after its surrender.[95] In addition to the vast destruction of their cities, the influx of a huge refugee population, and the scarcity of material resources, German civilian aid efforts would have to be carried out in the face of the paralyzing bureaucratic maze created by the four Allied powers, each occupying and governing a separate zone of Germany.

It became obvious even before the end of the war that the German *Landeskirchen* were the only ones capable of managing such a task, as they were the only civic institution that had survived the war intact and had the networks covering all four occupational zones required to coordinate such a task on a national scale.[96] German Protestant churches responded to these daunting challenges by founding Evangelisches Hilfswerk (Hilfswerk hereafter), which operated alongside the longstanding Innere Mission in looking after the material and spiritual needs of postwar Germany.[97] Formed in 1945 at the Treysa Conference, Hilfswerk became the emergency relief organization of the EKD. When aid from outside churches was finally allowed into Germany, Hilfswerk became the primary distributing agency for all such Protestant-based aid throughout Germany.[98]

In May 1946, when it became known that American churches would begin sending massive quantities of aid through CRALOG, Stewart Herman of the WCC approached Eugen Gerstenmaier, the director of Hilfswerk, about including the minority German *Freikirchen* as members of

Hilfswerk; this would make it a truly ecumenical organization. Gerstenmaier replied that he had sent the *Freikirchen* formal invitations to join,
but only two denominations had replied. Herman suggested to Gerstenmaier that a stronger and more personal invitation was called for in
order to overcome the longstanding suspicions most *Freikirchen* leaders
held toward the *Landeskirchen*. He tactfully pointed out that having the
Freikirchen represented in Hilfswerk's leadership structure "would benefit
[Hilfswerk] substantially [because] the rich giving churches in America,
which have small churches [among the *Freikirchen*] in Germany" would
be assured "that these churches were receiving fair treatment by the big
quasi-monopoly."[99] By August of that year Herman was able to report
back to the WCC's New York office that the *Freikirchen* were full members
of Hilfswerk. The arrangement signalled a new and unprecedented level of
cooperation between the *Landeskirchen* and the *Freikirchen*. In the judgment of American ecumenical leaders, the new spirit of partnership and
accountability among the German churches indicated that German Protestant leaders were adopting democratic models for their institutions.[100]

The actions of the WCC, and the role of American churchmen within
that organization, were instrumental in building bridges of reconciliation
with the postwar German people. While such ties were cloaked in ecclesiastical rhetoric, it was clear that these actions had a specific political goal
of cultivating democratic values of religious freedom and civic responsibility in the newly formed EKD. These initial gestures of democratic practice gave hope to American ecumenists that the EKD was in fact going to
break from its strongly nationalistic past. By the beginning of the 1950s,
there was growing optimism in the American mainline that a generation
of democratically oriented leaders, especially among the laity, was gradually gaining a dominant influence in the German church.[101]

A New Missionary Emphasis: Assisting the German Church in the Task of Self-help

A second, and more direct, emphasis in the ecumenical mission to Germany was that of enabling the German church to help its own people
in the tasks of material reconstruction and spiritual rehabilitation. Humanitarian aid, especially medical care, had long been part of the modern
Protestant missionary movement.[102] The significance of such material aid
in the context of the mission to Germany lay in its displacing the more
traditional missionary tasks of evangelism and teaching in the priorities

of ecumenical Protestants. In spite of Visser 't Hooft's early insistence that evangelism remain a priority in the ecumenical mission to Germany, this thinking was superseded by Sylvester Michelfelder's slogan, "Bread First, Catechisms Later."[103] As head of the WCC's Department for Reconstruction and Inter-Church Aid, Michelfelder was not ignoring the concern for spiritual renewal in Germany, but expressing the reality that basic humanitarian needs were so acute in postwar Germany (as well as in the rest of Europe) that it was vital they be attended to first.

Offering such assistance in the spirit of ecumenism, however, did not mean sending large brigades of missionary relief workers from America to hand out supplies and help re-Christianize Germany, but rather providing whatever material supplies the German churches requested in order to "re-establish the Protestant church as a major factor in the life of the German people."[104] Evangelism, or "re-Christianization" of the nation was the task of the German church; the ecumenical mission, as understood by supporters in both America and Germany, was to provide German Protestants with the resources they deemed necessary to achieve this goal.[105]

The mission of helping German Protestants help themselves took two main forms: sending basic humanitarian aid in the form of food, clothing, and medicine; and supplying "spiritual aid" in the form of hymnals, Bibles, and prefabricated church buildings specifically for the reconstruction of church life. Although both forms of aid were priorities of the ecumenical mission right from the start, Michelfelder's maxim of "Bread First" did reflect the urgency of the moment, and thus it became the initial basis of appeal issued by US ecumenical leaders in mobilizing the support of their constituents.[106]

In 1946, when the Truman administration changed its position and declared Germany eligible for American voluntary aid, Hilfswerk was in a position to receive and distribute such aid with a relative efficiency.[107] Michelfelder and the WCC were quick to endorse Hilfswerk as the official distributing agent of Protestant ecumenical aid in Germany.[108] What was needed next was an ecumenical agency in the United States for gathering and shipping aid to Hilfswerk.

Most of the US mainline denominations already had their own relief agencies, but in order to gather and then channel the massive quantity of material aid donated toward postwar recovery in Europe and Asia, FCC churches, in cooperation with the American Committee of the WCC, formed the Church World Service in 1946.[109] By 1948 the CWS had become the leading voluntary donor agency in the United States of material aid to Germany. During the period 1946–9, the CWS sent almost 18,000 tons of food, clothing, and medicine to Germany.[110] American Lutherans, through their own agency, Lutheran World Relief, were the second-highest contributor, sending 15,000 tons.[111]

When the Truman administration finally allowed voluntary aid from private agencies to enter Germany in March 1946, it insisted on dealing with only one single organization, not each agency individually. This led to the formation of the Council of Relief Agencies Licensed for Operation in Germany (CRALOG), an umbrella organization created specifically for this purpose.[112] Participating churches and voluntary relief agencies were required to gather and package aid materials from donor members and see that they were transported to a designated warehouse in New York. The US government then arranged for and assumed the cost of shipping these supplies to the German port city of Bremen. Once on German soil, CRALOG supplies were handed over to the two principal German relief agencies, Hilfswerk and Caritas, for sorting and distribution throughout the three Western Zones.

At the European end, the CWS relied on Michelfelder and Stewart Herman of WCC, working in partnership with the leaders of Hilfswerk, to channel US ecumenical aid to needy areas of Germany. From the outset the WCC saw its role in the ecumenical mission as consultative and facilitative.[113] Material aid gathered by the CWS was passed on to Hilfswerk for WCC-approved projects. As such the ecumenical mission was relatively minimalist in missionary personnel actually working in Germany. Only a small administrative staff of eight CRALOG workers was admitted initially to all three Western Zones (and Berlin) in Germany.[114] The labour-intensive activity of distributing actual material relief was undertaken by the Germans themselves. One reason for this had to do with the AMG's policy of restricting access by US civilian aid personnel of any kind to Germany. There was, however, another, philosophical reason, based on "the conviction that the [German] church could best be helped by enabling it to help its people in the name of Christ."[115] Self-help as the leading strategy for the ecumenical mission to Germany was fuelled by the belief that the German churches would be the most effective agents in using material and spiritual aid from America for the rebuilding of church life in their own country. Taking a more interventionist role in the actual distribution of such aid would seem patronizing and thus damage the fragile ties of ecumenical unity that the WCC and CWS were trying to strengthen.[116]

During the first two years of CRALOG's operations, it was the smaller denominational relief agencies (see chapter 3) who sent the most aid to Germany. By 1948, however, the CWS and Lutheran World Relief, with their much larger American constituencies, became the leading donors in CRALOG.[117] For the CWS, 1948 represented its most successful year of giving, in general aid. During that year it shipped 6,250 tons of clothing, bedding, shoes, food, and medicine to Germany. In comparison, during the same period US Lutherans and Catholics each contributed 3,250 tons of relief supplies, while Mennonites and Quakers contributed 2,150 and 1,000 tons respectively.[118]

Canadian ecumenical Protestants also fully supported the WCC's aid policy. Even though their financial contribution for relief work in Germany was proportionally smaller than their American counterparts, both the United and Anglican Churches faithfully promoted WCC aid to German churches – usually within the wider context of aid to European Protestants – in their respective journals. The *United Church Observer* was particularly committed to keeping the material needs of Germany in front of its members right up to 1950, when the Korean conflict began to compete for attention.[119]

Alongside this large quantity of general humanitarian aid, the CWS contributed to projects specifically targeted at aiding the spiritual life of the German churches. One project that found wide acceptance among American ecumenical supporters was the building of *Notkirchen,* or barracks churches. These churches consisted of placing prefabricated housing units, designed originally for the Swiss army, on a foundation made up of rubble caused by Allied bombs, on sites where original churches had once stood. Each unit could be constructed at a cost of just over US$9,000 and had a seating capacity of 500. The first *Notkirche* in Germany was built in the city of Pforzheim, near Karlsruhe, in May 1947. Forty more such churches were approved as projects by the WCC and received particularly strong support from American Lutherans, who sponsored the construction of thirty of these churches to replace destroyed Lutheran churches throughout the Western Zones.[120]

Examples of other spiritual aid projects supported by the CWS included funding the costs of training Christian teachers to give religious instruction in public schools, providing resources for Christian youth camps, sponsoring food and transportation stipends for German pastors, and supplying rolls of cellulose to publishers for printing church newspapers and Christian literature.[121] In all of this, CWS leadership took pains to avoid a posture of paternalism, which they believed was the blind spot of traditional missionary approaches. Instead they sought to offer their services and supplies in "a spirit of cooperation rather than an imposition of superior foreign ideas." Thus *inter-church aid* was a more apt term to describe their work, with missionary work being one subcategory of such aid and now was associated strictly with evangelism.[122] This missionary task was to be left to local churches, while spiritual aid focused on fostering ecumenical goodwill and cooperation, and was not tied to the emergency priorities of the immediate postwar needs. Such an approach was exemplified by the CWS sponsoring of five American youth workers to spend a year working in various churches in southern Germany with local youth leaders. At the end of their year of service the five reported that their work had been significant in two ways: first their mere presence as

> American Christians and representatives of ecumenical organizations has created a very real and very gratifying job as ambassadors for American and world Christianity. Especially in the present German atmosphere of isolation brought about by ... [AMG imposed] restrictions on travel, communications, commerce, etc., plus the wall of hate around Germany, the role of a living link in the world-wide fellowship of the Christian Church which transcends all such barriers takes on vital importance. Secondly, by counselling with leaders, initiating projects and making suggestions, we are able to influence the work itself by contributing some of the findings of American experience in the field, in such things as group work techniques, leadership responsibilities of youth, service projects, etc.[123]

Reports from German churches were so encouraging that CWS leaders recommended that more such qualified American personnel be sent to continue fostering these ties of ecumenical cooperation and goodwill. In an address to the CWS Board of Directors, Eugen Gerstenmaier could report, "A new spirit of the Church in Action lies behind the foundation of *Hilfswerk*, a spirit which we hope will have its consequences and in due course will bring about a change in the position of our Protestant churches within this our world."[124]

Similar hopes for the ecumenical mission of self-help came from the WCC Department of Reconstruction and Inter-Church Aid. As CRALOG aid began to flow into Germany, a WCC report pointed to the importance of a renewed German Protestant church for the revitalization of Christian life for the rest of Europe: "It has often been said that an adequate solution of the 'German problem' is the key to the peace of Europe. It may also be said that an adequate program of Christian reconstruction in Germany will provide the key to the solution of the 'German problem' ... Because of the trials and tribulations through which the German church has gone, it is highly likely that the Christians of Germany will ultimately be able to make a tremendous contribution to the spiritual reconstruction of Europe."[125]

By the early 1950s there were early signs that the Marshall Plan aid was beginning to rejuvenate the West German economy. At the same time a new international humanitarian crisis, triggered by the war in Korea, became the dominant priority for CWS and WCC aid. By the end of 1953 Korea was the leading recipient of CWS aid.[126] In light of these shifts, the ecumenical mission to Germany began to wind down. Although ecumenical aid from the United States continued to flow into Germany through the 1950s, it was at an ever-declining rate. By the middle of the decade the ecumenical mission was moving to its conclusion.

Conclusion: Developments in the American Ecumenical Mission, 1955–1974

With the crisis of postwar recovery fading into the background, the interest of US ecumenical Protestants in Germany did not abate, but it did change. The *Christian Century* continued to report on developments in Germany, but the primary object of its reporting became the plight of East German Christians under the rule of Soviet Communism.[127] Evidence that the mission to Germany was concluding, at least in the popular mind of American ecumenical supporters, can be seen in the nature of the articles. While the *Christian Century* sought to keep its readers informed on the state of the EKD in both East and West Germany, there was no longer a call for American aid.[128]

For leaders of the American ecumenical movement, the mission *to* Germany had changed to an ongoing ecumenical mission *with* Germany. Within the newly formed World Council of Churches, international ecumenical leaders welcomed the German representatives of the EKD as full participants.[129] In 1954 Otto Dibelius, EKD bishop for Berlin-Brandenburg, was elected as one of the presidents of the WCC, and was succeeded in 1961 by Martin Niemöller.[130] Other German clergy were active participants in discussions and debates during the plenary assemblies of the WCC.[131] German Protestant participation in the WCC was evidence of a new outward, ecumenical orientation and a repudiation of long-standing nationalistic tendencies within the German *Landeskirchen*. In light of their role as agents of democracy, US mainline Protestants could claim this as a measure of success for their mission to Germany.

Another tangible indicator of a democratic spirit in the German church can be seen in the impact of outside ecumenical aid on German Protestants. The great outpouring of ecumenical relief and spiritual aid from North America to Germany made a deep impression on the German churches. Most notably it produced a keen awareness among German Protestants of other needy areas of the world. As Steven Conway has pointed out, once German economic recovery was well underway, Germans became, and have remained, among the most generous donors to relief programs in other countries.[132]

Besides producing a new democratic outlook in the German *Landeskirchen*, the mission to Germany also affected how ecumenical Protestants in the United States understood the ongoing task of Christian mission elsewhere in the world. In spite of the fact that voices in the WCC continued to call for traditional evangelism as part of Christian missions, by the end of the 1960s their position reflected a minority report.[133] Debates on the nature of mission carried out at the WCC assemblies in New Delhi (1961) and Uppsala (1968) show a loss of consensus on what defined Christian mission, especially as the concept of Christendom came under increasing attack as a mere mask of Western cultural imperialism.[134]

By contrast, one aspect of mission on which ecumenicals could agree was the continuation of humanitarian relief work to suffering people as an expression of Christian witness. The principal ecumenical relief agencies that came into being as a response to the needs of war-torn Europe, and Germany in particular, continued to function as arms of ecumenical mission to crisis areas around the globe during the Cold War years.[135] As the consensus on evangelism collapsed, humanitarian relief work through inter-church aid became that aspect of Christian mission about which ecumenical Protestants could agree. The concept of self-help through humanitarian aid seemed to offer a more acceptable way to help one's neighbour instead of preaching a message of proselytization.[136] This new and more limited ecumenical consensus on Christian mission, which emerged from the postwar relief effort to Germany, continued to find effective ways to serve needy people in crises around the world, especially in underdeveloped countries of the Global South.[137] An article on the Church World Service, which appeared in a 1947 issue of the *Christian Century*, proved prophetic when it suggested that the humanitarian work of the CWS represented the most hopeful future for a united expression of Christian mission.[138] However, for Protestants who eschewed ecumenical channels in favour of denominational and sectarian mission agencies, saving Germany involved much more than offering assistance toward self-help. As we shall see in the next three chapters, denominational, and especially conservative evangelical missions adhered much more closely to a traditional approach of conversionist-oriented evangelism, while viewing relief work as one more means to that end. As ecumenical mission shifted its attention to the Third World, focusing on the goals of self-help and community development, it became apparent that the missionary agenda of American Protestantism was now divided between the ecumenical good Samaritans of self-help and the traditionalist apostles of global conversion.[139]

Denominational Protestant Missions to Germany, 1945–1974: Mennonites and Baptists Resuscitate and Rehabilitate the *Freikirchen*

From the earliest days of the postwar period, the North American Protestant mission to Germany was embraced not only by churches who channelled their resources through the World Council of Churches [in the Process of Formation] (WCC), but also by denominational mission boards who opted to work outside the emerging ecumenical movement. While the state of crisis in Germany immediately after the war drew all Protestant mission workers together in a variety of ad hoc cooperative relationships, a number of denominations chose to work primarily under their own banner. This group included Mennonites, Baptists, the Salvation Army, the Church of the Brethren, and the Society of Friends (Quakers).[1] All of the above registered with the CRALOG as independent relief organizations and thus were given official approval by the American government to carry out relief work in Germany under their own denominational banner.[2]

Of the denominations listed above who undertook their mission independently from the WCC, almost all could trace their roots back to Anabaptist or separatist bodies from the radical stream of the Reformation. They eventually came to be known as "believers' churches."[3] From this group it was the Mennonites and Baptists who undertook the most active and sustained missionary ventures in Germany during the Cold War period. As such, their respective missionary endeavours offer two illuminating case studies in analyzing and assessing the role of denominational

mission agencies in "saving" Germany.[4] These denominational missionary ventures evolved along similar lines, beginning with relief work; then
moving into some combination of community development, church
reconstruction, and refugee resettlement; and shifting finally to theological education.

In a similar way to their ecumenical counterparts, Baptists and Mennonites held to the dual priorities of material reconstruction and spiritual
rehabilitation in helping the German people rebuild their lives and their
country in the early postwar years. But unlike the ecumenical mission
effort, these two denominational mission agencies found avenues for
continued service in West Germany during the decades that followed her
economic recovery. Both denominations had relatively small, but active,
networks of indigenous churches in Germany, which had been in place
since the nineteenth century. Wherever possible, Mennonite and Baptist
missionaries worked through these denominational networks.[5] Although
these missionaries sought to bring material aid and spiritual care to all
Germans in need, they gave particular attention to their denominational
kindred and frequently used their German congregations as bases from
which to reach out to the wider German populace.

The denominational missionary response has significance primarily for
two historiographical areas: the development of postwar German Protestantism, and the American ideological influence in Cold War Europe.
The impact of denominational missions on German Protestantism was
most noticeable among the independent *Freikirchen,* under whose banner
German Baptists and Mennonites operated.[6] North Americans contributed to the growth of their respective branches of the *Freikirchen* in three
ways: (1) by undertaking relief programs to needy German Baptist and
Mennonite communities, who otherwise may have been overlooked by
relief work sponsored by the EKD; (2) by supporting the construction
and/or repair of church buildings for German sister congregations in their
respective denominations; and (3) by founding and staffing theological
schools to train German pastors and lay church workers.

North American Baptists and Mennonites were also conscious of
West Germany's geopolitical significance in Cold War politics and saw
themselves as ambassadors for democracy in Germany. For Mennonites this was evidenced initially by missionary relief workers seeking to
impart democratic principles to their German counterparts while working alongside them, and in later decades, by helping European churches

organize a visible peace witness in the face of escalating Cold War policies of military deterrence. Baptists worked to promote democratic principles primarily through church reconstruction projects. By supporting their denominational counterparts in Germany in these ways, missionaries saw their "believers' churches" as offering the wider German population a "bottom-up" democratic form of church governance, in contrast to the "top-down" hierarchical Evangelische Kirche in Deutschland (EKD). By practising an ecclesial governance model in which churches were not under state control, as were the *Landeskirchen*, but were directly account-able to their individual congregations, Baptists and Mennonites believed they were promoting personal religious freedom, which characterized a truly democratic society.[7]

In devoting most of their energy to assisting their denominational kindred in the *Freikirchen*, Mennonites and Baptists made their greatest impact on Protestant constituencies at the margins of German religious culture rather than in the mainstream. What follows is an examination of work of Mennonite and Baptist missionaries using the two themes intro-duced above.

Mennonites, Baptists and the *Freikirchen*: Legitimizing the German Protestant Minority

The Mennonites: Background and Overview of the Mission to Germany

North American Mennonites had been active in Europe as missionary relief workers as early as 1920. The widespread destruction in Eastern Europe caused by the First World War had left many Mennonite com-munities in southern Russia in a state of total devastation. To address the emergency need for food, clothing, and building materials, representa-tives of the major Mennonite denominations in North America agreed to form a joint aid committee to channel supplies to Mennonites in Eastern Europe. The result was the formation of the Mennonite Central Com-mittee (MCC), which was first convened in September 1920, and began sending aid to Russian Mennonites in conjunction with the American Relief Administration.[8] The MCC had been created as an ad hoc commit-tee, but a continued demand for its services – especially in helping Euro-pean Mennonite refugees emigrate to the Americas – eventually led to its permanent incorporation in 1937.[9]

When Europe was plunged back into war two years later, the MCC once again made preparations to send aid and relief workers into devastated areas, particularly into Germany. As described in the previous chapter, the American Military Government (AMG) in Germany was slow to allow any external aid from civilian agencies into the country, especially while the need in surrounding countries decimated by the Nazi forces remained high. By the middle of 1946 the American government had softened its position and allowed voluntary aid to flow into Germany through the creation of CRALOG.[10] As a charter member of this umbrella organization, the MCC positioned itself among the first private aid organizations to gain access to Germany.

Even before CRALOG's founding, MCC Director Orie Miller made it clear that once peace had arrived, his organization was interested in sending aid not only to the countries fighting Nazi aggression but to Germany as well.[11] There were several cultural motivations for such missionary interest by North American Mennonites: the ties of ecclesial kinship, ethnic heritage, ongoing familial ties, and in many cases, a common language.[12] The strongest motivator, however, was a theological one. As Miller explained in February 1943 to Herbert H. Lehman, director of Foreign Relief and Rehabilitation Service in the US State Department, Mennonites came from the pacifist stream of Anabaptism, and by bringing aid to the victims of war they were attempting to remain faithful to their pacifist convictions while satisfying their civic responsibilities.[13] Miller's observations provide a helpful summary of the Mennonite heritage and ethos that informed their postwar mission to Germany.

Mennonites have always been predominantly rural folk. Eighty-five per cent of the Church's membership still makes its living from farming as an occupation ... The total Church membership in the United States and Canada numbers about 200,000. Mennonites through their whole history have maintained their emphasis on simple living and in conscientious inability to participate in war ... As adherents to the foregoing ways of living we have appreciated the fine consideration granted our forefathers and us in the United States and Canada through the history of these two nations ... our constituencies feel that our appreciation for privileges granted us can be further shown in being ready to aid in relief of suffering wherever it may exist and particularly in bringing relief to those suffering from the effects of war. Abstention from the political order and being granted exemption from military service does not rule out works of mercy or activities of compassion.[14]

The MCC's mission to Germany during the three decades after the Seond World War falls into two successive phases. During the first phase, from the spring of 1946 to early 1950, Mennonites focused on relief and reconstruction work. During the second phase, which began in 1950, the MCC shifted its focus to theological education for both German- and French-speaking Mennonite young people.

By the end of the 1950s, with the material recovery of West Germany well under way, MCC activity was correspondingly reduced; however, North American Mennonites stayed on, serving primarily as Christian theological educators and peace workers. The impact of the MCC's work on German Protestantism was felt primarily in their aid and assistance to the Mennonite wing of the *Freikirchen*; however, in their work with the most needy victims of war they were careful not to use aid as a means of proselytizing. At the same time, when asked, they did point inquirers toward practices, beliefs, and ecclesial forms that distinguished the Anabaptist *Freikirchen* from the established EKD churches.[15]

Supporting the Mennonite *Freikirchen* through Material Aid and Community Centres

Twenty-seven-year-old Robert Kreider, the MCC's first full-time worker to be stationed in Germany, was a capable and shrewd choice. Kreider was born and raised in Ohio and was a member of the Mennonite General Conference Church. Prior to the outbreak of the war, he and a friend had spent the summer of 1938 hitchhiking and bicycling through Western Europe, experiencing Nazi Germany first hand. He also had served for four years in the Civilian Public Service program as an alternative to military service.[16] This combination of public service experience and familiarity with Germany made him a suitable candidate for such a venture.

On arriving in postwar Germany as an official CRALOG representative, Kreider was at first assigned to Berlin, but soon after was moved to Wiesbaden. This became an advantageous posting for the MCC because of its proximity to a dozen Mennonite congregations in the neighbouring southwestern province of Baden-Württemberg.[17] In Kreider's initial assessment of the needs of the German people, he recognized that the most eye-catching need was among the Mennonite refugees and *Volks-deutsch* expellees from the east, who crowded railway stations or huddled in little family groups with their few possessions anywhere they could find shelter. "Among these refugees are our own people who have fled from the East. The relief agency of the Evangelical Church has been aiding our own brethren in need. And these contributions which we now bring to Germany will find their way in part to our Mennonite refugee brethren. I have visited several of these little circles of Mennonite refugees. Their hearts leap up with joy and thanksgiving to know that we are seeking to help them, that our people are concerned and praying for them."[18]

The needs of the resident population in the American Sector were also great, but more difficult to detect. As a German mother of three small children summed up the plight of her fellow citizens to Kreider, "We have too much food to die and not enough food to live."[19] Summarizing his own thoughts on the future of the MCC mission to Germany, Kreider reflected, "I have a growing conviction that Germany's need is a material need, yes, but infinitely more a spiritual need. We of CRALOG are hoping that the door may be pried open so that additional personnel can come. A group of creative, Christian souls working together *with* the Germany people could do much for them in realizing their work and dignity as individuals."[20]

Kreider's observations provided the basis for the MCC's early operational strategy in Germany. They sought to bring aid to the most vulnerable among the population, while at the same time directing specific attention to the needs of fellow Mennonites in Germany. Underlying all of their relief activity was the belief that material aid needed to go hand-in-hand with Christian witness that addressed the spiritual needs of all people whom they served.[21]

As CRALOG supplies began to arrive in Germany, AMG senior officers made it very clear to all the CRALOG staff that decisions about distribution of aid would be made by the German Central Committee of Evangelisches Hilfswerk (Hilfswerk hereafter), and based solely on need and not religious partisan loyalties.[22] While Kreider and his fellow relief committee members were willing to comply with these stipulations, he was also on the lookout for ways in which he could attend to the specific needs of fellow Mennonites in Germany. In keeping with MCC principles, he was not satisfied with simply monitoring Hilfswerk's distribution of MCC aid, but appealed to AMG officials to allow additional MCC personnel into Germany and thus take an active role in the distribution of CRALOG aid.

In all of this Kreider was keenly aware of the delicate web of relationships in which he and the other CRALOG staff members found themselves. Writing to Sam Goering, the MCC coordinator for all of Europe, who was based in Basel, Kreider explained the competing priorities with which he and his team had to cope:

> At this stage … it does not appear that we can channel any of these [initial] supplies thru Mennonite distribution committees. There are four major German relief distribution agencies. Supplies will go – are required to go – thru their hands … The Lutherans and the Catholics probably will try very hard to get supplies for distribution to their coreligionists … Am I summarizing the MCC attitude correctly when I say this: As an MCC we are happy to cooperate fully with other agencies in this joint relief distribution effort of CRALOG … At the same time, we are interested in investigating the needs of Mennonite folk in Germany and developing indigenous Mennonite relief distribution committees among the Mennonites.[23]

Kreider realized how dependent he and other civilian personnel were on the ongoing goodwill of AMG leaders, and of their obligation to cooperate with the German Central Committee of Hilfswerk in determining how CRALOG supplies should be distributed. But he also wanted some of the MCC's efforts to benefit German Mennonites directly. His tentative articulation of the MCC's position turned out to be accurate, and during his two-year term of service in Germany, Kreider became the architect of the MCC's early mission in that country.

Right from the outset, alongside his responsibilities in Wiesbaden as a CRALOG liaison officer, Kreider devoted time to establishing connections with Mennonite churches in the American Sector in order to assess their needs. Anticipating that the AMG would soon allow civilian aid workers access to their zone, Kreider wanted to use Mennonite churches in the American sector as bases for a more comprehensive aid program to Mennonite congregations and their surrounding communities. As he outlined the plan to European Director Sam Goering,

> It seems that our first job in regard to German Mennonites is to make a simple survey of need, gathering such information as the following: 1. Clothing. How many in the congregation need

clothing, what kinds? 2. Food. Are there any in the congregation on a semi-starvation level? What types of food are needed? 3. What areas of critical need or needy institutions are there in the larger community, beyond the Mennonite *Gemeinde*? 4. Are there those in the Mennonite congregation who would be qualified and available for participation in a Mennonite relief program, contributing particular skills etc.? 5. What ties does the Mennonite congregation have locally with welfare or relief agencies such as *Innere Mission* (the German state-church Home Missions Society)?[24]

When the AMG resisted allowing more civilian aid personnel into its zone, Kreider found a warm reception for MCC relief workers in the British and the French Zones. The French and British military governments were much more open to the presence of civilian voluntary relief agencies, and in the autumn of 1946 the MCC was given permission to begin relief operations in both the French and British Zones under its own banner.[25]

For the MCC, the opening of the British Zone was especially advantageous. This zone included Germany's densely populated *Ruhrgebiet*, which, after heavy Allied bombing, was the area of greatest need. It also contained 90 per cent of Germany's Mennonite population.[26] This factor, along with the freedom to operate under their own banner and to supply their own staff to help with aid distribution, meant that from 1947 to 1952 the majority of the MCC's material and human resources were channelled into this area. By the end of 1947 MCC relief programs were operating in all three Western Zones with forty-three workers overseeing the distribution of 4,538 tons of food, clothing, and other supplies shipped through CRALOG channels. While a portion of this aid was still being distributed by Hilfswerk in the American Zone, the MCC increasingly was developing and working through indigenous Mennonite distribution networks. Christenpflicht and Hilfswerk der Vereinigung Deutscher Mennoniten were two German Mennonite relief agencies, working in Bavaria and the Palatinate respectively, which had with MCC help been granted official recognition by the AMG so that they could directly receive and distribute Mennonite supplies from CRALOG.[27]

In keeping with their commitment to seeking out the most needy victims, regardless of religious affiliation, the MCC ran child-feeding programs in cities such as München, Heilbronn, and Regensburg in the American Zone; and Kiel, Ludwigshafen, Lübeck, Kaiserslautern, and Krefeld in the

British and French Zones.[28] Collectively these programs provided a daily hot meal for up to 50,000 German children.[29] At the same time the MCC also served Mennonite congregations when the opportunity arose. The MCC's most ambitious child-feeding program was in Krefeld, where 6,000 children were fed daily. Here the local Mennonite church also acted as distribution centre.[30] Cornie Dyck, the MCC director for the British Zone, extended the relief program in Kiel to include direct Mennonite-to-Mennonite aid for 15,000 Russian Prussian and local Mennonites who lived in Kiel and the surrounding communities. As much as possible he sought to turn over the distribution side of the relief operation to local Mennonites so that "every one of our Mennonites that is really in need may be helped in proportion to the available supplies."[31]

While the Krefeld program reflected the ongoing concern the MCC had for its kindred in Germany, Kreider could still assure the leaders of Hilfswerk that only 10 per cent of all MCC aid was being earmarked specifically for German Mennonites, while the remaining 90 per cent continued to be distributed among Germans "without institutional prejudice" on the basis of the greatest need. In so doing, the MCC was attempting to "build bridges of cooperation and reconciliation among all groups and agencies" through its community-based relief programs.[32] Tangible evidence that the MCC was putting this into practice was to be found in cities of Kiel and Krefeld, where they worked alongside Roman Catholics and a number of Protestant denominations, and in cooperation with civic and military levels of government to bring food, clothing, and medical supplies to needy Germans.[33] Conservative estimates for the overall impact of MCC's feeding programs are as follows: 80,000 people were fed in 1947, and 140,000 in 1948, with forty-nine staff working throughout the three Western Zones of occupied Germany.[34]

The magnitude of the MCC's aid effort during the early postwar years can be seen when put alongside other non-government aid suppliers who made up the CRALOG consortium. In 1947 the MCC sent over 3,850 tons of food supplies to Germany, which constituted 39 per cent of the total tonnage of food shipped by all CRALOG agencies, as well as 50 per cent of the MCC's total relief effort to all of Europe.[35] During this same period other, much larger church denominations affiliated with CRALOG contributed food aid: Lutheran World Relief (LWR), 369 tons; the Church World Service (CWS), 2,045 tons; the American Friends Service Committee (AFSC), 2,007 tons; and the Roman Catholic War Relief Service

(WRS), 1,400 tons.[36] Baptists, the American Brethren, and the Salvation Army began shipping relief supplies through CRALOG only in 1948. In that year the combined total tonnage of food and clothing aid for all three denominations amounted to only 976 tons.[37] By 1948 the much larger donor constituencies represented by the CWS, LWR (see chapter 2), and the WRS had rallied to the cause of Germany, with the result that their total giving surpassed that of the MCC.[38] This new infusion of relief supplies allowed Mennonites to shift their attention to another avenue of missionary service: community development.[39]

Early in 1948 the MCC's focus began to shift from the immediate demands of emergency aid to the longer-term challenges of community development and reconstruction. At the same time their feeding programs continued to operate, mostly in cities in the British Zone. One reason for this shift was the opportunity it afforded them to place additional North American staff in the American Zone, especially in cities with Mennonite churches and refugees. While the AMG allowed few volunteer workers to come into their zone as relief workers, they did permit private agencies to bring in larger numbers of staff to help operate community development programs as part of their efforts to democratize Germans.[40]

Kreider decided to launch the first such MCC project in the city of Heilbronn. In 1944 Heilbronn had been the target of an Allied aerial firebombing that had destroyed the entire centre of the city and killed 60,000 people.[41] It was also home to a large Mennonite congregation whose meeting hall had been demolished. The MCC purchased a Swedish prefabricated wooden church, while the local congregation supplied the land, erected the building, and assumed the installation costs. The arrangement was that the local congregation could use the building for Sunday worship services, and during the week the MCC would use it for community service activities, in which local Mennonites were also invited to participate.[42] The goal of the community centres was "to provide self-help to the people and to interpret the spiritual significance that accompanies material aid distribution 'In the Name of Christ.'"[43]

This shift in mission strategy called for a change in the make-up of volunteer personnel. Feeding programs were staffed overwhelmingly by single young men and women, but the MCC preferred to have married couples, who could create more of a family-style atmosphere, in charge of their community centres.[44] They also needed people who were competent in a variety of trades and domestic skills in order to teach and supervise community residents who took advantage of the centre's services. The Heilbronn centre was staffed initially by Frank and Marie Wiens, a California couple who were able to establish good working relations with local Mennonites and non-Mennonites alike. Along with a support staff of two other married couples, the Wienses set up a sewing room, a shoe repair shop, a reading library, and music room. In addition to these services, the Heilbronn building was used as a drop-in centre where people could visit over a cup of coffee and attend weekly Bible studies.[45]

Alongside the above programs, the MCC used Heilbronn and its other *Nachbarschaftsheime* (as the centres became known) as bases from which to continue feeding programs for young children, elderly folk, and, increasingly, university students. Weekly worship services and training for Sunday school teachers were more direct forms of spiritual assistance the MCC offered to its constituents.[46] The multi-faceted services of this *Nachbarschaftsheim* exemplified the type of missionary program Kreider believed was best suited to the MCC's approach of spiritual rehabilitation through humble service. Community centres represented "projects with 'growing edges' and plus features."[47]

In reporting on the work of the Heilbronn centre after its first year of operation, Director Frank Wiens explained how such centres provided a measure of community stability and support for the *Freikirchen*. "[They] provide an opportunity for better acquaintance with others in the neighbourhood … Our aim is to establish acquaintance and working relations with the church groups within the area. Quite naturally closest would be the non-state protestant churches … Perhaps our ultimate goal in its finest terms is to create a cooperative community spirit; and more particularly encourage existing Christian churches to greater cooperation and understanding in building God's kingdom."[48]

At the gentle urging of MCC workers, the Heilbronn Mennonites worked in partnership with ministers from like-minded local Protestant churches and began a series Sunday evening meetings with the specific goal of reaching out to "churchless people." When the initial meetings were well attended, reluctance by the local pastors gave way to enthusiasm and plans to expand the program. Besides being a real help to un-churched people, Wiens reported that the meetings "served a function in bringing the ministers of various churches together and awaken[ing] them to a need for a more vital missionary program on their own doorstep … it is hoped that not only will non-Christians be won into the fellowship but also there will be a growth in the spiritual life of the local Mennonite congregation."[49]

By the end of 1948 the MCC had established four additional community centres in the cities of Krefeld, Hamburg (British Zone), Neustadt and Kaiserslautern (French Zone). Over the next two years they would establish another two *Nachbarschaftsheime* in the cities of Frankfurt and Berlin.[50] Whereas centres such as the ones in Krefeld and Heilbronn could draw on the support of previously existing Mennonite congregations, the Frankfurt centre signalled a newly planted Mennonite church where none had previously existed. The altered demographics created by refugee and DP migrations in the early postwar period thus provided opportunities for the MCC to establish new churches where new immigrant Mennonite communities were taking root.[51]

In the MCC's mission, the community centres functioned as a transitional step away from primary aid to community development. Initially the centres, such as the one in Heilbronn, were distribution points for material relief, a first step in the "weaning process" whereby local populations became decreasingly dependent on MCC aid and began to take responsibility for rebuilding their own neighbourhoods.[52]

By the middle of 1950 there were signs that the community centre program had served its purpose, and most, similar to the Heilbronn centre, were being turned over to local Mennonite churches. The Frankfurt *Nachbarschaftsheim* was also used as the MCC administrative headquarters for coordinating their volunteer service programs throughout Western Europe. Only the Berlin centre remained active as an MCC *Nachbarschaftsheim*, largely in response to the ongoing influx of impoverished refugees from the east.[53]

Supporting Mennonite Churches through Theological Education

Even as this second phase of mission work was winding down or being transferred to German Mennonites, the MCC found another way to support the growth and development of Mennonite congregations throughout German-speaking Europe. This new avenue was in Christian education. As an MCC youth worker, Milton Harder had observed the acute need for Christian instruction among Mennonite young people in the town of Neustadt, southwest Germany. Under Hitler's regime they had not been allowed to attend their church services but had been forced to participate in alternative Sunday youth programs mandated by the Nazi regime. Harder believed these young people would be discouraged from participating in church life for lack of biblical education, "which, of course, is necessary for a vision of Christian service."[54] The war years had robbed them of this. In addition there were few full-time pastors to look after multiple congregations, and no lay leaders with sufficient theological education and experience in youth work in local Mennonite congregations.

Harder's concerns were shared by Orie Miller, the MCC executive director, and Mennonite leaders in southern Germany, Switzerland, and France. European leaders were particularly concerned about the influences of "worldliness" among their young people in light of the demographic shift among Mennonites from rural farming communities to urban locations since the end of the war.[55] The trend toward urbanization was not unique to Mennonites in Germany, but mirrored a similar shift – along with its attendant religious concerns – in Mennonite communities in Canada and the United States.[56] Alongside this migration by North American Mennonites to urban centres was a correlating rise in the number of Bible schools and colleges begun by Mennonite groups to keep Mennonite young people faithful to their denominational and religious heritage.[57]

It was only natural that MCC missionaries such as Harder and Miller should see biblical education as an effective way to keep German Mennonite youth faithful to their spiritual roots. After meeting with Mennonite leaders early in 1950, the MCC European director, Henry A. Fast, recommended to MCC leaders in the United States that they should support the establishment of an international Bible school, which would educate Mennonite young people in biblical studies and the Mennonite heritage, and train them for service to their congregations and for mission work.[58]

The European Mennonite Bible School (EMBS) in Basel, Switzerland, offered two advantages: Basel was home to two of the largest and most strongly supportive Swiss Mennonite churches, and the school could benefit from the presence of the MCC's European headquarters in that city. In 1957 when the school outgrew this location the MCC helped EMBS purchase its property in the nearby village of Liestal. The school bought a bankrupt hotel, which was renovated and renamed Bienenberg, after a defunct beehive that had been part of the property.[59]

In order to get the Bible school up and running by the fall of 1950, the MCC made some of its office space available for classroom use, and provided two of the five full-time teaching faculty, one of whom was John Howard Yoder.[60] The school offered bilingual instruction, with all courses taught in German and French. Initially the program was a modest venture offering a six-week term of studies with courses in Old and New

Testament, Christian doctrine, Mennonite church history, and pastoral ministry.[61] During its first four years, the school's average attendance was around thirty students, but in its fifth year, enrolment climbed to fifty-one.[62] As EMBS prepared for its sixth year of operation it could boast increasing enrolment, a term of study now extended to ten weeks, a greater range of course offerings, and seven full-time teaching faculty. When the school moved to Bienenberg in the fall of 1957, EMBS had seen 278 students pass through its program with 106 of them from Germany – the country with the highest overall number of students who had attended the school.[63]

MCC faculty member Cornelius Wall, who served as the principal of EMBS from 1953 to 1958, kept North American supporters informed of the school's progress, while soliciting continued financial support for the purchase and renovation of the Bienenberg property.[64] During his years as principal, Wall continued to assure North American supporters that the school, or "their godchild in Europe," was realizing its original goals of teaching young people to know and study the scriptures, preparing students as "members of churches [to do] their part toward furthering the spiritual life of the church," and "enabling their graduates to present the claims of Christ to others in a winsome and effective manner."

In 1958 Sam Gerber, a Swiss Mennonite, took over the leadership from Wall. Echoing his predecessor, Gerber informed MCC supporters that the strength of EMBS was in its emphasis on training lay workers for service in their churches, but also for missionary work overseas. In its first seventeen years EMBS had enrolled 910 students, 340 of them from Germany, and 50 of its alumni were active as ministers, 17 had gone on to seminary training, and about 100 were active in youth and congregational work in their churches.[65] Gerber could say with some confidence that Bienenberg had "become a center for biblical education for [Mennonite] congregations" and was also beginning to attract students from other branches of the *Freikirchen*.[66]

The MCC in Germany from 1960 to 1974: Scaling Back the Mission

As the crisis of the early postwar years receded further into the background, Mennonites reduced their missionary presence in Germany to two centres of operation: the Bible school at Bienenberg, and the Volunteer Service Centre in Frankfurt. In Frankfurt the MCC continued to operate an office, which coordinated the volunteer service program for North American young people who came to Europe to work on short-term service projects. It also served as the centre for promoting peace initiatives as a distinctive aspect of Mennonite Christian witness, which will be examined in the second section of this chapter.[67]

The other centre of ongoing Mennonite mission in Germany was the EMBS campus in Bienenberg, just across the Swiss border. The primary contribution of the MCC to EMBS was ongoing financial support for the school and supplying at least one full-time member to the school's faculty. In some years the school's faculty included no more than a single North American teacher. In 1962 John Friesen and Herbert H. Janzen, both from Canada, were listed in the EMBS catalogue as members of the teaching faculty. As the school's enrolment increased during the latter part of the decade and into the early 1970s, the number of North American faculty did as well. For the 1969–70 school year, four of the fifteen teachers came from either Canada or the United States. In 1973 their number had increased to five.[68] Most were visiting faculty who taught their courses for a specific session, but their presence indicates an ongoing interest in and strengthening ties with EMBS by Mennonite congregations in North America.

Those bonds were nurtured during the 1960s and early 1970s by four North American concert tours undertaken by a choir of EMBS students. In 1961, 1965, 1968, and again in 1974, a choir of EMBS students travelled across North America, performing in Mennonite churches in order to cultivate goodwill and solicit financial support for the ongoing work of the school. The first two tours raised $20,000 for the school; the third tour, an additional $18,000.[69] Financial support remained strong into the early 1970s as EMBS recorded an income of just over SFR 315,000 (approximately $100,000 at that time) for 1972 from its North American constituency. This amounted to 11 per cent of the EMBS annual budget.[70] Thus even as the number of personnel from North America declined, such tours and financial support demonstrated that Mennonites in Canada and the United States considered themselves ongoing stakeholders in the mission of the school.

Overall it was the early postwar humanitarian aid efforts in which the MCC had its most dramatic impact, but its commitment to helping German Mennonite communities rebuild their lives and their places of worship and educate their young people had a longer-lasting influence. Through the latter practices, MCC missionaries helped local Mennonite

Freikirchen become a more visible and well-established part of German Protestant life.

Background to the Baptist Mission to Germany

American Baptist commitment to helping their German denominational kindred went back to the origins of the Baptist movement in that country. Unlike the Mennonites, whose religious and ethnic roots could be traced back to the Reformation, the Baptist *Freikirchen* were viewed – especially by church members in the established *Landeskirchen* – as an Anglo-American transplant whose congregants laboured under the stigma of being un-German.[71] As a result they too operated at the margins of religious life in Germany and had been a target of discrimination, and at times even persecution, at the hands of *Landeskirchen*.[72] The charge of being a foreign incursion into German church life was not without grounds. The founder of the Baptist mission to Germany, Johann Gerhard Oncken, was supported by missionary and Bible societies in England, Scotland, and America during the 1830s and 1940s. During these decades Oncken was responsible for founding twenty-five Baptist congregations in Germany. It is little wonder that Lutherans were quick to label the Baptist movement in their country as a "new English religion," alien to German culture.[73]

When the Second World War erupted a century later, German Baptists, in spite of having a membership of 80,000 across Germany, encountered the same prejudices and suspicions that Baptists – and the *Freikirchen* in general – had always received from the *Landeskirchen* members wary of these "sectarian" denominations.[74] Anglo-American Baptists were well acquainted with the long-standing discrimination suffered by their denominational kindred in Germany. Consequently North American Baptist participation in postwar reconstruction was guided by the priority of aiding German Baptists who might otherwise be overlooked or deliberately neglected by German relief agencies. Unlike the Mennonites, who subordinated denominational interests to distributing aid on the basis of greatest immediate need, Baptists gave greater priority to aiding those of their denomination, believing that their marginal religious status already placed them among the most needy segment of the German population.[75] Three factors help to explain this contrast. First, the two communities defined their mandates differently: for the MCC, relief work was primarily a form of Christian social justice; for the BWA, which existed more to promote international "fellowship and cooperation among Baptists," relief work served primarily as one more expression of denominational kinship.[76] Second, through the oversight of the relatively high numbers of its missionary personnel in Germany the MCC had assurance that the relief needs of German Mennonites would be met; in contrast, the BWA had only a small handful of missionaries in the German theatre, and thus relied on its agreement with Hilfswerk for the apportionment of BWA-provided aid to ensure that the needs of German Baptists would not be overlooked. Third, there was a significant difference in the tonnage of relief supplies donated by each agency. MCC donations of material from 1946 to 1949 distributed through CRALOG totalled over 11,000 tons, whereas BWA supplies for the same period amounted to just under 1,500 tons.[77] The sheer abundance of MCC supplies, along with the relatively small number of Mennonites in Germany, meant that it could designate a much higher percentage of its materials to non-Mennonite needs while still addressing the needs of its own people.

Following a similar pattern to that of the Mennonites, the trajectory of the Baptist mission in Germany fell into two successive but overlapping phases: relief work and church reconstruction undertaken by the BWA from 1947 to 1953; and the development of theological education, which began in 1949 with the founding of the International Baptist Theological Seminary and lasted through the entire Cold War era. During the first phase, Baptists, in contrast to the MCC, made their greatest impact in church reconstruction as opposed to relief programs. Baptists did operate a relief program, but on a much smaller scale than that of the MCC. It was through church rebuilding and founding a seminary that Baptists made their greatest impact on the *Freikirchen*. Even though the "fraternal assistance"[78] of Baptist missionaries from North America did not translate into a dramatic increase in the number of German Baptists, it produced a result similar to that achieved by the MCC: growing acceptance of the legitimacy of the *Freikirchen* in German Protestant life.

Relief Work among German Baptists through the Baptist World Alliance

As early as 1905 Baptists had founded an official transnational body, the Baptist World Alliance (BWA), to promote global fellowship among the national Baptist unions. The BWA was created at the Baptist World Congress in London that year, not to create a single Baptist "superchurch," but to be "a forum for fellowship, an agency of compassion, a voice for liberty, an instrument of evangelism and a channel of communication."[79] Following the First World War, the BWA promoted a cooperative relief effort for needy denominational kinfolk in Europe.[80] This initial effort by the BWA to bring material aid to needy Baptists in Central and Eastern Europe was led by a London pastor, Rev. J.H. Rushbrooke.[81] Fluent in German and possessing a network of ecumenical contacts on the European Continent from his earlier studies there, Rushbrooke was well suited for such a task.[82]

During the Second World War, Rushbrooke, now in his mid-seventies, was once again asked to organize the BWA relief effort for the postwar period. In a preliminary report to the BWA executive committee in 1943, Rushbrooke made several recommendations, which became the dominant themes of the Baptist mission to Germany during the early postwar period. While recognizing that Baptists were certainly in favour of broad humanitarian relief work, which sought to serve all who were in need, Rushbrooke called on Baptist unions to direct the efforts of their own denominational missionary and relief agencies specifically toward the needs of European Baptists. Mindful that Baptists in most European countries were marginalized religious minorities, and therefore easily overlooked by state and municipal reconstruction programs, he believed that it was up to Baptists from wealthier countries to make up for such indifference. In his report he noted, "It is also impossible that interdenominational bodies, including in many cases representatives of State and sacerdotal churches, should appreciate the religious values which we cherish who share these distinctive convictions: nor would it be consistent on our part to accept aid in doing our special work from those whose principles – as honestly held as our own – are in points we deem important definitely opposed to ours."[83]

His fear, with historical justification, was that the smaller bodies of the *Freikirchen,* such as Baptists, who cherished their ecclesial independence, stood to be overlooked by ecumenical and state-church agencies that viewed them as narrowly sectarian, and even subversive.

He would never see his plans come to fruition, however. On 1 February 1947, Rushbrooke died from a stroke while in the midst of organizing a congress for European Baptists. The mantle of leadership for the Baptist relief effort fell on Dr Walter O. Lewis, a missionary executive with the American Baptist Foreign Missionary Society who was also the general secretary of the BWA at that time.[84] In order to carry out his duties more effectively in this new capacity, Lewis moved across the ocean and set up his office in London, where he lived for the next four years.

As part of his responsibilities Lewis was designated as a special representative for dealing with Baptists in Germany. Assisting him in organizing relief efforts were two American missionaries who already had considerable experience working in Europe: Dr Edwin A. Bell, who was the Paris-based representative of the American Baptist Foreign Mission Society (ABFMS), and Dr Jessie Franks, based in Zürich, who represented the interests of the Southern Baptist Convention Foreign Mission Board (SBC-FMB).[85]

In the summer of 1947 Edwin Bell was appointed by Lewis to act as the on-site liaison officer for Baptists in Germany and Austria in order to assess needs and prioritize relief projects for North American aid.[86] In the fall of that year the BWA became a registered member of CRALOG and also reached a relief disbursement agreement with the EKD's Evangelisches Hilfswerk: 20 per cent of all BWA supplies would be turned over directly to Hilfswerk's general relief needs in Germany, while the other 80 per cent would be channelled to Bruderhilfe, the German Baptist relief agency, for distribution through the Baptist network of *Freikirche* congregations. Eugen Gerstenmaier, the leader of Hilfswerk, and Lewis agreed that "a reasonable amount of the supplies turned over to ... *Bruderhilfe* shall be used to relieve distress in churches of the Baptist Union."[87] The understanding was that Bruderhilfe, in addition to meeting the needs of Baptists, would use its distribution facilities and North American supplies to meet the needs of the wider German populace.

This arrangement assured American Baptists, and the BWA in general, that Baptist aid was reaching distressed German Baptists; and enabling Hilfswerk to recognize Bruderhilfe as a credible partner in bringing aid to the wider German populace gave German Baptists increased legitimacy in German Protestant circles. From 1948 to 1951, when the CRALOG program was operational, North American Baptists contributed $8.5 million in goods and cash gifts to Baptist world relief causes, the majority of which went to relief work in Germany.[88]

With a membership of just over 100,000, the German Baptist Union's highest concentration of members was in the British Zone (47 per cent), followed by the Russian Zone (33 per cent), and then the American (17 per cent) and French (3 per cent) Zones respectively.[89] In a way similar to MCC's work, these figures meant that BWA relief efforts would be channelled to the industrial area of northwest Germany, but in contrast to their Mennonite counterparts, Baptists also directed some of their aid to the Russian Zone.[90] By the end of 1948 Bruderhilfe was using BWA relief supplies to run sixteen different feeding programs, fourteen of which were specifically for members of Baptist congregations. By directing the vast majority of their aid to fellow Baptists, the BWA was working to ensure that a historically marginalized group in German Protestantism would be able to recover from the ravages of war and continue to be a viable independent alternative to state-subsidized *Landeskirchen*.

As the initial humanitarian crisis showed signs of gradually receding, Baptist relief workers focused their resources on specific lingering areas of physical need. The director of Bruderhilfe, Karl Koch, emphasized the appalling conditions faced by Baptists in the Russian Zone and Bruderhilfe's ongoing work in supplying food to needy congregations there. Jessie Franks called for Southern Baptists to continue supporting feeding programs for the elderly and for university students. Franks went on to praise the staff of Bruderhilfe, commending them for their organization and efficiency in distributing aid. As a result of their efforts, he observed, Baptists in Germany were being cared for much better than the average German.[91]

Like the MCC, the BWA also developed a community-based avenue of service once their material aid program was up and running. However, whereas the MCC focused on community centres, Baptists directed their resources primarily to church reconstruction and re-provisioning. Rushbrooke had anticipated such a development in his 1943 report and urged that priority be given to the provision of biblical literature and hymnbooks, the repair and reconstruction of church buildings, and funding for Baptist seminaries.[92] By the end of the war, the leaders of the BWA had already been made aware of the war damage inflicted on Baptist churches through information provided by US military chaplains stationed in Germany during AMG occupation. In the autumn of 1945, Baptist army chaplain Paul Gebauer had taken the initiative in assessing the immediate needs of German Baptists. Gebauer informed the BWA that two important Baptist institutions, the seminary in Hamburg and publishing house in Kassel, were both completely destroyed. He estimated that 240 German Baptist churches serving a congregational membership of 69,000 were now under Soviet control.[93] Figures for the size of the Baptist population and the number of churches that needed to be rebuilt in the Western zones emerged only several years later, once the large migrations of

Baptist displaced persons from Soviet-controlled regions to the west had been taken into account. From 1946 to 1950 the Baptist population in the Western Sector increased from 81,796 to 100,149, mostly through refugee and DP emigration from the east.[94] During this same period it was also reported that of the existing 165 churches in the Western Sector, 74 had been destroyed as a result of the war, and 190 additional churches needed to be built as a result of population shifts and the influx of Baptist DPs.[95]

Prior to the war, the majority of Baptists living in the part of Germany that would comprise postwar West Germany lived in the northwestern part of the country. By contrast many postwar Baptist refugees from the east ended up settling in the southern provinces of Bavaria and Baden-Württemberg. West Berlin and Western Zone cities just across the line from the Russian Zone also found themselves with a sudden influx of Baptist refugees fleeing Soviet occupation.[96] The results of this surge were that few of the existing churches could handle additions to their congregations, and the newly resettled Baptist refugee communities in the south found themselves with no church building at all. The plight of church building destruction, combined with Baptist refugee communities with no church access, was apparent in November 1947 to American Baptist minister G. Pitt Beers, who observed that two years after the war there was little noticeable improvement for German Baptists. As part of a touring delegation of American ministers, he described worshipping in a "repaired" Germany Baptist church on a rainy Sunday; the water dripping through the leaky roof made so much noise one could hardly hear the service. On a more hopeful note, he reported that eight new Baptist congregations had sprung up in Bavaria as the result of refugees from Eastern European states, where before the war there had only been one Baptist church, in München.[97]

Once the BWA relief program was finally operating, missionary representatives from both the Southern and Northern Baptist Conventions began pushing their respective mission boards to take a greater role in assisting German Baptists to address their spiritual needs. Through the BWA both conventions had contributed funds to rebuild the Hamburg Seminary and the publishing house in Kassel, but many opportunities to provide for the spiritual needs of fellow Baptists were being missed.[98] From his base in Switzerland, Southern Baptist missionary Jessie Franks wrote to the Foreign Mission Board regional director for Europe, George Sadler, "Southern Baptists are in a peculiarly favorable position in Europe now to render a great spiritual service, sharing with our Baptist brethren the fellowship of service, so richly inviting in fields of evangelism, education, missions and church reconstruction ... This is no time for Southern Baptists to do less for relief, but it is time when we should begin to shift our emphasis to the definitely spiritual side."[99]

In mid-1949 it seemed as if Frank's plea would go unheeded. The chairman of the BWA Relief Committee, Dr Paul Caudill, seemed lukewarm about the idea of church reconstruction in particular, noting that rebuilding churches was something that Germans would have look after on their own. The plight of refugee congregations with no meeting place for worship struck a more sympathetic chord with the committee, but in either case, resources for such a venture were not available.[100] A year later, much had changed. Not only was the BWA supporting the construction of church buildings for refugee congregations, they were also looking at helping with the rebuilding of existing churches.[101] While nothing in the BWA's records directly accounts for this about-face, a likely reason for it was the arrival of Kenneth Norquist in Stuttgart as the BWA's CRALOG representative in 1950. While his predecessor, former chaplain Otto Nallinger, had focused on relief projects, this phase of the BWA's work was already waning.

From 1950, with the arrival of Norquist in Stuttgart as the new CRALOG representative for the BWA, the construction of church buildings for refugee congregations and the rebuilding of churches became the major missionary priority.[102] From the outset of his time in Germany, Norquist devoted much of his energy to helping Baptist refugees resettle in West Germany, and as a result he became convinced that the best way to help the many Baptist refugees from Eastern Europe was not emigration across the Atlantic but permanent resettlement in the German communities where they were already placed in temporary refugee camps. Seeking to take advantage of the labour potential these refugees represented, the German government had introduced a program to help refugees find employment in the communities where they resided. Norquist estimated that 29,000 Baptist refugees had come to West Germany since 1945, and he believed that by working in harmony with the government's economic resettlement incentives, the BWA would help bring a permanent solution to the ongoing relief needs of refugees, and restore a sense of dignity to their lives.[103]

Norquist argued that an important step in the resettlement process for Baptist refugees would be the provision of a church building of their own, which could provide them with a sense of stability and identity. He pointed out that German communities with strongly established Lutheran or Roman Catholic populations discriminated against religious minority groups, such as Baptists, both socially and economically. Since the government plan involved group resettlement, it was possible to establish new Baptist centres and strengthen the fledgling ones that had recently sprung up in southwestern Germany. "Experience has shown in a unique way that wherever refugee churches have been established, favorable results have been felt in the community as a whole, the refugees have gained prestige, had the necessary social contacts and the split between the old and the new citizens in the community at large has become less pronounced ... An additional reason [to support chapel reconstruction] is the *great missionary opportunity* ... Out of 45 Baptist churches in Bavaria and Württemberg/Baden, 29 are without chapels, 26 of which are refugee churches in cities that have been without a Baptist witness before" (italics added).[104]

He went on to emphasize the importance of helping established congregations rebuild churches destroyed by the war, as well as helping new congregations construct a place of their own. Having their own church building helped Baptists gain a sense of belonging, while giving them legitimacy in the eyes of the community.

Norquist's portrayal of church construction as a missionary work found a favourable response with both the Southern and Northern Baptist Conventions, and given the advantageous rate of exchange, this kind of mission project could yield tangibly impressive results for a relatively low cost. For German Baptists, the period from the summer of 1951 to the summer of 1953 was characterized by the construction of numerous new chapels and the rebuilding of bombed-out churches. During this period the ABFMS and SBC-FMB, along with a number of smaller Baptist mission societies in Canada and the United States, sent just over US$250,000 to the BWA, specifically for chapel reconstruction. This was the largest budget item on the BWA's ledger, and double the amount given for relief work during this period.[105] The BWA used these funds to help in the construction of thirty-eight new chapels for refugee congregations, twenty-two of which were located in the southern provinces. Reconstruction of fourteen destroyed churches in major urban centres throughout Germany was also funded.[106]

Many of the new refugee chapels were *Notkirchen* or emergency churches, just like the ones the WCC supplied for the EKD in rebuilding many of the *Landeskirchen* destroyed during the war.[107] These chapel projects were usually joint efforts between American churches and local

German congregations in that overseas funding covered only part of the cost of each church, while local membership raised the remainder and often supplied volunteer labour for the actual construction. The chapel in the southern town of Schwenningen was a typical example. American Baptists provided DM 10,000 toward building materials, and the local congregation supplied the equivalent of the remaining DM 30,000 through a combination of some cash donations, but mostly through volunteer labour. As a result of this arrangement, German congregations began to feel a part of their surrounding communities and developed a missionary outlook of their own. Norquist noted this transformation among new refugee congregations.

> To see these people at work, both physically in building their chapels, and spiritually in making in-roads into the unsaved population, is an experience that makes one consider the greatest difficulties in providing help very insignificant in comparison with the results that can be achieved by investing our money in that kind of workers [*sic*]. The Baptist refugees in Western Germany are all potential missionaries. They are the most enthusiastic and the most spiritual of all the Baptists over here. In the effort that the Christians are making to use the unique opportunity for missionary work that the war-torn and socially defect country provides, it is these refugees who constitute the spearheads.[108]

The missionary theme in church construction was also evident when American Baptist chaplains stationed in Europe took up a collection to buy the land for construction of a new chapel in the Reformation city of Worms. The chapel site was located between the city's cathedral and a museum housing artifacts of the Reformation. Directly across the street was an early medieval church from the Merovingian era. Norquist observed the strategic and symbolic significance of such a location: "It is in the center of the history making part of the city – the places where the citizens like to stroll. Here in the midst of Catholic and state church surroundings the Baptist refugees of Worms want to make their lights shine. We can help them by aiding in the erection of a sanctuary where they can evangelize and invite the lost to their services."[109]

Such support for church construction indicates that North American Baptists understood the significance of their work as surpassing the mere restoration or provision of church buildings. They were helping German Baptists claim a legitimate place in the religious life of the communities in which they were resident and to thus be agents of spiritual renewal to their own people.

Church reconstruction represented the last phase of the BWA's missionary involvement in Germany, and with it the missionary work of the Northern Baptist Convention (NBC). Northern Baptists retained a "fraternal representative" in Western Europe sent by their mission society, the ABFMS. The ABFMS intended to adopt a spirit of partnership when working in Europe, in contrast to the SBC's aggressive approach, which marked the founding of the International Baptist Theological Seminary (IBTS).[110]

Spiritual Rehabilitation of the Baptist Freikirchen through Seminary Education

The ongoing Southern Baptist mission work in Germany after the early postwar years of crisis has to be understood in the context of the SBC-FMB's overall strategy of aggressive expansion during the Cold War decades. From 1947 to 1985, the SBC-FMB increased its missionary personnel from 625 to 3,432, and the number of countries in which they were active went from nineteen to eighty-four.[111] Under the successive administrations of M. Theron Rankin and Baker James Cauthen, Southern Baptists bolstered their efforts in the Roman Catholic countries of southern Europe, but also began to work in the predominantly Protestant countries of northern Europe.[112] It was this expanding missionary vision that fuelled the second phase of the Baptist mission to Germany: theological education.

Establishing a Baptist seminary for all of Europe was not a new idea for Baptists on either side of the Atlantic. The inspiration for such a seminary had been voiced intermittently in European Baptist circles since the European Baptist Congress of 1908, but no action had ever been taken.[113] In 1947 the leaders of the SBC-FMB sensed that the moment to proceed with such a venture had finally come. George Sadler, the SBC-FMB secretary for Europe, along with Jessie Franks, began to formulate plans to make the idea a reality. On the basis of their travels and relief work in postwar Europe, both men felt that the desolation of Europe was so overwhelming that its spiritual rehabilitation "was a responsibility that must be assumed largely by forces outside of Europe, chiefly by American Christianity."[114] In April 1948, Sadler made a formal proposal to the SBC-FMB's leadership to move ahead with such a venture, and received approval to do so, along with an initial budget of $200,000.[115]

In their enthusiasm Southern Baptist leaders acted unilaterally without consulting the national heads of the European Baptist Unions. When Sadler made the announcement about the SBC-FMB's plans for a seminary in Switzerland at a BWA Congress in London later that year, the response of Baptist European leaders was lukewarm.[116] While not opposed to the idea of a seminary, Europeans resented the high-handed way in which SBC-FMB delegates presented their plans as a *fait accompli*. In spite of this controversy the Congress delegates adopted the report of its Committee on Theological Education, which stressed "the need of a seminary in Europe which was more than a national institution … which may satisfy the educational needs of several countries … and may be more of a graduate school than some of the smaller seminaries." Such a seminary would in no way seek to replace existing national seminaries. The report concluded with an expression of appreciation to the SBC for its generosity in establishing such a school in Switzerland.[117]

On behalf of the SBC-FMB, Sadler sought to make amends with a much more conciliatory response when he addressed European supporters of the seminary at its first Board of Trustees meeting: "It might seem impertinent for one Baptist group to decide to establish an institution of this sort in a distant land, but we knew that such an institution was needed and decided to go ahead. We hope that you do not think that we were impertinent or presumptuous … We are not thinking in terms of supplanting but of supplementing the educational efforts of this continent."[118]

Sadler could point to the funds the BWA had contributed to the reconstruction of the Baptist seminary in Hamburg as evidence of goodwill. As a further demonstration of cooperation, the SBC-FMB gave an additional $16,500 to the seminary so that it could purchase the needed materials, pay its faculty, and discharge a heavy bank debt.[119]

In very short order Sadler and Franks took the next steps in getting the IBTS up and running by the fall of 1949. A country villa in the town of Rüschlikon, just outside Zürich, was purchased by the SBC and became the home of the new seminary. When its doors opened for its first classes in October 1949, the seminary had an enrolment of twenty-six students from twelve European countries, and five full-time teaching faculty, two of whom were American, along with Dr Arthur B. Crabtree from England, Claus Meister from Switzerland, and Dr Alexander Harasztl from Hungary.[120]

Sadler served as the seminary's interim first president until a suitable long-term replacement could be found in Joseph Nordenhaug, a man with a European heritage who had grown up and taken his undergraduate education in Norway, but received his theological training in the United States. Nordenhaug's appointment and subsequent ten years as president of IBTS signalled that the Southern Baptists were serious about giving the seminary a European orientation. Such a commitment was given further credence by Sadler when he invited European Baptist Unions to select candidates from their own countries to serve on the seminary's Board of Trustees.

The impact of the seminary on Baptist life in Germany was not as dramatic as the BWA's earlier church construction projects. The language of instruction at IBTS was English, thus greatly restricting the number of potential students from any European country, but during the 1950s and 1960s there was always German representation in the student body.[121] The seminary's proximity to southern Germany did prove to be a benefit for Baptist communities in this region. The co-curricular program at IBTS stipulated that students participate in ministry and service in nearby Baptist churches on the weekends during each term of study. By 1954 President Nordenhaug could report that students were engaged in such practical ministry – mostly preaching – at seven churches in the south German state of Baden-Württemburg, in towns such as Lörrach, Waldshut, Konstanz, and Friedrichshafen. Besides preaching in local churches, seminarians held services in refugee camps and visited newly resettled Baptists in their homes. Nordenhaug stressed the importance of these student ministries in supporting newly formed Baptist communities in predominantly Roman Catholic areas.[122]

An important indicator that German Baptists saw the value of the new seminary occurred at the end of the first year when the Board of Trustees met. One of the German trustees, Jakob Meister, praised the new school for effectively promoting a pan-European vision for Baptist ministry among the student body. He went on to say that German Baptists supported the work of the seminary, and that the recent trustee meeting showed that Southern Baptists were dedicated to making IBTS an important spiritual centre for European Baptists.[123] As the executive director of the Bund Evangelisch-Freikirchliche Gemeinden in Deutschland (German Baptist Union), the largest of all the Continental Baptist unions, Meister's endorsement carried significant weight.

As IBTS moved into its second decade of operation, Meister's early assessment was holding up. At the annual trustee meeting in 1962, Rudolf

Thaut, then executive director of the Bund, expressed thanks to the seminary's leaders for their continued support of Baptist churches in southern Germany. German graduates of IBTS were returning to Germany and either pursuing further studies at German universities or taking pastoral charges in Baptist churches. American faculty members from IBTS had also visited the Hamburg seminary in order to find out how IBTS could better serve the needs of German churches.[124]

Among the graduates to whom Thaut alluded were alumni such as Gunter Wieske, a member of the first IBTS graduating class who became the pastor of a Baptist congregation in Munster and went on to serve on the Executive Committee of the German Baptist Union. Another alumnus, Gerhard Claas, became one of the most prominent Baptist leaders both in Germany and internationally. After completing his studies at Rüschlikon, he pastored churches in Düsseldorf and Hamburg, before serving the German Baptist Union, first as youth secretary, then as general secretary during the 1970s. He became general secretary of the European Baptist Federation in 1976 and from 1980 until his death in a car crash in 1988 was general secretary of the Baptist World Alliance.[125] Other German graduates from the 1950s and 1960s went on to serve their national Baptist Unions as educators, missionaries, and itinerant evangelists.[126] In spite of its controversial beginnings, IBTS was having a significant impact through its graduates on Baptist life in Germany, providing pastors and educators who helped raise the profile of the *Freikirchen* in Germany.

Baptists in the 1960s and 1970s: Scaling Back the Mission

During its first two decades, IBTS's total enrolment rarely exceeded sixty students, and most years it hovered in the mid-forties. In that period the German student population averaged around six students each year. Over that same period the seminary's presidency, along with at least 50 per cent of its full-time teaching faculty, remained American.[127] The SBC-FMB continued to be the primary funding institution behind the seminary and saw the school as essentially a European missionary work, albeit a fraternal one. J.D. Hughey, who served as IBTS president during the period 1960–4 before going on to become area secretary for Europe with the SBC-FMB, held periodic discussions with European Baptist leaders that left him with the impression that while SBC-FMB missionaries were welcome in Europe, large numbers were not necessarily the best solution.[128]

As a result, the SBC-FMB would continue to send limited numbers of missionaries to work as "fraternal representatives" and promote a vision of Baptist internationalism through IBTS.[129]

For both Mennonites and Southern Baptists, the reduction of their missionary forces to West Germany in the wake of the *Wirtschaftswunder* reflected a growing confidence that their respective branches of the *Freikirchen* had the resources and infrastructure to be an ongoing presence in German church life. Both denominations had experienced moderate growth in their German churches, and by the mid-1960s the *Freikirchen* membership stood at 481,122.[130] This modest growth, fuelled by indigenous educational institutions, meant that the Anabaptist-Baptistic stream of the Reformation could continue in that country, with a stronger claim to be a genuinely German expression of Christianity.

Denominational Missionaries "Fight" the Cold War by Teaching Democracy

Mennonite Missionaries as Ambassadors for Democracy

A second theme that ran through the MCC's mission to Germany, particularly in the early postwar years, was the promotion of democratic principles, demonstrated most notably in two ways: through the practises of civic Christian service and democratic forms of church governance; and in reviving the historic Mennonite peace witness as a form of political engagement. In the former, Robert Kreider, the MCC's first staff worker in Germany, was a key figure in aligning the relief ministry of Mennonites with the task of rebuilding Germany based on democratic principles. John Howard Yoder was a key figure in the latter area.

Shortly after arriving in Germany in the spring of 1946, Kreider expressed his concern for a generation of young people who had been caught up in the thrall of National Socialism. In an open letter to MCC supporters back in North America, Kreider observed, "In the twelve years of power, Hitler completely possessed this younger generation. Cut out according to the common pattern, like little gingerbreadmen, this generation (ages 20 to 40) is ill prepared to spearhead the rebuilding of a new, democratic Germany. These youth are an unhappy lot ... Their old Nazi world – a complete world in itself – has been taken away, and the positive has not yet been found to replace it."[131]

Kreider realized that democratic values and ideas would not automatically rush in to replace the ideological void left by the demise of

Nazism, but would have to be intentionally cultivated. Implied in his letter was the belief that relief work presented an important and hopeful opportunity for Christian volunteer agencies, such as the MCC, to teach democracy as part of their mission.

Kreider's belief in the importance of twinning relief resources and democratic principles also found a receptive audience among the leaders of other North American volunteer agencies working in Germany. Early in 1947 at a CRALOG-sponsored conference of these leaders, Kreider was asked to present ideas for improving the relief effort of Protestant agencies in Germany. In addition to considering how to overcome denominational favouritism among both American and German Protestant groups in the distribution of material aid, Kreider was concerned that a cooperative infrastructure be established among German church groups. He called for a joint planning board, consisting of representatives from Evangelisches Hilfswerk, the *Freikirchen*, and American donor agencies, in order to establish an overall policy of aid distribution. "To insure the success of such a joint planning board it must be a committee in its truly democratic sense where the best judgment of each member is sought. Germans, with their limited experience with the committee principle, perhaps, have a tendency to fall back on the strong man leadership principle. But this cannot happen. Our joint planning board must seek to be broad, inclusive and democratic."[132]

While there is no evidence to suggest that such an over-arching cooperative body was ever set up, correspondence between Hilfswerk and the MCC indicates that Kreider's concerns for greater openness and accountability from German relief agencies, along with his call for closer cooperation between the EKD and Free Church groups, were being addressed.[133]

Kreider also appealed to the democratic nature of the MCC's mission when dealing with members of the military government, such as when Kreider petitioned the chief officer of the AMG, General Lucius Clay, to allow more MCC staff into the American Zone. Kreider argued that having more American relief personnel working alongside their German counterparts would be an effective way of helping the AMG achieve its goal of democratizing the German people: "With American relief workers actively participating in the distribution of CRALOG supplies, there would be opportunity to interpret and personally symbolize to the recipients that these are voluntary contributions from American citizens. We submit that this would be of immeasurable value in representing to Germans the democratic, humanitarian spirit of Americans … American relief teams, working together with German welfare agencies, could demonstrate to these agencies the American methods and philosophy of relief work."[134]

As mentioned in the previous section, Kreider's request for MCC relief staff to work in the American Zone was not granted by the AMG; however, permission was given to bring in staff for community centre projects. These centres were seen by the AMG as much more effective vehicles for instilling the values of democracy in German young people.[135] The one MCC *Nachbarschaftsheim* where political ideology combined most tangibly with Christian witness was in Berlin. As early as 1947 Kreider observed the growing international ideological tensions simmering in the national capital. Even before the blockade came into effect, he noted that Berlin was an Allied island in the sea of the Russian Occupied Zone, connected by three slender transportation threads to the other Western Zones.[136]

In 1949 Kreider's successor as the MCC's national director for CRALOG, Harold Buller, oversaw the construction of the Berlin *Nachbarschaftsheim*, and, along with the usual array of community services, included special educational programs for young people, which offered a combination of biblical instruction and philosophical discussion. By 1950 he could report modest success. In the midst of a daily atmosphere of Cold War crisis the MCC centre was offering a message of peaceful reconciliation in a democratic context. The centre functioned as the church home for the local Mennonite congregation, and was a base for what limited aid they were able to offer to Mennonites living in the Russian Zone. It also opened its doors to local non-churched community programs. As such the MCC was able to offer a "testimony not only of words, but of deeds" that promoted a Mennonite understanding of Christian faith in the context of democratic cultural pluralism.[137]

Promoting democracy was also an important part of the MCC's community service among German university students. By 1948, Mennonites sensed that the needs of the most vulnerable members of German society, such as children and homeless refugees, were being met by larger relief organizations. As a result, they began to look for other needy groups who might have been overlooked. Their search led them to impoverished university students. By running a feeding program specifically for these students, they hoped to bring a Christian influence to the generation of Germans who would lead in the near future: "The occupation has lasted nearly three years, and these years have brought untold suffering to the German people. Many are becoming bitter over what 'democracy' has meant to them. And these reactions find some of their strongest support from active student groups. We have felt that help to students 'in the name of Christ' would be an excellent witness. And we've not been disappointed."[138]

By meeting the material needs of university students, the MCC perceived that it was helping the future leaders of the country see a model example of democracy in action. Even the limited ability of the MCC program to relieve the hunger of a small group of students was considered a worthwhile investment in a stable future for the country. Thus MCC relief workers reasoned, "Student groups of any nation furnish the seed bed for a reactionary movement. It is the student groups of a nation that can see the sham of current international politics. To stifle the idealism of a nation's students is to breed malcontents for the oncoming generation."[139]

By the spring of 1949 the MCC was running four student feeding programs in the cities of Hamburg, Göttingen, Hanover, and Mainz. The program at Göttingen was significant in that the city was becoming a natural gateway for refugees from the Russian Zone to escape to the West. According to one local pastor, Göttingen had the largest number of refugee students of any German city. Hamburg also became a gathering point for many students who had fled the Russian Zone.[140] To address the many needs of these refugees who had fled the tyranny of Communism, as well as of local resident students who were still labouring under the after-effects of Nazi totalitarian rule, MCC staff members offered food and clothing, as well as counsel, conversation, or simply a sympathetic listening ear.[141] All this was done as a way of offering a more hopeful picture of democratic civic freedoms flowing from the spiritual liberation of Christianity. Harold Buller observed, "The students in Germany ... have never had a real feeling of freedom – they are cramped for free speech, free press, free religion. And farthest from all this, they have not come to the realization that before they can have these trivial freedoms, they must come to the basic fact that THERE IS A GOD WHO FREES ALL MEN – when men's hearts and souls are once free, these smaller freedoms will follow after in natural sequence."[142]

Buller's reflections reveal how closely Mennonites linked the Christian message of spiritual freedom for the individual with the derivative civic freedoms of a democratic society. It was this theology, incarnated in relief work and community development, that characterized the MCC's mission to German amidst postwar recovery and early Cold War tension. Writing his 1950 summary report for Germany to the MCC board in America, Buller stated that the MCC offered "a healthy balance of Christian Character and American Democracy ... that Germany needs in order to have its people find themselves again in the face of impending national crises."[143]

With the scaling back of relief efforts in Germany, the MCC found another avenue of missionary service that combined ecumenical dialogue with democratic civic engagement: the revival of the historic Mennonite peace witness in Europe. In 1949 Edward Yoder's book, *Must Christians fight?* was translated into German. That same year Harold Bender and C.J. Rempel, representing the Peace Section of the MCC, travelled throughout Europe to promote a broader Christian peace witness among other denominations.[144] These early itinerant tours were followed shortly by a series of inter-European Mennonite peace conferences, which featured Erland Walter and Guy F. Herschberger. Both men were faculty members of key Mennonite schools in North America.[145] In 1953, at the urging of W.A. Visser 't Hooft of the WCC, the Mennonites led the peace churches in producing a booklet, *Peace Is the Will of God*, which in turn was submitted to the WCC as a resource in formulating its own response to the growing threat of nuclear war.[146]

This cooperative effort between MCC representatives, European Mennonites, and other European peace churches led to a second joint initiative, namely a series of peace conferences, aimed at furthering the peace witness in Western Europe. The first conference was held in 1955 in the Swiss town of Puidoux, and the Puidoux Conference was convened five more times over the next twelve years. The purpose of these conferences was to invite like-minded leaders from the Protestant independent churches and established churches in Europe to support a wider peace witness in their ecclesial bodies.[147] In addition to contributing funding for these meetings, the MCC also sent delegates from its Peace Section to participate.

The most frequent and continuous MCC representative was John Howard Yoder.[148] Yoder came to Europe initially as an MCC relief worker in 1949 and served in France for five years. During the subsequent period, 1954–7, he was a full-time graduate student at the University of Basel, from which he graduated with a ThD in 1962. From 1959 until 1965 he also served as an administrative assistant in the Overseas Missions section of the Mennonite Board of Missions.[149] It was in this context that Yoder developed his ideas, which would in 1972 be published in his landmark work, *The Politics of Jesus*.[150] Through these conferences, Yoder was not so much promoting democracy as an ideology, developing a way by which the more isolationist peace churches could practise civic participation as full citizens in a democracy.

In addition to spreading the influence of the peace witness in the Protestant churches of Western Europe, Yoder was also promoting East-West dialogue among like-minded church groups on either side of the Iron Curtain. In 1965, and again in 1967 Yoder led a small group of North American theologians on a study tour of Czechoslovakia and East Germany. Yoder's early representation at Puidoux and ongoing activism in promoting the peace witness during his time as a graduate student in Basel, and then as an occasional faculty member at the EMBS, was instrumental in the MCC Peace Section's 1968 appointment of Marlin Miller as its first standing European representative.[151] Miller, who had represented the MCC Peace Section at the Puidoux Conferences in the early 1960s, had also been cultivating ecumenical contacts in Germany and Holland in an effort to help European churches formulate a stronger position on conscientious objection to military service.[152]

While these initiatives were limited in scope, they demonstrated that the MCC's ongoing mission work in German-speaking Europe was informed by Cold War politics. While eschewing the conventional political channels for expressing a voice on such a public issue, they nevertheless used and promoted the avenues provided by Western democracies to express their own voice on a matter of public policy. In doing so they also were educating members of the *Freikirchen* to take their democratic responsibilities seriously.

Baptist Missionaries as Agents of Democracy

Baptist missionaries also saw instruction in democracy as part of their relief and spiritual rehabilitation efforts. This was most noticeable immediately after the war when the BWA was distributing material aid and rebuilding churches. Once again J.H. Rushbrooke's assessment foreshadowed this aspect of the Baptist mission to Germany. In the concluding section of his 1943 report, Rushbrooke pointed out to BWA leaders that Europe at this time represented a unique field for Baptist relief and missionary endeavour. It was important for Baptists from prosperous countries, such as the

United States, Canada, and Britain, to support the often struggling work of their European counterparts, because the "one body offering a consistent and clear testimony against the State control and patronage of religion (in other words, defending a principle which is not only fundamental in our thinking but in the constitution of the USA) is the Baptist."[153] While the United States had been instrumental in training many European Baptist pastors for service in their own countries, now, more than ever, America needed to increase its support for European Baptists working in "lands feeling their way to the exercise of democratic liberty" so that the "Baptist message with its characteristic stress on the Gospel and freedom" could be spread during a time of great opportunity.[154]

This theme manifested itself in two parallel ways. First, by helping to establish Baptist congregations in West Germany, American Baptists, like the Mennonites, believed that their congregational model of church governance offered a microcosm of democracy in action. In contrast to the hierarchical, episcopal model of the EKD, Baptists believed their insistence on the accountability of church leadership to the laity was an effective way to help German congregations learn how to be members of a democratic society. Second, by promoting the *Freikirche* model of the church as a voluntary society instead of an instrument of the state, Baptists believed they were fostering the democratic values of personal and religious freedom in the wider civic community. These two aspects of democratic praxis acted like the twin rails of a railroad track over which the denominational train of the *Freikirchen*, pulled by a Baptist locomotive, could penetrate further into German society.

In seeking to implement the first of these strategies, American Baptists were confronted with an immediate problem that complicated their mission in a way that their Mennonite counterparts did not have to face: the possibility that the German Baptist churches themselves had been compromised by Nazi ideology and practice of authoritarian leadership. Signs that such a compromise had taken place were already were already evident in the behaviour of the German Baptist leaders during the pre-war years under the Third Reich. These signs were most visible in three international conferences during this period, at which German Baptist leaders were present. The first was the 1934 BWA Congress held in Berlin. The close association of the Nazi regime, particularly the ubiquity of its military symbols, with their German Baptist hosts, was disturbing for many of the international delegates. Participation of *Reichsbishof* Ludwig Müller also fuelled suspicion that German Baptists were in danger of becoming a religious propaganda tool of the Reich.[155] Growing confirmation occurred in 1937 at the ecumenical Life and Work Conference held in Oxford. When German delegates associated with the Confessing Church movement had their travel permits revoked by the Reich government at the last minute, it was left to German Baptist leader Paul Schmidt, and his *freikirchlicher* Methodist counterpart Bishop Otto Melle, to represent the German Protestant churches. When Schmidt and Melle failed to endorse a conference statement critical of the Nazi regime's treatment of the Confessing Church delegates, it placed their own presence at the conference in a highly compromising light. These optics were further fuelled by statements by both men praising the Reich government for its stand against Communism and for its recent recognition of the legitimacy of the *Freikirchen* as truly German churches.[156]

The third conference, of particular significance for American Baptists for its location on their soil, was the 1939 BWA Congress in Atlanta. Already tarred with severe criticism from the Oxford conference, Schmidt and his fellow German Baptist delegates were called to give their support to the Confessing Church movement and stand with them in protest against the tyranny of the Nazi government. In rebuttal Schmidt pointed out that Nazis still allowed Baptists and other denominations of the *Freikirchen* to evangelize in Germany so long as they remained neutral on political issues. He argued that, for German Baptists, the freedom to continue to evangelize must remain the overriding priority. Only Rushbrooke's diplomatic handling of the debate kept these differences from fracturing the strained relationship between German Baptists and the Anglo-American brethren.[157]

An additional issue that may have contributed to American Baptist fears of German Baptists having been significantly compromised by Nazism was the formation of the Bund Evangelischer-Freikirchlicher Gemeinde. This *Bund* or league united German Baptists with the Open Brethren denomination under one Free Church umbrella organization and came about with the aid and endorsement of the Reich government. Traditional Baptist ecclesial policy considered any such organization an "amalgamation of individual congregations," all with equal voice. However, this *Bund* was based on a hierarchical leadership structure, implying that the "Fuhrer principal" now undermined a hallmarks of Baptist ecclesial polity.[158] Not all German Baptists uncritically accepte their denomination's relationship with the Reich. Jakob Köbberling, a Baptist minister from East Prussia, declared that Baptist accommodation to Nazi demands, and the corresponding distancing of the Baptist leadership from the Confessing Church movement, meant that Baptists were "a church in bondage, an unfree church, even if it proudly calls itself a 'Free Church.'"[159] However, Köbberling's view expressed a small minority report among German leaders of the day. This record of compromise complicated renewal of relations between American and German Baptists during the early postwar period.

Paul Gebauer, a Baptist chaplain in the US army, was one of the first Americans to make official contact with the German Baptist leaders after the war. Gebauer was born in 1900 and raised in a Baptist family in Germany but emigrated to the United States in 1925. He began serving as a missionary with the North American Baptist Mission Society in Cameroon from 1931, but interrupted his work there to serve as an army chaplain from 1943 to 1945.[160] His position as an army chaplain, along with his German Baptist heritage and fluency in German made him well-suited to assess the needs of German Baptists. In the autumn of 1945 his reports to Rushbrooke at the BWA on the state of the German Baptist leadership in the US Zone were less than encouraging. Gebauer had heard rumours that Baptist leaders had not exercised their authority along democratic lines but had succumbed to the "Führer principle," and that the seminary in Hamburg had become a "hotbed of Nazi influence."[161] A month later, Gebauer notified Rushbrooke that his suspicions had been largely confirmed. In Gebauer's judgment, most Baptist pastors had "adopted the Nazi philosophy of life" and showed a "complete absence of a sense of guilt" over their conduct during the war.[162] Consequently, he urged leading pastors such as Paul Schmidt (who was also the *Bundesdirektor* of the German Baptist Union) and Hamburg seminary professor Hans Luckey to resign from their positions.[163]

The task of re-establishing fraternal relationships between Anglo-American Baptists of the BWA and German Baptists fell to Edwin Bell, the ABFMS representative to Europe who was instrumental in setting up the BWA's relief efforts in Germany. While Gebauer was reporting to Rushbrooke, Bell was writing to W.O. Lewis, head of the BWA's American relief division, who would later assume the role of associate secretary to Europe. His observations were more tempered and cautious than Gebauer's and took into account the realities and limitations in dealing with German Baptists. Bell advised Lewis that the BWA should first conduct a fact-finding trip to Germany before drawing conclusions about German Baptist collaboration with the Nazis. He went on to suggest that the BWA follow the AMG's recommended approach to denazification and urge

German Baptists "to clean their own houses as far as Nazi leadership is concerned." Bell believed that evidence of denazification by German Baptists was a necessary step in order to re-establish fraternal relationships with non-German Baptists, and he notified Lewis that he would point out to German Baptists that they would have to eliminate "whatever leadership among its pastors and elsewhere may have been compromised by its association with the Nazi movement in Germany."[164]

Lewis appointed Bell as the BWA's investigator, and by June 1946 Bell was able to assure Lewis that German Baptists had acted in accordance with his recommendations and that "Luckey and other members of the Seminary Faculty ... and that all of the members of the [German Baptist] Council who had Nazi connections had resigned." However, Paul Schmidt, unlike Luckey, was affirmed in his position as executive director (*Geschäftsführer*) "with expressions of confidence in him by [the Council]."[165] This assurance cleared the way for the BWA to re-establish connections with German Baptists so that relief and reconstruction aid could be channelled to them.

The conduct of the *Freikirchen* in their collaboration with the Nazis remains controversial at best.[166] Nicholas Railton, among others, has shown that leaders of the *Freikirchen* cooperated with the Nazi government during the years of the Third Reich, but as much for pragmatic reasons as for ideological ones. Railton rightly argues that the Nazi regime's willingness to grant the *Freikirchen* greater status and legitimacy in German religious life, in the face of calls from the *Landeskirchen* for dissolution of all *Freikirchen* denominations, was an opportunity for legitimation that Baptists and other denominations of the *Freikirchen* eagerly accepted. Such elevated status made leaders of the *Freikrichen* unwilling to condemn the Nazi government openly, and thus tainted them with the odour of collaboration, especially among supporters of the Confessing Church movement. While not seeking to exonerate the *Freikirchen* of any wrongdoing, Railton's careful analysis shows that the issue of church collaboration with the Nazi authorities was more complex than Baptists such as Gebauer and Bell were aware of at the time.[167]

Once American Baptist missionaries were satisfied that Nazism had been purged from German Baptist ranks, their concern for instilling democracy now became important as a means to resist Communism. In 1947 Herbert Gezork, a German Baptist seminary professor and national youth leader, sounded a more hopeful note, pointing out the importance of teaching democracy alongside the preaching of Christian renewal. In

1936 Gezork had fled to the United States when his opposition to the Nazi regime threatened to land him in prison. Shortly after the war he returned to his homeland as a member of the AMG's Department of Religious Affairs. In October 1948 as chief of evangelical affairs, Gezork noted the important contribution made by Christian American military personnel, along with their wives, in rehabilitating Germans from their Nazi past. These Americans had preached in German churches, procured paper for Christian publishing houses, and raised funds for local charitable causes. Some of the wives had organized kindergartens and youth clubs, where they took German children off the streets, gave them extra food rations, and taught them "Christian truths and democratic ways of life."[168]

At the same time, Gezork informed his readers, Communism beckoned from the east with the promise of a new utopia. With their state-supported religious institutions in tatters, German Christians would inevitably look to the Baptist *Freikirchen*, with their practice of the "Free Church principle," as the best way to bring spiritual renewal to their land.[169] Gezork's prediction of the imminent demise of the established church and his corresponding optimism about the future of the *Freikirchen* were patently unrealistic, but as an eye witness to the early postwar recovery of Germany, his conflation of spiritual renewal, free church governance, and democratic freedoms indicated how American Baptists viewed their contribution to spiritual renewal in West Germany. With Communism as the new enemy, purging the German church of its Nazi past became a lesser issue than preparing it to withstand the threat of its current enemy.

The blockade of West Berlin at the end of the decade fueledl this shift for leaders of the BWA as well. In his address to the eighth Baptist World Congress in 1950, W.O. Lewis proclaimed, "Europe is one of the battlegrounds of democracy. It may be that democracy and civilization and religion will continue to exist if these fail in Europe, but it will certainly be harder to maintain these values if they disappear in Europe." Thus Lewis saw the call to strengthen the Baptist community in Germany as a means to defend democratic freedoms.[170]

The connection between spiritual and political ideas was also put forward in the BWA's church construction program under the guidance of Ken Norquist. Not only had this program helped to integrate Baptist refugees from Eastern Europe successfully into West German communities, it had had a significant political effect. At the dedication of one such chapel in the Baden-Württemberg city of Schwenningen, a Lutheran professor from the University of Heidelberg remarked to Norquist that he "was in favour of bringing small evangelistic groups [such as the Baptists] into large industrial centers not only as a moral and spiritual influence, but also because of their educational function toward democracy."[171]

In a report to the BWA's leadership, Annamarie Oesterle, Norquist's German assistant at the CRALOG office in Stuttgart, offered her own assessment of the BWA mission to Germany. As part of her report to General Secretary A.T. Ohrn, she praised the BWA's work, referring to the comments Norquist had gathered from the Heidelberg professor. She informed Ohrn that similar commendations had also been made by German public officials in regard to newly constructed refugee chapels. As a resident German she believed that the American BWA staff were "helping to build goodwill and understanding between the German and American people both indirectly through relief work and directly through personal contacts, such as student exchange[s], immigration, etc."[172] Oesterle may have been only one German voice, but as someone who worked closely with American Baptists on behalf of her fellow citizens, and whom Norquist trusted to report accurately on the effectiveness of the BWA's efforts, it is reasonable to assume that her comments reflected the thinking of many other German Baptists.

A more modest variation of the same theme came from the ABFMS European Representative Edwin Bell in 1955. With American "fraternal assistance" Baptists had gained a more visible and respected place in German Christianity. Through a vibrant seminary in Hamburg, and many new churches throughout the country, 50,000 people had been baptized into their congregations since the end of the war, and many young people were seeing Baptist churches as a way to get beyond the indoctrination and disillusionment of Nazism. Relations with the EKD were now such that Baptists were decreasingly portrayed as a despised "nuisance sect" and gaining acceptance as legitimate expressions of German Christianity.[173] In a similar fashion to Gezork, seven years earlier, Bell warned his American constituency that the spectre of Communism loomed just across the Iron Curtain in East Germany. It was important that American Baptists continue their fraternal support of their German brothers and sisters in building strong churches, which would resist the "constant attempts at infiltration and spread" of Communist ideology from Russia and its satellite states in Eastern Europe.[174]

Southern Baptists, both through their support of BWA relief work and the founding of the IBTS, understood their role in Germany in much the same way. In the early postwar period the editors of the SBC-FMB

Commission ran regular editorials that warned of the growing Communist danger in Europe. Linked with Communism were the established Protestant churches of Western Europe and the Roman Catholic Church, which Southern Baptists viewed as exhibiting totalitarian tendencies similar to those of Communist regimes.[175] In justifying the promotion of democratic freedoms as part of the Southern Baptist mission work, the editors stated, "Political democracy is a by-product of Christianity. It has its roots in the Christian concept of God-given dignity of every human being. The words of the Declaration of Independence express this clearly."[176] The writer was not so naive as to confuse democracy with Christianity, but in calling for Southern Baptists to take up the task of spreading Baptist Christianity in Europe, he made it clear that democratic freedoms along the lines envisioned by the founding fathers of the United States would have ample opportunity to flourish.

John Allen Moore, an SBC-FMB missionary in Eastern Europe before the war, who worked in West Germany in the 1960s, saw the spread of Baptist churches in Europe as nurturing the democratic ideals inherent in the Protestant Reformation that could now be fully realized in the region of its birth. According to Moore, "Luther, Calvin and Zwingli stopped far short of the essential implications of the principles of individualism in religion which they early proclaimed," but "what had been arrested in Europe had been completed in America." In the United States greater freedom from the state had allowed Christianity to develop "according to its essential nature" along voluntaristic lines "utterly incomprehensible to most Europeans," whose churches are supported by taxes and often directed by the state. "American Christianity may therefore have a unique contribution to make to Europe in regard to religion ... and we are in a favourable position to help [Europeans]."[177] For Southern Baptists, democracy expressed through ecclesiastical polity played the dual role of fending off the external threat of Communism, and ameliorating and ultimately overcoming the internal threat of the oppressive hierarchical structures of the established churches.

Such a view was also put forward by the American faculty of IBTS. In a 1957 conference address, J.D. Hughey, professor of theology, recommended the importance of the *Freikirchen* as the best antidote against Communist encroachment, and for spiritual revival in Germany. By supporting national Baptist unions in countries with established Protestant churches, it was important for Baptists to "avoid unseemly competition with other churches," but at the same time to offer an unapologetic view of "the church as a fellowship of baptized believers."[178] For missionaries such as Hughey and Moore, Baptist voluntarism, which had come to full flower in the soil of American democracy, was now ready to return across the Atlantic and complete the work of Reformation – a project that would result in the spread of American democratic ideals.[179]

Conclusion

As this chapter has shown, the work of denominational missionaries has historical significance for the impact it had on Protestant life in Germany and for its contribution to understanding how Americans "fought" the Cold War in Western Europe outside official political and military channels. In the former area, the focus of denominational mission agencies such as the MCC and the BWA in offering relief and spiritual rehabilitation was to help their own denominational kindred rebuild their lives. While the historiography on the German *Freikirchen* has noted that their postwar recovery led to the strengthening of their place in German church life, sparse attention has been given to North American missionaries and the important role they played in helping their denominational kindred achieve this more secure status. Conversely the history of postwar relief and recovery in Germany has noted the important humanitarian contribution made by smaller voluntary religious agencies, such as the MCC, but has paid little attention to their wider missionary concerns. Assessing the activity of North American denominational aid workers and fraternal representatives as actual missionaries to Germany provides a more integrated perspective, adding a missing dimension to the postwar history of the *Freikirchen*. Denominational missionaries were instrumental in addressing the suffering of the minority *Freikirchen* congregations as they dug themselves out of the rubble of war, but North Americans then extended their mission, and hence their impact on German church life, by rebuilding denominational infrastructures that would give these marginalized communities a legitimate place in German religious life.

This chapter has also brought to light the significant role of Mennonite and Baptist missionaries as agents for democracy and thus participants in the ideological battles of the Cold War in Western Europe. The historiography of the Cold War has tracked the ideological contests that played out on the military-diplomatic stage. Recent works by cultural historians have also examined the media, arts, and even sports in which Americans deliberately promoted the growth of democracy in Western Europe, and Germany in particular.[180] But the role and significance of religious agencies in these contests has gone largely unnoticed. However, from the above material it is evident that instead of being naive about or immune to the ideological battles of the Cold War, denominational missionaries were knowledgeable and active participants in these battles. Operating outside official government channels and the main highways of cultural exchange, denominational missionaries promoted democratic values at the level of the local community. They took seriously their role of helping German Christians resist Communism as well as providing greater religious freedom vis-à-vis state church structures. Combining religious convictions and political ideologies is nothing new, and as seen in the previous chapter, it was clearly evident in the work of ecumenical missionaries. However, such ideological concern was not the exclusive purview of the mainline churches, but extended to churches that represented the Anabaptist end of the Protestant spectrum as well. Thus the record of Mennonite and Baptist missionary endeavour adds strength to the claim that Protestant missionaries in general played an important role, particularly at the grass roots, in spreading democratic ideals among the German people. It is also a call for political and cultural historians to take seriously the role of voluntary religious agencies in international relations.

As the West German recovery continued, and the need for relief and reconstruction help from abroad diminished, denominational missionaries continued to offer "fraternal assistance" to their brothers and sisters in Germany.[181] Invariably this meant a reduction in their numbers and limiting themselves to a more specialized set of roles as a way to define their fraternal relationship to their German kindred. In so doing, North American missionaries sought to strengthen their respective branches of the German *Freikirchen* and share in the common task of penetrating an increasingly secular, affluent society with the Christian message.

CHAPTER THREE

Conservative Evangelical Mission to Germany, 1945–1974: Two Case Studies

Defining and Contextualizing the Mission: Personal Revival and Democratic Freedom

In contrast to the ecumenical and denominational Protestant missions to Germany discussed in the previous two chapters, conservative evangelical missionaries understood their task almost exclusively in terms of evangelism and revival.[1] While not unconcerned about the great material needs of the German people, conservative evangelicals, for the most part, were willing to leave relief work to organizations that specialized in such services. As independent, non-ecclesial agencies, conservative evangelical missions also avoided aligning themselves with any one church denomination, seeking instead to form partnerships with interdenominational coalitions of local churches who were open to revivalist forms of evangelism – essentially some form of presenting the Christian message that called for a response from individuals to accept Christ into their lives – as a means of reaching their own communities with the Christian message. In most cases this led conservative evangelicals to work with local chapters of the Deutsche Evangelische Allianz, the German Protestant *Dachorganisation* open to this kind of evangelism.[2]

In the entrepreneurial spirit that marked the conservative evangelical missionary enterprise, independent agencies such as Youth for Christ (YFC) and Janz Team Ministries (JTM) concentrated their efforts on a few specific forms of Christian ministry, leaving other missions to find a spiritual "market niche" for their respective ministries. For YFC their signature event was the evangelistic youth rally, which drew heavily on the idioms of the American entertainment industry as means to invite young people to "accept Christ into their hearts." The staff of JTM focused on radio broadcasting and multi-week urban evangelistic "crusades" as their primary means to reach the German people with the Christian message. In both cases the conservative evangelical mission was characterized by a concern for the conversion or reawakening of individuals to the Christian faith, relying primarily on forms of revivalism, which had been a hallmark of Anglo-American evangelicalism from its eighteenth-century origins.[3] However, US conservative evangelicals in particular also linked their message to the ideological platforms of democratic political and religious freedom as defined by their own national mythology. For them, America was born as a result of persecuted refugees fleeing the oppression of a state-enforced religion, and the subsequent struggle of colonial subjects against the injustices of a tyrannical British monarchy.[4]

The efforts of conservative evangelical missionaries to save postwar Germany, like those of denominational missions, are significant beyond their evangelistic activities. Their work offers also provides insight into how missionaries were agents of the Cold War ideological battle in Western Europe and their influence on the German Protestant churches. This chapter will examine their activity in the light of these two historiographical contexts. In relation to the former, in a way to similar denominational missionaries, conservative evangelicals from the United States linked their revivalist work to the cause of democratic freedom, most noticeably during the early postwar period. Besides saving one's soul, American conservative evangelicals believed that "inviting Christ into your life" fostered the personal freedoms of democracy, thus immunizing people against Communism. Just as the Baptist and Mennonite missionaries promoted the values of democracy through congregational models of ecclesiastical governance, so conservative evangelicals promoted the same ideals through their conversionist forms of evangelism. Hence conservative evangelical missionaries believed they were contributing to the Cold War struggle, fighting on the side of democracy for the ideological soul of Germany.

The significance of the conservative evangelical mission for the historiography of the Cold War is thus twofold: first, study of conservative evangelical missions, even more clearly than of the ecumenical and denominational missions, uncovers a largely unexplored dimension of the US struggle against totalitarianism, showing that American engagement in the Cold War went beyond the more conventional military-diplomatic channels to include civilian religious avenues; and second, it reveals that conservative evangelicals believed that resisting Communism in Western

Europe was important to preventing its growth at home. One of the best ways to stop Communist advance was to evangelize Germany as quickly and aggressively as possible, using the methods and techniques of American revivalist Christianity. YFC, which exemplified this combination of hopeful revivalism and self-confident democracy, was one of the first conservative evangelical mission agencies to gain access to postwar Germany, and thus provides an insightful case study for this first thematic section of the chapter.

Conservative evangelical missionaries also had a significant impact on German Protestantism. The development of this second major theme is most clearly evident in the work of the Canadian Janz Team Ministries. JTM, while sharing the democratic commitments of YFC, did not make ideology a visible part of its message. Instead, through its large-scale evangelistic meetings, JTM was instrumental in making revivalism and the appeal to personal conversion acceptable practices in German Protestant life. From the late 1950s they took up residence in Germany, building up a strong network of supporters in both the *Freikirchen* and the *Landeskirchen*. In holding multi-week evangelistic crusades throughout the cities of German-speaking Europe, JTM established longstanding evangelistic partnerships with a network of like-minded churches. In so doing they helped move this form of evangelistic practice from the fringes of German Protestant life to a more visible and acceptable status. JTM's work also provided their German supporters with a way out of their Nazi-era isolation by reconnecting them with an international network of Christians who shared a revivalist/conversionist understanding of Christianity. The second section of this chapter analyzes and explains how JTM's work from 1954 to 1974 brought about this shift.

The chapter will conclude by briefly examining the contrasting priorities of these two mission agencies in the respective case studies. While both were committed to the traditional missionary task of evangelism, the contrasting nature of YFC's and JTM's approaches points to general differences between the character of Canadian and American conservative evangelicalism, particularly in their respective approaches to missionary work.

Saving Germany for God and Democracy: Youth for Christ Carries the Revivalist Torch

YFC's mission to Germany reflected its commitment to rapid worldwide evangelism through revivalist youth rallies. From an early date these rallies combined a conversionist message of Christianity with the ideological "brand" of American democratic freedoms.[5] In doing so, YFC's first president, Torrey Johnson, hoped to set Germany and the rest of Europe ablaze with the divine fire of spiritual renewal, which, in turn, would lead to moral rehabilitation – especially of young people. YFC was typical of American fundamentalism of the day, exuding optimism and confidence both in the power of its evangelistic message to bring about spiritual renewal in every land, and in American-style democracy as the best antidote against all forms of totalitarianism.[6] In evangelizing Germany, YFC also became a participant in waging the Cold War to save that country from the perceived threats of earthly totalitarian powers alongside threats from spiritual ones. In examining the record or YFC's work in Germany during the first three decades of the Cold War, this aspect of the conservative evangelical mission reveals itself in three related ways: (1) the role of the early anti-Communist rhetoric of YFC's leaders in providing the rationale for the mission to Germany; (2) the initial association of YFC's mission in Germany with US military servicemen and the frequent use of wartime metaphors by YFC leaders; and (3) the way in which YFC's distinctly American flavour was reinforced through its annual World Youth Congresses and the steady flow of youth missionary teams from the United States to Germany. However, before examining the role and impact of Youth for Christ in Germany, it is important first to understand its character and the formative context of its origins.

Background to the Mission: The Formation and Ethos of YFC

The precise origin of YFC is uncertain, as it did not begin as an organization, but as a catch-phrase adopted by American conservative evangelical pastors, radio evangelists, and youth workers in the late 1930s, to attract young people to their revival rallies. These rallies were not conventional church services, but up-tempo performances that combined elements of popular radio entertainment shows with an evangelistic message and appeal to surrender one's life to Christ; and they were highly successful in attracting large crowds of high school and university students.[7]

Part of their success lay with the charismatic young men who led these rallies. Most of them were not formally trained as ministers. A number of the YFC promoters, such as Jack Wyrtzen, had come out of the entertainment world and were attuned to the rhythms of current popular culture.[8] Others, such as Pastor Torrey Johnson, had attended a conservative evangelical Christian college before embarking on their chosen career (in his case, dentistry), and while at college sensed a call to Christian youth ministry. Some of the high-profile rally leaders, such as Percy Crawford and Cliff Barrows, attained celebrity status in conservative evangelical circles as YFC rallies took to the radio waves to reach a national audience.[9] Regardless of their varied backgrounds and levels of education, almost all YFC leaders reflected the entrepreneurial spirit of American capitalism, as well as exhibiting a contagious confidence and enthusiasm that reflected the country's national attitude since defeating the Axis powers.

There were three additional reasons why these events appealed to youthful sensibilities. First of all, these rallies drew on the techniques and format of popular entertainment shows, especially radio. One critic summarized YFC meetings as fast-moving performances "that combined Christian vaudeville and fervent revival-style preaching."[10] Taking their cue from contemporary radio variety shows, most rallies featured a mix of contemporary musical numbers, celebrity testimonies of conversion, and short homilies, which usually consisted of warnings about yielding to worldly vices.[11] The leader of the rally acted as the master of ceremonies for the evening's program and kept things moving along at a rapid pace. It was understood that no single item on the program could be more than fifteen minutes long. The purpose was to show skeptical young people that Christianity was not just for old folks, but spoke in a relevant way to the needs and aspirations of youth culture. The musical offerings proved especially controversial. Instead of church hymns, rally musicians introduced a wave of new upbeat choruses that drew on the contemporary styles of popular artists and used a selection of instruments previously considered the exclusive domain of the dancehall. Suddenly Christian music had a sound that matched its popular secular counterpart, and with access to airplay over commercial radio stations young people began to sit up and take notice.[12] Each rally concluded with an altar call, when those who attended were invited to "give their life to Christ" either with a show of hands, or by coming to the front of the auditorium.[13] And come they did, in record numbers. At the height of YFC's popularity, the organization managed to fill Chicago's Soldier Field with 70,000 young people for one of its rallies.[14]

Second, rallies were held on Saturday evening, deliberately competing for the time and attention of American young people on what had become known as "The Devil's Night."[15] YFC rallies offered an unconventional but intriguing alternative to the movies or the dancehall. Their success garnered support from unlikely sources outside of church circles. The war years had spawned a new social problem, identified as juvenile delinquency, and any organization or popular movement able to check the rising tide of teenage moral dissipation found allies among America's cultural gatekeepers concerned for the restoration of public virtue and civic religion. The media magnate William Randolph Hearst endorsed YFC in an editorial, and government officials, local chiefs of police, and even President Harry Truman praised the movement for its wholesome entertainment and its ability to check juvenile moral decline.[16]

The third reason was the venues in which the rallies were held. YFC rallies were not held in churches, in part because few churches could accommodate the size of the crowds. However, there was a deliberate effort to hold rallies in large concert halls, sports arenas, outdoor stadiums, and even on state fairgrounds. By the spring of 1944 YFC rallies were drawing capacity crowds of young people in the most prestigious entertainment venues, such as Carnegie Hall and Madison Square Garden in New York.[17] Not only did the sheer numbers give the movement a higher public profile, they demonstrated that YFC's form of revivalist Christianity could reclaim territory once thought to be the sole domain of "worldly" entertainment. While traditional churchgoers often looked critically at YFC leaders for their shallow theology or scandalously worldly music, few could argue with their success in attracting young people where most churches had failed.[18]

In August 1944 YFC rally leaders from various cities gathered informally at a Christian retreat centre at Winona Lake, Indiana, and agreed to develop a formal structure that could give the movement greater unity and effectiveness. By July 1945, YFC delegates agreed on a constitution, and the title "Youth for Christ International" was adopted as the official name of the new organization.[19] The constitution included four goals that reflected the energy and zeal of fundamentalists, who, since their national humiliation in the 1925 Scopes Monkey Trial, now had a new-found confidence and even a little swagger in their step.[20] They were to:

1 promote and help win youth for Christ everywhere;
2 encourage evangelism everywhere;
3 emphasize radiant victorious Christian living;
4 foster international service of youth through existing agencies.[21]

Torrey Johnson was elected president, and the Chicagoland chapter of YFC became the headquarters of the new organization.

Initially the inclusion of the word *international* indicated merely that YFC was already operating in both the United States and Canada, but it soon became apparent that the movement had spontaneously spread beyond North America. The Second World War provided the means for YFC's growth overseas. By 1944 weekly YFC rallies were being held in approximately 500 US cities, and a good number of those who filled meeting venues each Saturday night were servicemen, some of whom made professions of Christian faith as a result. When these soldiers were transferred to the Pacific or European theatres of war, they staged their own version of YFC rallies on their military bases as a way of giving witness to their newfound faith. As mail telling of these rallies overseas began to pour in to YFC headquarters, Johnson and his staff realized that the movement was much bigger and less controllable than even they had imagined.[22]

Liberating Germany from Communism and Fascism – with Revival!

Even if YFC had not reached Germany in this unexpected manner, it is clear from its founding in 1945 that Johnson intended to launch a revivalist campaign there as soon as possible. His inaugural address contained a clear indication that such a venture was an immediate priority, not just for the sake of Germany's spiritual welfare, but also, in Johnson's geopolitical reckoning, because the future of the free world hung in the balance:

I'm not interested in establishing YOUTH FOR CHRIST everywhere in America – I'M INTERESTED IN REACHING YOUNG PEOPLE FOR JESUS EVERYWHERE! ... there's one place in Europe more critical than any other place – Germany. As goes Germany so goes Western Europe. If Germany goes communistic, then you can write France, Italy, Spain and Portugal off in the same category, and you can shove England down the road of national socialism. What happens there will directly affect us, and so we need to get to Germany as soon as possible. We have no plan, but God has! If Hitler could make the youth in a nation move with his program, God, by the Holy Spirit, ought to be able to get the same youth into a program of His kind and it has to be done.[23]

Johnson's views, however bluntly expressed, actually anticipated future American President Eisenhower's "domino theory" of Communist expansion by nine years.[24] They also matched the views of influential Western political voices such as Winston Churchill, in his famous "Iron Curtain" speech, and President Truman, in formulating his policy of "containment."[25] Johnson's concerns were augmented by Harold Ockenga, a key YFC supporter who as pastor of Boston's prestigious Park Street Congregational Church was a leading conservative evangelical voice.[26] As the first president of the recently formed National Association of Evangelicals (NAE), an umbrella organization designed to foster greater cooperation among a new (and in some ways more moderate) generation of conservative evangelicals, Ockenga can be seen to represent a wide cross-section of American fundamentalism.[27] In an article in the influential conservative evangelical periodical *Moody Monthly*, Ockenga sounded the alarm about the pending threat of both Communism and Nazism after returning from a brief tour of Germany in 1947: "Though the Nazi party and philosophy have been discredited, [the German people] only await some other leadership. Into this vacuum comes communist propaganda ... There are many who sympathize with Communism today. If the minds of the German people are left without positive leadership, the normal and natural thing for them to do is to turn to Russia. The only alternative to ... democratization will be Communism ... Today we have an opportunity to democratize Germany."[28]

Ockenga went on to lament that democratization was the weakest aspect of the American Military Government's overall administration. Besides calling on American conservative evangelicals to contribute material relief to agencies working in Europe, he believed a missionary response was required, as in his view the only effective response to Europe's deep spiritual – and ideological – needs could come from American evangelicals.[29] At the same time, the ongoing threat of Communism to the United States was kept in the minds of American conservative evangelicals through the NAE's own periodical, *United Evangelical Action*. From its origin in 1942 well into the 1960s, this monthly publication ran a regular stream of articles warning its readers about the constant threat of Communism in the homeland.[30]

Johnson and Ockenga, however naive and simplistic their grasp of the ideological realities at work in Germany, reflected a typical conservative evangelical perception of the totalitarian threat in Germany and its implications for Western democracies. Their writing also reveals how closely conservative evangelicals linked their revivalist message with democratic political ideals. For Johnson, Ockenga, and other supporters of YFC, getting to Germany and spreading the fires of revival would consume the chaff of totalitarianism and provide a fertile seedbed in which democracy could take root. Checking the spread of Communism through a Christian revival in Western Europe would also weaken its ability to erode democratic freedom at home.

As noted in the previous chapter, civilian access to Germany in the early postwar years was extremely difficult and limited. As letters about soldier-organized YFC rallies being held on American military bases in Germany poured in to YFC's Chicago office, Johnson and other YFC staff members chafed at their inability to go there themselves.[31] However, in March and April 1946 Johnson, along with a small team of YFC evangelists, which included a fiery young evangelist named Billy Graham, embarked on a two-month preaching tour covering Great Britain, Scandinavia, France, and Holland. Even though they were not able to gain access to Germany, Johnson returned from the trip convinced that YFC's revivalist approach to Christian outreach was the key to evangelizing the European peoples. More generally, he believed that American Christians had a unique opportunity to meet Europe's spiritual needs: "Europe looks to America for leadership – particularly spiritual leadership. And we must give it to these countries filled with destitute and starving people."[32] The rhetoric was vintage YFC – both in its sweeping generalization and its hyperbole. It also carried with it an ideological undertone that American democracy was part of an export package to be delivered to needy Europeans. Such was the tone of many articles that appeared in YFC's own periodical, simply entitled *Youth for Christ Magazine*.[33] Through YFCM and in other public correspondence on behalf of YFC, Johnson presented a picture of Germany in peril, and thus as a key spiritual and ideological battleground where YFC urgently needed to commit its missionary energies.

In April 1947 YFC received clearance for another European tour, this time with permission to enter Germany. In soliciting financial and prayer support for the trip, Johnson sent an open letter to YFC supporters in which he stated some reasons for the trip to Germany, which included "the bitter and active opposition of God-hating forces who would capture German youth speadily [*sic*] if they are not won for Christ" and "the conviction that the destiny of all Europe's civilization will be determined with what happens in Germany within the next few years."[34] He concluded his speech in typical crisis mode:

This is the most critical hour in all history. This is America's hour of opportunity! If we in America seize our opportunity and in answer to pray[er] God opens up the door for us, our young people can be the means under God of not only bringing spiritual revival to Germany ... but stem the tide of Godlessness in Europe and turn many nations in the Old World back to God ... if we fail ... all of Europe will be overswept – yes probably America very soon will be engulfed in the bitter hatred of Godlessness that is rising in the Old World.[35]

Once again Johnson's comments reveal how closely conservative evangelical thinking conflated the Christian task of global evangelism with the role of the American nation in the postwar world. To see Germany fall to Communism would represent the failure of America, as well as the eventual capitulation of his own country to Communism.

Over eighteen days in April, Johnson criss-crossed the American and British Zones of occupied Germany, visiting military bases, YFC chapters, and German churches. He was encouraged by the YFC chapters that had sprung up on military bases in cities such as Frankfurt, Heidelberg, München, and Berlin. He was also enthusiastic about the strong response to his preaching among Germans. At Johnson's very first meeting on German soil, 1,100 people jammed into a Frankfurt auditorium to hear him, 800 of whom were Germans. Of the 500 who responded to his invitation to "receive Christ," most were Germans.[36] Over the course of his tour Johnson was gratified by the warm response from German pastors from both the *Freikirchen* and the *Landeskirchen,* and noted the many invitations to hold further meetings in German churches.[37] As will be evident below, the support of German pastors was not without qualification, but the initial responsiveness of the German people he met, and the limitations of communicating mostly through an interpreter would have made such nuances difficult to pick up, given the short duration of Johnson's stay. On the basis of initial support for YFC that Johnson and his team received, he had compelling evidence to believe that YFC's approach to evangelizing young people had struck a responsive chord among some German ministers.

During the early postwar years of YFC's mission to Germany, the ideological rhetoric was most noticeable. As the organization's most visible spokesman, Johnson was also the most frequent articulator of Christianity's battle with totalitarian ideologies in the race to save Germany's soul. But he was not the only one. Other YFC itinerant evangelists and ministers who spoke at YFC events echoed similar concerns. Oswald J. Smith, the conservative evangelical pastor of People's Church in Toronto travelled across Western Europe on a YFC-sponsored preaching tour in the summer of 1948. His impression of German adults was that on the one hand they harboured a hatred toward outsiders that was the residual fruit of Nazism, and on the other hand were fearful of Russian Communist occupation. He concluded that "the only hope for Germany is the gospel and the gospel in the hands of young people ... Youth For Christ has its greatest chance. There is no other organization more capable of getting a hearing in Germany."[38]

At its Annual Congress in 1955, YFC's president, Bob Cook, in his plenary address to congress delegates, described Germany as still in a state of ideological and spiritual crisis. According to Cook, the leaders of the German YFC chapter, Reinnie Barth and his wife, were at the time on a stress-related extended leave because "all the forces of Hell are focused upon a talented young couple who dared to bring their talents ... into a land, many sectors of which are still filled with heathenism and the hordes of hell – the land where the light went out."[39] Here again, the allusions to Germany's totalitarian past as well as its partial occupation by the current ideological threat were conflated with the spiritual opposition that conservative evangelicals viewed as their chief threat.

Into the 1960s the same theme and concern was voiced by YFC missionaries or YFC staff who went on to work as missionaries in Europe with other agencies. Robert Evans was among the first YFC missionaries to go to Europe and coordinated much of YFC's early work there from 1946 to 1948. He went on to found a small conservative evangelical Bible college in France, which in turn led to his founding Greater Europe Mission in 1952. In an address to the Billy Graham Evangelistic Association in 1963, Evans cited Communism as the chief threat to Christian renewal in Western Europe. Along with theological modernism, Communism was behind the greatest systematic attack on the Bible, and both of these threats had their origins in Germany. He warned Graham's staff not to be deceived by the emerging material prosperity and the visible "graces of civilization": Europe was still very much a mission field.[40]

As is evident from the material presented above, YFC, and American conservative evangelicals more generally, tended to conflate the spiritual forces that opposed them with the ideological adversary of Communism. Conservative evangelical missionaries were not so naive as to equate the ideas of democracy with the preaching of the Christian message, but they clearly saw the former as functioning synergistically with the latter. And by portraying Communism in essentially spiritual terms, conservative evangelical missionaries were implying that there could be no peaceful co-existence between Christianity and Communism. The best way to save Germany was through a robust combination of Christian revivalism and democratic freedom that would deny Communism the necessary spiritual-ideological atmosphere it required in order to breathe and spread. This approach allowed conservative evangelical evangelists to employ both spiritual and ideological rhetoric, depending on the needs of the moment.

On the Battlefield for Jesus: YFC's American Military Image

Another way in which YFC's work was connected to Cold War politics was through its close association with the American Military Government (AMG) in Germany. Such association was evident in two ways: the support of military chaplains, and the frequent invocation by YFC staff members of battlefield terminology and images when describing their mission. When Torrey Johnson began to hear reports of American soldiers stationed in Germany holding their own Youth for Christ rallies, he was quick to see the possible providential purposes being achieved through human military-diplomatic calculations. In addressing the first YFC congress at Winona Lake, Johnson exclaimed, "Who knows but what we've got an army of occupation for the purpose of establishing YOUTH FOR CHRIST!"[41] His words proved to be prophetic in that military personnel did play an important role in YFC taking root in Germany. At the height of the AMG's occupational presence in Germany in the early postwar decades, it was estimated that as many as 100 YFC rallies were being held each weekend on US military bases in the American Zone.[42] In a number of cases these YFC rallies were endorsed by military chaplains, who in turn became bridges for YFC activism to cross over into the surrounding

German communities. Even though chaplains and other military personnel who supported YFC were not as overt as Johnson in invoking anti-Communist or pro-democracy rhetoric, their early association with the establishment of a German YFC chapter, along with the frequent use of military imagery to describe their revivalist mission, kept YFC's identity associated with American foreign policy ideals.

Even before YFC became active in Germany, its leaders made frequent use of wartime analogies to depict the magnitude of the spiritual conflict in which they were engaged. YFC drew criticism from both religious and secular media for such depictions. A writer for the mainline *Christian Century* claimed that YFC's "smooth blend of religion and patriotism" made for an uncritical conflation of church and state. A secular journalist went so far as to label YFC's frequent military references as fascist.[43]

Once the movement had gained some traction on American army bases, the dramatic imagery of the battlefield became a convenient and evocative way to describe YFC's success and to garner support from their conservative evangelical constituency. Not surprisingly, Torrey Johnson was particularly adept at appropriating military language in describing the mission to Germany: "It may well be 'blood and guts' spiritual warfare ... we are battling for the lost souls of young men and young women for whom Christ died."[44] In October 1948, Colonel Paul Maddox, chief of US Chaplains for the US Army in Europe and a staunch YFC activist, described YFC revival rallies taking place across Europe as a "Gospel lift to win young people to Jesus Christ."[45] Thus Maddox was drawing an analogy between the American military's resistance to the Communist blockade through the Berlin airlift and resistance to the equivalent spiritual battle being waged by YFC. Such a close association between YFC's mission to Germany and the ideological showdown between American and Soviet troops over West Berlin made YFC look very much like an extension of the AMG's hegemony by religious means.

While inspiring to supporters in America, such rhetoric was potentially damaging to YFC's German constituency. In May 1947 Johnson, with a group of thirty-three German ministers, lay-leaders, and American military personnel gathered in Bad Homburg, just outside Frankfurt, for a conference that led to the official establishment of YFC-Germany. In preparation for the conference Willie Diezel, a pastor in the *Freikirchen* who would be appointed to YFC-Germany's first executive leadership committee, cautioned Johnson and other American YFC staff members against using such references. Military rhetoric, Diezel warned Johnson, would win him only the resentment and distrust of the German delegates.[46] Johnson must have taken the advice to heart, as Diezel, in a post-conference letter to Johnson, reported that because of Johnson's addresses at the conference, German delegates were now assured that the American YFC leadership had no political interests or agenda behind its work.[47]

More significant than battlefield rhetoric for the mission to Germany was the actual work done by army chaplains in using YFC rallies to evangelize German young people. As impromptu YFC rallies began springing up on American military bases, military chaplains played a vital role in establishing a sustained YFC presence there. In December 1946, as the result of support from a network of army chaplains, Youth for Christ was chartered in the headquarters of the US Occupational Government of Germany (OMGUS), thereby receiving official sanction to continue its work throughout the American Zone.[48] The unofficial flagship of YFC in Germany was the chapter that met on the military base in Frankfurt. It was here that YFC leaders decided to invite English-speaking Germans to attend their rallies. The initial enthusiastic response of German young people surpassed expectations, and YFCM went on to report that a number of German young people had become Christians as a result.[49]

The reality of military life in the form of frequent redeployment of chaplains and other military YFC leaders threatened to undermine any chance of sustained growth and continuity of leadership for this fledgling work among German young people. In order to make YFC's work less dependent on particular military personnel, American chaplains began working with interested German pastors and lay leaders to establish sustainable joint American-German YFC rallies held outside military bases. The first of these was held in a bombed-out church in Frankfurt in September 1946, and over 1,700 German young people attended.[50] During the early postwar years the same pattern of YFC missionary outreach through the initiative of army chaplains was replicated in cities such as Nürnberg, München, and Berlin.[51] While these chaplains showed a genuine concern for local German communities, at times using their influence with AMG authorities to channel relief supplies to needy German families, they also kept a predominantly American face on YFC's early mission work among German civilians.[52]

Two chaplains in particular, Colonel Paul Maddox and Captain John Youngs, were instrumental in helping YFC establish its German chapter.

Maddox, a Southern Baptist minister, used his position as chief of chaplains for Europe from 1946 to 1950 to promote YFC's presence both on military bases and in German communities. Youngs, a Presbyterian minister from Philadelphia, gave leadership to YFC in Nürnburg and Frankfurt as well as serving as YFC's coordinator for the European Theatre from 1947 until 1950 – an official military appointment made by the European Chaplaincy Office.[53] Both men helped set up the conference in Bad Homburg during Johnson's 1947 visit, which led to the official establishment of the German YFC, and both were part of the official delegation that represented the German YFC at the World Congress on Evangelism in Beatenberg, Switzerland, in the summer of 1948.[54] As such they were eager to see YFC take root in German soil, but they also believed that for YFC rallies to be successful in Germany they needed to follow the American format and approach.

In updating Johnson on the challenges facing the newly formed German chapter of YFC, Youngs noted the difficulty many of the German clergy had in moving the work forward. The solution was to have American leaders be more assertive in working with German young people and "training them in YFC principles." In Youngs's estimation, "German youth simply have lost faith in German Church leadership."[55] He realized that this deviated from the indigenization strategy originally mapped out at Bad Homburg, but in his judgment the need for ongoing American involvement to guide the fledgling organization was essential if it was to succeed. To give credence to his position, Youngs quoted Walter Hoffman, a *Freikirche* pastor in Berlin: "You Americans bring us the only hope for our youth by bringing your Youth For Christ groups to the German people."[56]

American chaplains were not averse to German leadership; in fact they encouraged it. But in seeking to indigenize YFC's leadership they made it clear that Germans needed to be faithful to "YFC principles," thereby assuring that even when dressed in German clothing, YFC evangelistic work would look and sound like it did back in America. In their willingness to bypass, or at best selectively engage, German church leadership, in building local support, YFC promoted a form of individualism in its presentation of the Christian witness that had as much to do with American values of personal freedom as it did with Christianity. Even with its Christian message tied to the ideals of democratic freedom, YFC's mission, aided by American chaplains, continued to penetrate small pockets of German society.

One more aspect of the influence of the US military in YFC's mission can be seen by noting the locations of YFC established long-term bases in Germany. As the transition to a full-time German leadership was accomplished and sustained during the 1950s and into the 1960s, YFC set up its permanent offices in Frankfurt and Berlin, mirroring the greatest concentration of American military strength in the country.[57] From the outset the Berlin chapter, as part of its mission, sought to supply pastors in the Russian Zone with YFC's literature and support materials.[58] Thus even the centres from which YFC operated during the Cold War decades continued to reflect the ongoing American presence in Germany. As will be evident in the next section, YFC's work further mirrored its fundamentally American DNA through a steady stream of both methods and short-term missionaries from the United States.

Franchising Revivalism: Promoting American Values through the YFC Brand

The third way in which YFC's mission played a role in advancing American ideological values in Germany during the Cold War was by successfully franchising its brand of revivalism in that country. There is little evidence in the YFC records that American leaders ever engaged in extended reflection and self-critique about the cultural presuppositions and biases embedded their own ministry. Even in the later decades of the Cold War, after the immediate crisis and uncertainty had settled down, and West Germany was safely in the fold of Western democracy, YFC's work there was sustained by continually adapting the methods of conservative evangelical revivalism to the current fashions of American youth culture. In exporting these methods and fashions, YFC's leaders assumed that young people around the world shared a generic set of "youth culture" values. In a way they were prophetic in that they anticipated – and to an extent even aided – the international acceptance of American pop culture as the global brand that it has become. YFC's annual world congresses were not only international evangelistic training sessions of the YFC faithful from around the globe, but also functioned as corporate religious exercises in franchise quality control and brand affirmation. YFC's itinerant missionary teams of young people that toured Germany throughout the 1950s and 1960s were not only ambassadors of American revivalism, but also apostles of American pop culture. These two aspects of YFC's work were important, not only as vehicles for YFC's spiritual message, but also, however unconsciously, for their role in promoting American cultural tastes and sensibilities among its German supporters. In this sense YFC missionaries continued to be Cold War participants, using the trends and fashions of American "Christianized" pop culture as their means of promoting the values of American democracy.

The first instrument of ongoing Americanization was YFC's annual world congress. In August 1948 YFC held its first world congress on evangelism in the alpine resort of Beatenberg, Switzerland. During his 1947 tour of Germany, Torrey Johnson had grown increasingly concerned that the opportunity to bring revival to Europe was already slipping away. From the earliest days he had used the metaphor of a torch lighter to describe the work of Youth for Christ. He saw YFC's cadre of American preachers and musicians who barnstormed across North America, and now around the globe, as individual torch carriers, each spreading small sparks of revival through their evangelistic rallies.[59] But on that May evening in his Berlin hotel room, Johnson realized how relatively feeble these torches were as long as they continued to work on their own. It was then that he had a new inspiration. Rather than having a limited number of American missionary evangelist torch lighters spreading sparks on their own, why not gather them, and like-minded torch lighters from other countries, together in one place for a world congress on evangelism? Using Johnson's metaphor, it was a case of bringing lots of smaller torches in the same place in order to create a revival fire of such combustible intensity that a great conflagration of revival would fan outward across the globe. Not only could Europe be swept up in a new wave of revival, but such a congress could be the means to "co-ordinate and accelerate ... the final complete evangelization of the world in [this] generation."[60]

When Johnson presented his vision for a World Congress to YFC's American leadership in the summer of 1947, it was endorsed enthusiastically. The Christian Bible School and retreat centre of Beatenberg, located in the Swiss Alps, was chosen as the conference venue, and in August 1948, 500 delegates from twenty-five countries gathered for YFC's first annual world congress.[61] The vast majority of the delegates came from North America and European countries. Germany alone was represented by eighty-two delegates, the largest contingent next to the United States; this number included twenty-five German nationals as well as American and British chaplains stationed in Germany.[62]

At the conclusion of a week filled with intense sessions of Bible study, prayer, and exhortation to evangelize, teams of delegates fanned out across ten European countries, holding revival meetings in the hopes that their sparks would ignite a wider and ongoing revivalist blaze.[63] Although participants were enthusiastic about the congress and afterward recounted stories of conversions, the actual picture tended to fall short of Johnson's optimistic projections.[64] Nevertheless, YFC's leaders were pleased with the results of the congress and the ability of such a model to ignite spiritual revival fires in Europe.

Beatenberg became the pattern for future congresses and laid the groundwork for a second YFC mission strategy: summer evangelistic teams of young people from the United States and Canada who would cross the Atlantic and hold meetings in Germany and other European countries well into the 1970s.[65] In the years following Beatenberg, YFC held annual congresses in major cities, such as Brussels, Tokyo, Caracas, São Paulo, and Mexico City. Besides the tourist appeal these venues held, especially for North American delegates, congresses provided opportunities for YFC leaders from various countries to meet each other as part of a larger missionary fraternity, and also receive a standardized training in conservative evangelical Bible-teaching and methods of evangelism. The congresses were thus a step toward fulfilling Johnson's dream for Germany: seeing "one hundred German evangelists on the field for God and trained in American techniques, adapted to the German mentality. It could turn the [spiritual] tide in many places throughout ... Germany."[66] While congresses could claim to have an international flavour because of the number of countries who sent delegates, it was also clear that the agenda of each congress was set by an American cultural orientation to evangelizing youth.

A second, related instrument by which YFC exported an American cultural voice to Germany was the steady stream of touring missionary teams of American college-aged young people. Known as Teen-Teams, these ensembles of seven or eight young people would go on month-long tours, visiting German schools and church youth groups, and appearing at YFC rallies. The concept was based on the belief that the most effective way to reach young people of any culture with the Christian message was through other young people – even if they were from a foreign culture – instead of through indigenous adult Christians. Johnson explained this in a letter to German EKD *Pfarrer* Martin Niemöller when first offering YFC's services in the spiritual rehabilitation of German youth in 1947, and the same philosophy continued to inform YFC's work in Germany in the decades that followed.[67] In the early 1960s, YFC staff in Berlin reported on the success of a recent visit by a teen team: "There was overnight change in [the German] young people when they saw what six [American] teenagers could do. It didn't matter that these teens were Americans. Far greater than national barriers is the age barrier. Foreign teenagers could convey to these German young people what older German people could not. The common age breaks down national and even language barriers."[68]

Under the banner of *"Jugend ruft Jugend,"* YFC Teen-Teams brought the message of conservative evangelical Christianity, often through music, or accompanied by a German evangelist, to youth venues and events set up by local YFC supporters.[69] In all of this, YFC was seeking to be faithful to its revivalist mandate of inviting young people to "accept Christ into their lives." However, the message was never culturally neutral, and as such YFC's own philosophy and methodology ensured that its evangelistic work invariably was intertwined with the aspirations and ideals of white, middle-class America. While not overtly waving the banner of democracy, the concentration of YFC's German work in cities such as Berlin and Frankfurt, where American military power was most visible, provided constant associations of YFC's links with a larger American ideological presence in its standoff against Communism. The frequent visits of Teen-Teams to Germany during the 1950s, a decade when air travel across the Atlantic was still considered affordable by only the relatively rich, further enforced the image of an American Christianity linked to the values of financial success, educational privilege, and the general optimism that came with the United States' postwar international ascendancy. James Hefley, who has chronicled the early growth of YFC overseas, has rightly observed that the confidence American conservative evangelicals derived from their country's victory in the Second World War often spilled over into their missionary proclamation: "Overseas, Americans enjoyed a liberator's popularity which they'd never known before (nor have since). They were from the wealthiest and strongest nation in the world."[70] Even as German attitudes toward the extensive American military presence in their country cooled, YFC's missionary zeal continued to exude the same confidence and revivalist optimism typical of Torrey Johnson and other early postwar leaders. The YFC mission to Germany is thus an apt illustration of historian Andrew Walls's epigram "Big boots in the temple" to capture the ethos of American missions during this period.[71]

Which segment of German Protestantism was the most receptive to a mission freighted so heavily with American cultural baggage? It is no coincidence that YFC's German branch found its greatest support among pastors and youth workers of the *Freikirchen*. As evident in the previous chapter, it was this spectrum of German Protestantism that most closely resembled the denominational character and congregational governance of many North American conservative evangelical churches. Its pastors were frequently leaders of local chapters of the Deutsche Evangelische Allianz, the organization most active in carrying out evangelistic missions in Germany.[72] Of the thirty-four church leaders who attended the Bad Homburg conference at which the German YFC was officially founded, twenty-one were pastors or church workers from the *Freikirchen*.

In addition to ecclesial affinity, another factor determining receptivity was personal connections of some German leaders to the United States. During the first three decades of the Cold War a number of YFC's *Freikirchen* staff, such as Willie Diezel, Reinhold Barth, and Werner Bürklin, had family or educational ties in the United States, by which they had become familiar with American forms of revivalism.[73] That this was the case well into the 1960s can be seen from minutes and reports from meetings held by YFC's European leaders and those of the German national chapter. It is evident from these records that these German staff members believed that American-style evangelistic rallies and youth activities sponsored by YFC were a suitable means of reaching young people in their own country with the Christian message.[74]

Campfires instead of Conflagrations

In the above analysis of YFC's efforts to save Germany, the focus has been on their role as emissaries of democracy during the ideological confrontation of the early Cold War decades. In concluding this section it is important to keep in mind that, its cross-cultural naïveté notwithstanding, YFC's priority was to help as many people as possible to embrace the Christian message. Twenty years after YFC's first official foray to Germany, Torrey Johnson's hopeful expectation of an immediate and far-reaching Christian revival had not come to pass. Compared with the dramatic rhetoric of sparks and torches and conflagrations of revival so typical of the earlier years, what materialized was more like a small group of warm, inviting campfires that attracted a relatively small but loyal German following. To label this a failure of missionary vision would be too harsh. Even if the results were not as spectacular as Johnson and other first-generation leaders of YFC envisioned, their energy, enthusiasm, and optimism had taken a haphazard revivalist movement and channelled it into a sustainable Christian ministry in a country with which its missionaries most recently had been at war.

Janz Team Ministries: Giving Revivalism a Legitimate Place in German Protestantism

The mission of Janz Team Ministries came directly out of YFC's work in Germany, but had an ethos and approach markedly different from that of YFC. Both organizations were committed to a revivalist/conversionist form of evangelism, but unlike their American counterparts, JTM's predominantly Canadian staff took up residence in Germany, became fluent in the German language, and developed long-term relationships with church leaders. This led to the creation of an indigenous network of German Protestants committed to holding large-scale evangelistic meetings known as crusades, or *Feldzüge*. JTM's mission through mass evangelism had a two-fold impact on German Protestantism: it brought mass evangelism from the margins of German Protestant life and gave it credibility as a legitimate way for German Protestants to evangelize their compatriots; and it helped their German supporters gain a tangible sense of identity by working with like-minded revivalists across German-speaking Europe, and by connecting them with an international community of conservative Protestants increasingly known as evangelicals. As we shall see in the next chapter, Billy Graham played a major role in this regard as well, but in many ways JTM's work nurtured and cultivated the growth of this movement in Germany between Graham's periodic visits. Before examining JTM's work under the above two themes, a brief overview of how JTM came to Germany and a summary of the defining contours of their work is in order.

Mass Evangelism: From the Prairies of Canada to the Cities of Germany

JTM began as a gospel music quartet on the prairies of western Canada. The quartet was composed of three brothers, Leo, Hildor, and Adolph Janz, along with Adolph's brother-in-law, Cornie Enns. All four had been raised in rural farming communities of the Canadian prairies and came from German-speaking Mennonite families who had fled the Stalinist purges in the USSR by emigrating to Canada in the late 1920s. They grew up speaking a dialect of German, known as Plattdeutsch, alongside English.[75] Their families belonged to the Mennonite Brethren Church, a branch of the Mennonites who in the mid-nineteenth century had embraced the evangelical teachings of personal conversion and biblicism through contact with Moravian revivalists.[76] As young men they all attended Prairie Bible Institute (PBI), a conservative evangelical Bible school located in the small farming community of Three Hills, Alberta. In large part through the influence of PBI's founder and principal, L.E. Maxwell, the four men became involved in evangelistic work. Maxwell was an enthusiastic promoter of missions and a charismatic preacher, who was well connected in conservative evangelical circles on both sides of the Canadian-American border.[77]

In 1948, now known as the Janz Quartet, Enns and the three Janz brothers joined the staff of PBI to sing on the school's weekly radio broadcasts and travel with Maxwell during his frequent summer preaching tours at the end of each school year. It was during one of these summer tours that the Janz Quartet came to the attention of YFC. Because they could speak some German, the quartet were invited to conduct evangelistic meetings under YFC's banner in Germany for three months during the summer of 1951. Interpreting this as a divine call to service, the quartet members agreed to go.[78]

In addition to singing as a quartet, all four members assumed responsibility for additional areas of the evangelistic work. Leo Janz, the second-eldest of the brothers and de facto group leader, was the preacher at each crusade meeting. Leo's younger brother, Hildor, acted as a vocal soloist. Cornie Enns was the master of ceremonies for each meeting and directed the volunteer choir of local singers, who were part of the musical at each crusade. Adolf Janz, the eldest of the three brothers, oversaw the training of volunteers from local churches who worked as crusade counsellors. These counsellors met with people who came forward at the end of each crusade meeting in response to Leo's invitation to "receive Christ into their lives." The evangelistic team was completed by keyboard accompanist Harding Braaten. In these roles, the five men formed a compact, mobile evangelistic team who used music and preaching in roughly equal measure to proclaim their message.

Their first set of meetings was held in the city of Solingen, at the southern end of the German industrial heartland, or *Ruhrgebiet*, where YFC had its German head office at the time. Leo Janz recalled,

Our meagre German did not deter them from listening and decid-ing for the Lord ... They had previously neither known nor heard of us. But there was a sense of fellowship immediately which erased from our minds the feeling that we were in a foreign land. We were cared for in families which received us so warmly that we were genuinely moved ... The [fellow Christians] from Solingen went to bat for us. Not only did they support our campaign ... but they also put us in touch with individual Christians and churches in other places. In one sense they became the springboard for our future work in Germany.[79]

Janz's reflections indicate an ethos that marked the quartet's initial min-istry experience in Germany that was noticeably different from the ear-lier YFC forays into Germany. Most American YFC teams had to work through interpreters and tended to use their relative wealth to stay in the best hotels.[80] This distance of language and in living quarters did not factor in the Janz Quartet's stay and gave them a more immediate connection to the German community. One further contrast to YFC implied in Janz's recollections is that the quartet were perceived by their German hosts as simple rural farm boys, and not urban entrepreneurs from large wealthy metropolitan centres. It was a quality that elicited sympathy from their German hosts and endeared them to those who attended their meetings.

During this first visit that the quartet worked alongside a well-known German tent evangelist by the name of Anton Schulte. It was through Schulte's connections in German Protestant circles, as well as his encour-agement to the young Canadian evangelists, that paved the way for their return to Germany permanently some years later.[81]

The strong turnout at the meetings and the warm hospitality shown to the Canadian farm boys by local church members set the stage for JTM's return to Germany full-time. Leo Janz promised his German supporters that if an opportunity arose for him to begin an evangelistic work through radio broadcasts in Germany, he would return.[82] The chance came five years later, and in 1956 Leo and Hildor, along with Harding Braaten, moved their families across the Atlantic and began producing a weekly fifteen-minute evangelistic radio program in German. This was then broadcast over Radio Luxembourg, the only privately owned radio station on Continental Europe at the time, and the only station that would sell Janz airtime for independent religious programming. All German radio stations at the time were state-owned and permitted only religious pro-grams produced by members of the officially recognized churches.[83]

Because Germany was still recovering from the devastation of the war, the missionaries and their young families decided to locate in Basel, Switz-erland, just across the border from the southwestern German province of Baden-Württemberg. They registered their mission in both countries under the name of Die Christliche Radiomission but eventually changed it to Janz Team Ministries, a name that seemed to resonate more strongly with their listeners.[84] Arranging a make-shift studio in the living room of Hildor's apartment, they began producing two fifteen-minute radio programs, which were broadcast over Radio Luxembourg each week.[85] Using the format that had worked successfully in their Canadian radio broadcasts, each consisted of a mix of musical numbers by Braaten and the two Janz brothers and a brief evangelistic message by Leo, concluded by an invitation for listeners to "accept Christ" into their lives. They were aired over both long- and short-wave transmitters twice weekly, reaching a potential audience of millions, not only in the German-speaking regions of Western Europe, but also deep into Communist Eastern Europe. The timeslot in which the programs were aired was the rather unpromising one of 6:30 a.m., and to get an idea if anyone was tuning in, Leo encour-aged listeners to respond by writing to the mission's mailing address. To the Janz brothers' surprise, listener response was immediate, and letters of appreciation began to pour in to JTM's office.[86] The living room of Leo's apartment doubled as the office for the mission, but the volume of mail would soon prove too great for the three men to handle. On several days up to 1,500 letters were delivered to the mission's post box.[87] Before long they were looking for more office and studio space as well as personnel to handle the high volume of mail correspondence from their listening audi-ence.[88] The popularity of the radio programs, as much due to the musical numbers as to the preaching, led to invitations from churches across Ger-many to hold meetings in their cities.

In September 1957, the two Janz brothers and Braaten held their first citywide, multi-week evangelistic crusade in Basel, just across the Swiss border from JTM's eventual headquarters in Lörrach, Germany. The posi-tive response to these meetings led to further invitations from churches throughout Germany, as well as German-speaking Switzerland, to hold evangelistic crusades. By 1960 the demands on the team called for more staff than the small three-man team could manage. In order to meet the challenge Adolph Janz and Cornie Enns joined Leo, Hildor, and Harding in 1961, reuniting the quartet. Over the next two decades the work of JTM would grow and diversify into areas such as theological education and camp work, but the core of its identity remained tied to crusade evangelism and to the members of the quartet.

Moving Mass Evangelism Closer to the German Protestant Mainstream

JTM helped make mass evangelism an increasingly credible and acceptable method of spreading the Christian message in the eyes of German Protestants through adopting two key strategies: first, their crusades were always cooperative ventures with coalitions of local church pastors who had invited them; thus JTM were never seen as rivals, but partners with existing churches; and second, JTM was able to convince a growing number of Protestant clergy that the most controversial aspect of crusade meetings – asking people to come to the front of the meeting hall "to receive Christ" – was not an American gimmick, but a legitimate way for Germans to respond to the Christian message. Before examining the impact of JTM's mission, it is important to understand the status of mass evangelism in Germany prior to their arrival.

Large-scale evangelistic meetings held outside of churches were not new for German Protestant pastors. Such meetings had been held in Germany as early as 1902 when Jakob Vetter founded the Deutsche Zeltmission with the specific purpose of evangelizing the working classes in the industrial centres of Germany.[89] Using meeting tents that could seat up to 1,000 people, Vetter and other itinerant evangelists from his mission conducted revival meetings in cities across the country. Shortly after the Second World War, German Baptists reactivated their own tent mission, which had been founded in 1934. By 1949 they had four evangelistic teams on three-week preaching missions in various regions of West Germany, using tents that held up to 1,500 people.[90] That same year Wilhelm Brauer, a *Pfarrer* in the *Landeskirche* in the province of Westphalia, along with Friederich Müller, an evangelist from the Methodist *Freikirche*, formed the Deutsche Evangelistenkonferenz (DEk). Originally intended as a support group for church leaders who also worked as evangelists, the DEk brought together as many as seventy pastors and church workers for periodic gatherings to discuss strategies and encourage each other in their common task.[91]

The largest Protestant organization dedicated to evangelistic work in Germany was the *Deutsche Evangelische Allianz* (DEA), which had been established in Berlin in 1851.[92] As a cross-confessional group for like-minded Christians from the *Freikirchen* and the *Landeskirchen*, its chief priority was to encourage evangelism and mission work both at home and abroad. The DEA did have a national executive body, but its members were all volunteers who held positions as pastors and church workers in local parishes. The national executive was not so much a governing body as a consultative one.[93] The strength of the DEA depended on the degree to which its local chapters took the initiative for evangelism and other forms of Christian witness.[94] Brauer and his coterie of evangelists were also members of local DEA chapters and frequently worked in conjunction with the DEA on local evangelistic initiatives.

In spite of this national infrastructure and commitment to traditional tent-meeting evangelism, Brauer and the members of the DEk represented a minority constituency in German Protestantism during the early post-war period.[95] Seen by many in the *Landeskirchen* as using an outmoded method of evangelism from nineteenth-century Pietism, the DEk increasingly was marginalized by the rising popularity of the *Kirchentag* movement founded by Reinhold Thadden-Trieglaff. The *Kirchentag* movement will be described in more detail in the next chapter, but at this point it is important to note that its approach to drawing German people back to church emphasized discussion over preaching, and focused more on instruction and sacramental worship than revivalist exhortation.[96]

Although the DEk participated in the biennial *Kirchentag* congresses, their members were not convinced that the congresses would render traditional tent evangelism obsolete. Already by 1953 it was apparent that in spite of impressive turnouts of up to 600,000 people to its five-day congresses, the *Kirchentag* congresses had brought no discernible increase in actual church attendance.[97] As such DEk members were skeptical about the effectiveness of such "modern" methods. At the same time they recognized the relative paucity of their own resources in the face of the great spiritual needs of their country. By the mid-1950s this sense of inadequacy made them open to outside help from North American evangelists, such as the Janz Quartet and Billy Graham.[98]

As stated above, JTM's radio programs over Radio Luxembourg led to invitations from pastors for these Canadian missionaries to hold evangelistic meetings in their churches. When first asked by pastors from the

Basel chapter of the Swiss *Evangelische Allianz* (EA) to do so in their city, Leo Janz stated up front, as he would time and again: JTM would not force itself on anyone and would go only where they were invited. However, once the Janz brothers began working with a specific group of pastors in planning a crusade, Leo insisted that pastors agree to certain conditions that became the operational norms of JTM's work: (1) all pastors in the EA had to pledge to work together in support of the crusade; there could be no half-hearted support from church leaders, as that would undermine morale, cause division, and lead to accusations of JTM favouring particular churches over others; (2) Leo would conclude every meeting with a *"Ruf zur Entscheidung,"* the invitation for people in the audience to come to the front of the auditorium "to ask Christ into their lives"; and (3) JTM would hold meetings every evening in one of the city's largest indoor facilities over an extended period of time: in the case of Basel it was to be for one whole month. Expenses for the rental of the auditorium would be covered by a free-will offering taken at each service.[99]

The latter two points were the cause of greatest resistance among local pastors. The sheer magnitude of such a venture was unheard of in church circles, and the financial risk was believed to be a recipe for certain failure and embarrassment for supporting churches. As well, it was a widely shared opinion that inviting people to come forward in immediate response to preaching was an "un-German" practice, and thus something that people would resist.[100] The Janz brothers gently persisted, and eventually won over Ernst Gilgen, the pastor of a local Methodist *Freikirche* and a highly regarded member of the Basel EA. With his endorsement the rest of the EA got behind the ambitious plan to hold meetings in a large auditorium in Basel's famous *Mustermesse* exhibition centre for the entire month of September. The high attendance and positive response to the crusade surpassed even the Janz brothers' expectations. Part way through the month the meetings had to be moved to a larger hall, which could seat up to 5,000 people because the one they had booked initially (seating capacity of 3,000) was too small to hold each evening's turnout. In addition to the high nightly attendance, a total of 1,200 people responded to the *Ruf zur Entscheidung* by coming forward for counselling, and the once skeptical pastors were now asking Leo to extend the meetings beyond the one month.[101]

The Basel crusade results could have been written off as an anomaly. However, in July 1958, attendance was just as high at a similar series of meetings when JTM was invited to Essen, Germany. Protestant leaders around the country began to take notice. Essen represented an even greater challenge than Basel. As a key city in the heart of the *Ruhrgebiet*, much of its population was made up of the "fourth class" of blue-collar industrial workers, who remained largely impervious to efforts by local churches to draw them into church life.[102] Ever since the quartet's first visit to Germany, Leo Janz had believed that ministry in the *Ruhrgebiet* was most crucial. Besides being the most densely populated region in West Germany, it had a reputation for being the most de-Christianized; less than 10 per cent of the population attended church regularly.[103] If one were to conduct mass evangelism in the Ruhr, Essen seemed the most strategic location for reaching as wide an audience as possible. It also had one of the largest auditoriums for holding such an event, the recently constructed Grugahalle.

Once again the local DEA issued the invitation to JTM and sponsored the meetings, but as in Basel, some clergy were doubtful of the crusade's success. Wilhelm Busch, one of the most respected *Landeskirchen Pfarrers* in the city, while not opposing the crusade, quietly refrained from publicly endorsing it, believing the credibility of his own ministry would be compromised if the crusade failed. Diplomatically, he planned to be away on vacation when the crusade was being held, yet did not discourage his parishioners from participating as crusade volunteers. The meetings were well attended; from the outset a steady stream of people came forward in response to Leo's invitation to "receive Christ" each evening. Busch was summoned home from his vacation prematurely by some of his excited parishioners, who informed him that he was missing out on a great work of God. Busch promptly cut short his vacation and returned home to throw his support behind the crusade. He later admitted to Leo, "I have been put to shame. What I am seeing here is simply unbelievable."[104] At the outset of the crusade the average nightly attendance was close to 3,000, but during the last two weeks, attendance rose to 7,000, almost filling the hall to capacity. At the conclusion of the month-long crusade, over 1,600 people had come forward for counselling.[105]

Besides pastors, the local press also took notice. In one case the *Neu Ruhr/Rhein Zeitung* favourably reported JTM's commitment to working with local pastors and not trying to lure people away from existing churches as part of a radical sectarian movement.[106] Another Essen reporter, writing in *Der Weg*, a weekly religious journal, described JTM's appeal using a comparative approach. He noted that during the month-long crusade the evangelists had to compete for people's attention with the soccer World Cup being held in Sweden, and with an election battle in the regional *Landtag*. While politicians gave campaign speeches to mostly empty chairs, the Grugahalle was comfortably full night after night. He noted that the Janz brothers made no reference to the electoral race or to anything political. The preaching of the gospel remained their central focus and attracted an intergenerational audience – adults, youth, and children – who responded each evening to the *Ruf zur Entscheidung*.[107]

If Essen was a test of mass evangelism in the eyes of German-speaking Protestant leaders, then JTM had passed with flying colours. Recalling that event some twenty years later, Leo Janz assessed its significance: "After the evangelistic meetings in Essen, the doors for our large-scale evangelism were wide open to us throughout Germany, Switzerland, and Austria. For over two decades since then, we have proclaimed the Gospel in all the major cities of German-speaking Europe, as well as in many rural areas; in large halls, in tents, and in the open air."[108]

For the next twenty years JTM held crusades throughout West Germany, as well as Austria and the German-speaking regions of Switzerland. By 1960 their work had settled into a recognizable pattern consisting of six to eight major crusade events annually, usually two or three weeks in duration, in halls or large tents with a seating capacity from 500 to 5,000.[109] Although major cities, such as Hamburg, Gelsenkirchen, and Braunschweig in Germany, and Basel, Bern, and Zurich in Switzerland, were the usual hosts for these events, JTM responded to invitations in smaller centres, such as Freiburg and Schaffhausen.[110] JTM also held meetings in cities in Bavaria; however, invitations from this region were less frequent, because there was a smaller Protestant presence in the largely Roman Catholic region.[111] While Leo Janz did keep a strategic eye on the larger cities of Germany and Switzerland, he frequently reminded supporters and news reporters alike that crusade venues were determined on the basis of invitation from local churches and the willingness of pastors to support the revivalist structure of the meetings.[112]

By the mid-1960s the demand for JTM's services was so popular among German Protestants that DEA chapters had to book the Canadian missionaries two years in advance if they wanted to host a crusade.[113] JTM demonstrated that they could work with churches all across German-speaking Europe, and their willingness to work not only in the big cities, but in smaller centres, such as Gummersbach (Germany), Liestal (Switzerland), and Linz (Austria), was an indicator that publicity and numbers were not their primary concerns. Leo Janz summed up JTM's position by frequently emphasizing that he and his mission were in Germany to serve the churches.[114] JTM's wide geographical reach generated coverage in local newspapers. In the mission's early years, press coverage tended to focus on the novelty and surprising popularity of JTM's evangelism. Such media curiosity frequently gave Leo Janz another platform from which to assure a wider public in each host city that the mission came as partners, not as rivals, with local churches.[115] In looking back on and assessing the JTM's impact on German Protestantism, *idea/Spectrum*, a Protestant periodical closely associated with the DEA, hailed Leo Janz as the "father of mass evangelism in German-speaking Europe." In a tribute to Janz, the article pointed out that the pioneering work of JTM's leader in the area of mass evangelism had inspired many German pastors and Christian workers to take up the task of evangelistic preaching.[116]

Alongside their ability to establish their reputation as partners in mission with the DEA, a second important way in which JTM helped mass evangelism gain credibility was by helping reluctant Protestant pastors support the use of a public invitation to "receive Christ" as part of each crusade. Leo Janz, in his efforts to educate pastors and a wider German public alike, used media interviews to explain why he asked people to come forward at the end of each meeting. It was not so much an "American method" as it was an important part of helping people to "come to Christ" and a way for people to identify publicly with the Christian message.[117]

It was ironic that, during the early years of JTM's mission, the group of people most opposed to the public *Ruf zur Entscheidung* were Protestant clergy and not the rank-and-file of the laity or even non-church folk.[118] In spite of Janz's rationale, many clergy at the time believed such an approach would not work with the German people. There was a strongly held belief, even among clergy who supported JTM through DEA invitations, that for Christian conversion to be truly genuine and lasting it needed to occur apart from anything that could be mistaken for coercion or manipulation. The latter charge was often brought up when JTM had its mass choir singing a popular hymn while people came forward. This was seen as emotional exploitation that yielded impressive short-term results but would not last. In a crusade in Mainz in 1963, Leo was willing to run an experiment to counter such charges. He offered to give the usual *Ruf zur Entscheidung* but without any kind of musical accompaniment – he would simply wait in silence for people to come. The experiment produced a result essentially no different from other meetings in which music was used.[119]

Beyond this kind of informal experimentation, pastors were won over by the results in church attendance. Not only did people respond to the crusades, but they could also see lasting growth in their congregations.[120] The charge that revivalist evangelism was only a *"Strohfeuer"* that would soon die out was undermined by the careful follow-up program JTM conducted alongside church leaders with people who came forward at their crusades.[121] Tangible results in local churches, especially the increase in the number of youth who joined congregations as a result of crusades, were noted by leaders such as Helmut Weidemann, a pastor of a *Freikirche* congregation in Giessen.[122] In a study of its follow-up conducted from 1968 to 1976, Larry Swanson, the director of that program, found that on average 90 per cent of those who went forward at JTM's crusades were still faithful church and Bible study attendees.[123] Such lasting results even caused some pastors to begin using altar calls in their own services.[124]

By the middle of the 1960s a growing number of clergy, especially those who were members of the DEA, became willing publicly to defend Leo's use of altar calls at crusade meetings. A typical example was Eberhard Müntiga, a *Landeskirche Pfarrer* in the city of Saarbrücken. In a letter to the editor of a local newspaper, Müntiga dismissed a skeptical journalist's claim that such a practice was manipulative, explaining that it had been part of proclaiming the Christian message from New Testament times onward.[125] Similar statements of support from other clergy were regularly published in JTM's monthly magazine, *Der Menschenfischer* – later changed to *Ruf* – in reports on recent crusades. As editor of the magazine, Janz made sure he included clergy endorsements from across the Protestant spectrum, quoting pastors from both the *Landeskirchen* and the *Freikirchen*.[126] For Janz it was important that the task of mass evangelism be seen as trans-confessional and not marginalized to a sectarian ghetto.

Such endorsements along with the number of requests JTM received for return engagements indicate that mass evangelism was finding a place among German Protestants as a credible and acceptable way to proclaim the Christian message. This was true of larger German cities, such as Essen and Hamburg, which hosted two or more multi-week crusades; and also of Swiss cities, such as Bern, Zurich, and Basel.

In 1958 when JTM held its first large-scale crusade in Essen, the media reported it as a surprising anomaly.[127] Almost twenty years later a regional newspaper covering JTM's crusade in the Black Forest city of Schwenningen announced with an easy familiarity that the Janz brothers were back in town, filling yet another exhibition hall with interested people. The reporter stated there would be no risk of a poor attendance at the meetings, as the name "Janz" was synonymous with thirty years of successful crusade evangelism that involved as many local churches as possible.[128] While not all German clergy were won over to the Janz Quartet's approach, by the mid-1970s it was clear that this form of revivalism had found acceptance among a wide-ranging network of Protestant churches in German-speaking Europe.

Radio, Records, and Ruf: Providing Touchstones for Evangelikaler Identity

Along with making mass evangelism an acceptable practice in German Protestantism, JTM also contributed to the formation of the *Evangelikaler* movement among German Protestants. As will be evident in chapter 5, *Evangelikaler* was the term coined by Germans who identified with the evangelical movement associated with Billy Graham's form of conservative Protestantism. Anglo-American Protestants who embraced "evangelical" as their identity saw themselves as rescuing historic evangelicalism from a strain of fundamentalism perceived as increasingly legalistic and separatist.[129] JTM's role in Germany vis-à-vis the nascent *Evangelikaler* movement was to plant and cultivate the field that Graham would harvest. Graham's crusades in Germany were conducted on a much larger scale and with more fanfare than JTM's, and thus gave a greater visibility to German supporters of the international evangelical movement crystallizing around Graham's leadership. But Graham's visits lasted only a few weeks at most, and it was during the intervening times that JTM's work continued to cultivate a community of supporters in Germany who would eventually identify themselves specifically as *Evangelikaler*, in addition to being *evangelisch*, which for Germans simply meant Protestant.[130]

Complementing its crusade evangelism, JTM developed a network of supporters through three interlocking aspects of its work: radio broadcasts, music recordings, and *Ruf*, its monthly journal. All three identified and sustained a community of like-minded supporters once the crusade was over and the Janz Quartet had moved on to another venue. For many supporters, participating as a crusade volunteer was frequently the gateway into a larger cross-confessional community based on the shared concern for evangelism. In his endorsement of JTM's crusade in Bern in 1959, *Landeskirche Pfarrer* Jakob Kurz pointed out the unity evident among the local participants: "The various Protestant [supporting organizations] from Bern, ones from the state churches, the free churches, and the fellowship groups worked together harmoniously. That was a joy and a source of refreshment."[131] Similar observations came from pastors and lay people who helped in local crusades as ushers, parking attendants, choir members, counsellors, and bus drivers.[132] Gustav-Adolf Potz, the pastor of a *Freikirche* in the town of Herborn in Hesse, noted that when Christians from across confessional boundaries worked together on such an "evangelistic offensive," such as JTM's 1973 crusade, "a strong image is presented to the unbelievers, and Christians are encouraged to see that they do not stand alone."[133]

JTM sought to assure crusade participants that they were part of a larger community by encouraging them to tune in to the mission's weekly radio broadcasts, to subscribe to the monthly magazine *Ruf,* and through the Janz Quartet's music records. As mentioned above, JTM actually began its work in Europe with evangelistic radio programs. Initially the mission was first registered as the Christliche Radiomission, before later adopting the more popular name of Janz Team.[134] The weekly fifteen-minute radio broadcasts acted as miniature crusades, and listeners were encouraged to write to the mission, especially if they had "come to Christ" as a result of listening to the program. From the early 1950s there was a steady stream of mail, which began to increase significantly after some of the large crusades in the *Ruhrgebiet*. Most were from the German-speaking countries of Western Europe, but because Radio Luxembourg's shortwave broadcasts could be picked up in Communist Asia and even South America, JTM also received a few letters from Communist Europe, informing them that they had listeners behind the Iron Curtain.[135] The programming was relatively simple and direct, and as such, it resonated with many Germans who not only tuned in and wrote letters of appreciation, but also supported the work financially through freewill donations.[136]

The demand for the Janz Quartet's music soon led to JTM recording gospel music under their own record label. As much as Leo's preaching with his *Ruf zur Entscheidung* was a hallmark of JTM's crusades, it was the musical offerings that generated some of the warmest and most appreciative responses from the German people. As Leo Janz told a Frankfurt newspaper, "We know that many church musicians look down on our music as an expression of religious sentimentality, [but] the people who attend our meetings want it this way. We have tested it and found that the simpler the melodies and texts, the more effective our music is."[137] Musical numbers made up at least half of each crusade meeting, featuring a mixture of quartet numbers, solos by Hildor Janz, congregational songs, and choral numbers from a volunteer choir of local church singers under the direction of Cornie Enns. In some of the larger cities such as Essen and Hamburg, the choir could be as large as 700 singers.[138]

According to the quartet's accompanist, Harding Braaten, one key reason for the popularity of Janz Team's music was that it tapped into a traditional stream of hymnody that ran deep in German Protestant culture.[139] Early on in their crusade ministry the Janz brothers used songs from a German hymnal known as *Reichs-Lieder*. These hymns were first produced in an 1897 songbook by Gustav Ihloff, a leader in the *Gemeinschaftsbewegung*, a renewal movement in the German state church begun in 1857. Ihloff had come across American Ira D. Sankey's revival hymnal, *Sacred Songs and Solos*, while attending revival meetings in England. As a result he oversaw the translation of over 300 nineteenth-century hymns from the Anglo-American revivalist tradition, which were then published in the above songbook.[140] By 1909 the first *Reichs-Lieder* hymnal was printed, containing over 600 such hymns, and shortly thereafter was adopted as the official hymnal of the *Gemeinschaftsbewegung*. By 1930 it had gone through forty-one printings, and there were 2.4 million copies in circulation.[141] In addition to *Reichs-Lieder* the Janz brothers also drew on German Anabaptist hymns they had learned in their Mennonite communities, which were also sung widely in German *Freikirchen* circles.[142]

In the early years of JTM's work, besides using their first make-shift recording studio to tape their weekly radio broadcasts, Hildor and Leo Janz recorded the duets and solos sung at crusades and then sold them as vinyl records – both the 45 rpm or "short play" records and the long play or LP editions. By 1962, with the quartet reunited, the JTM expanded its musical catalogue to over 200 musical recordings – mostly "short play" records – but with a growing number of LP offerings. Although JTM's offices have not retained the data for record sales during these early years, an article in their periodical, *Der Menschenfischer*, indicated that in they had received 12,000 orders during the last two months of 1963.[143]

Soloist Hildor Janz was the featured artist on most of the records released under JTM's label. In the German city of Essen he was described as not only having the good looks of a musical recording star but also the singing talent of one. Hildor's renditions of gospel songs, usually with an evangelistic message, struck a responsive chord with audiences. Unlike the more formal worship music heard in most German churches, Janz sang music that had more in common with folk tunes or even the popular hit songs of commercial radio.[144] When he was backed by a large crusade choir, the effect could be quite dramatic. Accompanied by Harding Braaten on either the piano or the Hammond organ, the resultant sound was labelled "worldly" by some German clergy. In Germany organ was associated solely with movie secular entertainment culture. Conservative clergy thought it scandalous to use it for Christian music. In their desire to comply with their German sponsors and co-workers, Braaten and the rest of the team initially agreed to go back to using only the piano, but popular response, especially among the youth, to the use of the Hammond was so positive that soon it continued to be included in the musical offerings at crusade meetings.[145]

In 1961, when the quartet members were reunited in Germany, they began recording German translations of American gospel songs as well as Negro spirituals in English – novelties that were enthusiastically received by radio and crusade audiences.[146] This musical combination of New World novelty and folk tradition familiarity found a strong positive resonance with the German people. It is not an overstatement to argue that music played an important role in Germans' being receptive to JTM's evangelism. New songs sung in English gave the quartet's music a "cool factor" particularly prized by postwar youth culture; at the same time their ability to identify with popular currents in German religious culture won over more conservative adult tastes. On the one hand, as North American outsiders they brought a new musical sound to German Christianity; on the other hand, they also showed an ability to breathe new life into a musical form already present in the German Protestant tradition. As one German news-reporter noted, "Radio, records and literature give the [Janz] Team the opportunity for Christians around the world to hear their message, both in word and song. In providing this service the Team does not want to start its own church but to strengthen existing congregations and to work together with them."[147]

Records, along with radio broadcasts, were a means of giving identity to German Christians who shared a concern for evangelizing their own country. They also helped JTM tap into an identifiable constituency of German financial supporters. Registered as a non-profit *Missionswerk* in Germany and Switzerland, JTM could assure its donors that the money raised through record sales was being reinvested into the work of the mission and not lining the pockets of the quartet members.[148] More importantly, JTM's radio and recording work gave shape to a network of supporters that was cross-confessional and rallied around the missionary priorities of the DEA.[149]

A third way in which JTM fostered a sense of community around the defining characteristics of the *Evangelikaler* movement was through its monthly magazine, *Ruf*. Initially called *Der Menschenfischer*, the magazine's name was changed in the mid-1960s to *Ruf zur Entscheidung* (the phrase that by now had become the watchword for the mission), and eventually reduced simply to *Ruf*. As editor, Leo Janz used *Ruf* to keep German supporters in touch with the activities of the Janz Team: reporting on the results of past crusades; soliciting prayer (and indirectly financial) support for upcoming crusades; advertising the musical offerings available in their record catalogue; and reminding readers how to access their radio broadcasts. In this way *Ruf* provided a sense of cohesion to the branches of JTM's work and made its supportive community more tangible through the magazine's subscriber base, which numbered 65,000 by 1970.[150]

Along with these notifications and reports, issues usually contained one of Leo's sermons, and an article of instruction for practical Christian living.[151] The emphasis of these articles, typical of much evangelical edification literature in the English-speaking world, was on the need for personal transformation by "coming to Christ." For the most part Janz avoided political issues and points of doctrine and ecclesial practice, which could prove divisive for German Protestants. Besides writing much of each issue's copy himself, Janz also ran translated articles by Anglo-American evangelicals, such as Theodore Epp and Bill Bright, as well as German authors, such as evangelist Werner Heukelbach.[152] In this way Janz was helping *Evangelikaler* to connect and identify with a wider international community of evangelicals. By avoiding contentious topics that could prove distracting from the task of evangelism, Janz directed his readers to focus on a minimalist Christian message that stressed personal salvation in Jesus Christ and the regular reading of the Bible. Through this means, *Ruf* was one more way in which JTM helped their German supporters gain a sense of identity around the key values that defined evangelicalism.

There is little in JTM's own documents to suggest that the forming of a discernible community of *Evangelikaler* was a premeditated goal; as Leo Janz regularly reminded the readers of *Ruf*, he and his mission came to serve German churches through evangelism that led to "lasting fruit" – Christian commitment that would be life-long.[153] However, by complementing their crusade work with gospel music, radio programs and edification literature, JTM was instrumental in shaping supportive German-speaking Protestants into an identifiable community under the eventual banner of *Evangelikaler*. While helping *Evangelikaler* Protestants define an indigenous identity, JTM also helped link them to the international evangelical movement which, by 1974, had established a visible transnational identity, with Billy Graham as its unofficial leader.

Conclusion

Conservative evangelical missions to Cold War Germany, represented by YFC and JTM, had an impact in two significant areas: the first was as ambassadors of a wider set of democratic values that American conservative evangelicals in particular associated with the Christian message. While "saving of souls for Christ" was paramount in the minds of YFC missionaries, they invariably invoked the ideological rhetoric of Cold War America in their proclamation. Their ongoing connections with the American military presence in Germany, as well as their uncritical application of methods developed in the laboratory of American popular culture, meant that the message of Christianity was closely linked with the ideological aspirations and cultural priorities of Americans.

JTM drew from the same fundamentalist heritage as YFC, but as Canadians they did not seem to carry the mantle of "Defender of the Free World" that weighed heavily on the mission work of their American counterparts. For Leo Janz the message of Christianity was "*die frohe Botschaft*," or good news. Where American evangelist Billy Graham was labelled by the German news media as "God's machinegun," the Janz quartet were dubbed "God's joyful singers."[154] JTM's willingness to take up residence in West Germany, to become fluent in the German language, and to wear their Canadian cultural clothing lightly gave them credibility in their role as cultivators of an *Evangelikaler* identity. They did so by drawing on some of the formative practices of the evangelical tradition: revivalist evangelism, individual conversionism, and gospel music.

From the above comparative analysis of YFC and JTM's work it would be easy to conclude that the Christian message of YFC's mission almost disappeared inside its American ideological clothing, thus limiting its effectiveness, while JTM was the perfect model of cross-cultural accommodation, and therefore more successful. Such over-simplification is misleading. Both forms of conservative evangelical mission work found a place in German Protestant life. During the Cold War years, YFC Germany continually hosted short-term mission teams from America, and this relationship seemed to work well. American evangelical enthusiasm and energy in short-term, limited doses played well in Germany. The growing attractiveness of American forms of popular entertainment in postwar Germany has been well-documented by cultural historians such as Jost Hermand, and YFC's positive reception by a segment of German Protestant youth suggests that this was also true of American religious forms that borrowed heavily from pop culture.[155] But like a gregarious extroverted relative in a more reserved family home, American revivalists could wear out their welcome if they stayed too long. However, in YFC's defence, two qualifications to the above evaluation are in order. First, YFC's goal was to turn the German work over to national leaders as soon as possible, and by the mid-1960s that goal had been largely realized.[156] Second, American YFC teams kept coming to Germany during the 1950s and 1960s at the request of the German Protestants who believed YFC's message and methods were appropriate for evangelizing German young people.[157] The purpose of the analysis of YFC's work in this chapter has not been to cast it as inferior to that of JTM, but to argue that its mission came packaged with the ideological aspirations of American democracy, at times intentionally and at others not.

The Janz brothers, by contrast, took a longer view of their ministry by developing fluency in the German language, taking up residence in the country, and building alliances with German Christians. In this way they brought the practice of mass evangelism from the margins of German Protestant life to a place of greater acceptance and familiarity. At the same time they helped their German supporters find a German way of identifying with revivalist evangelism by becoming indigenous *Evangelikaler*, while still enjoying some of its Anglo-American accents.

CHAPTER FOUR

Billy Graham's Mission to Germany, 1945–1974: From Cold War Crusader to Good Samaritan

As an itinerant evangelist who visited Germany only periodically during the Cold War era, Billy Graham's missionary work in Germany may seem relatively thin when compared with agencies who had long-term, resident missionaries in that country. However, Graham's impact both on North American missions to Germany and on German Protestantism was arguably greater than that of any other single missionary organization from North America. Part of this influence can be attributed to the sheer magnitude of his evangelistic crusades and congresses, and the widespread media coverage they attracted. Spectacle alone, however, is not sufficient to explain Graham's ongoing influence. The substance of his mission was also significant. In Graham's evangelism one can see a coalescing of the two divergent expressions of the conservative evangelical mission illustrated by Youth for Christ (YFC) and Janz Team Ministries (JTM). Therefore in assessing the significance of his mission to Germany, Graham's contribution can be analyzed according to the same two themes developed in the previous chapter: noting the way in which Graham's work contributes to mission as an extension of America's Cold War ideological confrontation with Communism; and the way in which his mission made an important contribution to German Protestant identity. This paradoxical mixture of brash Americanism and cross-cultural winsomeness form the internal tension in Graham's mission to Germany.

On the one hand, as with his conservative evangelical counterparts in YFC, Graham's missionary efforts were initially freighted with the ideological values and attitudes of democracy typical of postwar America. This was particularly true of his visits to Germany during the 1950s and 1960s. These aspects of Graham's ministry generated a negative, if not hostile, response from some German church leaders and in a segment of the secular press. Christian leaders, primarily from the Evangelische Kirche Deutschland (EKD), and skeptical reporters in the secular media saw Graham, not as an ambassador for Christ, but as an American ideological Cold Warrior, cloaked in the rhetoric of Christianity. Graham's early evangelistic efforts in Germany were well intended, but his lack of international experience, as well as the American ideological and cultural elements evident in his crusade ministry, all fed the prejudices of his German critics. Graham's visits were thus resented by some Protestant leaders as unwelcome intrusions into German religious life, and his evangelistic methods were considered inappropriate for addressing the spiritual needs of the German people. This aspect of Graham's mission work further explains how, during the Cold War, American missionaries combined Christian proclamation with an ideological agenda, in order to stop Communism from spreading westward.

On the other hand, Graham's methods and message did find a favourable reception among the German Protestants who were leaders of the cross-confessional Deutsche Evangelische Allianz (DEA). As was the case with JTM, regional chapters of the DEA sponsored most of Graham's visits to Germany. DEA leaders believed Graham's ministry was able to do for Germany what the German churches were incapable of doing on their own: attracting large numbers of youth and working-class adults to hear and respond positively to a clear presentation of the Christian message. The success of Graham's visits gave the host DEA chapters inspiration and confidence to press on with their own evangelistic efforts. By the late 1960s Graham had made a conscious effort to disentangle his ministry from an overtly American ideological and cultural agenda, with the result that he was perceived as a "Good Samaritan" to German Protestants who desired to evangelize their own people. In this manner he solidified his reputation as a truly international Christian leader among German Protestants. By the early 1970s this group of supporters became known as *Evangelikaler*. In addition to carving out a legitimate place in German Protestantism, the emergence of this identity signalled their connection to, and participation in, the growing worldwide evangelical movement.

This chapter will examine Graham's paradoxical identity: first as a Cold War crusader for democracy, and then as a Good Samaritan to German Protestant evangelism. Thus it will continue to develop and explicate the two respective themes of missionaries as ideological emissaries in the Cold War and as agents of influence on German Protestant culture. In order to examine how these two themes emerged in Graham's work, a brief summary of how Graham came to be a missionary to Germany is in order.

How Billy Graham Became a Missionary to West Germany

Graham began his preaching career as a typical product of American fundamentalism from the 1930s and 1940s.[1] Born into a conservative Christian home in 1918 in North Carolina, he underwent a conversion experience as a teenager at a local revival meeting in 1934.[2] Shortly after graduating from Florida Bible Institute in 1940, Graham sensed a divine call to a preaching ministry, but before taking up this vocation he enrolled in Wheaton College, just west of Chicago. Shortly after completing an undergraduate degree in 1943, Graham joined the staff of YFC as an assistant to Torrey Johnson. These years with YFC proved to be formative ones for his later ministry as an international evangelist. From 1945 to 1949 Graham travelled extensively across the United States, speaking at youth rallies and Bible conferences on behalf of the young organization. In the spring of 1946, Graham joined Johnson as part of the first YFC team to enter postwar Europe (see chapter 3). While Germany remained closed to them, they travelled extensively in Great Britain, Scandinavia, Belgium, and Holland, holding rallies arranged by YFC supporters in the US military.

In 1949 Graham had left YFC to pursue an independent evangelistic ministry, and in the fall of that year held his nine-week Greater Los Angeles Crusade, which catapulted him into the national spotlight. Already popular in conservative evangelical circles, it was the prominent and largely favourable coverage given to the Los Angeles crusades by newspaper magnate William Randolph Hearst that helped turn Graham into a national celebrity.[3] Over the next four years Graham continued to hold evangelistic crusades throughout the United States, which established his reputation as the most popular mass evangelist of his day.[4]

By 1950 Graham had formed his own mission organization, the Billy Graham Evangelistic Association (BGEA) and was working as an independent evangelist.[5] Similar to the expansion of YFC's ministry, Graham's early career as an international evangelist developed in a rather ad hoc manner: he simply preached where he was invited.[6] In the spring of 1954 he was invited to hold meetings in Great Britain, and it was at this time that his reputation outside of the United States began to grow. The dramatic twelve-week-long Greater London Crusade, held at Harringay Arena, brought Graham to the attention of the Western European press and church leaders. This included Wilhelm Brauer and his small group of German Protestant clergymen of the Deutsche Evangelistenkonferenz (DEk) (see chapter 3), who themselves were committed to a revivalist model of evangelism among their own people. A committed Lutheran, Brauer was also in tune with Pietist renewal impulses in German Protestantism and believed that revival was necessary at all levels of the reconstituted *Landeskirche,* as well as in the *Freikirchen,* if the people of Germany were to be truly won back to Christianity.[7]

From the earliest postwar days of American conservative evangelical missionary activity in Germany, Brauer proved to be an invaluable ally and unselfish supporter of these outside agencies. He was instrumental in connecting American YFC evangelists with the DEA, and later supported the Janz Team's crusade work as well. Throughout his career as a minister he championed a range of interdenominational and foreign mission initiatives in Germany that helped fulfil his life-long goal "to bring the people back to the churches."[8]

Brauer and a contingent from the DEk travelled to Harringay in 1954 to hear Graham preach in person and came away convinced that Graham's approach to evangelism would be effective in Germany.[9] They entered into negotiations with members of the BGEA, who were arranging a European tour for Graham once the Harringay crusade was over. The two organizations agreed on an arrangement that saw Graham hold two meetings in Germany near the end of June: the first in Düsseldorf and the second in Berlin.[10] These initial meetings proved so successful in the eyes of German supporters that over the next sixteen years Graham was invited back to Germany five more times to hold evangelistic crusades, from then on by the Deutsche Evangelische Allianz. In addition to these engagements he also hosted and/or participated in three international congresses on evangelism held in Europe, which played an important role in the formation of a German *Evangelikaler* identity.

Graham as an American "Cultural" Agent Provocateur and Cold War Crusader

An Overview of the German Crusades, 1954–1970

From 1954 to 1970, Graham came to Germany on five different occasions to hold evangelistic meetings. As mentioned above, his first visit in 1954 consisted of just two meetings in two separate cities; however, the large crowds that turned out for both occasions attracted substantial press coverage. In Düsseldorf an estimated 34,000 people turned out to the local football ground to hear Graham, and two days later 80,000 more crowded into the Berlin Olympic Stadium for the second meeting.[11]

A year later, Graham returned to Germany for a slightly longer tour of one-stop engagements, this time working with local DEA chapters.[12] For one week near the end of June, Graham held meetings in Frankfurt, Mannheim, Stuttgart, Nürnberg, and Dortmund. In each case the BGEA booked the largest venue available – usually a football stadium – and filled it to capacity.[13] During his five meetings in Germany, Graham addressed just over 250,000 people and saw 10,000 come forward and sign the decision cards to "accept Christ."[14]

It would be another five years before Graham paid another visit to Germany, but when he did, it was more along the lines for which the DEA had hoped already back in 1955, namely holding a longer series of meetings in fewer venues. In September 1960, Graham held three consecutive one-week crusades in the cities of Essen, Hamburg, and West Berlin. This time, instead of booking outdoor stadiums, the DEA rented a 20,000-seat tent and used it in all three cities.[15] Once again, Graham's crusades did not disappoint. The DEA recorded a total attendance of 750,000 over the twenty-one days of meetings, and 16,500 decision cards were filled out.[16]

Two more visits during the 1960s followed at three-year intervals. In 1963 Graham held a series of one-week crusades in Nürnberg and Stuttgart and then returned for another one-week engagement in West Berlin during the fall of 1966. This visit was timed to dovetail with the BGEA's first world congress on evangelism, held in West Berlin the week after Graham's crusade. As had been the case in all of his previous visits, Graham preached to full houses in all three cities.

Graham's last major crusade visit to Germany took place four years later in 1970. The city of Dortmund was selected as a host venue for what was originally supposed to be the German equivalent of the All-Britain Crusade from Earls Court, London, in 1966. In those meetings Earls Court had been used as a live venue, but the meetings also were simultaneously broadcast via closed-circuit television links to twenty-five additional venues throughout Great Britain. As a result, an additional 540,000 people turned out to hear Graham in the outlying venues, besides the 200,000 who came to Earls Court.[17]

As plans for Dortmund took shape, the crusade organizing committee realized that they could broadcast not just to a German audience, but to a wider European one. Dortmund thus became the broadcast base for Euro 70 – Graham's most ambitious mass evangelistic undertaking to date.[18] Thirty-five cities in ten different countries functioned as telecast venues for a week of meetings in April 1970 and reached an estimated audience of 840,000.[19]

Over this sixteen-year period, Graham's evangelistic ministry in Germany produced impressive statistical results, usually surpassing the expectations of his sponsors in the DEA. However, his work in Germany was not without its critics, in both the secular press and among church leaders. In the eyes of his detractors, Graham's form of mass evangelism was one more manifestation of American cultural and ideological imperialism.

"Billy Graham: Showmaster Gottes oder Prediger?"[20]

The above question was a headline for an opinion-editorial that appeared in the national German weekly periodical *Der Spiegel* shortly after Graham's Euro 70 crusade in Dortmund. The author, an EKD *Pfarrer*, was not voicing anything new, but rather echoing an ongoing debate that had surrounded Graham's ministry ever since his first visit to Germany in 1954: was Graham merely some kind of religious circus act from across the ocean, or was he an authentic preacher of the gospel? The views of German clergy and press that emerged through the German newspapers revealed a nation sharply divided on the matter. In assessing reader response to Graham's first visit, the editor of the *Der Kurier* of Berlin stated, "There doesn't seem to be any middle way."[21]

Graham's critics were not without warrant when it came to voicing their skepticism, and their arguments in opposition to his ministry revealed how differently Germans and Americans approached Christian belief and evangelistic practice.[22] Members of the German press and church leaders who viewed Graham's evangelism as a form of cultural imperialism provided a number of reasons for being wary of, if not outright hostile to Graham and his Americanized form of Christianity. The same set of criticisms tended to surface each time Graham visited Germany, and they can be summarized under three interrelated themes.

The first was the sheer immensity and scale of Graham's meetings, and the questions they raised about wise stewardship of scarce resources and the reduction of religion to a business enterprise. During his first Berlin crusade in 1954, one local newspaper, *Das Grüne Blatt,* ran an article entitled "Billy Wants to Convert Europe," along with the provocative subheading "William Franklin Graham's Crusade Costs Millions."[23] The article went on to describe how Graham used his connections among the rich, powerful, and famous back in America to raise the 8.4 million Deutschmarks (DM) necessary to advertise and broadcast his meetings over radio and television each year.[24] While never directly accusing Graham of any wrongdoing, the article did portray him as a big spender from America, who used expensive, state-of-the-art technology in the service of evangelism.

During his 1960 crusade in Hamburg, a local paper, *Die Andere Welt,* ran a story entitled "God's Well-Organized Machinegun." Besides using the unflattering military nickname Graham had acquired during his first visit in 1954 (discussed below), the article went on to describe the evening meetings as the product of a well-oiled American business machine. Everything was well organized, efficient, and seamlessly orchestrated: from the fleet of buses that transported people to the meetings, to the spotlights that flashed to life when Graham stepped up to the podium. It was all about business, statistics, precision, and efficiency.[25] Reiterating the theme of evangelism-as-business, Graham was periodically referred to *"Werbefachman Gottes"* or God's advertising agent, a modern crusader from the United States, who drove up to the meeting in a "heavenly blue Dodge" – not a more humble German car.[26]

The same critique was still being voiced in 1970 during the Euro 70 crusade. When the meetings were carried via closed circuit-television to thirty-five different venues and projected onto cinema-sized screens, the German press quickly labelled this as "Billys Monsterschau," which "lured the masses" to hear his message in ever greater numbers.[27] While the use of the term *monster* can simply mean "immense," the article was accompanied by a particularly unflattering close-up of Graham's face, further distorted by relatively low video resolution magnified on a large theatre screen. The juxtaposition of unflattering picture and sensationalist headline made it clear that a pejorative connotation was intended.

An even darker variation of this critique appeared in some newspaper articles that implied that Graham's form of revivalism was a thinly disguised form of mass manipulation on the same level as National Socialism. Graham was at times compared to Hitler, and his large meetings were portrayed as propaganda exercises in mass suggestion. Such suspicions were not without some justification for Germans who had only two decades before been seduced by the dramatic pageantry and mass rallies characteristic of the Third Reich's propaganda machine. The Graham organization's own flair for the dramatic may very well have added fuel for such speculation. Graham and his team understood the power of the symbols and the impact of drama as part of their evangelistic efforts, and did not hesitate to employ such devices when they provided the opportunity to show that Christianity could indeed triumph over the forces of evil. In his first visit to Berlin where his single meeting was held at the Olympic Stadium, Graham arrived at the venue under the escort of a large motorcade, which had travelled the identical route taken by Adolf Hitler to open the Olympic Games in 1936.[28] In 1955, on his second tour of West Germany, Graham held a crusade in Nürnberg at the Zeppelin landing field, which had been the site of Hitler's most memorable Nazi party rally. However well-intended such efforts were by Graham and his handlers, it is also plausible to see how such gestures could have been interpreted negatively by Germans, who saw these gestures as dredging up memories of a demagogue they were trying to forget.

While such associations may have been too inflammatory for the German media to use directly, the newspapers were willing to print these accusations when expressed in letters to the editor. One such letter to the editor of Berlin's *Der Kurier* sounded an ominously prophetic note in 1954: "The *Kurier* certainly hits the centre of the target when it asks the question: 'What does this unscrupulous provocation of calling people to repent en masse really mean?' ... this is exactly the same as it was with Hitler, who used the approval of the masses to establish his own godhood. Whoever has ears to hear, let him hear; and whoever has eyes, let him see, before it is once again too late."[29]

A second criticism, related to the first, was that Graham's evangelism was one more example of American show business; it was Hollywood entertainment masquerading as Christianity, with Graham as movie star.

One reporter, who attended the evangelist's 1960 press conference in Bonn, described him as exuding a clean-cut masculinity; elsewhere he was cast as a man who carried himself with the athleticism of a tennis player and possessed movie-star good looks.[30] From the time of his first visit in 1954, Graham's sharp, staccato style of preaching caused the German press to dub him variously as "God's Machinegun," the "Knight-Crusader," or the "Heavenly Hammer."[31] In later visits Graham's celebrity appeal with young people, especially among women, made the headlines: "Mensch, Billy ist 'ne Wucht!" (Man, Billy is a "stunner"!) ran the banner of both Hamburg and Berlin newspaper articles on Graham's 1960 crusade tour.[32]

Besides Graham's physical appearance and persona, German papers also criticized what they perceived to be the carnival-like atmosphere of his evangelistic meetings. In the early days of his ministry, crusade meetings included a mass choir, sometimes of up to 4,800 voices, and also an immense brass section of up to 700 trombonists.[33] These numbers represent the record high turnout at the Stuttgart crusade of 1955, but it was not uncommon for the preaching of the *"Maschinengewehr Gottes"* to be preceded by a choir of well over 1,000 voices and a brass section of over 200 horns.[34] A Hamburg paper covering his first crusade announced, "Billy Graham Converts 20,000 Berliners: The American Evangelist in the Olympic Stadium – Sausages, Coca-Cola, and Trombones." A disgruntled Frankfurt columnist portrayed Graham's crusades, not as worship, but as *"Volksbelustigung"* or mass merrymaking.[35]

The third theme of criticism had to do with Graham's theology more than his persona or the mechanics of mass evangelism. Graham's critics argued that his form of Christianity was unsuitable for Germans, and therefore not good for Germany. This suspicion was not a new thing for German Christians, but had a history that reached as far back as the mid-nineteenth century when the first *Freikirchen* were planted in German soil. As Nicholas Railton has shown, these first independent congregations of Baptists, Methodists, and Brethren were all introduced to Germany through the influence of Anglo-American revivalism of Pietist renewal movements in the German *Landeskirche*.[36] This association continued to taint members of the *Freikirchen* with the charge of being unpatriotic, or *Volksfremd,* and persisted right into the period of the Third Reich.[37] Graham's coming to Germany as a Baptist minister and evangelist served as a catalyst in bringing this prejudice to the surface among Germans once again, and particularly among those who had strong ties to the EKD.

Just before Graham began his 1955 campaign, an article appeared in the German national Sunday newspaper, *Die Welt am Sonntag*, entitled *"Das Rätsel Billy Graham."* The author could not figure out why Germans would be attracted to someone as utterly un-German as Graham. How could Germans be taken in by someone who travelled from America to Europe in a luxury suite of an ocean liner; was accompanied by a large, ostentatious entourage of brass players and publicity agents; who, reportedly in his own words, "sold religion like soap"; and then on any given evening would blithely summon his listeners to accept Christ? Such a crass approach trod clumsily over the refined cultural toes of Europeans.[38] In analyzing Graham's first visit to Germany, Robert Kennedy has identified the role played by the German press in exploiting long-standing prejudices of their countrymen when reporting on Graham. The church was seen as the most "purely German institution," and the only civic institution to survive the war intact. Graham represented a "foreign element" that now threatened the essential German-ness and cultural independence of the one remaining institution that had resisted the cultural encroachments of an occupying power.[39]

Evidence of this attitude was apparent a year later on the eve of Graham's second visit. A Hessen-Frankfurt regional newspaper, *Der Weilburger Tageblatt*, ran a story detailing the extended critique of Graham that had appeared in the official paper of the East German Communist Party, *Neue Zeit*. Beginning with his own provocative title, *"Amerikanisierung der Religion?,"* the West German reporter went on to make it clear that although he recognized the *Neue Zeit* article as a propaganda piece against capitalism, his extensive summary of its arguments amounted to an indirect endorsement of its conclusion: Graham's form of Christianity was essentially alien to German sensibilities. His own opinion was summed up in a colloquialism used by Berliners when expressing their dislike of something: Graham "is not our collar size."[40]

Graham's evangelism was considered un-German for another reason: his call for an immediate and public decision to accept Christ. As was evident in the last chapter, this was the same reason many German pastors took issue with Leo Janz's *"Ruf zur Entscheidung."* For Germans such as EKD *Pfarrer* Friederich Heitmüller, who believed that a more formal and reserved tone was the only suitable one for public proclamation of the Christian message, this was *Schwärmerei* – the German word of opprobrium for uncontrolled religious enthusiasm.[41] Above all, this kind of evangelism was regarded as not German. Heitmüller claimed that once Graham had moved on, German ministers would have to expend much time and effort restoring religious order to the chaos Graham had created and rebuilding what he so quickly had knocked to pieces.[42]

The same criticisms were raised again during Euro 70. Graham's message was considered a kind of "gospel lite," or as one newspaper headline put it, *"Biblisches Brot mit amerikanischem Zucker."* His preaching style was labelled simple, even naïve. The combination of such a simple gospel that demanded an immediate decision to accept Christ could only lead to a shallow and short-term faith. In using this quick-fix approach to becoming a Christian, Graham was simply starting "straw fires," which would quickly burn up and turn to ashes.[43]

The German media were clearly fascinated with Graham and often acknowledged that his personal charisma made him an appealing and winsome person, but at the same time the theatrical qualities of his evangelistic meetings preceded by an aggressive advertising blitz were clearly alien to German religious sensibilities. For many Germans, Graham's meetings were part of a wider postwar invasion of American pop culture. Richard Pells has described how the postwar trade arrangements between the United States and Germany gave American entertainment an unrestricted export market during the 1950s and 1960s. While American movies and music were eagerly consumed by members of the German working class, the professional classes and intellectuals in West Germany were harshly critical of American cultural fare, scorning it as unsophisticated and simplistic.[44] Pell's analysis helps explain why Graham simultaneously could draw such large crowds to his meetings and still rouse the ire of the professional media.

The three criticisms described above – evangelism as big business, entertainment, and un-German – were raised like musical variations on the underlying theme of resentment toward the ubiquity of American culture that had marked Germany's postwar reconstruction.[45] When Graham and his evangelistic team came to hold meetings in Germany, voices in the German media and church were quick to protest that Graham was one more manifestation of American cultural imperialism. Before examining the views of those in Germany who supported Graham and championed his ministry, we need to consider one more provocative aspect of Graham's evangelism, and that is his role as an ambassador of American Cold War ideology.

Billy Graham as a Cold War Crusader

Graham proved to be very much a product of his own time and culture in his views on Communism during the early years of the Cold War. In describing the anti-Communist "spirit of the age" that swept across America during the first two decades following the Second World War, Geoffrey Perritt has observed that "the American people had come up against the harsh, unwelcome fact of Soviet power and became so obsessed with it that, as Emmet John Hughes aptly remarked, 'they came close to losing sight of the world.' Every disappointment, every failure, every danger, was traced back to Moscow. It did not matter that these were just as likely to be the result of [factors besides ideology]; the Soviets were considered responsible."[46]

News that the Soviets had detonated their own atomic bomb in September 1949, followed in short order by the creation of Communist China and North Korea's invasion of South Korea, all fuelled American bellicosity toward Moscow. Describing the national mood of America in 1950, Perritt noted, "Given a choice between fighting a total (and potentially suicidal) war with the Russians and allowing further expansion of Russian power, seventy percent of the American people chose war."[47]

When Billy Graham came to national prominence during his 1949 Los Angeles crusade, he made his own strong anti-Communist pronouncements. The world was divided into two camps, he proclaimed: on the one side was Western culture, which had its foundations on the Bible and Christian revival; on the other side was atheistic Communism, which was hostile to the God, Christ, and the Bible. Communism was motivated by the Devil and was more rampant as a "Fifth Column" activity in Los Angeles than in any other city in North America.[48] In the following years he went on to rail against what he perceived to be the growing Communist threat in the United States, claiming that there were over 1,100 "social-sounding organizations," which were operated by Communists and controlled "the minds of a great segment of our people [by] the infiltration of the left wing through both pink and red into the intellectual strata of America."[49] At one point in 1954, Graham suggested that Germany should be armed with the most powerful weapons as a deterrent to war with the USSR.[50]

If Graham was typical of the American mainstream of the times, his ideas also reflected the general political outlook of conservative evangelicals. As shown in the previous chapter, the frequency of articles on Communism that appeared in leading conservative evangelical periodicals, such as *United Evangelical Action* (UEA) clearly indicates that it was an ongoing concern for its constituency during the 1950s and 1960s. Other flagship periodicals of American fundamentalism, such as *Moody Monthly* or the *Sunday School Times,* showed the same concern.[51] In fact, as Graham began to moderate his anti-Communist rhetoric, especially after extensive travels abroad, he drew greater criticism from conservative religious groups in America even as the liberal Protestant mainliners began to applaud him.[52]

As Graham became an increasingly public figure and a spokesperson – however unofficial – for evangelicalism in America, he learned to tone down his inflammatory rhetoric against Communism. But as Richard Pierard rightly argues, this in no way meant Graham had changed his views on the subject. Using Graham's correspondence with his friend, Vice-President Richard Nixon, Pierard shows that Graham continued to see Communism as a grave threat to democratic freedom at home and to peace and stability abroad well into the 1960s.[53]

As Graham prepared to travel to Germany for his first visit in 1954, his careless comments about the destructive nature of socialism to the British press had already caused an uproar in England. On the eve of the Greater London Crusade in 1954, a reporter for the London *Daily Herald* had got hold of a BGEA promotional calendar from the United States announcing the dates of Graham's upcoming crusade in England. As the result of an editorial oversight, one sentence in the calendar read, "What Hitler's bombs could not do, Socialism, with its accompanying evils, shortly accomplished." The word *Socialism* was to have been changed to *Secularism* but escaped correction in a first print run of 200 copies. When the *Daily Herald* first broke the story, it caused something of a feeding frenzy in the rest of the British media. The statement was seen as politically inflammatory, a perceived insult to the fourteen million members of the British Labour Party. Graham was portrayed as a political meddler even before he set foot on British soil. Fortunately, Graham and his BGEA team were diplomatically astute enough to issue a full apology and offer a means of seeking reconciliation both with key members of the press and offended political leaders.[54]

News of the controversy soon reached German clergy who were leaders of the DEA. Fearing that Graham would be too controversial a figure, the DEA did not participate in extending the official invitation to have Graham come and hold meetings.[55] When he first arrived in Germany, the BGEA's ill-considered decision to hold a preliminary meeting for military personnel on the American Forces base at Frankfurt seemed to fuel the DEA's suspicions. Not since General Eisenhower's farewell visit at the end of the war had the Frankfurt area seen such a large gathering of American military personnel. As one German paper noted, "The quiet residential streets around the Frankfurt Christ Chapel, where Graham addressed his countrymen, were crowded with American military vehicles. The military police were forced to work hard to bring order to the scene."[56]

Before coming to Germany, Graham had promised Brauer's DEk crusade committee that he would make no statements of a political nature; however, he seemed not to have realized that the German media would be covering his Frankfurt visit and how politically volatile remarks in such a setting could be. In an effort to let the servicemen and women know that their work in Germany was not going unappreciated, Graham stressed the goodwill American aid had brought in helping West Germany to undergo a *Wirtschaftswunder*. He noted in favourable terms the marked contrast between the robust economy of American-occupied West Germany and the noticeable poverty and backwardness of the Russian-occupied East Zone. Graham went on to say how important it was for the American military to make every effort to form a rearmament agreement with West Germany as the best way to deter aggression from the East.[57] German newspapermen present at the church gathering reported Graham's latter comments in isolation from the wider context of his overall address, making him sound like a political agitator. As had happened in England, Graham and the BGEA team were forced to go on the defensive.[58] With the help of Brauer and his associates they were able to set the record straight, but the event strained relations between Graham and his strongest German supporters.[59] It also fuelled media caricatures of Graham, portraying him as politically naïve, and a mere ventriloquist's dummy of the American secretary of state, John Foster Dulles.[60]

These early unintentional gaffes can be attributed to Graham's inexperience abroad in general, and his ignorance of German religious culture in particular. The instances when Graham was more intentionally provocative as a Cold Warrior were his visits to Berlin, particularly his week-long crusade in 1960. In order to understand the controversy that erupted at that time, one must go back to Graham's first crusade there in 1954. It reveals the interesting, if not paradoxical relationship between Graham and Berliners over the next dozen years. Unlike his problem-ridden meeting in Düsseldorf two days earlier, Berlin proved a much more positive experience. Under the adroit administrative leadership of Peter Schneider, Berlin's YMCA director, the crusade planning committee was much better prepared for such a large event. On his arrival in the city, Graham's reception by civic and religious leaders in Berlin could not have been more courteous and welcoming. He was met at Tempelhof Airport by local political and church dignitaries, and was given an official welcome by the Lutheran *Landesbischof* of Berlin-Brandenburg, Otto Dibelius. Later on he was granted an audience with the mayor of Berlin at city hall.[61] Even though the anticipated crowd of 100,000 people did not materialize at Sunday's meeting, it was still the largest single audience Graham had ever preached to up till that time. Some German reporters estimated that of the 80,000 in attendance, up to half had come from the East Zone.[62]

The German press published an array of critical stories playing on the themes discussed above. But there were also a number of positive media voices. A reporter for the Berlin daily *Der Abend* acknowledged that Graham's appeal was truly remarkable. He noted that people from all social classes were in attendance at the Olympic Stadium, and that many in attendance from the East Zone had braved harassment from their own *Volkspolizei*, or *Vopos*, and the possibility of being reported to the local authorities as subversives.[63]

In a markedly sympathetic and insightful article, the reporter for the *Neue Rhine Zeitung*, a Cologne-area newspaper, speculated on why Graham had chosen Berlin as the site for one of his first German crusades, and why Berliners had turned out in record numbers to hear him. She suggested that Graham chose the city because its population's temperament was in harmony with Graham's direct, no-nonsense approach to proclaiming the Christian message. He was an "up-tempo preacher," and Berliners, who had a reputation for being on-the-go and aloof, could appreciate his directness. Having survived the Soviet blockade just six years earlier and now surrounded by an increasingly hostile East German regime, West Berliners also understood what it was like to face a daily unremitting stream of Communist propaganda, which eroded people's capacity for any kind of Christian faith. Perhaps such people appreciated Graham's rapid-fire confrontational style, and his willingness to speak out against the tide of tyranny. But even more, Berliners responded to

Graham because he represented the hope that faith in God was possible amidst the constant barrage of voices to the contrary. For the people of Berlin just to see and be part of an event where tens of thousands gathered together to hear a gospel message and to pray was a sign of hope.[64] This same reasoning was echoed in the *Berliner Zeitung*, which noted that Graham's message about the promise of freedom through Jesus Christ struck a resonant chord with Berliners, who were all too aware of what it was like to live where the lack of freedom was painfully obvious.[65]

For Graham and his team, Berlin came to symbolize the spiritual heart of Europe. After 1954 Graham regarded the city with a special affection. Whether it was the particularly warm hospitality he sensed during his visit, the impressive turnout for his meeting, the plight of the East Berliners who risked personal attack in order to attend his meeting, or some combination of these factors, Graham formed a bond of kinship with Christians there who had supported his evangelistic effort. At one point Graham told Berliners how much he loved them, and how much at home he felt in their city.[66] This peculiar bond would bring him back to the city for an extended series of evangelistic meetings in 1960 and then again for the World Congress on Evangelism in 1966.

It seems highly likely that in addition to the above reasons, the dramatic appeal and geo-political significance of Berlin were factors that attracted the BGEA back to the city for a second visit. If Berlin was the spiritual heart of Europe, it was also Communism's backyard, and therefore a strategic place to preach the Christian message and strike a blow against an atheistic ideology. A convenient opportunity for Graham to return occurred when he received an invitation from the DEA in that city, so in the fall of 1960 he came to Berlin to hold a week-long crusade as the last stop on a three-city tour of Germany.

Before the week of meetings began, Graham went to great lengths to emphasize the non-political nature of his preaching, saying that he came to Berlin not as an American but as a "servant of God and a messenger of his kingdom." His coming to Berlin was not to preach against the Communist regime in East Germany, but because Berlin, one of the great cities of the world, had only 2 per cent of its inhabitants attending church.[67] This did not stop the East German press from accusing him of being an agent of Western politicians who was to be unleashed on Berlin to wage psychological warfare on behalf of American imperialist interests.[68] These accusations only intensified when the location for Graham's crusade meetings became known.

As a venue for the week-long campaign, the DEA organizing committee had opted to rent a massive tent, with a seating capacity of 20,000, and pitch it on a large open square only three hundred metres from the East German border. The name of the West Berlin square was Platz der Republik, lending further political overtones to Graham's presence. Citing this as a deliberate act of provocation by American imperialists, the mayor of East Berlin struck back. He protested to Willi Brandt, the mayor of West Berlin, demanding that the tent be taken down immediately.[69] In addition to the current news propaganda campaign to smear Graham, he authorized police harassment of people crossing from East Berlin into the West to attend the meetings. He also ordered a military show of force at the Brandenburg Gate to intimidate West Berliners from attending.[70] Brandt, who would go on to become *Bundeschancellor* of West Germany, was not intimidated and with the backing of his city council declared the tent would remain.[71]

Throughout the week of meetings, the propaganda campaign in East Berlin newspapers against Graham continued; he was denounced variously as religious charlatan, an agent of American imperialism, and as an agent provocateur unleashed by German authorities on West Berlin to engage in psychological warfare.[72] At times such tactics took on comical proportions, such as when the official Communist Party newspaper, *Neues Deutschland,* ran an article claiming that Graham had been seen in Paris in the company of a blonde escort named Beverly Shea. *George* Beverly Shea was in fact the BGEA's male baritone soloist who had been part of Graham's team since 1947.[73] On a more sobering note, the *Vopos* issued a warning to Graham, giving him twenty-four hours to leave town.[74]

In addition to the propaganda campaign, the *Vopos* stepped up their intimidation of East Berliners crossing the border each night to attend the meetings. Besides harassing East Zone residents, the authorities shut down the Brandenburg Gate border adjacent to the site of Graham's tent, forcing people to make a long detour to other crossing points in more remote parts of the city.[75] Most disconcerting was the array of army tanks and water cannons that pulled up to the Brandenburg Gate, their gun turrets pointing into West Berlin.[76] On some nights during the service, the East German artillery would fire off a rolling barrage of practice rounds in an effort to drown out Graham's preaching.[77]

The systematic campaign of harassment seemed to achieve an effect that was the exact opposite of what was intended. The West Berlin press became Graham supporters. Even if they were opposed to Graham's methods, they seemed more upset by the East German government's bullying. Berliners also showed their support with their feet. Every night of the campaign the tent was filled to capacity and, in spite of their heavy-handed efforts, the East German *Vopos* could not stop a steady stream of people crossing over from East Berlin each evening to attend.[78] At the official ecclesiastical level, West Berlin leaders of the EKD showed their support for Graham by sending a telegram of protest to the minister president and the chief magistrate of East Berlin, urging them to prevent the *Vopos* from bullying their own citizens. They argued that the Soviet constitution guaranteed its people freedom of religious practice.[79] Local West Berlin authorities also stepped up security around the tent. Against this backdrop of daily intimidation and harassment, the nightly meetings carried on.

Graham was careful not to make any direct references to Cold War politics, but he displayed his own creative flare for engaging in the indirect sparring that characterized so many Cold War exchanges. In the opening meeting he read a message of greeting to all German Christians from the president of the All Union Council of Evangelical Christians and Baptists in the USSR.[80] The significance of such a barb would not have been lost on the crowd. Graham became more provocative on the last day of the crusade, when the final meeting was held outdoors on a warm Sunday afternoon in early October. In a symbolic gesture, the service took place directly outside the burned-out shell of Hitler's Reichstag building. It also happened to be within 150 metres of the Brandenburg Gate and the border into East Germany. A banner had been erected behind the platform just below the stone inscription on the Reichstag facade. The carved inscription read, "To the German people," but the text of the banner acted (coincidentally, as it turned out) as a completion to the inscription in its proclamation: "Jesus said, I am the way, the truth and the life." Many in attendance noted the aptness of the linked texts for the occasion.[81] Ninety thousand people turned out for the meeting. Although the *Vopos* were out in force to block East Berliners from attending, powerful outdoor loudspeakers projected Graham's message so it could be heard by the crowd that had gathered on the east side of the Brandenburg Gate.

Instead of delivering a message full of Cold War allusions, Graham wisely opted for a safer historic example from Germany's past. His appeal was to Martin Luther and the Reformation cry of "sola scriptura."[82] In doing so, Graham was appealing to what Germans on both sides of the wall had in common, instead of emphasizing the obvious physical and ideological barriers that divided them. The meeting drew to a close with 90,000 voices singing Luther's great Reformation hymn, "A Mighty Fortress Is Our God."[83] Graham attempted to make it clear to his audience that it was Germany's spiritual heritage to which he was appealing, and their current spiritual condition for which he was concerned. The important decision he was calling Germans to make was not a political one about the nature of their country's government, but a spiritual one about the overseer of their individual souls.

Graham's return to Berlin six years later for his third and final crusade there lacked the Cold War tension and drama of the 1960 visit. By this time the Berlin Wall was in place, effectively cutting off any large-scale traffic from East to West Berlin.[84] This time the week of meetings were scheduled in the new Deutschland Halle, which had a seating capacity of 10,000. Attendance was again high, as Graham filled the hall on all but a few of the earliest evenings. Press coverage was once again extensive, but reported little that was new. Reflecting on the overall media coverage, Kurt Witting, a member of the DEA crusade committee, remarked that the degree of press coverage was encouragingly large, but it still reflected the same set of prejudices and commendations. There was no discernible shift in emphasis since the last crusade.[85]

In 1966 Graham continued to describe Berlin as an important city "on which the eyes of the world remain constantly fixed," but there were indications that his approach to Communism was becoming less confrontational. In an interview printed in the DEA's monthly periodical, the *Evangelisches Allianzblatt*, Graham emphasized that among all the *Führers* available for people to follow, none was able to provide a solution for the problem of the human heart. Neither ideological, moral, nor economic *Führers* could provide a way to peace with God. Graham seemed to be equating the hollowness of the spiritually empty values of both the East and West. He went on to discuss his increasing reluctance to use the word *crusade* to describe his meetings, and his ongoing disappointment in being labelled as the *Maschinengewehr Gottes* by the German press. On a more hopeful note, he mentioned that invitations to hold meetings in Hungary and Czechoslovakia were both being considered.[86]

By the beginning of the 1970s, Graham's stance toward Communism clearly showed signs of softening. Instead of being challenged about the Cold War in central Europe, Graham increasingly was facing questions about his country's involvement in Vietnam. By the time he returned to

Germany for the Euro 70 crusade, Graham avoided commenting on political issues of any kind. He repeated the claim he had made on earlier
occasions that he came not as an ambassador of the United States but an
ambassador of the kingdom of God. At one press conference a reporter
continued to press Graham about his views on American involvement in
the war in Vietnam. Graham answered,

> I believe you misunderstand my task. I don't represent the U.S.
> government, but the kingdom of God. I am an emissary in a foreign
> land. This world is a foreign land to me … My flag is the flag of
> Christ … I can't defend the United States any more than you can
> defend what happened in Germany during the 1930s and 40s. As
> far as Vietnam goes I can promise you this: if Germany were ever to
> be attacked by a foreign power and American troops came to your
> aid, you won't find me demonstrating [in front of the White House]
> against our sending [military] help to your country.[87]

While it can be argued that such a response is disingenuous and evades
the real issue, it does reveal that Graham was no longer uncritically endorsing his country's aggressive engagement against Communism. In a
moment of candour during an interview with the German national magazine *Der Spiegel*, Graham's reply to the question, "Do you continue to hold
an anti-Communist position?" was "That is a difficult question. For many
years now I have chosen not to discuss this. I can't go around the world
and judge who is right and who is wrong. That would distract me from
my life's calling, which is to preach Christ."[88] In distancing himself from
political engagement, Graham saw himself as taking up the mantle of John
Wesley. Like Wesley, he claimed, "The whole world is my parish."[89]

While Graham's views on Communism changed over the course of
his ministry in Germany, his behaviour still sent signals that undercut
these views, or at least communicated an ambivalence about his claim to
be apolitical. The fact that Graham continued to spend time with political leaders, especially heads of state, made it difficult to accept him as a
non-political figure. Communist leaders in Eastern Europe had legitimate reason to see him as a political agent of his country when he began
making regular calls at the White House each time he returned from a
crusade abroad.[90] His meeting with *Bundeschancellor* Konrad Adenauer
during his 1963 visit to Germany also fuelled such thinking. In spite of

Graham's claims to have acted only in the capacity of a friend and spiritual confidant of American presidents, his frequent appearances in the company of the politically powerful, both in America and abroad, must have made him aware that the optics of such a situation would raise suspicions of a hidden political agenda.[91]

A final point about Graham's role as an exporter of American political values can be made in the very nature of his message. In spite of claiming to preach a message free from political interests, Graham's emphasis on individual conversion and salvation, and his markedly low ecclesiology were closely aligned to American values of individual choice and initiative, voluntarism and open market competition for the affection and loyalty of individuals. For Christians who had been raised in the tradition of an established church, sacramental theology, and community obligation, as was the case for most Germans, it was understandable that, with the exception of Christians in the *Freikirchen*, most Germans would see much in Graham's method and message that was more about adopting American cultural accoutrements than about Christianity itself. As will be evident in below, these ideological and cultural biases notwithstanding, Graham's efforts to give visibility and identity to a transnational coalition of Christians around the tenets of revivalist evangelism found a positive reception among a segment of German Protestantism.

Billy Graham and the Formation of German *Evangelikaler* Identity

The Missionary Responsibility

During the summer of 1949 Horst Symanowski, an EKD *Pfarrer* in the industrial city of Mainz, wrote an article in the World Council of Churches' newly established periodical, the *Ecumenical Review*, titled "The Missionary Responsibility of the Church in Germany." The substance of his article was a heart-felt plea for members of the EKD to take seriously the evangelism of their fellow citizens, especially young people and members of the working class. These two groups were most conspicuously absent in the churches. Symanowski believed the German church had become preoccupied with internal matters in the postwar years, to the neglect of its missionary responsibility. He pointed to the great spiritual impoverishment in the East Zone, but then turned his attention to the west: "Is not the same thing going on in the industrial towns, in the mines and the factories? Can we bear, as we stand in our churches and listen to our noble services, to see what immense numbers of people pass around about these churches without going in at the door ... It seems to me that this is where we discover the missionary responsibility of the Church in Germany. It must come out from behind its walls ... its bourgeois surroundings, and betake itself to where the man of our day is living, working, suffering, amusing himself."[92]

Symanowski went on to say that members of the EKD needed to change their priority from setting up the "administrative machinery" of the church to going out among the people and presenting themselves as "messengers of the Lord, declaring His Lordship ... to all the people who don't understand what we are doing behind the walls of the Church – not waiting for them to come to us, but going [out] ourselves ... to the ignorant and estranged."[93]

Other German ministers and lay leaders shared Symanowski's concerns for the unchurched masses, especially in the *Ruhrgebiet*. Under the leadership of laity the EKD sponsored large yearly *Kirchentag* rallies, which consisted of a week-long series of meetings, presentations, and discussion groups aimed at renewing church attendance, strengthening people's beliefs, and encouraging Christian witness among parishioners in their communities.[94] The *Kirchentag* meetings were intended to reach out to the estranged and nominal members of the church who had been baptized but rarely if ever attended its service. The approach was dialogical and democratic, based on the belief that modern men and women needed to "be prepared over a longer period of time to receive the Word of God ... Meetings normally lasted a week and placed heavy emphasis on 'slowly ripening convictions.'"[95] In its early years the *Kirchentag* congress attracted impressive numbers of people; up to half a million people attended the 1951 congress in Berlin. But as mentioned in the previous chapter, *Kirchentag* rallies were not translating into increased church attendance during the rest of the year – especially among young people and blue-collar workers. One of the presumed strengths of the *Kirchentag* rallies may also have been the reason for their failure to achieve their desired results. Great emphasis was placed on the voluntary nature of participation in the rallies. Above all, religion was not to be force-fed to participants. This, supposedly, was a way of sharing the Christian message more in keeping with German sensibilities.[96] But as EKD *Landesbischof* Otto Dibelius noted, "The attraction of the rally – and at the same time its limitation – was that everything about it was entirely voluntary and without commitment. One could listen, one could discuss, but one did not have to undertake to do anything."[97]

Wilhelm Brauer and his group of evangelists in the DEk had a similar concern. They, along with other supportive clergy associated with the DEA, were the ones who invited Graham to Germany, supported his crusades, and promoted other evangelistic initiatives in their homeland. Over the next decades as Graham visited Germany for crusades and congresses, a visible indigenous network gradually took shape around Graham's evangelistic work and with his encouragement, principally through the DEA.[98] This loosely associated yet recognizable group became known as *Evangelikaler* and during the decades of the Cold War established a legitimate place in German church life. The term *Evangelikaler* was a neologism coined to distinguish this subset of German Christians from those who identified themselves as *"evangelisch"* (the direct translation of *evangelical*), which in German simply meant Protestant, usually of a *Landeskirche* variety.[99]

"What Do We Expect from Billy Graham's Ministry?"

After Graham's second visit in 1955, Wilhelm Brauer raised the the purpose of Graham's ministry in a report defending the legitimacy of Graham's work in Germany. Contrary to the German newspaper articles on Graham, which focused on the alien nature of Graham's evangelistic meetings, Brauer argued that Graham's ministry of revival and evangelism was consistent with currents of renewal that had a long history in German church life. Beginning with Martin Luther, but also in more recent times, the German church had experienced a regional series of "awakenings." He cited specific revival movements in regions such as the Minden-Ravensburger Land, the Siegerland, and the province of Baden-Württemberg.[100] Graham's crusades were in keeping with these legitimate spiritual awakenings and should not be confused with the uncontrolled religious *Schwärmerei* – uncontrolled enthusiasm – of charlatans and demagogues. Graham was not "narrow-hearted," not denominationally narrow or prejudiced. He came to Germany in order to work with Christians from all denominations: state church and independent churches alike. Brauer hoped that one day Billy Graham would be invited to exercise his important ministry in the *Kirchentag* rallies.[101]

Brauer could already point to how effective Graham had been in Germany in promoting revival and interdenominational cooperation. The statistics of Graham's crusades were impressive. In five meetings during 1955 a total of 256,000 people had attended. Of that number 10,000 had filled out decision cards to say they had received Christ. These meetings had also generated a high degree of participation from local churches. The number of musicians involved as choir members or brass players totalled 10,530. The crusade organizing committee of the DEk was a model of interdenominational cooperation. Of the fourteen-member committee, seven were *Pfarrers* and/or evangelists in the EKD, six were of the same status in various *Freikirchen*, and one was American: Robert Hopkins was a member of the Navigators, a mission agency that oversaw the follow-up program for the crusades.[102]

When the committee held its post-crusade meeting to review, they found that the participation of both church groups was a little more uneven from city to city. In Frankfurt the *Freikirchen* had the majority of participants. The *Landeskirchliche Gemeinschaften*, or fellowship societies within the *Landeskirchen*, were also well represented, but only a small number of actual EKD churches gave official support. In Mannheim and Stuttgart it was the local DEA chapters that took the lead, with the Mannheim effort being dominated by the *Freikirche* denominations of Methodists and Baptists. However, in both Stuttgart and Nürnberg the EKD churches also fully endorsed the Graham crusade and participated enthusiastically.[103] Both cities reported a strong sense of unity that crossed denominational fault lines among those who participated in crusade preparations.

Another positive aspect, in the eyes of the organizing committee, was crusade financing. The DEk's share of the crusade costs came to DM 56,000 which was to be met by taking free-will offerings at each of the five meetings. Not only were the costs covered, but a DM 27,000 surplus had been recorded.[104] Such tangible evidence of support was a strong indicator that Germans by and large saw this as an acceptable way of financing evangelistic work.

The most significant challenge to the organizing committee's unity was the issue of follow-up work: which churches were to receive the decision cards from those who came forward at the meetings for counselling? Most of the cards in the meetings had been filled out by people who already had a church connection, and therefore it was decided that counsellors needed to respect that and steer these people to a participating church of the denomination with which they were affiliated. There was to be no

"fishing in someone else's pond."[105] In this situation, having Robert Hopkins on the committee as the lone American proved helpful. As a neutral
outsider he was in a position to mediate between the EKD and *Freikirchen*
members, as well as remind them that they were all on the same side,
working toward a common goal.[106] The final statement on this issue in
the organizing committee's crusade review indicates that members knew
the importance of the issue for ongoing cooperation, and how fragile this
relatively young interdenominational unity still was. "All of the brothers
[in Christ] present at the meeting were united in the significance of follow-up work, and we want to stand side-by-side in support of each other,
in word and in deed."[107]

The report concluded with the observation that Graham's form of
evangelism was *a way*, but not the *only way* for effective evangelism to be
undertaken in Germany. It was important for members of the DEk not
to become reliant on Graham, but to use his visits to inspire a variety of
further evangelistic ventures, and for gathering prayer support so that
a revival would come to Germany.[108] As is evident from the above, the
BGEA had to work with German clergy to overcome many of the same
prejudices toward mass evangelism faced by Leo Janz during the early
days of JTM's work. Similar to his Canadian counterparts, Graham was
able to win over a growing base of support during his successive visits to
Germany and thus act as a catalyst for the growth of an indigenous *Evangelikaler* identity.

Graham and the DEA: Enlarging the Coalition

In the run-up to Graham's 1955 visit, the DEk had approached the national
committee of the DEA to enlist their full support. The chairman of the
DEA, Pastor Walther Zilz, decided not to do so at the time, mostly because
of some misunderstandings in a preliminary meeting between his national
committee and Graham's advance team. He did, however, encourage the
DEk to invite local chapters of the DEA to participate.[109] After seeing the
large response to Graham's preaching later that year, the national committee of the DEA extended an invitation to him to come as soon as possible.
In 1960 Graham returned for three consecutive one-week engagements in
Essen, Hamburg, and Berlin.

Structurally, the DEA was not a centrally controlled national organization, but a voluntary body whose strength and effectiveness came from
its regional or local chapters. The national committee was responsible

primarily for the annual *Gebetswoche* and a few other conferences each year. These limitations notwithstanding, the DEA still represented a broad coalition of EKD churches and fellowship groups, *Freikirchen*, and para-church mission agencies, along with individual Christians who wanted to build up the churches.[110] What the DEA lacked in infrastructure it made up for by providing a large pool of committed volunteer workers necessary to stage Graham's crusades. DEA member-groups as diverse as deaconess societies and the YMCA had signed on as crusade supporters. Perhaps most important of all, two EKD *Landesbischofs* gave their unqualified support to Billy Graham. Hans Lilje, the bishop of Hanover, and Otto Dibelius, the bishop of Berlin, were well-respected leaders in the EKD, who openly supported Graham's crusades.[111] Both had opposed Hitler during the war, and since 1945 both had been active in home-mission work.[112] Their support gave Graham's work a degree of credibility it had lacked in his two earlier visits.

At the national level of the DEA only five out of twenty members of the committee were EKD *Pfarrers*; the remaining fifteen were connected with various *Freikirchen*. In contrast, on the ad hoc crusade organizing committee the ratio was almost the reverse, with EKD-affiliated members holding eight of thirteen positions.[113] At the grass-roots level, all three cities reported afterward that there was substantial participation across the EKD-*Freikirchen* spectrum.[114] Thus Graham, similar to JTM, was able to help the DEA in various cities achieve a degree of cross-confessional ecumenicity in the common cause of evangelism.

Graham's crusades also echoed JTM's in that they required a large number of workers, and it was expected that pastors of participating churches would mobilize members of their congregations to get involved in volunteering to help. As was shown in the previous chapter, they required enlisting volunteers to serve as ushers, parking attendants, first aid staff, counsellors, musicians, and prayer group organizers.[115] The most novel and accessible way for lay people to become involved in the crusades was through a scheme called the Andreas-Plan. Based on the New Testament disciple, Andrew, the Andreas-Plan consisted of a short seminar that encouraged people to invite their non-Christian friends to the crusade meetings and then provided free transportation on chartered buses from several collection points in outlying areas. Inviting friends to a religious event was a new thing for most Germans, and the seminar included instruction on how this could be done in simple and friendly ways.[116]

Echoing pastors who worked in support of JTM, Billy Graham's crusade chairman for Berlin, Peter Schneider, reported that when hundreds of volunteers from both EKD and *Freikirchen* worked together in a common cause, it tended to break down denominational divisions, and also to form stronger bonds between participating pastors and their congregants.[117]

In its post-crusade report, the DEA enthused that the three one-week engagements had been an unqualified success. In the eyes of the organizing committee, the nine months of intensive preparation had paid an impressive dividend.

> The German public has come to realize the fact that evangelization is a reality and a necessity for the German people. This evangelization had reached large numbers of people outside of church circles and found acceptance by many who were only nominal church attendees ... Noteworthy was the full endorsement of Bishops Dr. Dibelius and Dr. Lilje, whose participation was important in gaining the support of a significant number of [EKD] pastors. The free churches, fellowship groups, and all manner of Christian organizations ... stood unwaveringly behind the work. The range of participants was incredibly wide and the number of stakeholders was, by German standards, the largest we have ever experienced.[118]

In a number of ways Graham's positive reception by the DEA at this point may have been due, in part, to JTM's mass evangelistic efforts of the previous three years. Key German evangelists who worked on Graham's crusade committee in 1960 had cooperated with JTM in previous years. This list included evangelists such as Wilhelm Brauer, Wilhelm Busch, and Gerhard Bergman.[119] By 1960 JTM had held crusades in Essen on two different occasions at the request of the DEA, and the high turnout at these meetings quite likely played a role in the city being selected as one of the three venues for the BGEA. The fact that Wilhelm Busch, who had been won over to JTM's crusade work in 1958, headed the organizing committee in Essen for Graham's meetings can be seen as a direct influence of JTM. As well, the DEA's insistence on a sustained series of meetings in one place may have come from the strong response they witnessed to JTM's month-long crusade in Essen two years earlier.[120] Just as JTM saw more un-churched and young people respond to the *Ruf zur Entscheidung* in the latter part of their crusades, the DEA now reported a higher percentage of youth and un-churched people coming forward for counselling than had done so at Graham's 1955 meetings.[121]

Alongside the continuing work of JTM, Graham's 1960 crusade showed that mass evangelism was a rallying point for a growing coalition of German supporters mediated through the DEA. The DEA was already an established and familiar entity in Germany and therefore did not come under the stigma of being foreign or sectarian. Its minimalist doctrinal statement provided a basis for cross-confessional cooperation that could span the EKD-*Freikirchen* divide. At the same time the DEA's concern to promote missionary ventures at home that would not put church denominations in competition with each other made it open to Graham's (and JTM's) trans-denominational form of evangelistic ministry.[122] Having the endorsement of two well-known and esteemed bishops of the EKD was further evidence that Graham's evangelistic work was appropriate for Germany, and that Germans could be faithful members of the EKD and part of a wider cooperative movement with other Christian groups.

Although this working coalition was not without its internal tensions and struggles, the 1960 crusade had laid the groundwork for future collaborations for Graham's visits to Germany in 1963, 1966, and 1970.

Giving Graham's Evangelicalism a German Voice

Increasingly the DEA sought to promote Graham not as an American evangelist, but as God's ambassador and a witness of Jesus Christ, who just happened to be an American.[123] The Janz Quartet had faced the same challenge as cultural outsiders from Canada, but had overcome it by learning to speak German fluently, thus having a German voice from the outset. Graham did not have the advantage of a German-speaking background, nor did his demanding crusade schedule allow him to master other languages. The DEA achieved a measure of success in bridging this gap largely through the effectiveness of his German interpreter, Peter Schneider.

Schneider was the head of the Berlin YMCA, and from 1960 onward, assumed responsibility on behalf of the DEA for organizing the Graham crusades in Germany. As a soldier in Second World War he had been captured and sent to a POW camp in Wisconsin after the war. While awaiting repatriation, he was given work as a custodian at a conservative evangelical college where he became fluent in English and embraced Christianity. Schneider not only possessed excellent command of the English language, he could also emulate Graham's rapid-fire delivery when interpreting his sermons in a sentence-by-sentence manner. Over the three weeks of meetings, Graham and Schneider developed a remarkable sense of timing, where it seemed as if they spoke with one voice. The result was that Schneider's interpreting was not so much a stilted relay of Graham's English sentences into German, but an intensification of them that produced an extraordinary immediacy between Graham and his German listeners.[124]

Schneider eventually became the BGEA's full-time representative for all of Germany. A gifted administrator as well as preacher, Schneider oversaw the preparation for each of Graham's evangelistic campaigns and other engagements in Germany during the 1960s and 1970s. Erich Beyreuther argues that this wider involvement with Graham's organization gave Schneider effective insight into the, BGEA which allowed him to interpret Graham's whole philosophy of mass evangelism to the DEA and its supporters.[125] The BGEA had, in Schneider, the ideal liaison officer: an efficient administrator, who could also broker a unity of understanding across a significant cultural/language divide. His leadership in the crusades of 1963, 1966, and 1970 continued to build on the foundation laid in the 1960 crusade, solidifying the place and identity of supporters of revivalist evangelism in German church life. Graham's biographer Sherwood Wirt observed that of all the countries of Continental Europe, Germany was the most responsive to Graham's message. Schneider has to be considered a key factor for this success.[126]

Another important factor in giving Graham a German voice, as well as nurturing a base of German supporters, was issuing a German edition of BGEA's quarterly periodical, *Decision Magazine*. Here again, Graham's work in Germany was following that of JTM, using a subscription-based periodical to give shape and identity to a growing group of German Protestants who supported revivalist evangelism. The first German issue, entitled *Entscheidung*, came out in the summer of 1963. While essentially a translated version of the flagship American magazine, it gradually acquired more of a German voice and look. By 1974 most of its articles were written by German contributors, and it was during the early 1970s that it reached its peak circulation with a subscription list of 33,000.[127] Similar to JTM's *Ruf* magazine, *Entscheidung* featured a range of articles on devotional meditations, sermons, Bible studies, personal testimonies, and crusade updates.

Periodicals such as *Ruf* and *Entscheidung* served at least two important purposes in shaping supporters' revivalist evangelism into an identifiable group: first, they continued to supply their readers with a contemporary vocabulary of evangelism, revival, and personal conversion, all of which was still relatively new to many German Christians. In so doing, this literature gave them a way to discuss their faith and interpret their own Christian experiences. Second, as already mentioned in the previous chapter, these magazines also drew German supporters into a wider international network of like-minded Christians. In being introduced to American and British evangelical writers through translated articles, German supporters were being made to feel part of an international network of Christian brothers and sisters who shared a common faith and could support each other's evangelistic endeavours.[128] Especially impressive were the large, wide-angle photographs of Graham crusades from around the world, which appeared regularly in *Entscheidung*. Seeing photographs of the Los Angeles Coliseum filled with 140,000 people, or the Melbourne cricket ground with 85,000, or even their own Stuttgart Neckar Stadium with 75,000 all impressed readers that they were supporters of a growing, international movement of Christians, who believed that Graham's evangelistic proclamation was for people in all parts of the globe.[129]

German Evangelikaler Become Part of the Global Evangelical Community

This growing sense among Graham's German supporters of belonging to a transnational movement was augmented by German participation in a series of international congresses on evangelism. The three congresses – Berlin in 1966, Amsterdam in 1971, and Lausanne in 1974 – were either sponsored directly by the BGEA or inspired by Graham's work, and brought German supporters into contact with a wider international body of leaders who identified themselves as evangelicals.[130]

The first of these, the World Congress on Evangelism (WCE) was especially significant for German supporters because it took place on German soil, in Berlin. On paper the WCE could boast an impressive international representation. Just over 100 countries were represented among the 1,200 delegates; however, two-thirds of them were from Anglo-American countries and Western Europe. Only one-third came from Latin America, Asia, and Africa.[131] The overall tone of the WCE reflected the strong American influence as well, but even in the midst of this cultural one-sidedness the congress played a constructive role in German evangelical identity.[132] The

DEA's monthly periodical, the *Evangelisches Allianzblatt*, gave the WCE extensive coverage in its pages and was very positive in its report. From the DEA's perspective the congress was a great source of encouragement to German participants, because it connected them more directly to evangelicals from around the world. Hearing dramatic testimonies of coming to faith, as well as sharing times of prayer and Bible study with delegates from other parts of the globe, provided German delegates with a new motivation to carry on the task of evangelism once they returned to their churches and ministries.[133]

The WCE also provided a powerful symbolic statement for evangelical identity that was simultaneously transnational and specifically German. On Sunday, 30 October, congress delegates assembled at Wittenberg Square in the centre of Berlin and, along with another 12,000 supporters, marched down the city's famed Kurfürstendamm in a "spectacle of Christian witness" to the Kaiser Wilhelm Memorial Church. On arriving at the cathedral the delegates were welcomed by two EKD bishops, Otto Dibelius and Kurt Scharf.[134] This *Zeugnismarsch*, occurring on Reformation Sunday, proclaimed that evangelicals "from all nations" were claiming an identity as faithful heirs of the Reformation and the keepers of its symbolic flame.[135] The *Zeugnismarsch* had special significance for Graham's German supporters: it gave them a way of simultaneously affirming their particular identity as *Evangelikaler*, and of laying claim to being the true heirs to Luther, and thus the real trustees of Reformation Protestantism in Germany. The term *Evangelikal* was given further credibility by having Dibelius and Scharf, two highly respected bishops of the EKD, place their imprimatur on the marchers. A sign that the new label was gaining traction in Protestant circles came in May 1968 when the DEA participated in a gathering of the World Evangelical Fellowship in Lausanne, Switzerland. Reporting on the Lausanne meetings, the *Allianzblatt* began using *Evangelikaler* to describe all the delegates.[136]

This same term came to define all German Protestants who aligned themselves with the movement. In 1972 Fritz Laubach, a theology professor and pastor of a *Freikirche* congregation in Hamburg, published a landmark book entitled *Aufbruch der Evangelikalen*. In it he chronicled the crucial role of Graham's crusade work in Germany, along with his international congresses on evangelism in the formation of a discernible *Evangelikaler* movement in Germany. The most recent events to bring this gradually maturing identity to fruition were Graham's Euro 70 in Dortmund, and the first ever European Congress on Evangelism, which had been sponsored by the BGEA in Amsterdam in 1971.[137] Laubach pointed out that as a direct result of Euro 70 the DEA had founded several key bodies that showed that an indigenous evangelicalism has taken root from Graham's work. Two *Arbeitsgemeinschafts* or "working groups" had been established by the DEA to sustain spiritual growth initiated by evangelistic crusades. The Arbeitsgemeinschaft für Hausbibelkreise and the Arbeitsgemeinschaft für Fernbibelkurse were appointed to develop resources for Bible study groups and distance learning courses for individuals who wanted to further their own biblical education.[138]

The third congress that played a key role in developing *Evangelikaler* identity was the BGEA-sponsored International Congress on World Evangelization (ICOWE) held in Lausanne in 1974. This was a watershed event for *Evangelikaler*, as it confirmed their identity on the landscape of German Protestantism. This confirmation came, in part, through German secular press coverage of the event. Newspapers used the term *Evangelikaler* when referring to the 180-member German delegation.[139] It was also apparent that German delegates, most of whom had some affiliation with the DEA, had come to accept the label as their own.[140] While ICOWE did not conclusively resolve the ongoing internal tensions and polarities that were part of German Protestantism, it was acknowledged that now they were being worked out within the context of this new identity.[141] Further confirmation of this distinctive identity was found in the fact that German Protestants from outside evangelical circles began using the term *Evangelikaler* to describe Graham's German supporters.[142] From their participation in ICOWE it was clear that Germans making common cause with Billy Graham and his fellow-travellers, such as JTM, under the flag of revivalist evangelism represented the flowering of a distinct and growing movement in German Protestantism. Graham's congresses, along with the wider evangelistic work of the BGEA and JTM, played a vital role in seeding and cultivating this movement on German soil, and simultaneously helped link *Evangelikaler* to the wider transnational evangelical movement.

Graham as the "Good American" to the German Evangelikaler

Graham cannot take full credit for the development of the *Evangelikaler* movement in Germany, but his mission in that country supports the claim that he was a primary influence in shaping and nurturing this identity.

The first part of this chapter focused more on the negative impact of Graham's ministry by identifying aspects of it that caused Germans to see him more as an agent of American cultural imperialism than an ambassador of Christianity. Graham's ministry also had political overtones, especially early on, as he uncritically twinned Christian revivalism with a bellicose form of anti-Communism. As with YFC's early work, this aspect of Graham's mission was freighted with an American cultural and ideological ethnocentricity that characterized not only conservative evangelical missionaries, but American Protestant missions to Germany more generally. Consequently Graham's mission encountered resistance, particularly among Germans aligned with the EKD, as well as the secular media.

At the same time Graham found a consistent and growing support base through Christians in the DEA. While that circle did include some highly placed leaders in the EKD, Graham and the *Evangelikaler* were never able to gain an unequivocal endorsement from the highest echelons of EKD leadership. A suitable metaphor for Graham's ongoing role and relationship to the budding *Evangelikaler* movement can be found in Bishop Otto Dibelius's address on the last night of his 1966 crusade in Berlin, honouring Graham for his service to the German people. That night the venerable bishop, who had supported the American evangelist's efforts in Germany from early on, expressed his gratitude to Graham for all his work in Germany. He concluded his remarks by likening Graham's mission in Germany to Jesus's parable of the Good Samaritan:

We all know the story of the good Samaritan, that he found a man beaten half to death and brought him to an inn. He told the innkeeper, "Care for him and I will pay whatever it costs." That is the end of the parable, but the story, of course, continues on, and I know how it continues. On the next day ... as the beaten man recovered, he asked the innkeeper, "Who was it who brought me here and paid for my care?" The innkeeper replied, "... the only thing I know about him is that he comes through these parts periodically and that he is a Samaritan. He does not believe as we do, and he is from a different people." On hearing this, the beaten man declared he would not accept any charity from this Samaritan. But then he thought about it further and said, "Even though he believes differently, if his belief leads him to practise such charity then I must have respect for that."

And that, I believe, is what the skeptical citizens here [in Berlin] have experienced. We don't have your belief yet, but when your faith leads one to have the freedom and joy you have, then one has to respect that. And if one returns to his home after this with respect for the Christian faith, that is not the deciding step, but it is the first step to Christ, and other steps will follow.[143]

In this description Dibelius effectively summarized the transformation of Graham's own persona in the eyes of many German Protestants, as well the growing impact of his mission to Germany. The man who began as the "Cold Warrior" – God's machinegun and anti-Communist crusader – had become the itinerant "Good American" who visited periodically in order to tend the wounds and offer encouragement to an embattled German church. Some Germans had begun to follow the steps recommended by Graham, but even from those not ready to follow, Graham and the evangelical expression of Christianity he represented had won a measure of respect from the wider German Protestant community.

Conclusion

As evident from the previous two chapters, the conservative evangelical mission to Germany played out in two paradoxical ways: on the one hand, much of YFC's work along with Graham's early crusades was loaded with a strong ideological flavour of American democracy; and on the other hand, the work of JTM and a more internationally astute Graham helped a minority group of German revivalists establish an indigenous *Evangelikaler* identity that found a legitimate place in German Protestantism. While the previous chapter suggested that one way of understanding this paradox was in terms of the differences in national character between American and Canadian conservative evangelicals, this chapter has shown that this paradox could also be resident in a single missionary. This analysis gets beyond a reductionist stereotyping of conservative evangelical missionaries as mere cultural imperialists and calls for a more complex and nuanced understanding of their work. That they were ambassadors of democratic ideals is beyond question, but that aspect of their work needs to be placed in the uniqueness of their mission field. Given Germany's recent totalitarian past and the immediate proximity of the Iron Curtain, political and religious freedom in West Germany was not a comfortable certainty, but a relatively new and precarious experiment that needed to be vigilantly protected and carefully cultivated. By championing democratic ideals, conservative evangelicals were no different from their ecumenical and denominational counter-parts.

What made the former group distinct was their ability to develop a constituency of German supporters apart from ecclesial structures. Conservative evangelicals eschewed the limitations of institutions, such as the World Council of Churches, as well as exclusive alignment with a particular church denomination. By making Christianity essentially a personal faith of the individual, evangelists such as Billy Graham and Leo Janz appealed to Germans primarily as individuals and not members of a particular class or denomination. Thus they gave Germans a new way of simultaneously being a German and a Christian, and a new label of identity – *Evangelikaler* – which did not bind them to the increasingly pejorative stereotypes of institutional Christianity in their country. This new identity also linked them to a growing international community of evangelicals, made visible by the BGEA's congresses on evangelism. In this sense Graham's, and by extension, JTM's, impact on German Protestantism is highly significant. By playing a key role in the formation of *Evangelikaler* identity, Graham was giving a group of German Protestants a new way of understanding their Reformation heritage. Being *Evangelikaler* challenged the prevailing German understanding of the Reformation that associated it primarily with established ecclesial bodies and fixed confessional documents. Graham's efforts in constructing an alternative basis for Protestant identity led *Evangelikaler* to see themselves as representing the true spirit of the Reformation. Erich Geldbach has noted that, beginning in the early 1970s, there was a growing sentiment among supporters of the DEA to see its initials as no longer standing for Deutsche Evangelische Allianz, but Deutsche *Evangelikale* Allianz.[144] Not all German Protestants embraced this individualized expression of Christianity; however, the growth of the *Evangelikaler* movement was evidence that the conservative evangelical mission had taken root in German soil.

CHAPTER FIVE

Mission to Germany after 1974: Responding to Post-Christendom Secularism

The 1974 Lausanne International Congress on World Evangelization (ICOWE) represents a watershed in the work of North American Protestant missions to Germany. While ICOWE may not have led directly to dramatic changes in missionary strategy in Germany, its timing, in the mid-1970s, coincided with several cultural and economic changes in the Western world that caused both evangelical and denominational agencies to adjust their approaches to missionary work in the years following the congress. But if ICOWE was a marker for these adjustments, it also represented a vindication of, and an apologetic for, North American missionary agencies active in Germany throughout the Cold War. In contrast to ecumenical missionaries who saw their task in Germany as having been completed once the Evangelische Kirche in Deutschland (EKD) had been successfully integrated into the World Council of Churches, denominational and conservative evangelical missionaries who subscribed to the traditional evangelistic-conversionist approach to missions could point to ICOWE and its statements as a justification for their presence in Germany. The very location of ICOWE in neighbouring Switzerland helped focus the attention of missionary agencies and supporters on Western Europe; but even more importantly, the global emphasis on evangelism, which dominated ICOWE's agenda, reinforced what the North American missionary presence in Germany had implied since 1945: that the European nations that comprised Old World Christendom now had become "legitimate" mission fields. Brian Stanley has argued rightly that ICOWE "revealed the first clear signs of a radical de-centering of the geographical and cultural identity of evangelicalism."[1] Sections VIII and IX of the Lausanne Covenant, ICOWE's official statement on evangelism, suggest that the "radical de-centering" also applied to missionary practice, and hence spelled the end of Christendom in any geographical sense: "The dominant role of the western churches is fast disappearing. God is raising up from the younger churches a great new resource for world evangelization, and thus demonstrating that the responsibility to evangelize belongs to the whole body of Christ. All churches should be asking God and themselves what they should be doing both to reach their own area and to send missionaries to other parts of the world ... Missionaries should flow ever more freely from and to all six continents in a spirit of humble service."[2]

While these statements seemed intended primarily to encourage missionary initiatives by churches in the developing nations of Africa, Asia, and Latin America, they also inspired North American conservative evangelical and denominational mission agencies in Germany to continue their efforts in there: the affirmation of mission "to all six continents" legitimized the status of Europe as a mission field.[3]

But what shape should these efforts take? Two emerging factors, concurrent with the staging of ICOWE, played a significant role in determining the nature and scope of missionary activity during the later years of the Cold War era. The first of these was the growing awareness by missionaries of a visible, aggressive secularism in an increasingly prosperous Europe. Secularism, combined with a growing popular resentment toward the ongoing American military presence in Europe, pushed many missionaries to consider new methods of proclaiming the gospel that would connect with a new generation of Germans, known as the '68ers. The name '68ers came from the year 1968, in which student revolts broke out on university campuses across Western Europe, largely in protest against a Western establishment that supported American military intervention in Vietnam. Thereafter it was used to identify a generation defined by student radicalism, often linked to Marxist ideology.[4] These young people were most unlikely to prove receptive to mass evangelism, with its stigma as an American import, as practised by missionaries in the earlier postwar decades. Thus mission agencies experimented with alternative ways to present their message.[5] In doing so, missionaries in West Germany found themselves participating in a wider missiological development encapsulated in the term *contextualization*. Contextualization was a Protestant variation on the long-standing missiological discussion over indigenization and was applied mostly to issues of Western missionaries working in developing countries in Asia, Africa, and Latin America.[6] However, some mission theorists also applied contextualization to mission work in Western lands, emphasizing the need for evangelists to exercise greater sensitivity to the post-Christian cultural landscape of their day.[7] While missionaries to Germany may not have been participating in the scholarly debate over contextualization, their concern to demonstrate the relevance of their message to a secular generation pushed them to practise it by experimenting with alternative methods. These new methods were often adaptations of aspects of North American popular music culture, which resonated strongly with German youth culture.

At the same time, the ongoing influence of Marxist thought in some strains of West German secularism, combined with greater missionary access to the Communist countries of Eastern Europe, meant that addressing Cold War ideological issues remained part of the missionary enterprise. By the early 1980s, missionaries found themselves having to walk a cultural tightrope, presenting a message critical of Marxist atheism while at the same time having to avoid being seen as mere religious ambassadors of American militarism, represented by the lingering spectre of Vietnam and the sabre-rattling posture of the newly elected President Ronald Reagan. As such, missionaries found themselves caught up in the ambivalence of German attitudes toward the United States, which on the one hand avidly appropriated American forms of popular entertainment, while on the other hand harshly criticized American foreign policy vis-à-vis Communist Europe.[8]

The second factor was the move toward greater indigenization of missionary institutions and ministries so that Germans themselves would assume greater responsibility for sustaining the enterprises begun by North Americans. The move toward indigenization was fuelled primarily by two developments: the rising cost of funding North American missionary work across Western Europe; and the belief that postwar recovery had put supportive German Christians in a position to supply staff and funds for the continuation of these mission enterprises. Beginning in August 1971, the drastic devaluation of both the US and Canadian dollar vis-à-vis Western European currencies led to a significant financial crisis for these same mission agencies by the middle of the decade. The withdrawal of Germany from the Bretton Woods monetary agreement with the United States at this time caused the dollar to decline by 7.5 per cent in value against the Deutschmark in three months. The falling value of the dollar, combined with a high inflation rate in an already strong German economy, resulted in some missionaries seeing the value of their funds decrease by over 12 per cent between 1971 and 1972.[9] In addition, the energy crisis of 1973–74, which saw the price of gasoline increase by as much as 300 per cent, meant the cost of the missionary enterprise in Germany by the mid-1970s had risen dramatically.[10]

These new financial realities led mission agencies to reassess, and in many cases reduce, the number of missionary personnel in favour of inviting nationals to take on greater responsibility for continuing their work. At the same time, conviction grew among some conservative evangelical and denominational missionaries that Germany's economic recovery mirrored a degree of spiritual recovery to the point where Germans could now take more of a leading role in operating and sustaining these missionary ministries to their own people. While the move to greater indigenization did not mean a full-scale withdrawal by North American personnel from Germany, it did lead Southern Baptists, and evangelical missionaries, such as Janz Team Ministries (JTM), to reassess and adjust their roles in working alongside Germans.

While it seems reasonable to assume that rising anti-Americanism in Germany during the 1980s, triggered by the US foreign policy shift from détente toward a more confrontational stance vis-à-vis Communist Europe, also contributed to indigenization, the missionary literature does not indicate this. A more typical response toward European anxiety and uncertainty over President Reagan's policies was expressed by Leo Janz, the leader of JTM. In his view, such difficult and dark times did not call for abandoning the mission, but for remaining faithful and active. Janz's view of world affairs was informed by a premillennial view of history, typical of many conservative evangelical Anglo-American missionaries of that day.[11] Present hostilities and uncertainties were not reasons to pull back, but to continue with courage, in the belief that these events were signs of Christ's imminent return.[12]

Thus the mission to West Germany after ICOWE, with its implications of living in a "post-Christendom" age, was increasingly defined by these two themes: finding effective ways to offer the Christian message as a compelling alternative to a more visible secularism; and, at the same time, moving toward greater indigenization of missionary institutions, thereby reducing the number of North American personnel and refocusing their roles as partners in a collaborative missionary enterprise. This chapter will examine these two themes in turn.

Mission to Germany amidst the Rise of Secularism and Demise of Christendom

Visible Secularism as Part of the Wirtschaftswunder

The debate over the effectiveness of the secularization thesis to explain the change in religious practices of twentieth-century Western Europeans continues. While its proponents see it as the most compelling explanation for decline of popular participation in religious institutions, other scholars contend that such decline did not mean that religion was no longer important to people, but rather that it had been channelled along less visible lines. The purpose of this section is not to enter that debate, but to point out that the increasingly visible signs of abstention from organized religion were seen as a serious challenge to Christianity by missionaries in Germany.[13] In his studies of institutional religious life in West Germany, Karl Gabriel has noted the dramatic exodus from religious institutions among the postwar generation of Germans. During the period 1968–73 regular church attendance declined by one-third, and the number of people officially leaving the church by opting out of paying their *Kirchensteuer*, or church tax, increased seven-fold. Gabriel's data also indicated that church members "displayed a growing detachment from the teachings and ethical norms espoused by the churches."[14] For missionaries and concerned German Christians alike, such changes were evidence of a visible secularism, which represented not so much irreligion as a rival religion.[15]

Concern among Christians about the growth of secularism in West Germany had already been voiced well before the 1970s. In 1962 Hans Lilje, EKD *Landesbischof* of Hannover, pointed out that while Marxism was an encroaching atheistic threat from Eastern Europe, a growing secularism, which amounted "in some places to complete paganization," was spreading through the countries of Western Europe. For Lilje this dual threat signalled the possible end of the Christian epoch in the history of Europe.[16] Indicators that measured popular participation in the religious life of West Germany supported Lilje's claims. In 1970 *Stern*, the leading German newsmagazine, ran a feature article chronicling the rapid decline of church attendance in general, but particularly among Protestants. On the cusp of a new decade, regular church attendance had fallen to 0.9 per cent of those listed as baptized members of EKD congregations. Church attendance among Catholics was considerably higher, at 40 per cent, but was also in significant decline.[17] While allowing that this decline was due in part to the privatization of religious belief, not necessarily its abandonment – what British sociologist Grace Davie has labelled "believing without belonging" – *Stern* attributed much of the exodus from the *Landeskirchen* to a growing secularist mindset among West German Protestants.

This assessment continued to predominate into the mid-1970s, particularly among German supporters of the *Evangelikaler* movement. In the summer of 1975 the *idea-Pressedienst,* a news service established by the DEA, announced that Germany, along with the rest of Europe, was truly a *Missionsland.*[18] If a "Christian West" still existed at all, it seemed that West Germany was no longer part of it.

North American missionaries in West Germany had also been aware of a more visible secularism in Europe since the early 1960s, and by the middle of the following decade their concerns about secularism's corrosive social effects, especially in promoting apathy toward Christianity, were being voiced more frequently and with greater alarm.[19] Denominational mission leaders, such as the Southern Baptist J.D. Hughey, observed that "Eastern Europe is officially atheistic, and western Europe is unofficially irreligious ... So long regarded as the center of Christendom, [Europe] has become a mission field."[20] Similar assessments of Europe's detachment from its Christian moorings and subsequent drift in the current of secularism were made by evangelical missionary leaders in JTM and Campus Crusade for Christ (CfC, but also referred to hereafter by its widely used abbreviated title, Campus Crusade).[21] Such assessments by missionaries and German church leaders continued well into the 1980s.[22] Consequently North American leaders began to see European mission work being not so much about helping a new generation recover a receding spiritual heritage as it was about introducing religiously skeptical people to something entirely new.[23]

Conservative Evangelical Missions Respond to Secularism: JTM and Campus Crusade

In 1979 JTM celebrated its twenty-five years of missionary service in Germany. Commemorating this landmark, Leo Janz, the founder and leading evangelist of JTM, sounded an optimistic note for the mission's future: "The doors for evangelization are wide open. God is granting us many opportunities ... If the [world continues to survive] through the 1980s, we believe that we will see the largest opportunities for evangelism in our generation."[24] Based on JTM's full schedule of, and continued strong attendance at, their evangelistic crusades, Janz had good reason for making that prognosis. Reports of crusades in both the secular press and JTM's own *Ruf* magazine indicated that the combination of gospel music and evangelistic preaching continued to draw sizeable crowds – in some cases up to 5,000 strong – to their meetings.[25] At the same time there were indications that the appeal of mass evangelism in Germany was on the wane. Apart from these evangelists, such as Leo Janz and Billy Graham, who themselves were approaching conventional retirement age, few other evangelists were able to draw such consistently large audiences among the next generation of missionary workers.[26]

JTM, along with other missions and native German evangelists, accordingly realized that they needed to adjust in order to relate the Christian message to generations of Germans who had not lived through the Second World War nor directly experienced the extreme hardships of the early postwar recovery. The current generation of young people increasingly had also grown up largely untouched by, and therefore were unfamiliar with, Christian institutions in Germany. While reaching youth with the gospel had been a concern right from the early postwar years, the student protest movements on German university campuses during the late 1960s and early 1970s were seen as one more symptom of the growing secularism that was eroding the moral fabric of the country.[27] Drawing inspiration from one of the themes of the Lausanne Congress, to find new ways of reaching skeptical "modern man," and from the fledgling – if not controversial – Christian pop music movement in the United States and Great Britain, JTM brought over a music team of college-age men from Canada in the hopes of attracting German young people to their meetings.[28] By marrying gospel song lyrics to a contemporary pop instrumental sound, this new team, known as the Janz Team Singers, used a model more akin to a touring band giving rock concerts than to a conventional evangelistic team holding a multi-week crusade in one fixed location. Their ability to attract youth to concert halls or even smaller venues, such as coffee houses, to hear an evangelistic message primarily through pop music, often using English lyrics as well as German ones, proved remarkably popular.[29] As Janz noted, "God speaks in many languages, and English is currently the fashionable [one]."[30]

This concern to reach young people was shared by Campus Crusade for Christ, a relatively new American evangelical mission agency to Europe. From the 1970s onward, CfC became the missionary successor to Youth for

Christ. YFC continued to be active in selected locations in Germany, but by the mid-1960s most of its work had been turned over to German staff members, who focused primarily on reaching youth of pre-university age. As a direct result of Billy Graham's 1966 Berlin congress on evangelism, Bill Bright, the founder of CfC, was inspired to send a fifty-member "Ambassador team" of American CfC missionaries to evangelize university students in Europe for two years.[31] As a young businessman, Bright had founded CfC in 1951 as a means of evangelizing students attending the University of California at Los Angeles.[32] Within fifteen years CfC had become one of the largest independent mission agencies in the United States, with chapters on university and college campuses across the country.

Two years after the Berlin Congress, CfC launched its work in Germany. The initial two-year European venture by the Ambassador team led to longer-term commitments by a small group of CfC American staff in four countries. Responding to an invitation from Bernhard Rebsch, a German evangelist and CfC supporter, nine American CfC missionaries took up residence in West Berlin and began to work among students at the Free University. By 1972 CfC had established an office in southern Germany to coordinate the work of over 100 American missionaries in seven Western European countries.[33] Most of CfC's early work consisted of training indigenous Christian university students in CfC's methods of evangelism to reach their classmates, not in church settings, but in the social spaces of the university campus. To facilitate this approach, Campus Crusade, like JTM, sponsored a travelling music team known as the Forerunners, who toured across Western Europe with an evangelistic message.[34] Performing in both campus and church venues, the Forerunners brought a contemporary sound and look to the gospel proclamation that CfC chapters used to draw young people into discussions about Christianity.

Rather than the elevated stage of the mass evangelistic rally, which typified previous decades, in the 1970s and 1980s, JTM and CfC tailored their approach to fit the sensibilities of the "jeans and coffee house" generation.[35] While this trend was not unique to Germany, Richard Pells has noted that German young people of this era were attracted particularly to American pop music, because it represented a means of protest against a stifling cultural conservativism.[36] By refining established methods to resonate with the prevailing cultural agenda, JTM and Campus Crusade showed they could adjust to changing times and sensibilities, while still focusing on the conversion of individuals.[37] In doing so they found themselves as part of the shift among missions toward contextualization. In this case, however, it focused on movement from one region of the developed world to another, not from developed to "developing" lands.[38]

This adjusted approach to small-scale or "micro-evangelism," using a concert tour format and booking smaller venues, came to define more of JTM's work through the 1980s. Bob Janz, also a member of the second generation of Canadian missionaries to join JTM's staff, led another musical team known as the Janz Team Ambassadors. Recalling the changes JTM was undergoing, which coincided with ICOWE, Janz pointed out the impact of Lausanne on independent mission agencies such as JTM. ICOWE had called for renewed emphasis on local churches becoming centres for evangelism, and as such, para-church missions such as JTM were left wondering how they should fit into this new model.[39] Rather than seeing this as the end of their missionary service, Bob Janz and other North American members of JTM found ways to adjust to this shift. Instead of holding large-scale evangelistic meetings that required extensive volunteer labour and the coordination of many participating churches, teams like the Ambassadors responded to invitations from individual churches to hold meetings, usually for just one week, right in their church buildings instead of larger concert or exhibition halls.[40]

Both JTM and CfC were concerned that one symptom of a more widespread secularism was that young people, especially university students, were growing increasingly attracted by the secular ideologies, such as Marxism. Fuelling this attraction was their increasing resentment toward the imperialist interventionism of American capitalism. This critical posture toward American adventurism abroad had become widespread on German university campuses as result of the Vietnam War.[41]

JTM's Leo Janz saw the situation as serious enough to address it openly. As a rule Janz did not make his evangelistic sermons and editorials overtly political, but there were times, especially in the midst of the ideologically charged climate of the mid-1970s, when he attacked ideological secularism directly. Commenting in 1975 on the state of global politics after the US withdrawal from Vietnam, Janz noted the pro-Communist sympathies and anti-American bias of the Western European media. Citing the French sociologist and political analyst Raymond Aron, Janz pointed out that each time a Communist party won greater power in a national election, it was perceived as a setback for the United States, but whenever the United States intervened to resist the spread of Communism it was labelled imperialism. Janz's point was not to justify US foreign policy, but to warn his German audience that Communism was, at best, a false messiah. He conceded that America was not without fault and its era as the world's leading power was already drawing to a close; in his view, God would judge the United States for its over-reaching hubris in due course. But Europe's time was also running out, and the solution was not Communist utopianism but the gospel of Jesus Christ. [42] Mindful of anti-American currents in Germany, Janz was careful not to identify himself uncritically with American political interests, while at the same time taking an unequivocal stance against Communism.

Some of Campus Crusade's methods in Germany showed a similar concern to combat ideological secularism. During the 1970s CfC's leaders in Europe viewed Marxism as a serious religious threat to Christianity in the Western world. [43] When CfC began its work in Germany, its first base of operation was the Free University of Berlin, a campus well known for its radical Marxist political activism. [44] CfC staff used the informal atmosphere of the student coffee house to sponsor seminars for students, which addressed a current cultural issue from a Christian perspective. One of the most popular seminars was "Marxism vs Christianity." Alongside these seminars, CfC staff operated a book table in the student cafeteria, where German translations of their own tracts and books about Jesus and Christianity appeared next to pamphlets and books about Marx, Lenin, and Mao. By positioning themselves in venues that encouraged ideological exchange and debate, CfC hoped to show that Jesus of Nazareth had a revolutionary personage superior to any Communist ideologues on offer. [45]

North American evangelicals' concern with the appeal of Marxism to the younger generation of West Germans also continued to reflect the ongoing realities of the Cold War standoff made visible by Germany's own political bifurcation along ideological lines. However, instead of overtly tying the Christian message to democratic ideals, as had been evident during the early period of postwar recovery, conservative evangelical missionaries were now more inclined to portray Christianity as the best way to fulfill the longings of a culture that increasingly was looking to secular "gods" as a source of hope for a better world.

Conservative Evangelical Responses to Secularism: Billy Graham and Evangelikaler

North American concern about the rise of secularism was shared by German *Evangelikaler* who continued to see Billy Graham as the international spokesman for their movement. Graham's visits to West Germany after the Lausanne Congress became less frequent, but his influence was still felt as those who identified themselves with the *Evangelikaler* movement drew inspiration from events sponsored by the Billy Graham Evangelistic Association (BGEA). In the summer of 1975 *idea*, the DEA's press service, announced a joint national congress of *Freikirchen* and *Landeskirchen* leaders on the topic "Evangelism and the Local Church."[46] The congress was proposed as a direct response to the Lausanne Covenant, produced at ICOWE, which called on churches to plan creative initiatives for evangelism in their own countries. The proposal, which came to fruition in the summer of 1976 as Christival, was launched by the German evangelist Anton Schulte, who had long been a supporter of both Billy Graham and JTM.[47] The primary reason given for holding the congress was recognition that the state of Christianity had undergone a radical decline across Europe in the last decade, and that West Germany in particular had become a *Missionsland*.[48]

In addition to inspiring such national initiatives, Graham was also credited by German *Evangelikaler* as the initiating force behind Eurofest, a Europe-wide congress held in Brussels during August 1975 to encourage and instruct young people from across Western Europe in the area of evangelism.[49] Among the 7,000 delegates who attended, Germans made up the single largest national delegation with 973 registered attendees.[50] In an interview with *idea* magazine, Graham pointed to materialism, science, and secular ideologies as the chief religious rivals to Christianity among European young people. While Communism had not ceased to be a source of concern, Graham and West German *Evangelikaler* were of one mind in recognizing that Marxist ideology was only one manifestation of a wider constellation of secular gods competing for the allegiance of German young people.

The following year, West German *Evangelikaler*, with the support of Billy Graham, hosted the above-mentioned evangelism training congress, this time focusing particularly on young people from German-speaking Europe.[51] The week-long event, entitled Christival '76, took place in Essen in June of that year. Ulrich Parzany, a Lutheran *Landeskirche* youth pastor in Essen, led the organizing committee for Christival. In his letter to Graham requesting the American evangelist's support and presence, Parzany attributed *Evangelikaler* evangelistic initiatives such as Christival directly to Graham's ministry, and particularly to the Lausanne congress on evangelization.[52] Thus it is evident that the leaders of the *Evangelikaler* movement saw themselves as the beneficiaries of Graham's work in Europe, and, in the spirit of ICOWE, were promoting missionary evangelism within their own country. With 8,000 registered delegates and an additional 30,000 visitors, the week-long event featured a variety of seminars that addressed the specific challenges of living in a secular culture, such as "Christianity and Marxism," "Sexual Ethics," and "Keeping a Christian Faith in School."[53] The defensive tone of these titles indicated a Christianity that was no longer part of the cultural mainstream but a minority voice under siege from a dominant secularism. In an interview with *idea*, Parzany went on to explain that the perception most Germans had of Christianity was that of a hollow shell of a tradition, no longer relevant to addressing the needs of a culture largely dismissive of things religious. Germany, and Europe more generally, had truly become a missionary land.[54]

Events such as Eurofest and Christival also indicated a shift in Graham's role as a missionary to West Germany. Graham's visits now focused on evangelism training events organized by German *Evangelikaler* groups themselves. Instead of playing the role of the principal evangelist, Graham took on the part of inspiring and training young people and an array of church workers who identified themselves with the *Evangelikaler* movement to evangelize their own people. These events were still mass gatherings, but the audience was made up of committed followers instead of inquirers, and the primary goal was instruction, not the invitation to conversion.[55]

During the years following ICOWE, Graham continued to play an important role in consolidating *Evangelikaler* identity as a legitimately German expression of Protestant Christianity. In her assessment of Graham's impact on German Protestantism, Uta Andrea Balbier concluded that Graham was significant in offering conservative German Protestants a way of coming to terms with modernity and democracy without caving in to secularism.[56] However, Balbier tends to portray religion only at the level of the personal experience of individuals, and thus misses the significance of Graham's role in the formation of organizational structures in German Protestantism that gave *Evangelikaler* a visible, sustained identity as a legitimate part of German Protestantism. Furthermore, *Evangelikaler* were not simply one more alternative indicative of the ongoing pluralizing of West German Protestantism; they understood themselves as offering an antidote to secularism that was superior to what was on offer in most churches of the established *Landeskirchen*. This was the view of Peter

Schneider, general secretary of the DEA in the later 1970s. When inviting Graham to participate in a DEA-sponsored evangelistic event in 1980–81 called "The Missionary Year," Schneider noted significant differences in West Germany since Graham's last visit in 1970:

> The situation in Germany has changed quite a bit since your last visit ... the evangelical part has grown and has become more respected ... The public media of press, radio and television have become more open toward evangelicals or at least more neutral ... Also disappointment with the church leadership among many church members has grown ... the average State Church services are terribly empty ... I am sure there will be great interest and openness for your message and the willingness of bringing fair reports about your work in the media.[57]

Rather than continuing in the role of a pioneer evangelist in West Germany, Schneider affirmed that Graham had laid the foundation on which Germans themselves were now building a structure that was taking on an increasingly important profile in defining the religious skyline of that country.

Alongside Graham's changing role in consolidating *Evangelikaler* identity, another significant element of these congresses was the presence of non-Western church leaders who were not merely observers, but were featured as keynote speakers. At Eurofest a full 50 per cent of the plenary addresses were given by Festo Kivengere, the Anglican bishop of Kigezi in Uganda, and Argentine-born evangelist Luis Palau.[58] The following year at Mission '76, the youth congress for world missions in Lausanne, Byang H. Kato, the general secretary of the Association of Evangelicals of Africa and Madagascar, was intended to be one of the featured speakers before his untimely death shortly before the congress.[59] Later that same year Bishop Kivengere was once again present at Christival 76.[60] While these examples did not indicate a flood of missionaries from the lands of the "younger churches" into Europe, their missionary presence in Germany and elsewhere in Europe indicated that Christian leaders from former "missionary-receiving" countries, especially from Africa, were now seeing Europe as a mission field. Kivengere's visits can be seen as foreshadowing not only the steady increase of African-planted churches in Western

European cities during the 1980s and after, but also further confirmation that European Christendom was a thing of the past.[61] As such, the impact of Graham's missionary work in West Germany extends to the wider growth of what has become known as "World Christianity," in which the missionary traffic from developing nations to European countries would grow from this early trickle into a much steadier and wider stream.[62]

A second aspect of Graham's response to secularism in Europe as a whole was seen in his preaching missions to Communist countries, and thus his continued connection to Cold War politics. Throughout the last decade of the Cold War, Graham's visits to Europe indicated that his focus had shifted from Western Europe to gaining access to countries behind the Iron Curtain. During this period he did not visit Germany for an officially scheduled event until he was invited to preach in a reunified Germany in 1990 at the Berlin Wall.[63] In contrast, during the period 1981–86, Graham conducted preaching tours of Hungary, Poland, Czechoslovakia, East Germany, Romania, and two in the USSR.[64]

Denominational Missions Respond to Secularism

Secularism in the mid-1970s was also a concern for Southern Baptist missionaries, and to a lesser degree was reflected in the ongoing work of the Mennonites in West Germany.[65] Both missionary groups were committed to working within denominational networks, but by 1974 it was evident that the nature of the relationship between North American missionaries and their respective denominational kindred in Germany was undergoing a change.

The work of Southern Baptist missionaries in Germany after 1974 was guided by J.D. Hughey, the SBC-FMB's missionary statesman and area director for Europe during the period 1963–81.[66] At a strategy conference for Southern Baptist missionaries in Europe in 1975, Hughey recognized that the postwar recovery of the German Baptist churches called for a reappraisal of the SBC-FMB's role there. Conference delegates concluded that "planning and work must be done in cooperation and consultation with the leaders of the German [Baptist] union. A certain amount of freedom in planning and action must be relinquished. German Baptists are not now and never have been a child of Southern Baptist missionary endeavor."[67] As will become apparent in the section of the chapter dealing with the theme of indigenization, the SBC-FMB realized that German Baptists were not opposed to working with Americans, but wanted to do so as equals and on their terms.

As Günter Wieske, leader of the German Baptist Union, explained his denomination's stance, "We have no right to refuse missionaries when we have not evangelized our own country … we have no right to say that the cultural differences between North Americans and Europeans are too great to be overcome for effective missionary work," but these missionaries needed to be highly trained in the German language and evangelism.[68] The implication of Wieske's comments was that no amount of energy and goodwill would compensate for a lack of cultural preparedness; Germans would not suffer fools – no matter how enthusiastic – gladly. "German-speaking people are less tolerant than many cultures to those who speak their language poorly."[69]

By 1981, with this understanding in place, Wieske invited Southern Baptist missionaries to work alongside German Baptists in ministry situations where American strengths complemented German needs. By this time Wieske's tone had become less defensive and more amiable: "The German [Baptist] Union, as a minority church, did not have sufficient resources and means to undertake the evangelism of Germany on its own. On these grounds we can have nothing against our American fellow Baptists if they desire to work in unity with us in evangelizing Germany."[70] The German leader saw American missionaries as invaluable co-workers when it came to planting churches in areas with no previous Baptist witness. Their pioneer spirit and commitment to evangelism made them in his view more suitable candidates for planting new Baptist churches in Germany than many German Baptist ministers. With English as their native language – the dominant language of rock music – Americans had a cachet with German young people, which made them good candidates for youth work.[71]

In 1981, in response to an invitation from Wieske, and as a follow-up to Hughey's policies, four American pastors became SBC-FMB appointees to the German Baptist Union to take charge of newly planted German churches.[72] After five years Wieske reported back to the SBC-FMB that the partnership was working well, as two new Baptist churches had been established in predominantly Roman Catholic areas.[73] In the future Wieske hoped to see an expanded number of such partnerships develop to assist German Baptists.[74]

Reflecting on the benefits of this new collegial arrangement, John Merritt, a veteran Southern Baptist missionary in Europe, observed, "We can't pastor a German Baptist church as well as a German Baptist can, but we can be supportive of that work. We want to be as much help to the German Baptists as we can."[75] This was also consistent with Hughey's philosophy of missions in a world in which a geographical Christendom was no longer recognizable: "A mission field is any part of the world, regardless of its background or history, where there are large numbers of people with spiritual needs which are not being adequately met in the name of Christ. Europe is such a place; America is also ... The distinction between Christian and non-Christian countries has broken down. The whole world is a mission field."[76]

In the light of the increasingly visible secularism evident in the traditionally Christian countries, Hughey and the SBC-FMB recognized that mission work had increasingly become de-centred from its Western points of reference and that the new reality for missions was "from everywhere to everywhere."[77]

Mennonites also had been aware of secularism in Europe for some time. As early as 1954, David Shank, a Mennonite missionary working in Belgium, described Western Europe as a de-Christianized or post-Christian society. According to Shank, secularism was but one of a plurality of European voices declaring that, for all practical purposes, "God is dead."[78] By the beginning of the 1970s the MCC European office reported a similarly gloomy outlook: "There is material prosperity and there is little or no evidence of church renewal."[79] While such an awareness was present in Mennonite missionary circles from an early point in the Cold War, the missionary activity of the Mennonite Central Committee (MCC) in West Germany from the mid-1970s to the end of the Cold War took a more indirect approach to confronting secularism. With the German economic recovery now well established, the MCC realized that its original program of rebuilding, relief, and education largely had run its course. At the same time MCC staff continued to see two opportunities for ongoing mission work consistent with MCC's historic commitments to serving the most needy members of society, and to promoting a pacifist, or "peace witness" agenda as part of a Christian countercultural response to Cold War militarism.[80]

By 1975 a small but steady trickle of Mennonite emigrants had obtained permission to leave the Soviet Union and move to West Germany, where they had family connections. Not officially considered refugees, these *Um-siedler*, or "resettlers," left Mennonite communities in the region of the southern Ukraine and were resettled in, or close by, existing Mennonite communities in West Germany.[81] Recognized as ethnic *Volksdeutsch* by the government, *Umsiedler* received some financial assistance from the West German government as well as help in language acquisition. However, the prejudice they encountered in local communities where they were resettled made the transition difficult for many. The *Umsiedler* were arriving in West Germany at a rate of around fifty per month. The MCC, in partnership with the European Mennonite Christenpflicht, contributed financial assistance and spiritual support in helping these arrivals make the transition to a radically different culture. Three full-time MCC missionaries were appointed to work full-time with these *Umsiedler*.[82]

The second avenue of ongoing mission involvement was promoting the ongoing peace witness of the historic peace churches in Europe. This was done primarily through continued support for EIRENE, the official program of European peace churches to promote pacifism at home and abroad. The MCC developed a further initiative in the 1970s when they established a full-time East-West Research office, located in their European headquarters in the city of Neuwied. The office existed to promote peace concerns alongside like-minded organizations in both East and West Germany, and to give support to Mennonites living behind the Iron Curtain.[83] The East-West Research Office also worked to update North American Mennonites on the state of Cold War relations and mobilize support for the peace movement at home.[84] The activity of the office was severely limited by having minimal personnel – only one full-time MCC staff member – but even so, during the 1980s, it did manage to conduct regular study tours of Eastern Europe for Mennonite students from North America, as well as place several missionary workers in East German cities as university students.[85]

In both avenues of missionary work, the MCC operated primarily through denominational channels and networks. Thus the impact of its work was limited to the relatively small peace church constituency in Western Europe. Consequently the mission work of the MCC during the latter stages of the Cold War, in contrast to its higher profile relief work in the early postwar decades, flew quietly under the radar of most Christian organizations active in West Germany. While the European Mennonite Bible School that it had helped to establish in 1950 continued to thrive, it was now operated entirely by European Mennonites and had only one MCC faculty member. Similar to other North American mission agencies, the MCC not only retooled its program of service in Germany after the mid-1970s, but also scaled back its personnel commitments, allowing the ongoing missionary task it had begun to be taken over by indigenous personnel.

Mission to Germany and the Move to Indigenized Ministry

Billy Graham and Conservative Evangelicals

The second development to note regarding the mission to Germany in these years was the move toward greater German control. In part this was driven by the changing financial realities, briefly described at the outset of this chapter, which came into play from the early 1970s onward. Most of the funds supporting missionaries in Europe came from donors in North America, so when these currencies lost ground against their European counterparts, missionary budgets were placed under sudden severe strain.

The changing economic conditions coincided with the growing sense that native supporters of mission in that country were ready to assume greater leadership in missionary ventures begun by North Americans. To say that the former directly caused the latter might be overstating the connection, but the increased cost of carrying out missionary work in Germany was concurrent with the deliberate move among some mission agencies in the direction of indigenization. The move toward indigenization was also fuelled by a number of support structures created by German *Evangelikaler* designed to sustain and give greater visibility to *Evangelikaler* life and mission.

In the case of the evangelical missions, such as JTM, the move toward indigenization was fuelled by a combination of financial stresses and the aging of its primary evangelist, Leo Janz. As Janz reduced his crusade schedule, by the early 1980s JTM had turned much of the crusade work over to two younger German evangelists: Albert Jansen and Bernhard Scharrer.[86] Neither of these two men held meetings on the scale that Janz had done during the 1970s, but, with the overall strategic shift to smaller-scale evangelism noted above, JTM's leadership was pleased that Germans were coming to the fore in an aspect of the work that had initially been the prerogative of North Americans. By 1981, it was noted in the minutes of JTM's annual meeting of its leaders that such a combination, and the move toward greater indigenization that it signalled, was an important step for the mission: "The work in Europe is becoming more indigenous both in the administrative field and in the various public ministries – a development which is healthy in view of the political trends. This development should continue, but North Americans are still needed in specialized fields – especially music. A combination of North American and European workers is advantageous for the work and should be continued."[87]

The record indicates that JTM did not see a full-scale withdrawal of North American personnel as a desirable goal, but rather anticipated a continued partnership in mission, which allowed North Americans to contribute in areas of relative strength. The 1980s saw a continuation of this kind of partnership, but with German personnel taking on greater leadership. Increasingly Germans now were at the forefront of running camps, short-term Bible school classes, and children's meetings, with North Americans playing a supporting role, mostly in a music-based ministry.[88]

CfC also followed a trajectory of indigenization. In their case it was a primary goal of their work in Europe from the outset. This is evident in an early manifesto put forward by Gordon Klenck, CfC's European director during the early 1970s. CfC's aim was to see "the Great Commission fulfilled in Europe – both east and west – by 1980. By 'fulfilled' we mean that the population of each country will be continually saturated with the claims of Christ, by every possible means and media … Our immediate objective is to recruit and train nationals in every country with national support and national leadership."[89]

Reflecting the confidence and enthusiasm of their predecessors from Youth for Christ, CfC had twenty-two American missionaries working in their European headquarters, located near JTM's offices in southern Germany, by 1974. Another thirty-two CfC American staff were active in the West German cities of Erlangen, Freiburg, and West Berlin.[90] With its commitment to efficiency and haste, CfC sought to develop self-supporting national chapters of its work across Europe in the shortest time possible.

The main thrust of its work consisted of training Christian young people in methods of "person-to-person" evangelism, so they could evangelize their peers on university campuses, and then nurture newly won converts in their faith.[91] Frank Kifer, Gorden Klenck, and Dennis

Griggs were among the American leaders pioneering the early CfC work in Europe. Looking back at their initial efforts they admitted their expectations were unrealistic: "When we came [to Europe] we thought we could get the ministry started, recruit plenty of Europeans to take over leadership, and then leave after two years. That was an illusion."[92] In spite of such initial false hopes for a short-lived missionary venture, CfC continued its efforts, albeit at a more realistic but still aggressive pace, towards indigenizing its European operations and making them self-supporting as early as possible.

By 1977, Kalevi Lehtinen, a Finnish staff member, had taken over the directorship of European operations, and by the following year, CfC's German staff consisted of thirty-four full-time nationals and only twelve Americans. By 1983 the approximate ratio remained the same – two-thirds German staff to one-third American – although the actual numbers on both sides increased to fifty-nine and twenty-three respectively.[93] The work of CfC also began to diversify during the 1980s, and while some American-based techniques of evangelism continued to be imported by the national staff, it was also evident that Germans themselves were finding ways to give CfC more of a native voice.[94]

Along with conservative evangelical missions, Billy Graham's work in Germany also underwent indigenization. After 1974 this was most noticeable in the ongoing publication of the BGEA's monthly magazine, *Decision*. Under the German title, *Entscheidung*, the magazine continued to find a solid readership base in West Germany. Until 1974 the magazine consisted mostly of translated pieces of its English counterpart. But that year the BGEA hired Dr Irmhild Bärend to be the full-time editor of *Entscheidung*. Bärend, who held a PhD in German literature, opened up a new publication office in Berlin and over the next decade slowly reshaped the magazine so that it had a more authentic German voice while still informing supporters of the BGEA's activities around the world. Of the six non-English-language translations of *Decision* magazine launched by the BGEA, only the German one survived.[95] At its peak popularity *Entscheidung* had a circulation of 33,000, but with the emergence of new Christian periodicals in the later 1980s that number was reduced to 10,000.[96]

Even with such a reduced profile and infrequent presence, Graham's influence among German *Evangelikaler* continued to be felt through a series of initiatives by the Germans themselves. Two examples are the formation of the Arbeitskreis für evangelikaler Theologie in 1977, and the series of evangelistic events across Germany under the banner of Das Missionarisches Jahr held in 1980. The former was a society of German theologians formed as a direct result of the Lausanne Conference, and designed to promote the research and publication of German evangelical theologians and to supply educational materials to churches and other Christian groups.[97] The group included members from the *Freikirchen* and the *Landeskirchen* and worked in close conjunction with the DEA.

The events that made up Das Missionarisches Jahr also drew their impetus from the Lausanne Congress. Spearheaded by the DEA, these events represented the first ever Germany-wide evangelistic efforts organized by Germans themselves.[98] Although Billy Graham was invited to participate, the DEA made it clear that this was a made-in-Germany effort designed to "mobilize every individual Christian at the grass-roots level for witnessing and serving the Lord." The fact that such an event was even possible was directly attributable to Graham's motivation and encouragement to German Christians over the years.[99] For DEA General Secretary Peter Schneider, *Evangelikaler* Christians now had the resources to continue the mission to Germany that Graham had helped initiate.

Denominational Missions and Indigenization

A similar trend was occurring in denominational missions during this period as well. For Southern Baptists this was most noticeable in the SBC-FMB's decision to reduce its financial support to the International Baptist Theological Seminary (IBTS) in Switzerland. In a 1978 report to the European Baptist Federation, J.D. Hughey, the SBC-FMB's director for Europe, summarized the increasing financial stress under which IBTS had laboured during the 1970s. This was due largely to the dramatic decline of the US dollar against the Swiss franc. At the beginning of that decade one American dollar could buy 4.25 francs. By 1978 the dollar could only buy 1.60 francs. During the same period the SBC-FMB's annual subsidy to IBTS doubled from $140,000 to $280,000, yet this amounted to only a 20 per cent increase in Swiss francs. Allowing for the rate of inflation, the subsidized budget actually had less buying power in the Swiss economy than the earlier amount. Hughey also pointed out that in 1977 the SBC-FMB served notice to European Baptists that the "continuation of the seminary depends upon their sharing with Southern Baptists the financial support of the institution."[100]

Hughey's statement was not intended as a threat, but as a warning to European Baptists that the SBC-FMB believed it had reached its financial ceiling of support for IBTS. For the seminary to remain open, European Baptists would have to assume a greater share of its operational costs. European Baptists, particularly those of the German Baptist Union, were quick to affirm both their appreciation of the Americans for bringing the seminary into being, and its ongoing value in sustaining Baptist life in Europe. Gerhard Claas, a German Baptist leader and the newly appointed director of the European Baptist Federation (EBF), called the seminary the "father-house" of European Baptists, because most of the current generation of European Baptist leaders had been trained there. As a member of the IBTS board of trustees, Claas assured Hughey that European Baptists would work to cover the seminary's short-term financial deficit as well as look for new sources of funding for the future.[101]

In addition to Claas's endorsement, a second expression of German Baptist support came in a letter from the collective faculty of the Baptist seminary in Hamburg to Hughey and Isam Ballinger, the president of IBTS. Expressing their shock at hearing that the IBTS might have to close its doors in 1979, the Hamburg faculty assured the Americans of how much they valued the service of the seminary, and how important it was for Baptist life in Europe that IBTS continue operating.[102] Such unequivocal support indicated that the initial resentment of European Baptists toward the SBC-FMB for the high-handed way they had gone about establishing the seminary (see chapter 3) had since given way to appreciation for the role of IBTS in training indigenous Baptist leaders.[103]

In June 1978, the SBC-FMB had reached an agreement with the EBF on a five-year plan to transfer the operational and financial responsibility for IBTS to the EBF Council. Southern Baptists would continue to subsidize the seminary until 1983, while relinquishing the administrative responsibility for the school at the start of 1979. In spite of the restructured financial and administrative arrangements and assurances of goodwill by both parties, the seminary faced ongoing financial and leadership struggles throughout the 1980s, yet in spite of chronic budget shortfalls, coupled with a high turnover rate of its presidents during this same period, IBTS managed to keep its doors open through these years of instability. In 1988 Southern Baptists and the EBF agreed on full transfer of the seminary property into European Baptist hands, as well as a plan gradually to eliminate all American financial subsidy of the seminary.[104] In an official ceremony that year, Keith Parks, the SBC-FMB president, handed over the "key of ownership" of the seminary to EBF General Secretary Knud Wumpelmann.[105]

The indigenization of the IBTS continued after the Cold War with the seminary's eventual relocation to Prague in 1995. The process was accelerated by the emergence of a militantly conservative fundamentalist theological stance in the SBC's leaders. They in turn began to accuse IBTS faculty – and, by implication, the EBF – of taking the seminary in a theologically liberal direction.[106] However, amidst the deteriorating relationship between the EBF and the SBC, the seminary, as the most prominent institution of Southern Baptist mission work in German-speaking Europe, made a successful transition to European indigenization.[107]

The move toward greater indigenization was also noticeable in the Mennonite Central Committee's (MCC) work in German-speaking Europe. From 1975 until the end of the Cold War, the MCC's work was focused in two areas: the European Mennonite Bible School (EMBS) in Bienenberg, Switzerland, and the MCC's European office in Neuwied, West Germany. In the case of EMBS, the MCC's commitment to the school remained consistent with the pattern already established by the later 1960s: the MCC maintained one representative on the school's board, continued to supply and pay the salary for a full-time teacher on the EMBS staff right up until 1989, and contributed funds for capital projects as the school continued to expand its campus at Bienenberg.[108] By the end of the Cold War, evidence that indigenization was now practically complete can be seen in the report on the EMBS given at the MCC's 1990 annual board meeting. The relationship between EMBS and the MCC was now described as "informal … though as always very cordial." Both in governance and staffing, the school no longer relied on the MCC. The report expressed concern over a decline in enrolment during recent years, yet it was clear that it was up to European Mennonites to come up with made-in-Europe solutions to the challenge.[109]

The MCC's European office in Neuwied, Germany, was the other base of the MCC's ongoing work in Europe. Although MCC staff numbers in the office varied from nine to thirteen, this presence was muted by two factors: first, only two or three of these were long-term appointments, while the rest served mostly for two-year terms; and MCC personnel were not in positions of leadership, but served in support roles to German Mennonite communities. As already outlined in the previous section, these roles included working with *Umsiedler* Mennonites entering West Germany from the USSR; raising the profile of the Mennonite peace witness in Europe in partnership with EIRENE, the European Mennonite peace organization; and supporting Mennonites in East Germany.[110] Justification for this selective and more reduced role in Germany was stated at the MCC's annual meeting in 1978: "Germany is affluent and well able to take care of itself and others."[111] In pursuing a policy of deliberate indigenization, the MCC's mission during the last decades of the Cold War brought it to the point where it was now willing to undertake joint ventures with European Mennonite groups as one among equals.

Conclusion

Missionary Responses to Secularism

An increasingly dominant theme of the North American mission to Germany from 1974 to 1989 was the response to secularism by conservative evangelical and denominational missionaries. These responses are significant for three wider areas of historical inquiry. First, for the history of Protestant missions, the actions of missionaries to Germany give insight into the rising concern for contextualizing the Christian message in ways that called for great cultural sensitivity and acuity. As explained above, contextualization was not only a reality for missions moving from developing countries of the West to nations in the developing world, but also increasingly shaped missions to other developed countries as well as conservative evangelical home missions in North America itself.[112] The story of how this played out in the mission to Germany thus adds greater depth to the history of how North American Protestants became more aware of relativity of their own cultural context.

Second, for the history of World Christianity, the work of North American missionaries during this period can be seen as a forerunner to a growing convoy of missionary traffic to the lands of Old World Christendom. Missionaries were among the first to see that secularism was changing Europe into a "post-Christian" mission field, but the growing number of Christian immigrants from countries in the Global South were not far behind in recognizing that Europe was in need of re-Christianizing.[113]

Understanding North American missionaries as the advance guard of this movement brings a new dimension to the narrative of World Christianity and the demise of the traditional conceptualization of Christendom.

The third area for which this chapter has significance is the history of the final phase of Cold War relations in Europe. While the role of missionaries during the presidential administrations of Jimmy Carter and Ronald Reagan should not be overstated, they did play a part, mostly in West Germany, in promoting a plausible and viable Christian alternative to the secular Marxist rhetoric that had come into fashion on university campuses across the Western world.[114] In doing so, missionaries continually drew attention to the spiritual and religious implications of the Cold War ideological debates of the day. In the case of Billy Graham and the MCC, they were also involved in promoting peaceable dialogue across the Iron Curtain at various ecclesiastical levels. These were not merely efforts to promote goodwill; missionaries in this role clearly wanted to have their voices heard and taken seriously by policy-makers on both sides of the Iron Curtain.[115] Hence this chapter points to the significance of religious voices in the complexity and wide-ranging nature of Cold War relations.

Mission to Germany and Indigenization

In a way similar to the missionary response to secularism, the theme of indigenization that came to the fore in these years has a wider significance for three areas: Protestant missiological inquiry as it relates to the issue of contextualization; the issue of German/European perceptions of Americans during the final phase of the Cold War; and recent developments within German Protestantism.

First, as in the case of secularism, the move toward indigenization by North American missions is connected to the missiological discussions on contextualization taking place at the time. Challenges to the traditional thinking and methods of conservative evangelical missionaries had already been voiced at the Lausanne Congress by delegates from developing nations, such as René Padilla, Orlando Costas, and John Gatu.[116] The move toward indigenization of mission work in Germany in the period after Lausanne suggests that Padilla, Costas, and Gatu were not expressing concerns limited to Christian workers only in developing nations. Instead this move to indigenization in an intra-Western context points to contextualization as indicative of the zeitgeist of missions on a more global level. Consequently traditional patterns of cross-cultural missionary activity were yielding to strategies that privileged local initiatives, respected regional particularities, and valued customized made-at-home solutions over larger-scale productions from abroad.

Second, the significance of indigenization for America's image abroad may, at first glance, be seen as a reaction to the prevailing anti-Americanism in Europe triggered by the more confrontational foreign policy of the United States under the Reagan presidency toward Communist countries. However, evidence from mission organizations themselves suggests that indigenization was fuelled more by economic concerns and a sense that the Germans themselves were now in a position to take the lead in these tasks. If anything, the evidence suggests that, at least in some cases, indigenization provided North American missionaries who continued to work in Germany with the opportunity to demonstrate a growing cultural sensitivity that worked to mitigate anti-Americanism.

Finally, the growth of indigenization after Lausanne is significant for understanding the recent history of German Protestantism. Indigenization signalled a certain coming of age for the German *Evangelikaler* movement, and the growing resourcefulness of its Baptist *Freikirchlicher* wing. During the early postwar decades, both groups had existed at the margins of German Protestantism and were viewed as alien entities by many Germans. Stephan Holthaus has pointed out that although there is no indication of a dramatic growth in numbers of either group after 1974, it is significant that in the final decades of the twentieth century German *Evangelikaler* made up the majority of the most regular church attenders not only in the *Freikirchen*, but also increasingly in the *Landeskirchen*. As overall regular Sunday attendance in the *Landeskirchen* continued to decline, it was self-identifying *Evangelikaler* who remained among the faithful in their respective congregations. So while overall numbers fell, *Evangelikaler* Protestants made up a growing percentage of those congregations.[117] As such, their role in German Protestant church life became more prominent. Even as the Cold War came to a conclusion, Billy Graham continued to inspire the formation of indigenous evangelistic organizations in which *Evangelikaler* Christians played key roles. One such organization was ProChrist, led by evangelist Ulrich Parzany, who, as mentioned earlier in this chapter, had worked closely with Graham at Christival in the 1970s. By 2007 the overall number of *Evangelikaler* was estimated to be 1.3 million (or 1.7 per cent of the overall German population).[118] On the surface, such a statistic may not look impressive, but in the increasingly tough, thorny secularizing soil of German cultural life the *Evangelikaler* movement had taken root and showed signs of ongoing vitality. During these final years of the Cold War, from 1974 to 1989, the significance of North American missionary efforts became fully apparent in nurturing and shaping this increasingly influential constituency in German Protestantism.

Saving Germany: The Significance of the Mission

In 2004, Alan Kreider, a Mennonite missionary and historian, offered a re-flection on a half-century of his denomination's mission work in Europe: "How do we evaluate the labors of North American Mennonite mission-aries in Europe over the past fifty years? This is a task for historians, not a participant."[1] Most missionaries to Germany would have agreed with Kreider. They were too busy with the task at hand to speculate on what the legacy of their work would be. As is frequently the case when historians analyze and assess events, they realize that the actions of the people they are studying have consequences and significance beyond the immediate intentions and awareness of the historical actors themselves. This is cer-tainly the case when examining the activities of North American Protest-ant missionaries in their efforts to "save Germany." From the outset I have argued that the story of the missionaries in Germany during the Cold War period makes an important contribution to four fields of study: North American Protestant missions; German Protestantism; American foreign relations in Cold War Europe; and the development of World Christianity. In each of these four areas, the activities of North American missionaries have significance well beyond – yet still related to – the immediate goal they were trying to reach, namely restoring a vibrant Protestant presence in Germany. The remainder of this chapter will offer a summative ap-praisal of the importance of Protestant mission to Germany for each field in turn.

North American Protestant Missions: Two Rival Visions of Christian Internationalism

As is evident from the previous chapters, the plight of postwar Germany generated a strong missionary response from a wide spectrum of Protestant groups in North America. In doing so, it brought to the surface the underlying rifts within Protestantism over the nature and purposes of missions that had been developing during the interwar decades. Dana Robert and Robert Wright have traced the shift away from the central priority of conversionism by the mainline Protestant denominations in the United States and Canada respectively.[2] While not removed from the missionary agenda, conversionism was an increasingly junior partner alongside other priorities, such as promoting ecumenical partnerships and indigenized expressions of mission, and practising a more tolerant attitude toward non-Western religions. Concurrent with this shift in Christian internationalism was the move toward a formal institutional expression of Protestant ecumenism in the World Council of Churches (wcc).

On the other side of the divide were those who continued to favour the traditional missionary emphasis of evangelism. This position increasingly came to be represented by conservative evangelical independent mission organizations.[3] The resultant loss of a "Protestant missionary consensus" was one more outworking of the fundamentalist-modernist theological controversy that was occurring in North America at the time.[4] For conservative evangelicals, the vision of Christian internationalism promulgated by mainline Protestants and promoted through the ecumenism of the wcc amounted to an unacceptable deviation from the true task of missions, namely evangelistic proclamation.[5]

In looking at both the ecumenical and conservative evangelical missionary efforts to save Germany, my research has shown how these two divergent expressions of Christian internationalism worked out in practice. Most of the research on this theme in the history of North American missions has focused on the missiological debates between ecumenists and conservative evangelicals since the formation of the wcc.[6] Few, if any, historical treatments take a comparative approach to actual missionary practice, showing the range of Protestant missionary responses to a common mission field. The picture that emerges in the chapters of this book is that postwar Germany acted as a kind of missiological laboratory in which the contrasting approaches of ecumenicals and conservative evangelicals were enacted side by side. By including denominational

Protestant agencies whose missionary practices included a mixture of ecumenical and conservative evangelical affinities, this study also shows that, in the wake of the fundamentalist-modernist controversy, Protestant missionary work did not necessarily neatly divide into these two broad camps. What does come to light is a more nuanced, complex range of responses that comprise the range of the North American Protestant missionary spectrum of the day.

The mission to Germany also suggests that the ways in which the success or worth of a missionary work was determined were also changing. For the fledgling World Council of Churches "in process of formation," participating in Germany's reconstruction and spiritual rehabilitation set a precedent for ecumenical missionary practice in the years that followed: a model was established of entering into partnerships with Christian organizations in needy countries with the goal of providing resources that contributed toward indigenous self-help. Even though Visser 't Hooft, the WCC's first general secretary, reminded American ecumenists to attend to the spiritual needs in Germany, as well as relief and reconstruction projects, it was the latter category that found sustained support among ecumenicals, not only once Germany had recovered, but as the Church World Service and the WCC's Department of Reconstruction and Inter-Church Aid increasingly turned their attention during the 1950s to other needy areas of the globe.[7]

By 1953 Hilfswerk had requested that all further ecumenical aid to Germany go exclusively to East Germany because West Germany could look after its own needs. By 1957 West German Lutherans were themselves no longer recipients but contributors to ecumenical aid, recording $250,000 in donations to the Lutheran World Service for distribution through WCC channels. Richard W. Solberg, who oversaw American Lutheran relief work in Germany from 1948 to 1955, concluded that ecumenical aid toward self-help had been effective not only in addressing German needs, but also in producing among the German people a sensitivity toward the needs of less fortunate peoples elsewhere.[8] Robert C. Mackie, associate secretary of the WCC during the period 1948–55, concurred when he affirmed that while the WCC's Department of Inter-Church Aid would always have a role in providing countries such as Germany with provisions for spiritual ministry to the un-churched masses, the main burden of this task was on the shoulders of the German churches themselves. The crowning achievement of the WCC's postwar work of reconstruction in

Germany, and elsewhere in Europe, could be found in having fostered "an increased understanding of other people and a stronger sense of Christian solidarity. These are the things which make for peace."[9]

Further significance of the mission to Germany for this growing emphasis on relief and reconstruction as a leading component of Protestant mission emerges from examining denominational mission agencies. Both the Mennonite Central Committee (MCC) and Baptist World Aid had already been operating prior to the Second World War, but largely on an ad hoc projects that targeted the needs of their denominational constituencies abroad. As a result of their postwar mission to Germany, both organizations became permanent humanitarian relief missionary agencies in their respective denominations. Together with the establishment of the Church World Service, Lutheran World Relief, and the above-mentioned WCC Department of Inter-Church Aid, the MCC and Baptist World Aid represent a significant commitment by a wide range of Protestant groups in North America to see mission as much more encompassing than conversionism. The analysis offered in this book opens up the way to examine the ongoing significance of this shift for the present-day concern of missions with the concept of "development" and for the contribution of the above agencies to current development theory. While such a discussion falls outside the scope of this present work, the possibility for such a linkage is an intriguing avenue for further investigation.

Another important contribution to the historiography of Protestant mission emerging from this study on missions is the non-doctrinal basis for Christian internationalism that resulted from the ecumenical mission. As is evident from the material in chapter 2, the estrangement and isolation of the German churches from Protestant Christians in other Western nations at the end of the Second World War presented an awkward problem for which there was no ready solution. It was ecumenical missionaries working through WCC-supported networks who were key figures in building bridges that would allow the German *Landeskirchen* a way out of isolation and into restored ecumenical fellowship. The elements of enabling toward self-help, renewing bonds of ecumenical fellowship, and motivating German Protestants to participate in the ongoing ecumenical mission of inter-church aid provided the foundation on which to construct a vision for Christian internationalism that contrasted markedly with that of conservative evangelical missionaries, who continued to emphasize evangelism, conversion, and a measure of doctrinal consensus.

Mackie's remarks indicate that along with this alternative vision, leaders of the ecumenical mission were invoking a set of criteria for evaluating the relative success of a missionary venture that were different from the statistical record-keeping of individual conversions or the founding of new church congregations, which commonly used by conservative evangelical and denominational missionaries. Support for these shifting priorities by American mainline churches was voiced through the *Christian Century*. By the end of the 1950s, the *Christian Century* noted with approval the new spirit of voluntarism and ecumenical mission through international relief that pervaded German churches. The best expression of this spirit could be seen in the 18 million Deutschmarks that Germans contributed in 1959 alone to Brot für die Welt, West Germany's own ecumenical relief agency created as a response to its own postwar experience.[10] Such evaluations, it was claimed, indicated that in spite of the fact that the hoped-for resurgence in church attendance by the German population never materialized, the missionary investment in that country had achieved a measure of success.[11] Mackie's criteria of solidarity, understanding, and peace were therefore one more signal that there had been a significant divergence in Protestant missions, and as such point to the value of my research in showing the mission to Germany as a watershed in the history of North American missions.[12]

This did not mean the demise of traditional missionary practices. As is also evident from my research, conservative evangelical and denominational missionaries found ongoing support in their efforts to keep evangelistic conversion and planting new church congregations at the centre of their work. It was this latter group of missionaries who played a significant role in altering the landscape of German Protestantism, which brings us to the next major historical theme.

German Protestantism: The Radical Reformation Comes Home to Roost

As Nicholas Railton and Karl-Heinz Voigt have shown, the *Freikirchen* had traditionally been perceived as a foreign transplant and not as a legitimate expression of German Protestantism.[13] Unlike the *Landeskirchen* of the EKD, which could trace their establishment back to the magisterial Reformation credo of *Cuius regio, eius religio*, members of the *Freikirchen* understood the church as a voluntary society of the faithful and not the religious arm of a state bureaucracy. Hence the members of the

Freikirchen were viewed by most Germans as not truly *evangelisch*, and thus not truly German. In addition to the charge of being un-German, members of the *Freikirchen*, along with radical pietists, were accused of fostering excessive emotion, or *Schwärmerei*, an accusation fuelled by distant memories of sixteenth-century Anabaptists. Such a charge stemmed from their association with revivalism, which in turn was identified with nineteenth-century Anglo-American evangelical preachers who had conducted periodic preaching tours in Germany.[14] *Freikirchlicher* Protestantism grounded in the voluntary association of private individuals motivated by a personal faith stood at odds with the civic Protestantism of the confessional *Landeskirchen*, in which church membership went hand-in-hand with citizenship.[15]

Although some members of these two contrasting styles of Protestant church polity had found common ground through the Evangelische Allianz, North American Protestant missionary work during the Cold War period helped legitimatize the place of voluntary Christianity in German Protestantism. I have highlighted the important role of conservative evangelical and denominational mission agencies in bringing about this changed perception. The significance of this change for the wider scope of the history of German Protestantism is that after nearly five centuries the German Protestant establishment was at last making its peace with the radical wing of the Reformation.[16] Conservative evangelical mission agencies, such as the Billy Graham Evangelistic Association (BGEA), Youth for Christ (YFC), and Janz Team Ministries (JTM), along with Southern Baptist and Mennonite missionaries, acted as key brokers in bringing it to fruition. They did this primarily in two ways. First, as explained in chapter 3, denominational missions helped their kindred to rebuild churches and establish new congregations in the immediate postwar period. These new congregations emerged from the chaos of postwar population displacement and resettlement, which also shattered the confessional homogeneity (and hegemony) of numerous *Länder*. This shifting pattern of demography gave Baptists a greater visibility in German church life than they had had before the war. Southern Baptist and Mennonite missionaries were also instrumental in founding educational institutions to train indigenous pastors and Christian workers for their respective denominations. These theological schools nurtured denominational life and also contributed to these denominations' gaining greater respect and legitimacy in the communities where they were present. Postwar aid from North American Baptists and Mennonites also contributed to the *Freikirchen* being included as full members of Hilfswerk, and thus recognized as legitimate members of the German Protestant church relief effort. In summary, denominational missions, through church reconstruction, education, and material aid, helped raise the profile and improve the status of the *Freikirchen* in the Cold War decades.

Second, chapters 4 and 5 outlined a second way in which the ideals of the Radical Reformation were promoted through the work of conservative evangelical missionaries. As noted in these chapters, conservative evangelicals worked primarily through the Deutsche Evangelische Allianz (DEA) to promote a more voluntaristic expression of Christianity. By working in cooperation with local chapters of the DEA, JTM, the BGEA, and to a lesser degree, YFC, German Protestants were encouraged to transcend denominational boundaries in the cause of evangelism and thus helped forge an indigenous *Evangelikaler* identity. Erich Geldbach has rightly argued that the *Evangelikaler* movement did not require novel foreign additions to German Protestantism, but was a unique coalescing of elements already resident in it.[17]

North American conservative evangelicals can thus be seen as catalysts in the synthesis of this new form of Protestant identity, making it a tangible reality in German church life. When missionary evangelists such as Billy Graham and Leo Janz worked with the local DEA in holding large-scale crusades, they were able to bring together Christians from the *Landeskirchen* and the *Freikirchen* in the common cause of seeing individual Germans make a personal commitment to the Christian faith.

Two defining moments that revealed the importance of North American missionaries in the formation of *Evangelikaler* identity took place in 1966 during Billy Graham's crusade and congress in Berlin. These moments were analyzed at some length in chapter 5, but their significance bears recapitulating here. The first involved the last public address of Otto Dibelius, the venerable Lutheran *Landesbischof* of Berlin-Brandenburg and icon of German political and religious conservativism. In the final evening of the crusade, Dibelius expressed his appreciation for Graham's work in Germany. In the first part of his address (quoted at length on pp. 173–4) he acknowledged that the American evangelist not only had helped win respect for Christianity among skeptical Berliners, but that he had also shown German Christians the importance of helping their unbelieving compatriots to a personal decision for Christ. In his conclusion Dibelius likened Graham to the Good Samaritan in Luke's Gospel, who, as a foreigner, had come to the aid of a beaten and hurting people, and won many of them over. Even though Graham's ways, as an outsider, might seem unusual, the Christian message he proclaimed was one that Germans could and should embrace.[18] In other words, one could practise being *Evangelikal* and still be a good Lutheran. Through such an endorsement Dibelius was signalling that Graham's form of personal voluntaristic Christianity had a place in the *Landeskirchen,* and not merely in the *Friekirchen* minority. Reflecting the same trans-denominational spirit, Leo Janz ensured that he included endorsements for JTM's crusades in *Ruf* magazine from both state-church *Pfarrers* and free-church pastors.[19]

A second event that affirmed this dual identity and went on to imply that the *Evangelikaler* movement reflected the true spirit of Luther's Reformation was the *Zeugnismarsch,* which took place during the congress on evangelism. As Anglo-American evangelicals marched alongside German *Evangelikaler* from Wittenberg Square to the Kaiser Wilhelm Memorial Church on Reformation Day (31 October 1966), the association of the marchers with these symbols of the Lutheran Reformation was a powerful statement about who were the true heirs of the Reformation.

Billy Graham's role in the development of *Evangelikaler* identity has been acknowledged in passing by several historians of German Protestantism, but the significance of his role and that of other mission agencies largely has been left largely unexplored.[20] My research has brought to light the importance of conservative evangelical missionaries from North America in shaping and sustaining *Evangelikaler* identity. In doing so it develops further Nicholas Railton's account of the nineteenth-century Anglo-German evangelical network. Where Railton's work traces the foundation of evangelical links across the North Sea from the latter half of the nineteenth century, my work shows that after the Second World War the evangelical network expanded across the North Atlantic to include North America. By the middle of the twentieth century what had begun as an Anglo-German fellowship of equal partners had shifted dramatically to reveal a North American dominance.[21] During the early decades of the Cold War the traffic flowed predominantly west to east, and the intent was not so much mutual fellowship as it was missionary.

My analysis of Billy Graham's work in Germany also makes an important contribution to the argument put forward by Uta Balbier. As Balbier has suggested, Graham's presentation of Christianity (and, by extension, that of other evangelical North American missionaries) allowed Germans a way to reconcile overt Christian commitment with modern culture and thus practise a form of Christianity in tune with the times and apart from formal church structures.[22] While insightful, Balbier's thesis goes only part way in explaining Graham's appeal, largely because it fails to deal with people's spiritual experiences beyond a sociological level. Mark Noll's recent work on the global appeal of evangelical Christianity mediated through American missionaries adds a dimension missing from Balbier's argument, namely that conservative evangelical missionaries such as Graham and Janz offered a form of Christianity that, although it did not eschew church structures entirely, promoted a personal voluntaristic style of religious association that helped people to see church, and Christianity in general, as a voluntary fellowship of the like-minded.[23] My findings add strength to Noll's assessment and widens its applicability. Although Noll was concerned only with evangelical missions from North America to the pre-Christian societies in Asia, Africa, and Latin America, my work suggests that his portrayal of conservative evangelicalism as the progenitor of contemporary World Christianity in the Global South would be applicable to parts of the post-Christian North as well.

Conservative evangelicals did more than provide an alternative and more individualized spiritual experience as part of the make-up of German Protestantism. I have explained how their work led to the formation of indigenous structures that made the *Evangelikaler* movement sustainable as a truly German entity, and also connected the German movement to the wider international movement of evangelical Christians.

Here again, the historiography of German Protestantism has noted the emergence of such structures but has not analyzed or credited the role of American missionaries in bringing this about. JTM, Billy Graham, and YFC established branches of their own on German soil, all of which in turn became members of the DEA, which has since become the most visible organization associated with the *Evangelikaler* movement.[24] North American missionaries were also directly involved with founding and/ or supporting other aspects of the *Evangelikaler* network. In 1972, *idea*, the first Christian press service in Germany, was founded by the DEA as a result of Graham's Euro 70 crusade. As a direct result of the Lausanne Congress, *Evangelikaler* founded the Arbeitskreise für evangelikale

Theologie, a standing workshop to promote the publication of materials by *Evangelikaler* theologians.[25] Space has not allowed inclusion of another significant American mission organization, Trans World Radio (TWR), and its influence in the *Evangelikaler* movement. A brief note here will suffice to show that my case studies portray only a representative selection, and not the whole story of American missionary influence. The creation of Germany's first Christian radio and television studio, Evangeliums-Rundfunk Deutschland, which would go on to become a cornerstone of the *Evangelikaler* movement, was due in large part to the efforts of missionary Paul Freed, who began its religious broadcasting over TWR from Monte Carlo in 1960.[26]

One can make the case that in spite of these achievements, the overall impact of conservative Protestant missions on German church life fell far short of the sweeping spiritual renewal for which missionaries and their like-minded German *Evangelikaler* had hoped. While it is clear that missionary-inspired *Evangelikaler* movement was felt most noticeably among the *Freikirchen* segment of German Protestantism, these churches made up a very small percentage of the official overall Protestant population of the country. The *Evangelikaler* movement never managed to thoroughly capture or permeate the dominant structures of the *Landeskirche* where the vast majority of Protestants were registered. However, as Stephan Holthaus has pointed out, even though self-identifying *Evangelikaler* in the *Landeskirche* number only 700,000, they are among the most active and devout members of their respective congregations. On average, only 4 per cent – just over a million people – of registered members in the *Landeskirche* attend church regularly. This difference between the statistical record and the Sunday-to-Sunday operational reality of church life suggests that *Evangelikaler* influence in the *Landeskirche* is disproportionately high because of their commitment to church life.[27]

Additional evidence of the ongoing significance of the *Evangelikaler* movement in German religious life is the press coverage it receives from German national media outlets, such as ARD.de and Taz.de. In recent years both of these media outlets ran stories on the movement and its place on the German cultural landscape.[28] *Evangelikaler* also have received media coverage when they stage large outreach events led by home-grown evangelists such as Ulrich Parzany (see chapter 5) and his ProChrist organization.[29] Thus despite their relatively small numbers when compared to those officially registered as Protestants, *Evangelikaler* continue to have a significant presence in German religious life and would seem to punch above their weight in the ability of their activism to attract secular media attention.

As I have demonstrated in the previous chapters, much of this ongoing activism and vitality can be traced back to the work of North American missionaries such as YFC, Janz Team, and Billy Graham. Therefore it can be asserted that North American conservative evangelicals and denominational missionaries exercised significant influence in German Protestant life, not merely because of the novelty of their creative approaches to evangelism, or the massive investment in postwar reconstruction, but in offering a compelling form of Christianity that emphasized the role of the individual as a member of a voluntary society. In so doing they were helping some segments of the German population overcome their historic antipathy toward Anabaptist forms of Christianity, and demonstrating that this expression of the Christian faith had a legitimate place in German Protestant life.

Cold War Relations: Missionaries as Agents of Democracy and Cultural Ambassadors

It is in this historiographical area that examining missionaries from a transnational perspective has paid large dividends by bringing to light ways in which the Protestant mission to Germany played out beyond its explicit religious or spiritual objectives. As members of private transnational religious organizations, missionaries found themselves playing roles normally reserved for government personnel or working with official government sanction. These roles were both intentional and incidental. When missionaries took on the role of agents of democracy, it was largely deliberate and intentional. In cases in which they acted as cultural ambassadors, it was more of an unintended by-product of proclaiming the Christian gospel.

Once Germany surrendered, Nazism was no longer seen as the primary totalitarian threat; but as the Allied occupation of Germany showed, Communism represented a "clear and present danger" to a Europe only just released from Hitler's grasp. A common concern among all strands of North American Protestant mission to Germany was fostering democratic ideals, especially religious freedom, in the German population. Although their approaches varied widely, missionaries were conscious of promoting democratic freedoms as part of their mission. In the case of conservative evangelicals, such as Billy Graham, this involved an uncritical linking of the Christian message with democratic ideology; for Mennonites and Baptists it meant offering a democratic church polity as an alternative to what they perceived as the authoritarian hierarchical ecclesiastical structures of the *Landeskirchen*; for ecumenical Protestants it included drawing the leadership of the *Landeskirchen* into the democratic structures of international ecumenism.

Once Allied occupation gave way to a divided Germany, missionaries could see the fruit of their labours in West Germany's firm commitment to nation-building along democratic lines. Living on the frontier of the Iron Curtain, however, meant that the spectre of Communism was always present. For missionaries in West Germany this meant being concerned not so much with the ideological barbarians at the eastern gates, but with the Marxist wolves in democratic sheep's clothing who were already inside the pen. Much attention has been given to the Communist threat present in America itself during the Cold War, usually by examining aspects of the "Red Scare" fuelled by Senator Joseph McCarthy.[30] Alternatively mission chroniclers have looked at developments taking place behind the Iron Curtain, and instances of cross-border tension between the rival superpowers when writing on aspects of the Cold War.[31] The material in the preceding chapters has shown that there was at least one more theatre of operations where Americans were active in contesting the spread of Communist influence, namely West Germany. In their efforts to integrate democratic ideals into their proclamation of the Christian message, missionaries saw this as a cure for Nazism and, more importantly, an inoculation against Communism. The emergence of the theme of missionaries as agents of democracy during Europe's postwar recovery invites further inquiry into the nature and extent of American activity in Western Europe more generally, as a means of checking Marxist influence in this region.

Missionaries never worked in an apolitical context, nor has their message been politically neutral. But this aspect of their work has begun to receive scholarly attention during recent decades. Jeffrey Cox, Andrew Porter, and Brian Stanley are only some of the scholars who have explicated this theme, in all its complexity, in the activities of British Protestant missions in the nineteenth and twentieth centuries.[32] James Reed, and, more recently, Andrew Preston's research on the religious influences on American foreign relations have opened the way for similar explorations of the political dimension of American missionary activity.[33] Thus the story of missionaries in Germany helps map new territory in this relatively uncharted historiographical terrain. It also invites further studies of North American missionary activity in other geopolitical regions such as Southeast Asia and Latin America, where American political interests were increasingly defined by resistance to perceived Communist encroachment. Such studies could compare the role of missionaries as agents of American democracy in these theatres of operation with that of their European counterparts. The fruit of such investigation would shed significant light on the ongoing interplay between ideological and religious commitments of those who served under the banner of transnational mission agencies.

Related to their transnational role as agents of democracy, a second aspect of missionary influence in Germany during the Cold War years covered in this book is their role as cultural ambassadors. Only recently have cultural historians, such as Uta Balbier, become aware of the wider cultural significance of Billy Graham's visits to Germany.[34] While Graham was probably the most famous missionary from North America to Germany, other missionaries who were long-term residents, not itinerants, arguably had as great a cultural impact as did Graham. Such a case could be made for the founding members of Janz Team Ministries. As was noted in chapter 4, to many of their German supporters, the members of the Janz Quartet were just as well known for their musical recordings as for evangelistic preaching. The quartet frequently featured songs from the Negro spiritual tradition during their crusades, as well as on their numerous LP records.[35] These were something of a novelty for German audiences during the 1950s and 1960s, as was the use of the Hammond organ for playing explicitly Christian songs. In both cases these innovations were well received by German audiences.[36] By the 1970s both JTM and Billy Graham were among the first to introduce Christian songs in the style of rock music into German Protestant circles.[37] Leo Janz was also among the first in Germany to use radio broadcasts as a form of evangelism. Applying the format used by American variety programs, which Youth for Christ had already made popular back in the United States, Janz drew on American entertainment culture in his efforts to present the Christian message in an attractive, contemporary way. Such forms would eventually be picked up and further modified by German Christians, but it was missionaries from across the Atlantic, acting as the cultural conduits, who made these later developments possible.[38]

These are only a few examples of the ways in which missionaries acted as cultural ambassadors. Through their denominational networks, and especially through their educational institutions, Southern Baptists and

Mennonites performed a similar role. Ecumenical missionaries, in a more limited way, also participated in cross-cultural exchanges designed to promote not only goodwill, but also the exporting of American ideas and methods for German church leaders and theological students.[39] As mentioned in the introduction of this book, the importance of American religious influence has gone unnoticed by the leading cultural historians writing on American influences in Europe after the war. Scholars have examined American cultural penetration of Europe through a variety of lenses including music, movies, race, and gender.[40] Religion has been conspicuous by its absence in this discussion. By bringing to light the significance of religion as a key aspect of American cultural influence, and of missionaries as its principal purveyors, this book fills this void, and it widens the historiographic horizons of this field pioneered by cultural historians such as Alexander Stephan, Mary Nolan, Richard Pells, and Jessica Gienow-Hecht.[41]

Anticipating World Christianity: Mission to the Post-Christendom West from ... the West?

The final historiographical map to which the preceding chapters make an important contribution is that of World Christianity. The term *World Christianity* has been widely applied to the results of the twentieth-century shift of Christianity's critical mass from a geographical Christendom defined primarily by the countries of Europe and North America in the northern hemisphere, to the countries of the Global South.[42] The paradigm emerging from this process, as described by Andrew Walls, is not a new, relocated Christendom, with a different set of geopolitical boundaries, but a realization that Christianity is now a global faith connected by a worldwide polycentric network of hubs.[43] With the shift in the numerical preponderance of Christians from the Anglo-European countries that comprised the Christendom of the North to the developing nations of the Global South also came a reassessment of Christian missions. As mentioned in the previous chapter, the Lausanne Congress of 1974 was a milestone among evangelical Protestants in calling for global missionary strategy in which mission flowed from "everywhere to everywhere." Support for such a strategy came from the growing realization that secularism, or pragmatic atheism, was becoming a dominant world view in the cultural gatekeeping institutions of the North.[44]

Scholars who study the flow of missionary traffic in World Christianity have described how the formerly Christian countries of the North – most notably in Western Europe – have now become a mission field in the eyes of churches in the Global South.[45] While this narrative has been helpful in mapping the missionary contours of World Christianity, my research challenges the simplicity of such a narrative by showing that there was another significant source of missionary activity from one region of the North to another, well before Christians from the Global South began their missionary efforts in Europe. Thus it is apparent that the story of religious transformations in the North – both toward secularism and then back toward re-Christianization (not to mention the growing presence of Islam) is more complex than the current historiography suggests. Secularism did not spread uniformly across the North, nor did it rob some regions of the North of an ongoing missionary impulse that now saw other parts of Northern Christendom as a mission field. If anything, this book makes the case for North American Protestants being in the vanguard of the reorientation of missionary priorities within the new geography of World Christianity.

Gerrie ter Haar, Claudia Währisch-Oblau, and other scholars have traced the development of missionary concern among churches of African diaspora communities in Europe, but these activities, at least until quite recently, have been directed at reaching other Africans, not secular Europeans.[46] Such studies have brought to the fore the ongoing issue of racism in Western Europe, particularly its presence in the indigenous Protestant churches in German-speaking regions. However it is now apparent that North American missionary activity worked in the opposite direction: beginning with the intention of reaching native Europeans, and then discovering opportunities among immigrant minority groups from Middle Eastern and African countries. As briefly noted in the previous chapter, this was particularly true of Southern Baptists as they formed church-planting partnerships with local German Baptist congregations.

While the current research has provided an interesting account of missions after Christendom, my research suggests that the current conventional narrative is too simple. The new missionary traffic of the late twentieth century was not merely unidirectional from South to North, but also involved other paths that ran from one northern region to another. This opens up possibilities for further development of this particular narrative in order that a richer story can emerge.

Internal Assessments of the Mission to Germany

As is evident from the preceding chapters, the goals and activity of Protestant missionaries in Germany varied widely during the period from 1945 to 1974. Because of the wide variance in their goals, the criteria by which ecumenical, denominational, and conservative evangelical missionaries evaluated the progress and worth of their endeavours also differed. For all three groups, the mission to Germany involved a large investment in that country, in material and human resources. As voluntary organizations it was important for these mission agencies to inform their supporting donor constituencies about the results and relative success of their work. Consequently, in the midst of their activism, missionaries paused occasionally to take stock of their efforts, assess the value of their work, and assure supporters that their investment was worth it.

For ecumenicals, material aid was intended to help Germans in the spiritual recovery of their people. In November 1945 Robins W. Barstow of the Church World Service summarized the goal of the ecumenical mission by stating that all aspects of material aid were designed to do "everything possible to re-establish the Protestant church as a major factor in the life of the German people. Our program is based upon the conviction that political and ecumenical readjustments are vain unless there be a substantial foundation of moral and spiritual values upon which community life can build securely."[47]

In its coverage of the American ecumenical aid effort, the *Christian Century* offered an essentially positive evaluation of the efforts of the CWS and WCC. Overall the cooperation among American churches, coupled with the wider international reach of the WCC was seen as a triumph of ecumenical missionary cooperation.[48] At the end of 1948, Lutheran theologian E. Theodore Bachmann wrote in praise of the ecumenical spirit evident in the German church on his return from a recent tour of the country. Bachmann reported that ties of goodwill between Germany and the Allied nations were being rebuilt, and that American aid was also facilitating ecumenical cooperation within German Protestantism, allowing Hilfswerk to bridge the long-standing divide between the *Landeskirchen* and the *Freikirchen*. According to Bachmann, Americans could not give too much in order to help out. Every donation given in Jesus's name meant one more ray of hope for the people of Germany.[49]

This early optimism would be tempered by a growing sense of concern during the 1950s and 1960s as the hoped-for spiritual resurgence within the EKD and greater ecumenical cooperation between *Landeskirchen* and *Freikrichen* never really materialized.[50] Thus, while there was disappointment that the ecumenical mission had not seen a widespread spiritual renewal of the nation, there was a consensus among ecumenical supporters and analysts that it had achieved other notable goals, such as putting the Protestant churches in a position of self-help, renewing bonds of international ecumenical fellowship, and motivating German Protestants to participate in the ongoing ecumenical mission of inter-church aid in other needy parts of the globe. For ecumenists these indicators made the mission well worth the investment of material and human resources.[51]

During the immediate postwar crisis, it was relatively easy for Baptists and Mennonites to justify their mission work, not only by showing how material aid was helping to save German lives, but also by holding out a vision of hope for a spiritual revival to come to Germany as a result of the work. In 1947 Cornelius Dyck, one of the Mennonite Central Committee's relief coordinators, saw the work of his mission as bringing hope to Germany, and the possibility that "out of the fires of tribulation there may arise a new and glorious Church, a purer and nobler community of Christian witnesses, [and] perhaps ... another Luther, who ... may point out a new and brighter road – with Christ – to Germany and the world."[52] His Southern Baptist counterpart, Jesse Franks, echoed Dyck when evaluating the contribution of his fellow citizens to European relief and reconstruction. Not only had material needs been met, "a spiritual contribution [also] has been made of rich and vital significance, which will continue to bear fruit in the years ahead for the glory of Christ and his Gospel."[53] While circumspect in their language, both Dyck and Franks were implying that a key criterion for measuring the success of their respective mission works was the degree to which spiritual renewal in Germany translated into the adoption and furtherance of Anabaptist types of church life.

Once the immediate crisis of postwar recovery had passed, and the expectations of widespread spiritual renewal had been tempered by the return of material prosperity and rising secularism, denominational missionaries settled for more modest goals. Given their belief in a *Freikirchliche* vision of Christianity as the key to spiritual renewal in Germany, it is no accident that Mennonites and Southern Baptists established educational institutions to train church leaders as part of their missionary mandate. For both the MCC and Southern Baptists it meant changing their roles: moving from being benevolent benefactors to becoming partners in education. By making this shift, North American Mennonites and Southern Baptists saw themselves as fortifying the ongoing work and witness of these relatively tiny minority congregations who faced a two-fold challenge: first, offering an alternative ecclesial expression of Christian community praxis to the established-church model; and second, seeking to win over an increasingly secular society to their respective visions of Christianity.[54] Both mission agencies used their respective print media to inform their supporting constituencies of the value of their schools to their denominational kindred in German-speaking Europe.[55] Even though theological education may not have had the same kind of dramatic impact as the reconstruction work of the early postwar period, Mennonites and Southern Baptists continued to support this new phase of the work through financial contributions and missionary personnel.[56]

Conservative evangelical mission agencies lacked the ecumenical ideals and metrics of the WCC, and the ecclesial networks and solidarity of denominational mission groups. Instead, they operated as religious entrepreneurs and relied more on consumer feedback mechanisms associated with market economies to measure the relative value of their work. In its starkest reduction, such a market philosophy of religion held that North American missionaries were delivering a Christian product for which there was demand by German religious consumers.[57] Thus if missionaries could maintain the investor confidence of their financial supporters at home, and if German church leaders were willing to invite these missionaries to work their communities, then the mission could be considered successful. Most conservative evangelical missionaries would have been shocked by the use of such language to describe what for them was a sacred calling. Yet it helps explain the use of crusade statistics in missionary newsletters, and the frequent testimonials from German pastors and lay leaders who participated in the evangelistic rallies. For conservative evangelical missionaries and their supporters, such data, in the context of a shared understanding of Christian activism and Providential leading, helped confirm their missionary calling and demonstrate the value of their work to North American and German supporters alike.[58] Even if the results were not always as tangible and dramatic as hoped for, in the eyes of their supporters at home and in Germany, mission agencies

demonstrated that the investment of finances and personnel was producing a valuable return. For conservative evangelicals the cost of striving to
save Germany was worth it.

An Academic Assessment of the Mission to Germany

For the academic historian a more measured evaluation of the mission
to Germany from a vantage point outside the missionary community is
considerably more difficult to achieve. Nevertheless at least three things
can be said about the work of North American missionaries in Germany
that make their mission worthy of serious academic attention.[59] First, on
a humanitarian level, the great outpouring of aid by Protestant relief organizations saved countless German civilian lives and helped ameliorate
the negative image of the German people to the point where they too were
now seen as victims of the war. The postwar humanitarian effort was initially focused on Germany, but this crisis saw the establishment or reacti-
vation of a number of Protestant relief agencies that soon became global
and increasingly prominent in patterns of global religious philanthropy.
They continue to carry out humanitarian aid around the world and have
played an important role in reshaping the contours of Christian internationalism. The Church World Service, the WCC Department of Inter-
church Aid, the Mennonite Central Committee, Lutheran World Relief,
and Baptist World Aid were all constituted as permanent relief agencies
as a result of their participation in German reconstruction, thus making
humanitarian aid – and increasingly development – a staple of Protestant
internationalism around the globe.

Second, both the humanitarian and evangelistic endeavours of North
American Protestants were important in establishing or re-establishing
ties with significant sections of German Protestantism, letting Germans
know that they were not alone or doomed to indefinite isolation for the
stigma of Nazism's war-time atrocities. Even if missionary efforts to promote democracy proved naïve or clumsily heavy-handed at times, their
desire to promote democratic freedom as the best available road to postwar recovery was in harmony with the aspirations of most Germans. A
divided Germany proved to be an interesting ideological laboratory, and,
as Billy Graham rightly understood when making Berlin a strategic crusade venue, almost all the emigration traffic between the two Germanys
flowed from the Communist East to the democratic West *because* of

ideology. Protestant Christianity thus played an important part in reconnecting Germany to the Western world.

Finally, most missionaries ended up in Germany because the organizations they represented had been invited there by the Germans themselves. They did not come as interlopers or postwar profiteers, nor were they part of the Allied military occupation forces. Mostly they drew on altruistic motivations when responding to requests to help their former enemies. This does not mean that they were always cross-culturally adept or virtuous in their conduct when they came, or that they were the best stewards of the resources at their disposal. However, it is important to point out that, having set aside the relative prosperity and security of living in their native culture, they came as a response to a call for help. Such willingness, as EKD Bishop Dibelius reminded Berliners about Billy Graham, exemplified the heart of the Christian witness found in Jesus's parable of the Good Samaritan. In coming to Germany in her time of need, missionaries, for all their shortcomings, were seeking to live in a manner consistent with the message they professed.

NOTES

Introduction

1 Keller was a Swiss minister who had directed an inter-church aid program initiated by the Federal Council of Churches during the 1920s. He went on to head up the Ecumenical Committee for Refugees from 1939 to 1941. Even though it did not play a central role in relief work, it did cooperate with active Protestant relief agencies during this period. Genizi, *American Apathy*, 256. Although the WCC was not officially founded until 1948, the Utrecht Conference of 1938 produced a Provisional Committee that was responsible for carrying on the work of "The World Council of Churches – in Process of Formation." Visser't Hooft, *The First Assembly*, 14. Keller served as a consultant for the Provisional Committee. See Visser't Hooft, *Memoirs*, 91, 128; and *The Ten Formative Years*, 78.

2 Keller was invited by the FCC to participate in the National Preaching Mission. This was a program organized by the Federal Council of Churches to stimulate a stronger Christian witness in American communities. Keller was one of eighty clergy and lay preachers who participated in the mission. The mission itself was a series of conferences held in twenty-five of the largest cities in the United States between September and Christmas 1936. See Cavert, *American Churches*, 129, 154.

3 Keller, *Christian Europe Today*, 225.

4 Ibid., 225–6.

5 Ibid., 228.

6 Railton, *No North Sea*, 137–68.

7 For evidence of this among Protestants committed to the ecumenical movement, see Stanley, *World Missionary Conference*, 281–302; and Hutchison, *Errand to the World*, 130–1. For a Canadian perspective, see Wright, *World*

Mission, 23–4. For transatlantic links between conservative evangelicals, see Fiedler, *Story of Faith Missions*, 224–5.

8   The original intent was to cover the entire Cold War period up to the fall of the Berlin Wall in 1989, but in addition to the reasons enumerated above, the paucity of sources and records detailing the work of Protestant mission organizations during the 1980s was an additional factor to find a suitable alternative.

9   Sanneh, *Disciples of All Nations*, xx.

10 Douglas, *Let the Earth Hear His Voice*, 6.

11 See Genizi, *America's Fair Share*, 37–63. For a wider contextual study of refugee emigration from Germany, see Proudfoot, *European Refugees*; and Marrus, *Unwanted*. See also Gimbel, *German Community*, 37–44; see also his broader treatment of the AMG, *American Occupation*; and Davidson, *Death and Life of Germany*, 308–10. Accounts focused specifically on humanitarian relief work include Woodbridge, UNRAA; Egan and Reiss, *Transfigured Night*; Reiss, *American Council of Voluntary Agencies*; Lissner, *Politics of Altruism*; Zink, *United States*; Ziemke, "Formulation"; Schwartz, *America's Germany*; Tent, *Mission on the Rhine*; and Speier, *Ashes of Disgrace*. For an anecdotal but highly insightful account of both spiritual needs and the ambivalent response of American soldiers as they encountered these among the German civilian populace, see Sandifer, *Binding Up*.

12 McSweeney, *Amerikanische Wohlfartshilfe*. See also Sommer, *Humanitäre Auslandshilfe*; and Stüber, *Der Kampf*.

13 See Pells, *Not Like Us*; Stephan, *Americanization and Anti-Americanism*; and Nolan, "Anti-Americanism." Other valuable cultural analyses of the American presence in postwar Germany include Browder, *Americans in Post–World War II Germany*; Goedde, GIs and Germans; Ninkovich, *Germany and the United States*; Willet, *Americanization of Germany*; and Wilson, "American Religious Sects." For politically focused treatments, see Mai, "Germany and the Integration of Europe"; and Rupieper, "American Policy."

14 Albaugh, *Who Shall Separate Us?*; and Pierard, "Baptist World Alliance Relief"; also Patterson and Pierard, "Recovery from the War."

15 On the work of the Mennonite Central Committee (MCC), see Unruh, *In the Name of Christ*; and Redekop, *Pax Story*. Beyond these histories, a couple of notable memoirs of MCC staff members who worked in Germany are Kreider and Goossen, *Hungry, Thirsty*; and Kreider, *My Early Years*. See also Dyck, *Up from the Rubble*. On the LWF, see Solberg, *As between Brothers*; Solberg, *Open Doors*; and Bachman, *Together in Hope*. On the history of Quaker relief work in Germany, see Wilson, *Quaker Relief*; Welty, *Hunger Year*; and Pickett, *For More Than Bread*. On the relief efforts of the World Council of Churches, see three works by Visser't Hooft, *First Assembly*, 95–7, 167–72; *Ten Formative Years*, 32–49; and *Memoirs*, 175–6, 187–8, 215. For a brief celebratory account of WCC aid to Germany, see Thimme, "Receiving Church," 12–29.

16 Hutchison, *Errand to the World*; and Hutchison, "Americans in World Mission"; Wacker, "Plural World."

17 In contrast to the development of the mainline understanding of mission, evangelical missions continued to be firmly rooted in a nineteenth-century theological tradition with strong ties to pre-millennial eschatology. For background on the theological roots for evangelical missionary zeal, see Weber, *Living in the Shadow*; Stanley, "Future in the Past"; and Robert, "'Crisis of Missions"; and also Carpenter, "Propagating the Faith."

18 Typical examples would be accounts of evangelistic work conducted by Youth for Christ, Billy Graham, and Janz Team Ministries. See Pollock, *Billy Graham, Authorized Biography*; Martin, *Prophet with Honor*. On the work of Youth for Christ, see Larson, *Youth for Christ*. Some other popular accounts of a mission work written by a missionary leader include Freed, *Trans World Radio*.

19 McAlister, *Europe*; and Thiesen, *Survey of World Missions*. More critically reflective accounts of Protestant mission work in Europe include Evans, *Let Europe Hear*; Detzler, *Changing Church in Europe*; Wagner, *North American Protestant Missionaries*; Henley, *Europe at the Crossroads*; and Moennich, *Europe behind the Iron Curtain*.

One exception to the above is Koop, *American Evangelical Missionaries*, which looks specifically at one country, but, as the title implies, examines only the work of evangelical Protestant missionaries.

20 Robert, "First Globalization," 52–8; Hutchison, "Americans in World Mission," 158–9; and Anderson, "American Protestants," 106–8. For the development of this rift among Canadian Protestants, see Wright, *World Mission*, 142–77.

21 While images of the death camps caused many North Americans to see Nazism as uncivilized barbarism, the mass displacement caused by the Allied Potsdam Agreement very quickly turned the German population as a whole into victims, thus separating them, in the minds of many North American mainline Protestants, from Nazi barbarism. For evidence of this perspective, see articles from the leading media voice of US mainline Protestantism, *Christian Century* (CC hereafter): "Germany's Regeneration" CC 62 (13 June 1945), 702–3; "What Is Mass Starvation?" CC 62 (26 December 1945), 1439–40; and Elizabeth Gray Vining, "If Thine Enemy Hunger" CC 64 (27 February 1947), 268–270.

22 *Wirtschaftswunder* refers to the "economic miracle" of West Germany's rapid rebuilding and economic recovery during the 1950s.

23 Silk, *Spiritual Politics*; Herzog, *Spiritual-Industrial Complex*; Jewett and Lawrence, *Captain America*. See also Boyer, *By the Bomb's Early Light*; and Boyer, *When Time Shall Be No More*.

24 Mead, *Special Providence*; and McDougall, *Promised Land, Crusader State*. See also Toulouse, *Transformation of John Foster Dulles*. For more on Dulles's

Christian vision expressed in his foreign policies in opposing Communism in Europe, see Dulles, *War or Peace*; and Dulles, *One Germany or Two*.

25 Schäfer, "'What Marx, Lenin and Stalin Needed'"; and Preston, "Death of a Peculiar Special Relationship."

26 Besier, "Protestantismus"; and Jarausch, *After Hitler*, 19–129.

27 Toulouse, *Transformation of John Foster Dulles*, 195–203.

28 Jewitt and Lawrence, *Captain America*, 90–1. See also Dulles, *War or Peace*. For more thorough studies of the religious nature of Dulles's foreign policy toward West Germany, see Dulles, *One Germany or Two*; and Felken, *Dulles und Deutschland*.

29 The *Christian Century* ran a number of articles that portrayed various socialist experiments in western democracies in a positive light, thus showing that socialism was not incompatible with democratic freedom. For examples, see "Britain: Socialist and Free," CC 65 (15 September 1948), 938–40; and "Socialism No Longer a Bugaboo," CC 60 (18 August 1943), 931–2.

30 While this book emphasizes the role of ecumenical Protestants in promoting democracy in West Germany, Andrew Preston has shown how the American ecumenical Protestant internationalism produced a simultaneous critique of the increasingly confrontational foreign policy of the US government toward Soviet Communism. See Preston, *Sword of the Spirit*, 440–95. See also Inboden, *Religion and American Foreign Policy*, 29–104.

31 See Schwarz, *You Can Trust*. The book went through ten printings in the first two years after its initial publication and was endorsed by such high-profile conservative evangelical leaders such as Bob Pierce, founder of World Vision.

32 There are no ready one-to-one English equivalents for these ecclesial terms, but the sense of each could be translated as follows: *Landeskirche* – state church, or established church within each German province or region (*Land*); *Volkskirche* – the people's church or church of the nation; *Evangelisch* is the German equivalent of *Protestant*, however the EKD is the specific title given to the official federation of all the regional state churches.

33 For examples of the first theme, see Hockenos, *Church Divided*, 75–80; Knappen, *And Call It Peace*, 101. See also Scheerer, *Kirchen für den Kalten Krieg*; Helmreich, *German Churches under Hitler*, 413–33. See also Spotts, *Churches and Politics*. Ruh's *Religion und Kirche* is less a history, as it is an overview of how the EKD is organized and how it functions in its federal responsibilities as well as regional ones.

On the second theme, see Boyens, "Die Kirchenpolitik." Boyens argues that the misjudgments of the Education and Religion Branch of the AMG were the main cause of negative relations between German church leaders and the Allied occupiers.

On the third theme of war guilt and anti-Semitism, see Lammersdorf, "Question of Guilt"; Foschepoth, "German Reaction." On this same theme, see Boyens, "Das Stuttgarter Schuldbekenntnis." For treatment by American historians, see Herman, *Rebirth of the German Church*; Barnett, *For the Soul of the People*; and Hockenos, *Church Divided*.

34 The *Freikirchen*, in contrast to the *Landeskirchen*, exist as independent churches with no financial support from the state. They include denominations such as Baptists, Mennonites, Pentecostals, and the Salvation Army. For a complete list of the churches officially recognized under the *Freikirchen* umbrella, see Vereinigung Evangelischer Freikirchen, http://www.vef.de/wer-wir-sind/. For a survey of the most prominent *Freikirchen* denominations, see Geldbach, *Freikirchen*. For a historical overview of the *Freikirchen*, see Voigt, *Freikirchen in Deutschland*.

35 Railton, "German Free Churches," 85–8, 94.

36 Geldbach, "'Evangelisch,' 'Evangelikal.'"

37 Ohlemacher, "Gemeinschaftschristentum," 371–92; Jung, *Die deutsche Evangelikale Bewegung*; Jung, "American Evangelicals"; and Jung, *Was ist Evangelikal?*; Laubach, *Aufbruch der Evangelikalen*; and Holthaus, *Fundamentalismus in Deutschland*. For a more descriptive survey of the *Evangelikaler* movement, see Holthaus, *Die Evangelikalen*. For a treatment of the evangelical movement specifically within the state churches, see Scheerer, *Bekennende Christen*.

38 Kerkofs, "How Religious Is Europe?"; McLeod, *Religion and the People*, 132–54; Brown, *Death of Christian Britain*; and also Davie, *Religion in Britain*. For a missiologist's perspective, see Kuzmic, "Europe." A good overview of the scholarly arguments for European religious decline in the face of advancing secularization can found in Cox, "Master Narratives." On the decline of institutional Christianity and changing moral attitudes specifically in Germany, see Hölscher, "Semantic Structures"; and Herzog, "Sexual Morality."

39 For some examples, see Evans, *Let Europe Hear*, 15–45; Shank, "Missionary Approach"; and Detzler, *Changing Church*.

40 Carpenter, *Revive Us Again*, 161–81; and Pierard, "Pax Americana," 155–79.

41 Visser't Hooft. "Evangelism among Europe's Neopagans"; and Davie, *Europe*.

42 Jenkins, *God's Continent*, 55–102.

43 ter Haar, *African Christians*; and Gerloff, "Religion, Culture and Resistance."

44 Adogame, "African Christians."

45 Carver, *Course of Christian Missions*, 278–85; and Clark and Clark, *Gospel in Latin Lands*, 1–169.

46 See Nazir-Ali, *From Everywhere to Everywhere*.

47 I am indebted to Andrew Preston for pointing me in this direction.

48 Tyrrell, "American Exceptionalism," 1050.

49 Iriye, "Culture and Power," 116, 118, 126–8. For more detailed discussion of the nature and methodologies of transnational history that distinguish it from other subfields such as global history and international history, see Bayley et al., "AHR Conversation"; Iriye, "Transnational Turn"; and Seigel,

"Beyond Compare," 62–3. For a more comprehensive overview of the field, see Iriye and Saunier, *Palgrave Dictionary*.

50 The academic literature examining the nature of US cultural influence in Europe is considerable, and while all sorts of cultural categories are used as means of analyzing and assessing the extent and significance of American cultural influence, religion is conspicuous by its absence. Given the extensive writings on the religious nature of American foreign policy during the twentieth century, and the prominent role of religion in civic and private life in America during this century, it seems all the more incongruous that this remains largely a non-category when the impact of American cultural influence abroad is examined. For treatments on American cultural exports, see the essays in Stephan, *Americanization of Europe*; Ramet and Cmkovic, *Kazzm! Splat! Ploof!*; Pells, *Not Like Us*; Markovits, *Uncouth Nation*. For studies that focus specifically on Germany, see Stephan, *Americanism and Anti-Americanism*; Goedda, GIs *and Germans*. For a German perspective, see Doering-Manteuffel, *Wie westlich sind did Deutschen?* Related works include Wagnleitner, *Coca-colonisation*; and Poiger, *Jazz, Rock, and Rebels*.

51 For Canadian contributions to Baptist World Alliance relief efforts leading up to the Second World War, see Wright, *World Mission*, 75–106.

52 For more on Canadian Lutheran World Relief participation in partnering with the World Council of Churches in relief efforts in Germany, see Canadian Lutheran World Relief Collection, MG 28-V 120, Library and Archives Canada, Ottawa.

53 I am indebted to both John Briggs and Andrew Preston for suggesting the term *conservative evangelical*, as it is a clearer and more historically nuanced descriptor than either *fundamentalist* or simply *evangelical*.

54 Three archival collections comprise the majority of the primary source material on the ecumenical mission. The documents of the RAS are housed in the US National Archives as part of the AMG's official records from governing postwar Germany. Combined with Marshall Knappen's memoirs as the first head of the RAS, these sources reveal the plans, policies, and responsibilities carried out by the churchmen who were RAS officers. The second archival collection is that of the WCC at the WCC headquarters in Geneva, as well as the Yale Divinity School Library. These records give a detailed account of logistical and bureaucratic challenges faced by the WCC when delivering relief supplies to postwar Germany. They also supply extensive statistical data on the distribution of aid, and the cooperative agreements worked out with *Evangelisches Hilfswerk*, the leading German relief agency. The third important collection of primary documents is that of the CWS, housed in the archives of the Presbyterian Historical Society in Philadelphia. These documents provide extensive statistical records of the value of aid shipped to Germany during the first ten years after the war, and reveal the missional and philosophical priorities that shaped CWS policy

and activity in Germany. The *Christian Century*, the chief periodical of the American mainline, will also be used as the representative journalistic voice of American ecumenical Protestantism. Two denominational journals from Canada, the *United Church Observer* (United Church of Canada) and the *Canadian Churchman* (Anglican Church of Canada) will also be used to provide a Canadian ecumenical perspective alongside the American one. What becomes apparent from this comparative approach is that ecumenical Protestants in North America were strongly united in support of the goals and methods of the World Council of Churches' mission to postwar Germany.

55 For the development of this new vision among American ecumenical Protestants, see Hutchison, *Errand to the World*, 146–75; Warren, *Theologians of a New World Order*, 56–116; and Robert, "First Globalization." For developments in Canadian ecumenical Protestantism, see Wright, *World Mission*, 142–77.

56 Four archival collections are the source of most of the primary data. The records of the Baptist World Alliance (BWA) housed in Valley Forge, Pennsylvania, and in Regents Park College, Oxford. They contain data on the efforts of the BWA to mobilize and channel American Baptist relief efforts toward Germany. These records focus mostly on the work at the administrative level, but also provide helpful on-site reports from key BWA personnel in Germany. A third important collection, which documents the work of the Southern Baptist Foreign Mission Board (SBC-FMB), is housed in the Southern Baptist Historical Library in Nashville. These records offer an extensive and detailed picture of SBC-FMB contributions to postwar relief and to the founding and development of the International Baptist Theological Seminary in Switzerland. As such, these documents offer insight into the ongoing mission of Baptists in Germany once relief and reconstruction were no longer needed. The important fourth collection is the records of the MCC in the Mennonite Church-USA archives in Goshen, Indiana. Beyond providing documents pertaining to the executive-level administration of MCC aid to Germany, these records contain a wealth of first-hand observations of MCC relief workers in Germany, as well as extensive records of the Bible school established by the MCC in German-speaking Switzerland in the 1950s.

57 For a brief summary on the origin and character of these mission agencies, see Fiedler, *Story of Faith Missions*, 11–56.

58 Marsden, *Fundamentalism and American Culture*, 141–70, 184–95; and Carpenter, *Revive Us Again*, 13–109.

59 Carpenter, *Revive Us Again*, 124–60. See also Carpenter, "From Fundamentalism"; Marsden, "From Fundamentalism to Evangelicalism"; and Marsden, "Evangelical Denomination"; and Rosell, *Surprising Work*, 127–60, 213–23.

60 Unlike the ecumenical and denominational mission agencies, no formal archive exists for JTM. An assortment of records has been kept by the mission: these include back issues of missions' monthly magazine, scrapbooks of newspaper reports on crusades, and a variety of administrative documents, both in their German and Canadian offices. In order to fill out the material, especially on the early days of JTM's work, I interviewed three missionaries who were part of JTM's early work. One of these interviewees is my father, and as such, situates me as an "insider" when researching and writing on JTM's work. In using the data gleaned from these interviews I have tried to corroborate them with printed sources. Realizing my personal connection to JTM, I have been particularly conscious of the need for objectivity in assessing the work of the mission, while at the same time realizing that researching from an insider position also offers unique insights that a more disinterested approach might overlook.

In 2009 Janz Team Ministries changed its name to TeachBeyond: Transformational Educational Services. For more on the transition of JTM to TeachBeyond, see "History of TeachBeyond," http://teachbeyond.org/site-content/uploads/History-of-TeachBeyond-2014-12-02.pdf.

The records of YFC's mission to Germany are found in the Billy Graham Center Archives (BGCA) in Wheaton, Illinois. These records focus mostly on the early postwar period, particularly the activity of its leader, Torrey Johnson. Even though later records are slightly less consistent, there are sufficient data to trace the evolution of YFC's work in Germany in the 1970s.

61 Other conservative evangelical independent missions active in Germany during this period were Greater Europe Mission and Trans World Radio. Both of these missions were also, in part, influenced by YFC to begin working in Germany. Unfortunately the records of the former were incomplete, and the German branch of the latter, the Evangeliums Rundfunk Deutschland, was unwilling to make its archival records available for this project. While access to these records would have proved helpful, YFC and JTM as two representative case studies bring to light the important characteristics and themes of the conservative evangelical mission. For popular historical treatments of these mission agencies, see the following: for Greater Europe Mission, see Campbell, *Light for the Night*; for Trans World Radio, see Freed, *Towers*; and for Evangeliums Rundfunk Deutschland, see Lutzenberger, *Gottes Wort*, and Marquardt, *Meine Geschichte*.

62 The Billy Graham Evangelistic Association (BGEA) has been conscious of preserving Graham's legacy right from the start, and its extensive and detailed records in the BGCA offer great insight as to how Graham was received by the German public. Alongside that, the records of Graham's German crusades held by the Deutsche Evangelische Allianz in Bad Blankenburg, Saxony, reveal how German church leaders worked alongside the BGEA and how they assessed the impact of Graham on German church life.

63 Pierard, "Billy Graham and the Wende," 5.

Chapter One

1 Hans Lilje, an open letter to churches outside Germany included in *The State of the German Churches*, Brussels, September 1945, folder "Clippings, 1945," box "Foreign Service 1945, Germany, Collection: Post WWII Reconstruction Europe, Asia and Africa," Archives of the American Friends Service Committee, Philadelphia, Pennsylvania; also Egan and Elizabeth Reiss, *Transfigured*, 37.

2 Elizabeth Grey Vining, "If Thine Enemy Hunger," *Christian Century* (CC hereafter) 63 (27 February 1946): 268.

3 E. Theodore Bachman, "Wilderness of Want," CC 64 (3 December 1947): 1482.

4 Thimme, "Receiving Church," 17.

5 Solberg, *Between Brothers*, 35.

6 Ninkovich, *Germany and the United States*, 41.

7 Newman, *Three Germanies*, 64–5; and Marrus, *Unwanted*, 327.

8 Marrus, *Unwanted*, 325.

9 Alexander Boeker, "The Atrocity of Mass Expulsions," CC 64 (9 April 1947): 462.

10 Marrus, *Unwanted*, 326. Quotation taken from United Nations, Official Records, Plenary Meetings of the General Assembly, First Session (15 January 1946), part I, p. 424.

11 Clay, *Decision in Germany*, 313; Marrus, *Unwanted*, 330.

12 Newman, *Three Germanies*, 65.

13 Churchill quoted in Marrus, *Unwanted*, 327.

14 "What Is Mass Starvation?" CC 62 (26 December 1945): 1439.

15 Hertha Kraus, "What Germany Needs Most," CC 62 (18 December 1946): 1553–4.

16 Samuel McCrea Cavert, "What Hope for Germany?" CC 63 (23 October 1946): 1274.

17 For more on the formation of the FCC and its member churches, see Schneider, "Voice of Many Waters"; Marty, *Righteous Empire*, 183–4; Hutchison, *Modernist Impulse*, 174–84; and Sandford, *Origin and History*. The World Council of Churches was not officially constituted until the Amsterdam Conference in 1948 but had been in the "process of formation" since 1937. With this acknowledgment and for the sake of economy, I have chosen not to use the official pre-1948 title of the "WCC – in process of formation," when discussing the operations of the WCC prior to the Amsterdam Conference. I will use the less cumbersome term WCC when referring to both the pre- and post-1948 activities of the World Council of Churches.

18 Hutchison, "Protestantism as Establishment," 4.

19 Bachman, *Together in Hope*, 14–15; and Solberg, *Between Brothers*, 40–4.
20 Solberg, *Between Brothers*, 42–3; and Herr and Riegel, "Stewart W. Herman Jr."
21 Visser't Hooft, *Memoirs*, 175, 190.
22 "Germany's Regeneration," CC 62 (13 June 1945): 703.
23 Cecil Northcott, "The Treatment of Germany," CC 62 (14 February 1945): 205. On the issue of the CC as the representative voice of American Protestant mainline churches, see Coffman, "Long Ride on the Mainline," 22; and Marty, "Peace and Pluralism." That American conservative evangelicals also perceived the CC as the national voice of the mainline can be found in Rosell, *Surprising Work of God*, 208.
24 "Germany's Regeneration," CC 62 (13 July 1945): 703.
25 Hutchison, *Errand to the World*, 158–75.
26 Robert, "First Globalization," 54–8.
27 For more on the United Church of Canada and its place in Canadian church life during the early postwar decades, and its role in developing a new Protestant internationalism during the interwar period, see Airhart, *Church with the Soul*, 126–53; and Wright, *World Mission*, 142–77.
28 Knappen, *Call It Peace*, back cover. The Religious Affairs Section was itself a subdivision of the Department of Religious and Educational Affairs.
29 Ibid., 49; and McClaskey, *History of US Policy*, 16–17.
30 Knappen, *Call It Peace*, 19.
31 Marrus, *Unwanted*, 329–30. On the issue of DPs as potential sources of political radicalism, see Buscher, "'Great Fear,'" 206–11.
32 "Report on the U.S. Occupation of Germany (Religious Affairs Program) 23 September, 1947," file "Church Reputation," box 942, record group 260 (RG 260), United States National Archives (USNA), College Park, Maryland; and Spotts, *Churches*, 51–4, 76.
33 Knappen, *Call It Peace*, 112.
34 McClaskey, *History*, 17. The Religious Affairs Section was itself a subdivision of the Department of Religious and Educational Affairs.
35 Spotts, *Churches*, 59, 75, 79; McClaskey, *History*, 18; and Knappen, *Call It Peace*, 48–9.
36 McClaskey, *History*, 19–20, 32. Out of a total staff of fourteen, eight ranking officers were stationed at headquarters as an administrative section, and six additional professionals served as field officers.
37 McClaskey, *History*, 17.
38 Knappen, *Call It Peace*, 136.
39 Clay, *Decision in Germany*, 281.
40 "Memo from Military Government Office in Würzburg to Director of the Military Government for Bavaria, 17 October, 1945," file 45, box 55, RG 260: OMGUS—Bavaria, Records of the Educational and Cultural Affairs Division: Religious Affairs Branch, 1946–49, USNA.

41 Knappen, *Call It Peace*, 49, 135–6. For more on the unpopularity and failure of the AMG's denazification program among German clergy, see Hockenos, *Church Divided*, 7; Herman, *It's Your Souls We Want*, 121; Ninkovich, *Germany and the United States*, 46; Stolper, *German Realities*, 56; Barnett, *For the Soul of the People*, 224.

42 McClaskey, *History*, 27n79.

43 "Summary of FY-1949 Program of the Religious Affairs Branch, Educational and Cultural Division," 21, file 9, box 204, RG 260, OMGUS, Records of the Evangelical Affairs Sections, USNA.

44 McClaskey, *History*, 28; and "Summary of FY-1949 Program of the Religious Affairs Branch, Educational and Cultural Division," 14.

45 McClaskey, *History*, 71–2.

46 "Summary of FY-1949 Program of the Religious Affairs Branch, Educational and Cultural Division," 19.

47 Knappen, *Call It Peace*, 101.

48 Ibid., 48.

49 The English title is Working Federation of Christian Churches in Germany. McClaskey, *History*, 77; and "Semi-annual Report, Religious Affairs Branch, 1 July–31 December 1949," folder 3A, box 8, RG 260, OMGUS, Records of the Evangelical Affairs Sections, USNA, 10.

50 "Summary of FY-1949 program of the Religious Affairs Branch, Educational and Cultural Division."

51 "Semi-annual Report, Religious Affairs Branch 1 July–31 December 1949," 2.

52 Ibid., 3–4, 8; and "Progress Report for February 1949," 1, file 4A, box 10, RG 260, OMGUS, General Records of the Research and Planning Section, USNA.

53 "Semi-annual Report, Religious Affairs Branch 1 July–31 December 1949," 2.

54 "Summary of FY-1949 Program of the Religious Affairs Branch, Educational and Cultural Division," 16.

55 Knappen, *Call It Peace*, 104.

56 For more on the fundamentalist/modernist disputes in the major American denominations during the 1920s, see Marsden, *Fundamentalism and American Culture*, 164–84.

57 Knappen, *Call It Peace*, 104–5. The finalized constitution for the EKD was not in place until June 1948, when it was ratified at the Eisenach conference, but its initial framework was already in place at Treysa. See Helmrich, *German Churches*, 419–22.

58 "Report on the U.S. Occupation of Germany, 23 September, 1947, Religious Affairs Program," 7, 10, 15, file "Church Liaison Representatives," box 942, RG 260, OMGUS, Baden-Württemberg, Records of the Educational and Cultural Relations Division, Religious Affairs Branch Chief, Memos and Reports, 1945–49, USNA.

59 "Report on the U.S. Occupation of Germany, 23 September, 1947, Religious Affairs Program," 9–10. Youth were defined as all young people ages ten to eighteen; and "Semi-annual Report, Religious Affairs Branch 1 July–31 December 1949," 3–4, 8; and "Progress Report for February 1949," 52–5.

60 Genizi, "Problems of Protestant Cooperation," 165; Egan and Reiss, *Transfigured Night*, 94; "Minutes of the Department of Church World Service Executive Committee, 19 December, 1952," file "Executive Committee, 1952," box 82, RG 8, Presbyterian Historical Society, Philadelphia (NCC-CWS, PHS hereafter).

61 Solberg, *Between Brothers*, 41.

62 "German Churches in the Crucible," CC 63 (6 February 1946): 174; and "For a Democratic Offensive," CC 64 (12 February 1947): 200.

63 "What Germany Needs Most," CC 63 (18 December 1946): 1534.

64 "Christian Prescription for Germany Today," *United Church Observer* (UCO hereafter) 11 (15 May 1949): 5, 24.

65 "Churches behind the Iron Curtain," UCO, 11 (15 March 1949): 5, 28; "Turning Points in History," *Canadian Churchman* (CCM hereafter) 75 (16 September 1948): 5, 11; "What about Communism?," CC 76 (20 January 1949): 21, 23; and "A World Mission, Christianity or Communism," CCM 77 (20 April 1950): 126.

66 An exception can be made for the American Friends Service Committee, whose leader, Clarence Pickett, had close connections with Presidents Roosevelt and Truman. For more on Pickett, see Miller, *Witness for Humanity*, 129–46, 233–5. American churchmen from the mainline denominations had a long history of public service in high government offices. During the early postwar period the convergence of ecumenical Protestant theology and American foreign policy found its strongest expression when John Foster Dulles, a Presbyterian churchman, helped draft the Preamble to the United Nations Charter, and then served as secretary of state under President Eisenhower in the 1950s. For more on Dulles and the influence of mainline Protestantism in American foreign policy, see Toulouse, *Transformation of John Foster Dulles*, 198–207; Mead, *Special Providence*, 139–62; Silk, *Spiritual Politics*, 94–5; Jewett and Lawrence, *Captain America*, 75–8; and Dulles, *War or Peace*, 17–21, 79.

67 "What Is Mass Starvation?," CC 62 (26 December 1945): 1440–1.

68 Fry to Herman, quoted in Bachman, *Together in Hope*, 23–4.

69 "Washington Bars Relief Anywhere in Germany," CC 63 (30 January 1946): 131–2.

70 Solberg, *Between Brothers*, 36–7.

71 "Germany's Regeneration," CC 62 (13 June 1945): 702–3; and "What Is Mass Starvation?," 1440. For a wider context of American impressions of the German people by the end of the war, see Hönicke, "'Know Your Enemy.'"

72 Bachman, *Together in Hope*, 25.

73 Solberg, *Between Brothers*, 36. The index of the *Christian Century* for this period reveals that the weekly periodical ran over one hundred articles relating to socio-political and religious issues in Germany.

74 For a good example of this contrast from the early postwar period, see Max Rheinstein, "The Ghost of the Morgenthau Plan," CC 64 (2 April 1947): 428–30; alongside the following conservative evangelical articles: Douglas A. Clark, "Unconditional Surrender," *Moody Monthly* 46 (November 1945): 125, 161; and "Building the Brave New World," *Evangelical Christian* 40 (January 1946), 5–6. For more on the dominant themes of conservative evangelical periodicals during the Second World War, see Enns, "Sustaining the Faithful."

75 Adolf Keller, "Why They Fear America," CC 65 (18 February 1948): 206–7.

76 "What Is Mass Starvation?," 1440–1; and "For a Democratic Offensive," CC 64 (12 February 1947): 199–201.

77 "Way Opened for Direct Aid to Germany," CC 63 (20 May 1946): 612–13.

78 "The New Directive for Germany," CC 64 (30 July 1947): 915.

79 Visser 't Hooft, *Memoirs*, 173–81.

80 Ibid., 173–4; and Conway, "How Shall the Nations Repent?," 605.

81 Hockenos, *Church Divided*, 16, 43–4, 75–81.

82 "Protestant Thinking in Europe," CC 62 (18 July 1945): 831. For a sampling of more detailed treatments of the Confessing Church and its relationship to the Reich government during the war, see Gerlach, *And the Witnesses Were Silent*; Conway, *Nazi Persecution*; Bergen, *Twisted Cross*; and Prolingheuer, *Der ungekämpfte Kirchenkampf.*

83 Cavert, "What Hope for Germany?," 1276.

84 Other members of the WCC delegation included Visser 't Hooft, Anglican Bishop George Bell, and Methodist leader Gordon Rupp from England, Alphonse Koechlin from Switzerland, Pierre Maury from France, and Hendrik Kraemer from the Netherlands. For a more detailed treatment of the Stuttgart meeting and aftermath, see Conway, "How Shall the Nations Repent?," 622; and Hockenos, *Church Divided*, 75–100. For German perspectives, see Besier and Sauter, *Wie Christen ihre Schuld bekennen*; Boyens, "Das Stuttgarter Schuldbekenntnis"; and Bodenstein, *Ist nur der Besiegte schuldig?*

85 Conway, "How Shall the Nations Repent?," 607. *Gleichschaltung* was the Nazi policy toward the established churches with the purpose of turning these churches into one more organ of the Nazi party itself. For more on the Nazi policy of *Gleichschaltung* and the resistance of the Confessing Church, see Barnett, *For the Soul*, 30–3, 62, 71–2.

86 Conway, "How Shall the Nations Repent?," 605.

87 Visser 't Hooft, *Memoirs*, 191.

88 Hockenos, *Church Divided*, appendix 4, 187. Original text reads:
Mit grossem Schmerz sagen wir: Durch uns ist unendliches Leid über viele Völker und Länder gebracht worden. Was wir unseren

Gemeinden oft bezeugt haben, das sprechen wir jetzt im Namen der ganzen Kirche aus: Wohl haben wir lange Jahre hindurch im Namen Jesu Christi gegen den Geist gekämpft, der im nationalsozialistischen Gewaltregiment seinen furchtbaren Ausdruck gefunden hat; aber wir klagen uns an, dass wir nicht mutiger bekannt, nich treurer gebetet, nicht fröhlicher geglaubt und nicht brennender geliebt haben. *Die Stuttgarter Schulderklärung*, official website of the Evangelische Kirche in Deutschland, http://www.ekd.de/glauben/bekenntnisse/stuttgarter_schulderklaerung.html.

89 Samuel McCrea Cavert, "The New Birth of the German Church," CC 63 (23 October 1946): 1380–1.

90 A similarly favourable perspective was evident among Canadian ecumenists. See "German Protestantism Reverses Former Policy," UCO 7 (1 October 1945): 19.

91 Wilhelm Mann, "German Hopes for Amsterdam," CC 65 (7 April 1948): 310.

92 "Germans at Amsterdam," CC 65 (20 October 1948): 1101–2.

93 JCS 1067, vol. 8, *Occupation and the Emergence of Two States, 1945–1967*, German History in Documents and Images, http://www.germanhistorydocs.ghi-dc.org/docpage.cfm?docpage_id=2966.

94 Ibid.; and Solberg, *Between Brothers*, 28.

95 Kreider and Goosen, *Hungry, Thirsty, a Stranger*, 72.

96 Theodore Bachman, "Self-help for the German Churches" CC 64 (31 December 1947): 1609.

97 The Innere Mission had been formed in 1948 as an arm of the German *Landeskirchen*, which administered charitable aid and promoted spiritual renewal. For a detailed discussion on the relationship of *Evangelisches Hilfswerk* to the Innere Mission, see Wischnath, *Kirche in Aktion*.

98 The Roman Catholic equivalent to Evangelisches Hilfswerk in Germany was Caritas.

99 "Herman to Barstow, 1 May, 1946," file "General Correspondence, 1946," box 91, RG 8, NCC-CWS, PHS.

100 Bachman, "Self-help in the German Churches," 1610.

101 E. Theodore Bachman, "Laymen Rouse German Churches," CC 68 (11 July 1951): 818.

102 Walls, "Domestic Importance."

103 Visser 't Hooft, "Reconstruction and Inter-Church Aid in Europe," file "Exploratory Conference on Church Relations with Post-war Europe, 15 May, 1942," box 425.03.082, WCC Records on the Commission of Interchurch Aid, Refugee and World Service, WCCA; and Bachman, *Together in Hope*, 22.

104 "Fact Book on Foreign Relief," file "CWS Predecessor Agencies," box 91, RG 8, NCC-CWS, PHS; "Barstow to the American Council of American Voluntary Agencies, 13 February, 1945," file "Europe Committee," box 91, RG 8, NCC-CWS, PHS; Solberg, *Between Brothers*, 29–36.

105 For German perspectives, see Symanovski, "Missionary Responsibility of the Church in Germany"; and Weckerling, "Germany: A Mission Field." A more internationalist approach was advocated by Keller, the Swiss ecumenist, in *Christian Europe Today*, 231–2. For American perspectives, see Robert Root, "Church Relief: For How Long?," CC 64 (12 March 1947): 334–6; Cavert, "What Hope for Germany?," 1275; and "Robbins W. Barstow Report to the Board of Directors of the Church World Service 14 April 1948," file "Board of Directors January–May 1948," box 82, RG 8, NCC-CWS, PHS.

106 "Report on Germany, 1948," Department of Reconstruction and Inter-Church Aid, folder 4, box 301.43.21, WWII-WCC, WCCA.

107 Bachman, "Wilderness of Want," 1489–90; and Bachman, "Self-help for the German Churches," 1609–10; and Cavert, "What Hope for Germany?," 1274–5. For more on the contribution of Cavert to the ecumenical movement, see Schmidt, *Architect of Unity*.

108 *Drei Jahre Hilfswerk*, promotional booklet published by Evangelisches Hilfswerk (1948), 8. Found in folder 7, box 301.43.14, WWII-WCC, WCCA.

109 American Lutherans sent almost all their aid to Germany under the denominational banner of Lutheran World Relief (LWR), created in 1945 specifically to send aid to Germany. LWR was also thoroughly ecumenical in that it channelled its aid through the WCC and Hilfswerk. See Solberg, *Between Brothers*, 41, 98.

110 McSweeney, *Amerikanische Wohlfartshilfe*, 69–72.

111 Ibid., 72.

112 For a detailed history of CRALOG, see Egan and Reiss, *Transfigured Night*.

113 "Fact Book on Foreign Relief Prepared for Use at the Special Meeting of the Federal Council of Churches of Christ in America, 6–8 March, 1946," file "CWS Predecessor Agencies," box 91, RG 8, NCC-CWS, PHS; and "Memo to General Dwight Eisenhower from the WCC Department of Reconstruction and Inter-Church Aid, 6 November 1945," file "General Correspondence 1945," box 91, RG 8, NCC-CWS, PHS. See also "Report on Germany, 1948."

114 "Announcing a Relief Program of the Churches for Germany through CRALOG," file "CWS Predecessor Agencies," box 91, RG 8, NCC-CWS, PHS.

115 "Germany," report from the Department of Reconstruction and Inter-Church Aid [1947?], folder 9, box 301.43.14, WWII-WCC, WCCA.

116 "Report to the Board of Directors of the CWS by Executive Director, Robbins W. Barstow, 14 April 1948," file "Jan–May, 1948," box 82, RG 8, NCC-CWS, PHS; "Germany" report from the Department of Reconstruction and Inter-Church Aid; "Address for the Church World Service Board of Directors, by Dr Eugen Gerstenmaier," 14 April 1948, folder "January–May 1948," box 82, RG 8, NCC-CWS, PHS.

117 McSweeny, *Amerikanische Wohlfartshilfe*, 73.

118 "Church World Service Treasurer's Report," CWS-B-51C, folder "June–December 1948," box 82, RG 8, NCC-CWS, PHS; and McSweeny, *Amerikanische Wohlfartshilfe*, 70.

119 For examples, see "Aid to Protestant Churches of Europe," UCO 7 (10 February 1945): 31; "Canadian Council of Churches to Increase Aid to Europe," UCO 8 (1 December 1946): 1; and "Am I My Brother's Keeper?," UCO 8 (15 June 1947): 5. For Anglicans, see "Why Anglicans Must Raise $4,300,300," CCM 73 (2 May 1946): 24. The CCM showed a much more parochial orientation in its articles promoting aid for European Christians. Articles on the needs of British clergy and churches far outnumbered those reporting on the needs of churches on the European Continent.

120 "Notkirchen," file 7, box 301.43.14, WWII-WCC, WCCA.

121 "Memo: Approved CWS Projects Voted in January 1948," folder "Europe 1943–1949," box 90, RG 8, NCC-CWS, PHS; "Memo I, Validations by Business Committee of the Reconstruction Department, Geneva, 21–22 January 1947," folder "CWS General 1946," box 91, RG 8, NCC-CWS, PHS; and "Report on Germany, 1948.

122 "Report to the Committee on Cooperation with the Churches in Europe, 14 October, 1949," folder "Board of Directors, 1949," box 82, RB 8, NCC-CWS, PHS.

123 "Report by Roswell P. Barnes to the Committee on Cooperation with the Churches in Europe, 15 June, 1949," box 82, RB 8, NCC-CWS, PHS.

124 "Address for the Church World Service Board of Directors, by Dr Eugen Gerstenmaier," 14 April 1948, folder "January–May 1948," box 82, RG 8, NCC-CWS, PHS. Support for and commendation of Hilfwerk's work in cooperation with the WCC was also echoed by Canadian ecumenical Protestants. See "The Need I Saw in Germany," UCO 11 (15 April 1949): 5; and "The Hour of Destiny for the Churches of Europe," UCO 11 (15 June 1950): 7.

125 "Germany," report from the Department of Reconstruction and Inter-Church Aid.

126 "Exhibit C-2, Minutes of the Executive Committee 21 January 1954," folder "Board of Managers 1954," box 82, RG 8, NCC-CWS, PHS.

127 See "East German Churches Face Grave Trouble," CC 77 (28 September 1960): 1111; and "A Sunday in East Berlin," CC 81 (13 May 1964): 1502–4.

128 For two examples, see Paul Hutchison, "Protestantism in the Crisis of These Times: Part I," CC 74 (13 March 1957): 321–3; and James E. Wagner, "Today's German Church," CC 72 (12 October 1955): 1170–2.

129 Visser 't Hooft, Memoirs, 193.

130 Conway, "How Shall the Nations Repent?," 619.

131 For an example, see The New Delhi Report, 16–17.

132 Conway, "How Shall the Nations Repent?," 620–1; Solberg, Between Brothers, 190; and Murray, "Joint Service as an Instrument of Renewal," 225.

133 "Discussion on the Report on Renewal in Mission," in Goodall, Uppsala Report 1968, 25–7.

134 Newbigin, "Mission to Six Continents," 175.

135 Gaines, World Council of Churches, 528.

136 Newbigin, "Mission to Six Continents," 174.

137 Murray, "Joint Service as an Instrument of Renewal," 199–232.

138 "Protestant World Relief," cc 64 (14 May 1947): 614.

139 The term *Third World* was coined by French economic historian Alfred Sauvy in 1952. He used it to refer to countries not aligned with either the United States or the USSR. See Wolf-Phillips, "Why 'Third World'?," 1311.

Chapter Two

1 The Church of the Brethren in North America is an offshoot of the German Brethren, not the Plymouth Brethren. For an overview of the history of the Church of the Brethren, see Durnbaugh, *Fruit of the Vine*. For a brief history of the American Society of Friends' contribution to postwar recovery in Germany, see von Borries, *Quiet Helpers*.

2 Egan and Reiss, *Transfigured Night*, 25; and McSweeney, *Amerikanische Wohlfartshilfe*, 26.

3 For more on those denominations who belong to this category, see Durnbaugh, *Believers' Church*. Two possible exceptions to the "believers' church" label among the independent denominational missions licensed by CRALOG were the Unitarians and the Salvation Army.

4 While American Quakers made a greater relief contribution to postwar Germany than Baptists, the Quaker mission to Germany, along with those of the Brethren and Salvation Army had largely ended by 1950, while Mennonites and Baptists carried on sustained missionary activity well into the next decades. For a comparison of relief contributions of the various American religious bodies to Germany, see McSweeney, *Amerikanische Wohlfartshilfe*, 69–73; and von Borries, *Quiet Helpers*, 53.

5 For a brief history of early Mennonite communities in Germany, see Fehr and Lichdi, "Mennonites in Germany." For an introduction to the history of the Baptist denomination in Germany, see McBeth, *Baptist Heritage*, 464–98.

6 For a brief overview of the main denominations that make up the *Freikirchen* in Germany, see "Vereinigung Evangelischer Freikirchen," http://www.vef.de/wer-wir-sind/. For historical treatments, see Voigt, *Freikirchen in Deutschland*, 108–81.

7 Space does not allow inclusion of additional ways in which the theme of promoting democracy as mission played out. Other – if perhaps less direct – ways in which these denominational missions wedded Christian mission to democratic political values included setting up refugee emigration programs for Baptists and Mennonites fleeing religious persecution in Eastern Europe, and supporting their denominational kindred who ended up behind the Iron Curtain in the German Democratic Republic.

8 Unruh, *In the Name of Christ*, 16–19.

9   Ibid., 35.

10   For a detailed account of CRALOG's work, see Egan and Reiss, *Transfigured Night*.

11   Ibid., 58.

12   Unruh, *In the Name of Christ*, 150; Robert Kreider to Sam Goering, 29 March 1946, file 67, box 2, Robert Kreider Correspondence, 1946, IX-19-3, Mennonite Central Committee Archives Collection (MCCAC), Archives of the Mennonite Church, USA (AMC), Goshen, Indiana; and Bender, "New Life," 148–9, 167; see also Toews, *History*, 433.

13   Miller to Lehman, quoted in Egan and Reiss, *Transfigured Night*, 59; and Toews, *Mennonites in American Society*, 141–2; and Dyck et al., *Mennonite Central Committee Story*, 2:28–9.

14   Miller to Lehman, quoted in Egan and Reiss, *Transfigured Night*, 59.

15   "Motivation for Relief Work," *European Relief Notes* (ERN hereafter), November 1946, 1; and "From Social Service to Missions," ERN, May 1951, 2–3, both in IX-40-2, MCCAC, AMC.

16   Kreider, *Looking Backwards*, xv. For more on Kreider, see Kreider, *My Early Years*, 71–83.

17   Kreider to Sam Goering, 20 March 1946, file 67, Robert Kreider Correspondence, box 2, IX-19-3, MCCAC, AMC.

18   "Germany," ERN, June 1946, 9, IX-40-2, MCCAC, AMC.

19   Ibid.

20   Ibid. Emphasis in the original.

21   Ibid.

22   Kreider to Goering, 29 March 1946; and letter to friends, 7 April 1946, both in file 67, Robert Kreider Correspondence, box 2, IX-19-3, MCCAC, AMC.

23   Kreider to Goering, 20 March 1946, file 67, Robert Kreider Correspondence, box 2, IX-19-3, MCCAC, AMC.

24   Kreider to Goering, 29 March 1946.

25   Ibid.; and "Germany," ERN, July 1946, 6–7, IX-4-2, MCCAC, AMC.

26   Kreider to Gerstenmaier and Luckowicz, 3 February 1947, file 67, Robert Kreider Correspondence, box 2, IX-19-3, MCCAC, AMC.

27   "Relief Section," MCC *Workbook, 1947*, MCC Annual Reports/Workbooks IX-5-2.1, MCCAC, AMC.

28   Ibid.

29   "Germany," ERN, May 1947, 6–7, IX-40-2, MCCAC, AMC.

30   Ibid.

31   Ibid.

32   Kreider to Gerstenmaier and Luckowicz, 3 February 1947.

33   "Germany," ERN, February 1947, 3–4; and "Germany" ERN, May 1947, 2–3, both in file 3, IX-40-2, MCCAC, AMC.

34   Unruh, *In the Name of Christ*, 151–2; "Relief Section, MCC *Workbook, 1948*, MCC Annual Reports/Workbooks IX-5-2.1, MCCAC, AMC.

35 Letter to Headquarters No. 104, January 1948, file "MCC Headquarters Letters 1945–51," box 1, IX-40-2, MCCAC, AMC.

36 McSweeney, *Amerikanische Wolfahrtshilfe*, 69–70. The MCC's overall contribution to CRALOG that year made up roughly 31 per cent of the total material aid sent to Germany – an astonishing figure in view of the donor base of 200,000 at the most. Where the MCC focused mostly on food aid, LWR, the CWS, and the WRS gave a higher tonnage of clothing supplies. See also Stüber, "Kanadische Deutschlandhilfe," 48.

37 McSweeney, *Amerikanische Wolfahrtshilfe*, 69–70.

38 Ibid., 70–1. McSweeney's statistics show that during the crisis years of 1946–49 the MCC was the fourth-largest contributor of CRALOG relief agencies, behind the CWS, LWR, and WRS. If giving were measured on a per capita basis of denominational membership, the magnitude of MCC aid would be even more remarkable.

39 Another aspect of MCC service in Germany during the early postwar period was sponsoring refugee emigration to Canada and the United States. While this kind of work can be considered an aspect of missionary service, I have chosen to limit my treatment of "mission" to the activities of North Americans directed to people who actually remained resident in the country.

40 Unruh, *In the Name of Christ*, 153–4.

41 Ibid., 153.

42 Ibid., 153–4.

43 "Relief Section," *MCC Annual Workbook, 1948*.

44 Ibid.

45 "A Reality: Heilbronn," ERN, March 1949, 5–6, IX-40-2, MCCAC, AMC.

46 Ibid.

47 Robert Kreider, "Report to the MCC Relief Director's Conference, April 13–15, 1947," file 67, box 2, Robert Kreider Correspondence, 1947, IX-19-3, MCCAC, AMC.

48 "As We See It," ERN, March 1949, 12, IX-40-2, MCCAC, AMC.

49 "A House of Worship …," ERN, March 1949, 10–11, IX-40-2, MCCAC, AMC.

50 "Relief Section," *MCC Annual Workbook, 1949*; and "The Frankfurt Center," ERN, September 1950, 3–4, IX-40-2, both in MCCAC, AMC.

51 The difference between DPs and *refugees* is that the former term was used to describe those who were expelled from their homeland as a result of the Allied agreement reached at the Potsdam Conference, and the latter designates those who fled East Germany of their own volition to escape living under Communist rule. See Newman, *The Three Germanies*, 62.

52 "A Beginning: Kaiserslautern," ERN, March 1949, 4, IX-40-2, MCCAC, AMC.

53 "Relief Report," *MCC Annual Workbook, 1952*; and "Relief Report," *MCC Annual Workbook, 1953*, both IX-5-2.1, MCCAC, AMC.

54 "Working Together with Mennonite Young People of South Germany," ERN, December 1951, 8–9, IX-40-2, MCCAC, AMC.

55 Samuel Gerber, "A Dangerous Venture," translated by Peter J. Dyck, MCC News Service, 12 July 1968, file "European Mennonite Bible School 1965–1974," IX-12-6, MCCAC, AMC.

56 Pannabecker, *Open Doors*, 226–33; Toews, *History*, 323–35; and Kauffman and Driedger, *Mennonite Mosaic*, 47–55.

57 Kauffman and Driedger, *Mennonite Mosaic*, 129–30.

58 Gerber, "Dangerous Venture." See also catalogue of the "Europäische Mennonitische Bibleschule" (EMBS hereafter) for 1950, file "European Mennonite Bible School (EMBS) 1949–1965," box 2, IX-12-4, MCCAC, AMC.

59 "Bible School Minute Record," file "EMBS 1949–65," box 2, IX-12-4, MCCAC, AMC.

60 Catalogue EMBS 1950, and "Bible School Minute Record," both in file "EMBS 1949–65," box 2, IX-12-4, MCCAC, AMC. John Howard Yoder would go on to become one of the most renowned Mennonite scholars, especially in theology and political thought. After teaching at Mennonite colleges in Europe and the United States, Yoder spent the last twenty years of his life as a full-time faculty member of the University of Notre Dame, South Bend, Indiana. For a brief overview of Yoder's life, see Nation, *John Howard Yoder*, 1–29. For Yoder's most influential work, see Yoder, *Politics of Jesus*.

61 Catalogue EMBS 1950, file "EMBS 1949–65," box 2, IX-12-4, MCCAC, AMC.

62 Catalogue EMBS 1955/56, file "EMBS 1949–65," box 2, IX-12-4, MCCAC, AMC.

63 Catalogue EMBS 1957–58, file "EMBS 1949–65," box 2, IX-12-4, MCCAC, AMC. France was a close second with 105 students, but during the most recent three years, German annual enrolments had jumped dramatically from around ten to twenty-nine, while French numbers showed more of a holding pattern at around eighteen students per year.

64 "Flash Glimpses into the European Mennonite Bible School," file "EMBS 1949–65," box 2, IX-12-4, MCCAC, AMC.

65 Gerber, "A Dangerous Venture."

66 Ibid.

67 "Annual Report," MCC *Annual Workbook, 1967*, IX-5-2.1, MCCAC, AMC.

68 Ibid.; and *Schulprospekt EMBS 1969/70*, and *Schulprospekt EMBS 1972/73*, file "EMBS, 1965–74," IX-12-6, MCCAC, AMC.

69 "Bienenberg Says Thanks," MCC News Service, 18 October 1968, file "EMBS 1965–74," IX-12-6, MCCAC, AMC.

70 "Proceedings of Europe Mission Study Conference"; Bienenberg Choir Tour Letter, 23 April 1974, and *Schulprospekt EMBS 1972/73*, both in EMBS 1965–74, IX-12-6, MCCAC, AMC.

71 Railton, "German Free Churches," 88; and Voigt, *Freikirchen in Deutschland*, 31–4.

72 Railton, "German Free Churches," 87.

73 Ibid., 88. For more on Oncken, see Donat, *Wie das Werk begann*; and Balders, *Theuer Bruder Oncken*.

74 Railton, "German Free Churches," 92–4. Statistics taken from "An Open Door" in *Prospectus Neus Leben*, a Baptist World Alliance pamphlet, 1953, file 3, box 2A, Baptist World Alliance Collection (BWA), Angus Library Archives (ALA), Regents Park College, Oxford.

75 Bell, *Europe's Jericho Roads*, 9–10.

76 Pierard, "Baptist World Alliance," 718, 723; and J.H. Rushbrooke, "Post-war World Relief the Special Responsibility of Baptists, 12 October 1943," folder X.1.1.B, Baptist World Alliance – Record Group 503 (BWA-RG hereafter), American Baptist Historical Society and Archives (ABHSA), Mercer University, Atlanta, Georgia.

77 McSweeney, *Amerikanische Wohlfartshilfe*, 69–73.

78 The preference for the term *fraternal worker* instead of *missionary* was indicative of both Northern and Southern Baptists in the United States. See *Europe: Where American Baptists Cooperate*, 9; and J.D. Hughey, "Europe Needs the Gospel" (Foreign Mission Board tract, 1956), file 25, box 2, Arr. 711, Papers of J.D. Hughey, Southern Baptist Historical Library and Archives (SBHLA), Nashville, Tennessee.

79 Pierard, "Baptist World Alliance," 711.

80 Richard V. Pierard, "Baptist World Alliance Relief Efforts," 1.

81 For more on Rushbrooke, see Green, *Biography of James Henry Rushbrooke*.

82 Pierard, "Baptist World Alliance Relief Efforts," 2. Baptist World Aid continues to be involved in relief work as a division of the BWA. See Baptist World Aid, a division of Baptist World Alliance, https://www.bwanet.org/programs/baptist-world-aid. For a more detailed account of Rushbrooke's work with the BWA during the First and Second World Wars, see Green, *James Henry Rushbrooke*.

83 Rushbrooke, "Post-war World Relief the Special Responsibility of Baptists."

84 The BWA had a two-person executive structure consisting of a general secretary and a president. The former was the senior position and the only salaried one. The latter was essentially a voluntary position, to which one could be elected at BWA Congresses. See Richard Pierard, "The Baptist World Alliance: An Overview of Its History," 713, 719.

85 Pierard, "Baptist World Alliance Relief Efforts," 7–10; and Caudill, *The Romance of Relief*, 3, copy available in X.1.1.D, BWA-RG, ABHSA.

86 Chaplain Paul Maddox to W.O. Lewis, 21 May 1947, folder I. 2.12 H, BWA-RG, ABHSA. The letter contains a list of twenty-four Baptist chaplains who were stationed in the American Zone and who planned to attend the Copenhagen conference. See also Caudill, *Romance of Relief*.

87 "Minutes of the Baptist Alliance Relief Committee, 7 October 1947," folder X 1.1 C; and Gerstenmeier to Lewis, 4 November 1947, folder I 2.6 R, BWA-RG, both in ABHSA.

88 Caudill, *Romance of Relief*, 6–8. American Baptist Relief published statistics only of total donations made by each country to world relief in general.

According to their reports, at least 50 per cent of that went to relief work in Germany.

89 Jacob Meister, "The Bi-Annual Convention of the Baptists in Germany, Dortmund, 19–23 September 1951," file 3, box 2A, BWA – Europe 1931–1970, ALA. Meister's report shows an increase in the German Baptist population from 81,796 in 1946 to 101,506 in 1948.

90 "American Baptist Relief Committee Minutes, 3 May 1948," folder X 1.1 C, BWA-RG, ABHSA.

91 "Relief Meeting Minutes, 29 July 1949," folder X 1.1 C, BWA-RC, BHSA; and Franks to Sadler, n.d., file 3, box 251, Arr. 551–1, Southern Baptist Convention – Foreign Mission Board, Mission Minutes and Reports 1949–1990, SBHLA.

92 Rushbrooke, "Post-war World Relief the Special Responsibility of Baptists."

93 Gebauer to Rushbrooke, 11 September 1945, file 2, box 2A, BWA – Europe, ALA, Regent's Park College, Oxford.

94 Meister, "Bi-annual Convention."

95 "Prospectus: Europe – An Open Door," 1952, file 3, box 2A, BWA – Europe, ALA.

96 "Shadows and Light in War-Ravaged Germany," Missions 35 (December 1945): 528; "Bi-annual Convention of Baptists in Germany, 19–23 September 1951"; and "Prospectus: Europe – An Open Door," 1952, both in file 3, box 2A, BWA – Europe, ALA.

97 "What Was Unimaginable Is Now Indescribable," Missions 37 (November 1947): 525.

98 Farnum to Lewis, 10 May 1948, folder I 2.2 A, Lewis; and Schedule of Projects for Baptist Relief Program in Germany, Winter 1948–49, folder X 3.14 J, BWA-RC, BHSA.

99 Franks to Sadler, 6 April 1949, file 3, box 251, Arr. 551–1, SBHLA. For a similar appeal on the Northern Baptist Convention side, see Bell to Ohrn, 8 March 1948, folder I 2.2 A, BWA-GS, BHSA.

100 "Minutes of Relief Meeting, 29 July 1949," folder X 1.1 C, BWA-RC, BHSA.

101 "Minutes of the Relief Committee of the BWA, 16 June 1950," folder X 1.1 D, BWA-RG, ABHSA.

102 "Minutes of the Relief Committee of the BWA, 16 June 1950," folder X 1.1 D, BWA-RG, ABHSA.

103 Norquist to Caudill, 16 April 1951, folder X 3.14 E, BWA-RG, ABHSA. In its own published material on relief work in Germany, the BWA put the number of Baptist DPs in West Germany after the war at 28,200. See "Prospectus: Europe – An Open Door" (1951), file 3, box 2A, BWA-Europe, ALA. Yet Norquist consistently used the slightly higher rounded-up figure in his correspondence. See also Norquist, "Opportunities for Our Contribution in Germany," August 1951, X 3.14 F, BWA-RG, ABHSA.

104 Norquist to Caudill, 16 April 1951, folder X 3.14 E, BWA-RG, ABHSA.

105 "BWA Stuttgart Financial Report Oct. 1, 1950–June 1953," folder X 3.14 F, BWA-RG, ABHSA.

106 Ibid.

107 Edwin Bell, "Report on Notkirchen," folder I 2.3 N, BWA-GS; and "Minutes of the BWA Relief Committee, 16 June 1950," folder X 1.1 D, BWA-RG, ABHSA.

108 "Opportunities for Our Contribution in Germany."

109 "Baptist Refugees in Worms, 1 February 1953," folder X 3.14 F, BWA-RC, BHSA.

110 Bell, "Our Program of Assistance in Europe," *Mission* 45 (October 1955): 19.

111 Crawley, *Global Mission*, 24–5.

112 Estep, *Whole Gospel, Whole World*, 277, 300.

113 Woodfin, "Rüschlikon," 1–9.

114 Franks, "Europe Must Have a Baptist Seminary," *Commission* 11 (June 1948): 4.

115 "Minutes of the Semi-annual Session of the Foreign Mission Board, 6 April 1948," accession number (AN) 2005, International Mission Board Archives and Records Services, https://solomon.imb.org/public/ws/oldmin/www2/minutesp/Record?parenttreeid=9302864&sessiondepth=2&parenttreeid=9302864&sessiondepth=2&w=NATIVE%28%27MIN_DATE+%3D+%27%27April+6%2C+1948%27%27%27%29&upp=0&order=native%28%27MIN_DATE%2FDescend%27%29&rpp=10&r=1&m=1.

116 Woodfin, "Rüschlikon," 27; and Hughey, "Baptist Theological Seminary," 4. This journal is a Southern Baptist publication out of Nashville and is not to be confused with the British *Baptist Quarterly*, the journal of the British Baptist Historical Society.

117 Hughey, "Baptist Theological Seminary," 4.

118 "Minutes on the First Annual Meeting of the Board of Trustees of the Baptist Theological Seminary, 10–11 March 1950," file 26, box 251, Arr. 551–1, SBHLA.

119 Franks to Sadler, 6 July 1951, file 3, box 251, Arr. 551–1, SBHLA.

120 Woodfin, "Rüschlikon," 51–2.

121 In 1953 IBTS began to publish the *Rüschlikon Link*, a quarterly, then later, semi-annual newsletter, which included articles on current life at the seminary as well as alumni news. Most editions included a demographic profile of the student body. For example, the first issue recorded that fourteen of the thirty-four students that year were from Germany. Issues of the *Rüschlikon Link* from the 1950s and 1960s show that Germans consistently comprised 10 to 20 per cent of the student body. See file 14, box 7, Arr. 711, and file 18, box 252, Arr. 551–1, SBHLA.

122 Nordenhaug, "Tower for Europe's Homes," *Home Life* 8 (September 1954): 10.

123 "Rüschlikon Reports, April 1950," file 15, box 252, Arr. 551–1, SBHLA.

124 "Minutes of the Annual Trustee Meeting, 20–21 March 1962," file 26, box 251, Arr. 551–1, SBHLA.

125 "Transcript of Oral Memoirs of Gerhard Claas," ref. no. b2500136x, Texas Collection, Baylor University Library, Waco, Texas; and "Gerhard Claas," http://de.wikipedia.org/wiki/Gerhard_Claas.

126 Selected issues of the *Rüschlikon Link* from December 1955 to December 1965, file 18, box 252, Arr. 551–1; and file 14, box 7, Arr. 711, both in SBHLA.

127 Hughey, *Europe*, 106.

128 Ibid., 15; and "Strategy Report from Europe: 1975," 2, file 10, box 1, Arr. 711, SBHLA.

129 Hughey, *Europe*, 91–5, 104–11.

130 Evans, *Let Europe Hear*, 407. Within the *Freikirchen*, Baptists were listed at around 100,000 members and Mennonites at 65,000.

131 Kreider letter to friends, 30 May 1946, file 67 – Robert Kreider Correspondence, box 2, IX-19-3, MCCAC, AMC.

132 "An Operating Program for Germany, 5 February 1947," file 67 – Robert Kreider Correspondence, box 2, IX-19-3, MCCAC, AMC.

133 Lorhman to Kreider, memo, 4 July 1947, file 67 – Robert Kreider Correspondence, box 2, IX-19-3, MCCAC, AMC.

134 Kreider to Clay, 13 July 1946, file 67 – Robert Kreider Correspondence, box 2, IX-19-3, MCCAC, AMC.

135 Petra Goede, *GIs and Germans*, 127–8.

136 "Berlin," *ERN*, March 1947, 6, IX-40-2, MCCAC, AMC.

137 "Activity Reports – Berlin, August and September 1949," file 37 – Harold Buller Correspondence, 1949; and "European Area Report, Relief Section 21 July 1950," file 41 – Harold Buller Correspondence, 1950; both in IX-6-3, MCCAC, AMC.

138 "Need, Need, Need," *ERN*, May–June 1948, 10–11, IX-40-2, MCCAC, AMC.

139 "Supplementary Feeding for University Students," *ERN*, July 1948, 7, IX-40-2, MCCAC, AMC.

140 "For Want of a Room," and "How the MCC Is Helping," both in *ERN*, April 1949, 5, 8–9, IX-40-2, MCCAC, AMC.

141 "A Galaxy of Problems," "Beyond Material Aid," and "Student Christmas," in *ERN*, April 1949, 2–3, 10–11, IX-40-2, MCCAC, AMC.

142 "Galaxy of Problems," *ERN*, April 1949, 3, IX-40-2, MCCAC, AMC (capitalization in the original).

143 "Summary of Relief Activities Program Planned by the MCC within Germany," file 41 – Harold Buller Correspondence, 1950, IX-6-3, MCCAC, AMC.

144 Lapp, "Peace Mission," 292.

145 Waltner worked at Mennonite Biblical Seminary, and Herschberger was on the faculty of Goshen College. Herschberger was also well qualified to take up this role, as he had recently completed an account of the Mennonite Church's wartime ordeal. See Herschberger, *Mennonite Church*.

146 Peachy, "Puidoux Conferences," *Global Anabaptist Encyclopedia Online*, 1989, http://www.gameo.org/encyclopedia/contents/P856.html; Durnbaugh, "John Howard Yoder," 375.

147 Lapp, "Peace Mission," 293, and "Peace Section Report," MCC *Annual Workbook, 1960,* IX-5-2, MCCAC, AMC.

148 Lapp, "Peace Mission," 293; and Durnbaugh, "John Howard Yoder," 371, 376–9.

149 Nation, *John Howard Yoder,* 16–21; and "Biographical Sketch," John Howard Yoder Collection, Historical Manuscripts 1–48, MCCAC, AMC. For more on the development of Yoder's political theology see Yoder, *Discipleship* and "Theological Basis."

150 Durnbaugh, "John Howard Yoder," 379.

151 "Peace Section Report – Europe," MCC *Workbook, 1960,* IX-5-2, MCCAC, AMC.

152 "Peace Section Report – Europe," MCC *Workbook, 1964,* IX-5-2, MCCAC, AMC.

153 Rushbrooke, "Post-war World Relief the Special Responsibility of Baptists."

154 Ibid.

155 Green, *European Baptists,* 47–52. See also Strübind, "German Baptists and National Socialism."

156 Railton, "German Free Churches and the Nazi Regime," 121–2, 124; and Green, *European Baptists,* 52–5.

157 Green, *European Baptists,* 65–70.

158 Ibid., 70–1.

159 Jakob Köbberling, "Stellungnahme zur Freikirchen Vertretung zuer Weltkonferenz in Oxford 1937," quoted in Railton, "German Free Churches," 126.

160 For more on Gebauer, see Effa, "The Legacy of Paul and Clara Gebauer."

161 Paul Gebauer to the BWA, 12 September 1945, file 3, box 2A, BWA – Europe, ALA.

162 Gebauer to Rushbrooke, 10 October 1945, file 3, box 2A, BWA – Europe, ALA.

163 Ibid.

164 Bell to Lewis, 15 October 1945, I.2.3.N, BWA-RG, ABHSA.

165 Bell to Lewis, 19 June 1946, I.2.3.N, BWA-RG, ABHSA.

166 On the relationship of the *Freikirchen* to the Third Reich, see Zehrer, *Evangelische Freikirchen;* Strübind, *Die unfreie Freikirche;* and Railton, "German Free Churches."

167 Railton, "German Free Churches," 111, 121–4. Bernard Green is also careful to show the complexity of the political pressures faced by German Baptists under the Reich. This was further complicated by pietistical theological tendencies among Baptists. See Green, *European Baptists,* 53–5, 67–71. See also Briggs, "Theology Meets History," 236–43.

168 Herbert Gezork, "Today and Tomorrow in Postwar Germany," *Missions* 38 (October 1948): 477.

169 Ibid., 476–7.

170 Lewis, "Importance of Europe," 107.

171 Kenneth Norquist, "Opportunities for Our Contribution in Germany, August 1952," folder X 3.14 E, BWA-RG, ABHSA.

172 Oesterle to Ohrn, 2 September 1951, folder X 3.14 E, BWA-RG, ABHSA.

173 Bell, "Our Program of Assistance in Europe," 20.

174 Ibid., 21.

175 "Can Communism Win?," *Commission* 12 (September 1949): 1; "Toward Holy War?," *Commission* 12 (April 1949): 18; and "Return to Despotism," *Commission* 13 (February 1950): 20.

176 "Toward Holy War?," 18.

177 Moore, "What about Europe?," *Commission* 9 (October 1946): 11.

178 J.D. Hughey, "Men and the Gospel," unpublished conference paper, 1957, file 22, box 2, Arr. 711, SBHLA.

179 Moore, "What about Europe?," 11.

180 For example, see the essays offered in Stephan, *Americanization and Anti-Americanism*.

181 Shank, "Missionary Approach to a Dechristianized Society," 39–44; David A. Shank, "Review of Political Economic, Social and Religious Developments in Europe over the Last Decade That Have an Effect on Our Mission," paper presented at Mennonite Board of Missions and Charities, Europe study conference, July 1967, file 47, IX-12-4, MCCAC, AMC; Gordon Lahrson, "Annual Report – Europe, 1968," folder "Europe: Annual Reports, Lahrson, 1961–69," BWA, ABHSA; and Hughey, *Europe: A Mission Field?*, 14–15.

Chapter Three

1 Richard Pierard, "Pax Americana," 166–73; and Carpenter, *Revive Us Again*, 177–86.

2 The Deutsche Evangelische Allianz (DEA) will be introduced at greater length later in the chapter. For more on its founding and early history, see Beyreuther, *Der Weg*, 9–60.

3 For more on the revivalism and early evangelicalism, see Noll, *Rise of Evangelicalism*; and Ward, *Protestant Evangelical Awakening*.

4 See Marsden, *Fundamentalism and American Culture*, 206–11, 221–8; and Pierard, "Pax Americana," 160–4.

5 Fey, "What about Youth for Christ?," *Christian Century* 62 (20 June 1945): 729.

6 Pierard, "Pax Americana," 167–75; and Carpenter, *Revive Us Again*, 178–86. See also Rosell, *Surprising Work of God*, 115.

7 "Wanted: A Miracle of Good Weather and the 'Youth for Christ' Rally Got It," *Newsweek* 12 (11 June 1945): 84; and Carpenter, *Revive Us Again*, 166-7; Larson, *Youth for Christ*, 53-60.

8 Jack Wyrtzen never officially became part of YFC, preferring to shepherd his own multifaceted Christian organization, known as Word of Life. However, he gave support to YFC through his own rallies and his weekly radio program, which reached thousands of listeners in New York state. For more on Wyrtzen's role in the conservative evangelical resurgence, see Forbes, *God Hath Chosen*.

9 Larson, *Youth for Christ*, 17-20, 47. *Newsweek* magazine dubbed Torrey Johnson as the religious counterpart of Frank Sinatra; see "Wanted: A Miracle of Good Weather," 84.

10 Hefley, *God Goes to High School*, 17; Johnson and Cook, *Reaching Youth for Christ*, 35-62.

11 Carpenter, "Introduction," 6; Johnson and Cook, *Reaching Youth for Christ*, 44-5.

12 Larson, *Youth for Christ*, 77.

13 Hefley, *God Goes to High School*, 14; and "What about 'Youth for Christ'?," *Christian Century* 62 (20 June 1945): 729.

14 Larson, *Youth for Christ*, 42; Carpenter, *Revive Us Again*, 166.

15 Hefley, *God Goes to High School*, 13.

16 Carpenter, *Revive Us Again*, 168-9. The editorial in the Hearst newspapers, titled "Youth's New Crusade," was reprinted as "William Randolph Hearst's Editorial Endorsement of 'Youth for Christ,'" *United Evangelical Action* 4 (15 July 1945), 13. Larsen, *Youth for Christ*, 26-9.

17 Larson, *Youth for Christ*, 20, 30.

18 Hefley, *God Goes to High School*, 31; and Fey, "What about 'Youth for Christ'?," *Christian Century* 62 (20 June 1945): 730-1.

19 Even after adding the word *international* to its title, Youth for Christ was still referred to in its initially abbreviated form of YFC. For the sake of consistency, this chapter uses YFC throughout, as it emerged as the more commonly used reference for the organization.

20 George Marsden, *Fundamentalism and American Culture*, 184-95.

21 Larson, *Youth for Christ*, 88.

22 At the height of the American occupational presence in postwar Germany it was estimated that there were as many as 100 YFC weekly rallies being held on military bases in the American Occupational Zone. "Progress Report on Youth for Christ Movement in Germany," file 28, box 5, collection (CN) 285, Papers of Torrey Johnson, Billy Graham Center Archives (BGCA), Wheaton, Illinois.

23 Torrey Johnson, "Accepting the Challenge," First Annual Conference of Youth for Christ, Winona Lake Conference Grounds, Indiana, 28 July 1945, file 26, box 3, CN 285, BGCA. Capitalization his.

24 Gravel, *Pentagon Papers*, 597–8.

25 See Winston Churchill, "Sinews of Peace, 1946," speech delivered at Westminster College, Fulton, Missouri, 5 March 1946, https://www.nationalchurchillmuseum.org/sinews-of-peace-iron-curtain-speech.html; and Spalding, *First Cold Warrior*, 37–60.

26 Rosell, *Surprising Work of God*, 73–80. For more on Ockenga, see Lindsell, *Park Street Prophet*.

27 Carpenter, *Revive Us Again*, 142–51; and Rosell, *Surprising Work of God*, 91–106.

28 Harold J. Ockenga, "This Is Our Problem," *Moody Monthly* 48 (November 1947): 222.

29 Ibid., 223.

30 For examples, see "How We Can Defeat Communism without War," *United Evangelical Action* (UEA) 20 (January 1962): 11–12; and "Communists on Campus," UEA 22 (April 1964): 28.

31 "Another One in Germany!," *Youth for Christ Magazine* (YFCM), August 1946, 4; "Salvation Echoes from Frankfurt, Germany, YFC," YFCM, October 1946, 41; and "Memos from Munich, Germany!," YFCM, November 1946, 53.

32 "Great After-Meeting at Los Angeles," YFCM, September 1946, 38.

33 For similar examples of such rhetoric in other conservative evangelical periodicals, see "Germany Today," *Moody Monthly* 48 (August 1947): 830–1; and "Germany ... a Challenge and an Opportunity," *Evangelical Christian* 44 (November 1948): 576–8.

34 Torrey Johnson, YFC rally speech, "Why Is Youth for Christ Going into Germany? April 1947," file 5, box 28, CN 285, BGCA.

35 Ibid.

36 Johnson, "Report from Germany," YFCM, August 1947, 19.

37 Karl Gronenberg to Torrey Johnson, 24 July 1947, file 5, box 26; and Albert Rönick to Torrey Johnson, January 1947, file 1, box 27, CN 285, BGCA.

38 Oswald Smith, "Miracle of Youth for Christ in Europe," *People's Magazine*, first quarter 1949, 18–19. Copy found in file 16, box 21, CN 48, BGEA.

39 "YFC Annual Congress Report, July 1955," file 29, box 8, CN 285, BGEA.

40 "Bob Evans: Team Meeting 1963," file 13, box 22, CN 506, BGEA.

41 Johnson, "Accepting the Challenge."

42 "Progress Report on Youth for Christ Movement in Germany."

43 "What about 'Youth for Christ'?," *Christian Century* 62 (10 June 1945): 729; and "Who Is behind Youth for Christ? Rally Has Fascist Tone," *Daily World*, n.d., file 29, box 12, CN 285, BGEA.

44 Johnson, "Why Is Youth for Christ Going into Germany?"

45 "Youth for Christ Is Registering New Victories," *Sunday School Times* 90 (24 October 1948): 881.

46 Diezel to Johnson, 22 May 1947, file 5, box 26, CN 285, BGCA.

47 Diezel, circular letter, 30 May 1947, file 5, box 26, CN 285, BGCA.

48 Johnson, "Progress Report on Youth for Christ in Germany."

49 "GIs Gospelize Germany," YFCM, February 1947, 17, 20–1; and John B. Youngs, post chaplain, Nürnberg, letter to the editor, *United Evangelical Action*, 1 November 1947, 22.

50 Youngs, letter to the editor, *United Evangelical Action*; and "German-American YFC Rally," *Frankfurt Youth for Christ News*, May 1947, 3–4, file 45, box 5, CN 285, BGEA.

51 Wolfgang Müller to Johnson, 9 October 1948, file 26, box 5, CN 285, BGEA; "Memos from Munich," YFCM, November 1946, 53; and Paul Fine to Johnson, 7 July 1949, file 27, box 13, CN 285, BGEA.

52 Johnson, open letter to YFC supporters, 7 July 1947, file 26, box 7; and Paul Fine to Johnson, 28 April 1949, file 27, box 13, both in CN 285, BGEA.

53 Youngs, letter to the editor, *United Evangelical Action*.

54 Johnson to Youngs, 6 May 1948, file 27, box 13, CN 285, BGEA; and "Youth for Christ Is Registering New Victories," 881.

55 Youngs to Johnson, 15 December 1947, file 27, box 13, CN 285, BGEA.

56 Youngs, post chaplain, letter to the editor, *United Evangelical Action*.

57 "Report on Germany YFC," *Overseas Manual for 1966*, file 16, box 41, CN 48, BGEA.

58 John H. Jones to Johnson, 25 November 1947, file 26, box 6, CN 285, BGEA.

59 Hefley, *God Goes to High School*, 38–40.

60 "Youth for Christ World Congress," *Moody Monthly* 48 (October 1947): 85.

61 Ibid.; Hefley, *God Goes to High School*, 40, 42; "Youth for Christ World Congress on Evangelism," news release, n.d., file 24, box 11, CN 285, BGEA; "Youth for Christ Is Registering New Victories," 881; and Robert J. Campbell, *Light for the Night in Europe* (USA: Robert Campbell, 1999), 13. There is a significant discrepancy over the actual attendance figures. Hefley and Campbell cite a lower figure of 230 delegates, while the *Sunday School Times* article and a YFC news release immediately following the congress claimed an attendance at around 500 delegates from twenty-five countries. A possible source of confusion was that some pre-congress reports called for 250 delegates from North America and another 250 from the rest of the world. Hefley and Campbell may have taken one of these numbers as a total number of delegates.

62 "Budget Report Beatenberg Congress," file 1, box 25, CN 285, BGEA; and "Youth for Christ Is Registering New Victories," 881.

63 "Youth for Christ Is Registering New Victories," 881.

64 Ibid.; and Smith, "Miracle of Youth for Christ in Europe."

65 Hefley, *God Goes to High School*, 137–43.

66 Johnson, "Progress Report on Youth for Christ Movement in Germany," file 5, box 28, CN 285, BGEA.

67 Johnson to Niemöller, 18 March 1947, file 26, box 5, CN 285, BGEA. For more on Niemöller and his role in German Protestant life, see James Bentley, *Martin Niemöller.*

68 "Report of European Youth for Christ conference, October 3–6, 1961," file 23, box 16; and "Report of Germany YFC, 1966," file 41, box 16, both in CN 48, BGEA.

69 For an example, see "Jugend ruft Jugend," *rally: Nachrichtenblatt der Jugend für Christus in Berlin* 4 (April 1962): 1; and "Youth for Christ's European Outreach '71," – promotional leaflet, file 22, box 16, CN 48, BGEA.

70 Hefley, *God Goes to High School,* 29.

71 Walls, "Missionary Dimension," 3.

72 See Beyreuther, *Der Weg;* and Railton, *No North Sea,* 51–6.

73 Spencer, *Story of the German Evangelist,* 37–40; Diezel to Johnson, 22 May 1947, file 26, box 5, CN 285, BGEA; "Report of Germany YFC," folder 16, box 41, BGEA; "Minutes of YFC Annual Convention 1952, July 1952, Winona Lake," file 13, box 39, CN 48, BGEA.

74 "Report of European Youth for Christ Conference, October 3–6, 1961," file 23, box 16; and "Report of Germany YFC, 1966," file 41, box 16, both in CN 48, BGEA.

75 Janz, *Janz Team Story,* 34–7. Also known as Low German, Plattdeutsch was a dialect native to northern Germany and the eastern Netherlands.

76 For a broad historical survey of the Mennonite Brethren, see Toews, *Pilgrimage of Faith;* and Faber and Jost, *Family Matters.*

77 For more on Maxwell, see celebratory histories on Prairie Bible Institute by Keller, *Expendable;* and Callaway, *Legacy.* For a scholarly analysis of PBI's early years, see Enns, "Every Christian a Missionary"; and Callaway, "Training Disciplined Soldiers."

78 Janz, *Janz Team Story,* 41.

79 Ibid., 43–4.

80 Hefley, *God Goes to High School,* 40.

81 Ibid., 44. For more on Anton Schulte, see Spencer, *Story of the German Evangelist.*

82 "Interview mit Leo Janz," *Ruf zur Entscheidung* (*Ruf* hereafter) 18 (March 1974): 6.

83 Maase, "From Nightmare to Model?," 79–81.

84 Kraska, "Es begann mit Musik," 4.

85 Braaten, "JTM: Historical Facts" (unpublished manuscript for Janz Team 50th Anniversary Celebrations, 2004, author's personal copy).

86 Harding Braaten, interview with author, 19 September 2006, Calgary, Alberta. Interview notes in possession of the author.

87 Ibid.

88 Braaten, "JTM: Historical Facts"; and Janz, *Janz Team Story,* 69.

89 For more on Jakob Vetter, see Bruns, *Jakob Vetter*. For more on evangeliza-
    tion movements in modern Germany, see Beyreuther, *Kirche in Bewegung*.

90 "Report to the Bundeskonferenz des Bundes Evangelische Freikirchlicher
    Germeinden in Deutschland, Kassel, 13–16 Oktober 1949," file 2, box 1, Bap-
    tist World Alliance – Europe, Angus Library Archives, Regents Park College,
    Oxford.

91 Eissler, *60 Jahre Deutsche Evangelistenkonferenz*, 4–5; and Waldorf, "Mis-
    sionarische Bemühungen," 9–10. For more on Brauer and the early years of
    the DEk, see Kennedy, "Best Intentions," 381–6; and Parzany, *Im Einsatz für
    Jesus*.

92 Beyreuther, *Der Weg*, 19.

93 Ibid., 11–23.

94 Jung, *Die deutsche Evangelikale*, 42–4.

95 Kennedy, "Best Intentions," 386. For a summary of indigenous evangelis-
    tic initiatives in Germany during the early postwar years, see Scharpff,
    Geschichte der Evangelisation, 312–20.

96 Reinhold Thadden-Trieglaff, "Neue Bewegung," *Sonntagsblatt*, 1 September
    1950. Cited in Kennedy, "Best Intentions," 387.

97 Kennedy, "Best Intentions," 389.

98 Eissler, *60 Jahre*, 6, 9.

99 Braaten, interview with author; Kraska, "Es begann mit Musik," 7; and Janz,
    Janz Team Story, 70.

100 Kraska, "Es begann mit Musik," 8.

101 "Rückblick," *Ruf* 22 (February 1979): 5; and Janz, *Janz Team Story*, 70.

102 Kennedy, "Best Intentions," 389.

103 "Ruhr-Feldzug für Christus," *Der Menschenfischer* (DMF hereafter) 2 (May/
    June 1958): 1.

104 Janz, *Janz Team Story*, 71–2; and "Rückblick," *Ruf* 22 (February 1979): 5.

105 Braaten, "JTM: Historical Facts."

106 "'Ruhrfeldzug für Christus' – : ein phänomenaler Erfolg," *Neu Ruhr/Rhein
    Zeitung* (NRZ), 19 June 1958, in Crusade scrapbook binder, "Echo der Veran-
    staltungen des Janz Teams" (Echo hereafter), Janz Team Crusade Files, JTM
    Records Room (JTMRR hereafter), Kandern, Germany. Janz Team's collec-
    tion of articles from the early part of their work is highly irregular. While
    most of the articles they did keep on record were positive, some are also
    more critical, suggesting that the compilers were interested in more than
    just gathering data that cast their mission in a positive light. The paucity of
    articles in the records makes it impossible to assess what the overall media
    response to Janz Team was. However, the articles that have survived corrob-
    orate Janz Team's own reports that during these early years Germans were
    curious enough to turn out to these evangelistic crusades in high numbers,
    and many responded positively to the music and preaching of the Canadian
    missionaries.

107 Quotation from an untitled article in the news journal *Der Weg*, Essen, in Echo folder, Janz Team Crusade Files, JTMRR.

108 "Rückblick," *Ruf* 22 (February 1979): 5. The quotation in the original German reads: "Nach der Evangelisation in Essen standen die Türen für unsere Großevangelisationen in ganz Deutschland, in der Schweiz und in Österreich weit offen. Über 2 Jahrzehnte haben wir in allen größeren Städten des deutschsprachigen Europas sowie in vielen ländlichen Gebieten das Evangelium in großen Hallen, Zelten und im Freien verkündigen dürfen."

109 Kraska, "Es begann mit Musik," 5.

110 See issues from JTM's monthly periodical *Ruf*, from the 1960s and 1970s. Each issue carried the yearly calendar of crusade engagements.

111 Braaten interview with author, 19 September 2006, Calgary, Alberta.

112 Kraska, "Es begann mit Musik," 7; "Drei Brüder kamen aus Kanada," *Oberbergische Volks-Zeitung*, 30 June 1961; and "Groß-Evangelisation mit Musik," *Hannoversche Presse*, 4 October 1967, both in Echo, Janz Team Crusade Files, JTMRR; "Lieber Freunde," *Ruf* 15 (September 1971): 3.

113 "19 Tage 'Ruf zur Entscheidung'" *Ruf* 12 (June 1968): 8.

114 "Ein persönliches Wort," DMF 7 (August 1963): 2; "Liebe Freunde," *Ruf* 12 (May 1968): 4; and "Liebe Freunde," *Ruf* 15 (September 1971): 3.

115 "'Ruhrfeldzug für Christus' – "; and "Drei Brüder kamen aus Kanada"; and "Evangelisation durch Wort und Lied," *Altenaer Kreisblatt*, 6 September 1967, all articles in Echo, Janz Team Crusade Files, JTMRR.

116 "Das Geheimnis der 'Feldzüge für Christus,'" *idea/Spectrum* 34 (6 September 2006): 22.

117 "Im Janz-Team-Studio entsteht Sendung aus Gummersbach," *Oberbergischer Anzeiger*, 30 June 1961, 12, Echo folder, Janz Team Crusade Files, JTMRR.

118 Braaten interview with author.

119 Ibid.

120 "4 Antworten," *Ruf* 23 (June 1979): 10.

121 A fire fuelled by straw that leapt quickly to life but died out just as quickly. "Nur ein Strohfeuer?" *Ruf* 14 (January 1970): 9.

122 "Nach 5 Jahren wieder in Giessen," *Ruf* 16 (February 1972): 11–12.

123 Swanson to Enns, 2 October 2006, letter in possession of the author; and Larry Swanson, "Hausbibelkreise innerhalb der Gemeinden," *Ruf* 12 (October 1968): 8–9.

124 Braaten interview with author.

125 "Ein Feldzug für Christus," *Saarbrücker Zeitung*, 6/7 April 1968, Echo, Janz Team Crusade Files, JTMRR.

126 For examples, see "Bilder und Berichte vom Feldzug für Christus in Bern," DMF 9 (September 1959): 4–10; and "Feldzug in Saarbrücken," *Ruf* 12 (June 1968): 8–11.

127 "'Ruhrfeldzug für Christus.'"

128 "Janz-Team – Feldzug für Christus," *Schwarzwälder Bote*, 1 September 1976, Echo, Janz Team Crusade Files, JTMRR.

129 See Henry, *Uneasy Conscience*; Bebbington, *Evangelicalism in Modern Britain*, 2–17, 220–8; Carpenter, *Revive Us Again*, 141–60; Rosell, *Surprising Work of God*, 161–223; Marsden, *Understanding Fundamentalism and Evangelicalism*, 62–83; and Marsden, *Reforming Fundamentalism*, 153–71.

130 For more on this distinction in German Protestantism, see Geldbach, "'*Evangelisch,' 'evangelical,'*" 156–7.

131 "Der Herr hat Großes an uns getan, des sind wir fröhlich," DMF 3 (September 1959): 5. Original text reads: "die verschiedensten evangelischen bibelgläubigen Kreise von Bern aus Landeskirche, Freikirchen und Gemeinschaften arbeiten in schönster Harmonie zusammen."

132 "Ein Wunsch geht in Erfüllung," DMF 5 (June 1961): 5.

133 Quoted in Janz, *Janz Team Story*, 78.

134 Kraska, "Es begann mit Musik," 4.

135 Braaten, "JTM: Historical Facts."

136 "Ein persönliches Wort," DMF 2 (December 1958): 2.

137 "'Gedränge um 'Gottes fröhliche Sänger,'" *Frankfurter Rundschau*, 23 June 1962, Scrapbook 292, Collection 360, BGEA. Original German text reads: "Wir wissen dass viele Kirchenmuiker unsere Lieder als fromme Schnulzn abtun. Die Menschen die zu uns kommen wollen es aber so. Wir haben sie getestet. Je einfacher die Melodien und Texte, desto ergriffener sind sie."

138 Cornie Enns, interview with author 6 June 2006. Interview notes in possession of author; and "Liebe Freunde," *Ruf* 15 (September 1971): 3.

139 "Gedränge um 'Gottes fröhliche Sänger.'"

140 See http://www.reichslieder.de/. The title, *Reichs-Lieder*, was a play on words. Where the term *Reich* was normally associated with the German government, in revivalist circles it referred to the heavenly kingdom or Reich Gottes.

141 "Die Reichslieder," http://reichslieder.de/geschichte.php.

142 Braaten, interview with author.

143 "12,000 Schallplatten bringen Freude und Segen ins Haus und Familie," DMF 8 (March 1964): 7.

144 "'Ruhrfeldzug für Christus' – "; and "Janz-Team fordert Entscheidung für Christus," *Allgemeine Zeitung* – Giessen (2 November 1971), both in Echo, Janz Team Crusade Files, JTMRR.

145 Braaten, interview.

146 Ibid.; and "Im Janz-Team-Studio entsteht Sendung aus Gummersbach," *Oberbergischer Anzeiger*, 30 June 1961, 12, Echo, Janz Team Crusade Files, JTMRR.

147 *Altenaer Kreisblatt*, n.d., Echo, Janz Team Crusade Files, JTMRR.

148 "Drei Brüder kamen aus Kanada."

149 "Janz Team-Internationales überkonfessionelles Missionswerk," *Evangelischer Allianz-Brief* 28 (June 1981): 17–18.

150 "Kennen Sie das Janz-Team?," *Der Korbacher Bote*, October 1970, Echo, Janz Team Crusade Files, JTMRR.

151 For a typical issue, see DMF 2 (December 1958).

152 For sample issues, see Theodore Epp, "Was sagt Gott zur Ehescheidung?," DMF 7 (July 1963): 10–11; Bill Bright, "Kein Wunder dass alles schiefgeht," *Ruf* 17 (June 1973): 4–5; Werner Heukelbach, "Ungeduld ist Mange an Vertrauen," *Ruf* 12 (May 1968): 8–9.

153 For examples, see the opening column, "Liebe Freunde," *Ruf* 14 (January 1970): 3; and in *Ruf* 16 (February 1972): 3.

154 "'Gedränge um 'Gottes fröhliche Sänger,'" *Frankfurter Rundschau*, 23 June 1962, Crusade Scrapbook 292, Collection 360, BGEA.

155 Hermand, "Resisting Boogie-woogie Culture," 71–3.

156 "Overseas Manual for 1966: Report of YFC Germany," file 16, box 41, CN 41, BGEA; and "Zeltplan 1964 der JFCD: – Jugend für Christus in Deutschland," *Evangelische Allianzblatt* 67 (March 1964): 59.

157 "Jugentevangelisation," *rally: Nachrichtenblatt der Jugend für Christus in Berlin* 3 (May 1962): 4; and "Neuer Mitarbeiter," *rally: Nachrichtenblatt der Jugend für Christus in Berlin* 4 (February 1963): 7, both in file 26, box 16, CN 46, BGEA.

Chapter Four

1 For more on the ethos and milieu of American fundamentalism, see chapters 2–5 of Carpenter, *Revive Us Again*; Marsden, *Fundamentalism and American Culture*, 199–229; and Brereton, *Training God's Army*. For an overview of fundamentalism in the southern states, see Beale, *In Pursuit of Purity*.

2 "Billy Graham and the Billy Graham Evangelistic Association: Historical Background," Billy Graham Center Archives, Wheaton College, http://www.wheaton.edu/bgc/archives/bio.html.

3 Ibid.

4 For more details on Graham's early crusade ministry, see Frady, *Billy Graham*, 209–318; Martin, *Prophet with Honor*, 123–269; and Pollock, *Crusades*, 121–95.

5 The biographies of Graham are numerous; two of the best treatments of both the man and his vocation as an evangelist are listed above: Frady, *Billy Graham*; and Martin, *Prophet with Honor*.

6 Graham, *Just as I Am*, 146, 167–8.

7 Kennedy, "Best Intentions," 381–2.

8 Ibid., 383–4.

9 Brauer, *Europas goldene Stunde*, 23–34.

10 For a more detailed account of how these meetings were arranged, see Kennedy, "Best Intentions," 403–90.

11 Graham, *Just as I Am*, 244; and "Der himmlische Holzhammer," *Der Kurier* (Berlin), 28 June 1954, Crusade Scrapbook (CS) 61, collection 360 (CN), Billy Graham Evangelistic Archives (BGCA), Wheaton, Illinois.

12 Brauer, *Europas goldene Stunde*, 50–4; and "Protokoll der Sitzung des erweiterten Vertrauensrates der Deutschen Evangelistenkonferenz, 30 June, 1955," folder 2, Berlin, 1960, Crusade Manual (CM), Archives of the Deutsche Evangelische Allianz (ADEA), Bad Blankenburg, Germany.

13 For the attendance statistics of Graham's crusades, see "Select Chronology," BGCA, http://www.wheaton.edu/bgc/archives/bgeachro/bgeachro02.htm.

14 Brauer, *Europas goldene Stunde*, 56.

15 "Bericht an das Zentralkomitee über die Evangelisationen Billy Grahams in Deutschland," folder 4, 1960, CM, ADEA.

16 Ibid.; "Select Chronology Listing of Events in the History or the Billy Graham Association," BGCA, http://www.wheaton.edu/bgc/archives/bgeachro/bgeachro02.htm.

17 Booklet on Closed Circuit TV Crusades, file 22, CN 17, BGEA.

18 Foster, *Euro 70*, 35–6.

19 "Europa – Tele – Evangelisation 1970," *Entscheidung*, May–June 1970, 5; and "Der Herr hat Großes an uns getan …!" *Evangelisches Allianzblatt* (EAB hereafter) 73 (June 1970): 106.

20 "Billy Graham: Showmaster Gottes oder Prediger?," *Der Spiegel* 16 (1970): scrapbook (SB) 151, CN 360, BGEA.

21 "Für und wider die Mission Dr. Billy Grahams," *Der Kurier*, Berlin, 3 July 1954, SB 61, CN 360, BGEA. The original statement reads, "Einen Mittelweg scheint es nicht zu geben."

22 Media records of Graham's crusade events are extensive and well preserved by Graham's own organization. Since the BGEA's formation in 1949, its officers have been meticulous in gathering and preserving material published in the news media about Graham's work over the years. This is true not only of his ministry in North America but all over the world. Newspaper clippings on Graham's crusades have been organized in scrapbooks as part of the BGEA's archival collection. The priority of this collection seems to be documenting the extent of media coverage given to Graham, instead of assessing the editorial nature of that coverage. The scrapbooks have no editorial shaping other than having the articles grouped by event, chronology, and country. Thus it is possible to get a sense of the wide range of opinions as well as representative responses of the German media to Graham.

What the scrapbooks underscore is that Graham was big news whenever he visited Germany. Another source of German media coverage comes through the DEA crusade files and their monthly newsletter, the *Evangelisches Allianzblatt*, which included excerpts of newspaper articles, or gave an overall assessment of the bias of media coverage for a given crusade. When these materials are coupled with the crusade scrapbooks, it is possible to get a good sense of the German media's views – pro and con – on Graham and his ministry.

23 "Billy will Europa bekehren, Der Kreuzzug William Franklin Grahams kostet Millionen," *Das Grüne Blatt*, 24 June 1954, SB 52, CN 360, BGEA.

24 Ibid.

25 "Das gutorganisierte Maschingewehr Gottes," *Die Andere Zeitung*, Hamburg, 24 August 1960, SB 291, CN 360, BGEA.

26 "Werbefachman Gottes in Düsseldorf," *Lübecker Nachrichten*, Lübeck, 26 June 1954, SB 61, CN 360, BGEA.

27 "Billys Monsterschau lockt die Massen" *Filder Zeitung*, Stuttgart, 7 April 1970. The scrapbook notes that this article, or portions of it, appeared in twenty-four other German newspapers as well. SB 293, CN 360, BGEA.

28 Pollock, *Billy Graham*, 184.

29 "Für und wider die Mission Dr. Billy Grahams," *Berlin Kurier*, 3 July 1954, B 61, CN 360, BGEA. The German text reads: "Der Kurier trifft ins Schwarze wenn er die Frage aufwirft: 'Aber was bedeutet eigentlich dieser hemmungslos provozierte Bekennermut der Masse?' … Jawohl genau wie bei Hitler, der mit Zustimmung der Massen eine Selbstvergottung trieb. Wer Ohren hat zu hören, der höre, und wer Augen hat, der sehe, bevor es wieder einmal zu spät ist."

For a later example, see "Unsere Leser schreiben," *Die Kirche*, Hamburg, 23 October 1960, SB 42, CN 360, BGEA; and "Billy Graham in Widerstreit unterschiedlichster Urteile," *Sudwest Presse*, Ulm, 11 April 1970, SB 293, CB 360, BGEA.

30 For an example, see "Billy Graham: 'Nur Christus wirkt,'" *Aachener Nachrichten*, Aachen, 11 September 1960, SB 42; and "Der Kreuzfahrer aus Minneapolis," *Deutsche Volkszeitung*, Düsseldorf, 3 July 1954, SB 61, both in CN 360, BGEA.

31 "Der himmlische Holzhammer," *Der Kurier*, Berlin, 28 June 1954; "Kreuzritter Billy Graham will Deutschland bekeren," *Abendpost*, Frankfurt, 18 June 1954; "'Gottes Maschinengewehr' – Made in USA," *Freie Presse*, Berlin-Ost, 4 July 1954; "Das 'Maschinegewehr Gottes' sprach," *Der Taunusbote*, Bad Homburg, 23 June 1955, all found in SB 61, CN 360, BGEA. It was the British press that coined the nickname "God's Machinegun," but the German press was quick to adopt it. One Berlin journalist, after hearing Graham, suggested that a better metaphor would be God's Flamethrower, because of the double intensity of hearing Graham's sharp delivery immediately followed by his equally emotive translator. See "Eindruck eines Zuhörers," *Berliner Zeitung*, 28 June 1954, SB 61, CN 360.

32 "Mensch, Billy ist 'ne Wucht," *Welt am Sonntag*, Berlin and Hamburg, 18 September 1960, SB 291, CN 360, BGEA. Historian Marshall Frady noted that women comprised 60 per cent of Graham's crusade audiences. See Frady, *Billy Graham*, 226.

33   Brauer, *Europas Goldene Stunde*, 60.

34   Ibid.

35   "Billy Graham bekehrt 2000 Berliner," *Die Zeit*, Hamburg, 1 July 1954; "Das ist kein Gottesdienst mehr sondern Volksbelustigung," *Die Abendpost*, Frankfurt, 15 May 1955, both from SB 61, CN 360, BGEA.

36   Railton, "German Free Churches," 87–90.

37   Ibid., 91–2.

38   "Das Rätsal Billy Graham," *Die Welt am Sonntag*, Berlin, 26 June 1955, SB 61, CN 360, BGEA. Translated, the article title reads, "The riddle of Billy Graham."

39   Kennedy, "Best Intentions," 484.

40   "Amerikanisierung der Religion?," *Weilburger Tageblatt*, Hessen-Frankfurt region, 18 July 1955, SB 61, CN 360, BGEA. The original reads, "Das ist nicht unsere Kragenweite."

41   Friedrich Heitmüller, "Ein Rückblick auf die Großstadt-Evangelisation mit Dr. Billy Graham in Hamburg," folder 2, CM 1960, ADEA. For a brief biography of Heitmüller, see "Heitmüller, Friederich," Biographisch-Bibliographisches Kirchenlexikon, Verlag Traugott Bautz, http://www.bbkl.de/lexikon/bbkl-login-2.php?art=./H/He/heitmueller_fr.art.

42   Heitmüller, "Ein Rückblick auf die Großstadt-Evangelisation." See also Kennedy, "Best Intentions," 510.

43   "Biblisches Brot mit amerikanischem Zucker," *Tages Post*, 9 April 1970. This same article was carried in twelve other newspapers; "Überfüllt Westfallenhalle hörte Billy Graham," *Siegener Zeitung*, 6 April 1980, also carried in six other newspapers; "Interview mit Probst D. Heinrich Grüber," *Spandauer Volksblatt*, 16 June, 1960, folder 4, Berlin 1966 CM, ADEA.

44   Pells, *Not like Us*, 157–68, 204–20.

45   Ermarth, "Counter-Americanism," 30–5, 46.

46   Perritt, *Dream of Greatness*, 158. John Emmett Hughes served as the Rome and Berlin bureau chief for *Time* magazine in the late 1940s, before becoming editor of *Life* magazine from 1949 to 1953.

47   Ibid., 159.

48   *Revival in Our Time*, 54–5. This book is a compilation of some of Graham's sermons and eye-witness accounts of some of his early crusades.

49   Ibid., 144.

50   "Billy in Germany," *Time* 31 (5 July 1954): 48. Found in Barnhart, *Billy Graham Religion*, 234.

51   For examples, see "Is Your Church Ready if the Bombs Should Fall?," *Moody Monthly* 59 (February 1959): 15, 17; and "A Survey of Religious Life and Thought," *Sunday School Times* 100 (10 May 1958): 360–1.

52   Pierard, "From Evangelical Exclusivism," 429.

53   Ibid., 167–8. Especially influential in feeding Graham's antipathy were the suppression of the Hungarian uprising in 1956, and the disastrous Bay of Pigs

insurgency in 1961. For Graham's own assessment of his anti-Communist statements during these years, see Billy Graham, *Just as I Am*, 381–2.

54 Graham, *Just as I Am*, 214–15; and Pollock, *Billy Graham*, 157–8.

55 Kennedy, "Best Intentions," 377–9.

56 "Billy Graham: Seelsorge mit Schocktherapie," *Pforzheimer Zeitung*, 29 June 1954, SB 61, CN 360, BGEA. The original reads, "Die stillen Wohnstrassen um die Frankfurter Christ Chapel in der Billy Graham während seines Deutschlandbesuches vor seinen Landsleuten predigte, waren vollgestopft mit Autos. Militärpolitzisten hielten mühsam Ordnung."

57 Ibid.

58 "Graham und die Politik," *Lübecker Nachrichten*, 26 June 1954, SB 61, CN 360, BGEA.

59 Kennedy, "Best Intentions," 442–4.

60 "Kreuzritter Billy Graham will Deutschland bekehren," *Abendpost*, Frankfurt, 25 June 1954; and "Maschinengewehr Gottes, eine Katholische Kritik," *Deutsche Volkszeitung*, Düsseldorf, 3 July 1954, SB 61, CN 360, BGCA.

61 Kennedy, "Best Intentions," 448.

62 "Einen weg au Gott," *Neue Rhine Zeitung*, Cologne, 10 July 1954, SB 61, CN 360, BGCA. Calculations for attendance based on the amount of East German currency collected in the crusade offering put the figure closer to 30,000.

63 "Graham: Entscheidet Euch für Gott," *Der Abend*, Berlin, 28 June 1954, quoted in Kennedy, "Best Intentions," 540n1183.

64 Kennedy, "Best Intentions," 540n1183.

65 "Jeder kann die Welt verändern" *Berliner Zeitung*, 28 June 1954, SB 61, CN 360, BGCA.

66 "Billy Graham: Ich liebe die Berliner," *Berlin Morgenpost*, 8 October 1966, SB 292, CN 360, BGCA.

67 "Billy Graham: meine Arbeit ist unpolitisch" *Niederelbe Zeitung*, Ottendorf/Cuxhaven, 27 September 1960, SB 291, CN 360, BGCA.

68 "SED und Maschinengewehr Gottes," *Haller Tagblatt*, Schwäbische Hall, 26 September 1960, SB 291, CN 360, BGCA. SED stands for Sozialistische Einheitspartei Deutschland and was the official name of the East German Communist Party.

69 "Ostberlin: Grahams Zelt abreißen," *Die Welt*, Berlin, 29 September 1960; and "Graham macht Ostberlin nervös," *Badische Neueste Nachrichten*, Karlsruhe, 29 September 1960, SB 291, CN 360, BGEA.

70 "SED und Maschinengewehr Gottes," *Die Freiheit*, Mainz, 26 September 1960, SB 291, CN 360, BGEA.

71 "Senate antwortet der SED. Billy Grahams Zelt bleibt!," *Spandauer Volksblatt*, Berlin, 29 September 1960, SB 291, CN 360, BGEA.

72 "SED und Maschinengewehr Gottes" and "Graham: 'Ich bin nicht Brandts Maschinengewehr,'" *Oldenburgische Volkszeitung*, Oldenburg, 27 September

1960, SB 291, CN 360, BGEA; and "Brandenburger Tor gesperrt, weil Graham predigt," *Telegraph-Wochenspiegel*, Berlin, 2 October 1960, SB 291, CN 360, BGEA; and Wirt, *Billy*, 108–9.

73 Pollock, *Billy Graham*, 68.

74 Wirt, *Billy*, 108–9.

75 "Brandenburger Tor gesperrt, weil Graham predigt."

76 Wirt, *Billy*, 108–9.

77 Frady, *Billy Graham*, 375.

78 "Sperren am Brandenburger Tor," *Die Welt*, Berlin, 28 September 1960, SB 291, CN 360, BGCA; and Wirt, *Billy*, 109.

79 "Protest gegen Gotteslästerung der Vopo," *Wiesbadener Kurier*, 30 September 1960; and "Kirche protestiert bei Grotewohl," *Heimat Rundschau*, Stuttgart, 30 September 1960, SB 291, CN 360, BGCA. The minister-president was the Moscow-appointed head of East Germany.

80 Wirt, *Billy*, 109. Wirt uses the title "Evangelical Baptist Union for Moscow," but there is no record of such an entity. He likely was referring to the All Union Council, which had been created in 1944 when the Union of Evangelical Christians merged with the Russian Baptist Union.

81 Pollock, *Billy Graham*, 280.

82 Ibid.

83 Wirt, *Billy*, 110–11.

84 Untitled article from *Der Telegraf*, Berlin, 21 October 1966, folder 4, Berlin 1966 CM, ADEA.

85 "Der Großevangelisation mit Dr. Billy Graham im Spiegel der Presse," folder 4, Berlin 1966 CM, ADEA.

86 "Graham in Berlin," EAB 69 (November 1966): 213–14, 216. Graham did not make it into Hungary until the mid-1970s, but he did hold meetings in Zagreb, Yugoslavia, in July 1967. See Pierard, "From Evangelical Exclusivism," 455.

87 Foster, *Euro 70*, 71–2. For more on Graham and his views on Vietnam, see Frady, *Billy Graham*, 421–33; and Pierard, "Billy Graham and Vietnam," 37–51.

88 "Auch Jesus nannte keine Prozente," *Der Spiegel*, Hamburg, 6 April 1970, SB 152, CN 360, BGEA.

89 "Graham: die ganze Welt ist mein Pfarrei," *Haller Kreisblatt*, Halle, 14 April 1970, SB 293, CN 360, BGEA. The article was carried by two other German regional papers.

90 Frady, *Billy Graham*, 258–9.

91 For an extended discussion on Graham's association with American presidents, see Frady, *Billy Graham*, 250–71, and 437–80; and Gibbs and Duffy, *The Preacher and the Presidents*.

92 Symanowski, "Missionary Responsibility," 421.

93 Ibid., 422. For an expanded discussion of Symanowski's ideas of how to reach urban industrial workers with the gospel. see Symanowski, *Christian Witness*.

94 For more on Thadden Trieglaff, see Hühne, *A Man to Be Reckoned*. For a history of the *Kirchentag* movement, see Palm, *"Wir sind doch Brüder!"*; and Schroeter, *Kirchentag*.

95 Kennedy, "Best Intentions," 386–8.

96 Ibid.

97 Dibelius, *In the Service of the Lord*, 248.

98 For an introduction to the role and identity of the DEA vis-à-vis the *Evangelikaler* movement, see Jung, *Was ist Evangelikal?*, 18–30.

99 For more on this distinction and the origin and development of the term *Evangelikal*, see Geldbach, *"'Evangelisch,' 'Evangelikal,'"* 156–60. See also Laubach, *Aufbruch*, 82–7.

100 Brauer, *Europas Goldene Stunde*, 61. It is interesting to note that these three regions form a north-to-south axis down the centre of Germany.

101 Ibid., 61–3.

102 Ibid., 60; and "Protokoll der Sitzung des erweiterten Vertrauensrates der Deutsche Evangelistenkonferenz, 30 June 1955" (DEk Protokoll hereafter), folder 2, Berlin 1960 CM, ADEA.

103 "DEk Protokoll, 30 June 1955."

104 Ibid.

105 Ibid. The German expression used was "Nicht in fremden Teich fischen."

106 "DEk Protokoll, 30 June 1955."

107 Ibid. The original reads: "Alle anwesenden Brüder sind sich über die Bedeutung der Narcharbeit einig, und wir wollen einander darin mit Rat und Tat zur Seite stehen."

108 "DEk Protokoll, 30 June 1955."

109 Zilz to the DEk Board, 10 June 1955, folder 2, Berlin 1960 CM, ADEA.

110 Paul Schmidt, "Billy Graham in Deutschland," folder 7, Berlin 1960, CM, ADEA; see also Jung, *Was ist Evangelikal?*, 19–30, 92–3.

111 For more on Lilje and Dibelius, see Siegmund, *Bischof Johannes Lilje*; and Stupperich, *Otto Dibelius*.

112 For the wartime memoirs of these two men, see Lilje, *In the Valley of the Shadow*; and Dibelius, *In the Service of the Lord*.

113 DEA letter to supporters February 1960, "Aufruf an alle die unsern Herrn Jesus Christus kennen und liebhaben," folder 2, Berlin 1960 CM, ADEA; and "Protokoll der ersten Sitzung des Zentralausschusses für geplante Groß-Evangelisationen mit Billy Graham (Protokoll ZA hereafter), 6 November 1959"; and "Protokoll ZA 1 October 1960," both in folder 1, Berlin 1960 CM, ADEA.

114 Peter Schneider, "Report: … und was kam dabei heraus?," folder 7, Berlin 1960 CM, ADEA.

115 "Protokoll ZA, 22 August 1960," folder 5, Berlin 1960 CM, ADEA.
116 "Der Andreas-Plan," folder 7, Berlin 1960 CM, ADEA. In the New Testament Gospel accounts, Andrew is mentioned only in a few instances but in almost every one of these he brings people to meet Jesus.
117 "Schneider, "Report … und was kam dabei heraus?," folder 7, Berlin 1960 CM, ADEA.
118 "Bericht und des Zentralkomitee über die Evangelisationen Billy Grahams in Deutschland," folder 4, Berlin 1960 CM, ADEA.
119 See "Protokoll der fünften Sitzung des Zentralausschusses für Gross-stadte-vangelisationen mit Billy Graham, 23 February 1961, Essen," folder 1, Berlin 1960 CM, ADEA; and "Janz Team 1954 bis 1974," Ruf 22 (February 1979): 4–5; and Eissler, 60 Jahre, 6–9.
120 "Das Janz Team in der neuen Grugahalle in Essen, 9 November 1958," Der Menschenfischer 2 (December 1959): 9; "Protokoll der 'Brüderlichen Besprechung' in Fragen geplanter Evangelisationen mit Billy Graham in Deutschland, 12 August 1959," folder 1, Berlin 1960 CM, ADEA.
121 "Bericht des Zentralkomitee," folder 4, Berlin 1960 CM, ADEA; and Paul Schmidt, "Billy Graham in Deutschland," folder 1, Berlin 1960 CM, ADEA.
122 Schneider, "Report: … und was kamm daraus?," folder 7, Berlin 1960 CM, ADEA; see also "Die Aufgabe der Evangelischen Allianz: Einheitsbewegung!" EAB 66 (September 1963): 167–70.
123 "Billy Graham in Deutschland," folder 1, Berlin 1960 CM, ADEA; "Bedeutung der Evangelisationen Billy Grahams für Deutschland," EAB 63 (August 1960): 180.
124 "Maschinengewehr Gottes: nebst Dolmetscher," Die Zeit, Hamburg, 23 September 1960; "Billy Graham sprach vor fünfunddreißigtausend," Hamburger Morgenpost, 17 September 1960; and "Billy Graham: Nur Christus wirkt," Dürener Nachrichten, Düren, 17 September 1960, all from SB 291, CN 360, BGEA; and Beyreuther, Der Weg, 132–3, 164–5n204; and Wirt, Billy, 107.
125 Wirt, Billy, 107.
126 Beyreuther, Der Weg, 165n204.
127 Interview with Dr Irmhild Bärend, 19 February, 2008. Interview notes in possession of the author. Dr Bärend was editor of Entscheidung from 1974 to 2004.
128 For examples, see Norman P. Grubb, "Das Geheimnis des Lebens," Entscheidung, January 1966, 8–9; "Interview with Rosemary Murphy (a Former Miss America)," Entscheidung, September 1965, 6; and Dr Alan Redpath, "Der Wille Gottes," Entscheidung, Summer 1964, 8–9. For reports on Graham's crusades around the world, see "Gott war im Coliseum," Entscheidung, Winter 1963, 8–9; "Geboren in Melbourne," Entscheidung, July 1969, 8–9; and "Grossevangelisation in Deutschland," Entscheidung, Fall 1963, 8–9.
129 "Gott war im Coliseum," Winter 1963, 8–9; "Geboren in Melbourne," July 1969, 8–9; and "Grossevangelisation in Deutschland," Fall 1963, 8–9, all in Entscheidung.

130 The Berlin Congress was actually the work of American evangelical magazine *Christianity Today*, but came about as a result of Graham's influence. Amsterdam was sponsored by the European Evangelical Alliance, but again was the direct result of his evangelization work in Europe the previous decade. In all three cases Graham was either a keynote speaker or honorary chairman.

131 "The World Congress on Evangelism," *Watchman Examiner* 54 (15 December 1966): 781.

132 "Haile Selassie, Billy Graham und Otto Dibelius sprachen," *Die Welt*, Berlin, 27 October 1966, SB 292, CN 360, BGEA.

133 "Eine Menschheit, ein Evangelium, ein Auftrag," EAB 67 (December 1966): 228, 230.

134 Mooneyham, "Introduction," 1:3.

135 "Eine Menscheit, ein Evangelium, ein Auftrag," EAB 67 (December 1966): 228, 230.

136 "World Evangelical Fellowship Lausanne 1968," EAB 71 (July 1968): 132.

137 Laubach, *Aufbruch*, 84–5.

138 Ibid., 85.

139 "Lausanner Verpflichtung – mehr als unverbindliche Erklärung Erlebnisse und Erkenntnisse der deutschen Teilnehmer beim Weltkongress für Evangelisation," *Stuttgarter Zeitung*, reprinted in *Evangelischer Allianz-brief* (AB hereafter), Sondernummer Lausanne, September 1974, 41.

140 "Lausanne 74: Rückblick und Ausblick," and "Persönliche Eindrücke von deutschen Kongressteilnehmern," both in AB, September 1974, 1–3, 35–9.

141 "Mögliche Kooperation bei notwendiger Abgrenzung," AB, September 1974, 25–6.

142 "Die Deutschen in Lausanne," AB, September 1974, 27–8. This was a copy of an article written by the Evangelischer Pressedienst, the news service of the EKD.

143 "Schlußwort von Bischof D. Dr. Dibelius in der Deutschlandhalle," folder 4, CM Berlin 1966, ADEA. The original text reads:

> Also, wir kennen alle das Gleichnis vom barmherzigen Samariter, daß der Samariter den Halbtodgeschlagenen in die Herberge bringt und sagt zu dem Wirt, "Pflege ihn, ich werde alles bezahlen." Das ist das Ende von dem Gleichnis. Aber die Geschichte geht natürlich weiter, und ich wieß wie sie weitergeht. Am nachsten Tag … als der Man zur Besinnung gekommen ist, da hat er natürlich den Wirt gefragt: "Wer war denn das, der mir hierhergebracht hat und alles bezahlen will bis ich wieder gesund bin?" Und da hat der Wirt gesagt … "alles was ich weiß ist, daß er ein Samariter ist; er hat nicht unseren Glauben, und er gehört nicht zu unserem Volk." Und dann hat dieser Halbtotgeschlagene zunächst [gesagt] … "Von solch einem Samariter nehme

ich keine Wohltaten an." Aber dann hat er überlegt: "Er hat gesagt,
er hat wohl einen anderen Glauben, aber wenn der Glaube von dem
Mann ihn zu dem bringt, was er getan hat, dann muß man Respekt
davor haben."

    Und das, denke ich, haben auch die skeptischen Bürger hier in
diesen Tagen erlebt. Wir haben Ihren Glauben noch nicht. Aber wenn
Ihr Glaube dazu führt, daß man so froh und frei und natürlich wie sie
wird, dann muß man auch Respekt davor haben. Und wenn man-
cher nach Hause geht mit einem tiefen Respekt vor dem christlichen
Glauben, dann ist das nicht der entscheidende Schritt, dennoch is das
der erste Schritt zu Christus, und dann müssen die anderen Schritte
folgen.

144 Geldbach, "'Evangelisch,' 'evangelikal,'" 157.

Chapter Five

1 Stanley, "Lausanne 1974," 533–1. This view is also echoed by missiologist
Charles Van Engen. See Van Engen, "Broadening Vision", 217–24.
2 Douglas, *Let the Earth Hear His Voice*, 6. For more on the impact of ICOWE
on fundamentalist missionary work, see Tizon, *Transformation after Lausanne*. For a complete version of the Lausanne Covenant, see "Lausanne
Covenant," *Ecumenical Movement*, 358–63.
3 "Janz Team Singers Tour," *Janz Team Reporter*, January–March 1975, 3,
Newsletter Files, Office Records, Janz Team Ministries, Winnipeg, Manitoba
(JTMW hereafter); interview with Cornelius Enns, 6 August, 2006, Three
Hills, Alberta. Interview notes in personal files of author.
4 For more on the 68er movement in Europe in general and Germany in
particular, see Gilcher-Holtey, *Die 68er Bewegung*; and Dutschke, *Rudi
Dutschke*. For a journalistic portrayal, see Kurlansky, *1968*, 143–77.
5 On German anti-Americanism, see Gassert, "With America against America"; and Markovits and Rensman, "Anti-Americanism in Germany,"
168–72; see also the collection of essays in Stephan, *Americanization and
Anti-Americanism*.
6 Honeycutt, "Contextualization," 9–10. For more on missiological applica-
tions of contextualization, see the range of essays in Costa, *One Faith, Many
Cultures*; and Padilla, "Contextualization of the Gospel."
7 Taber, "Contextualization," 35; Bjork, "Model for Analysis"; Newbigin, "Mission in the 1980s," 154; and Krass, *Evangelizing*, 152–69.
8 Berman, "Anti-Americanism and Americanization," 12–16; Nolan, "Anti-
Americanism," 110–11; and Markovits, "On Anti-Americanism," 16.
9 "Report of Secretary for Europe and the Middle East," IMB Minutes 10
April 1972, Record 1317, International Mission Board Archives and Records

Services, https://solomon.imb.org/public/ws/oldmin/www2/minutesp/
Record?parenttreeid=13419636&sessiondepth=2&parenttreeid=13419636&
sessiondepth=2&w=NATIVE%28%27MIN_DATE+%3D+%27%27April+10
%2C+1972%27%27%27%29&upp=0&order=native%28%27MIN_DATE%2
FDescend%27%29&rpp=10&r=1&m=1. For more on the currency devaluation of the 1970s, see Frum, *How We Got Here*, 295–8.

10 For more on the impact of the energy crisis, see Merrill, *Oil Crisis*.

11 Stanley, "The Future in the Past," 116–17.

12 "Liebe Freunde," *Ruf* 24 (February 1981): 3.

13 For more on the secularization thesis in the latter half of the twentieth century, see Brown, *Religion and Society*, 177–314; Brown, *Death of Christian
Britain*; Bruce, *God Is Dead*, 106–84; Davie, *Europe*; Martin, *On Secularization*, 47–90. For an assessment of the rise of secularism in Western Europe,
see McLeod, *Religious Crisis*, 188–256.

14 Gabriel, "Post-war Generations," 114.

15 For a missionary perspective, see "One Vision to Catch," special issue, *Europe
Report*, newsletter of Campus Crusade for Christ Europe, Correspondence
File, Documents on the History of Campus Crusade – Europe, Records of
the Director of Communications Office, Campus for Christ – Europe (DCO-
CfCE hereafter), Kandern, Germany. For a German perspective, see Lohse,
Erneuern und Bewahren, 150–1.

16 Lilje, "Christianity in a Divided Europe," 10. Lilje can be seen as echoing
even earlier statements made by Swiss churchman Adolph Keller in 1933. See
Keller, *Religion and the European Mind*, 7.

17 "Der Bruch mit der Kirche," *Stern* 22 (25 January 1970): 14–20.

18 "Kongreß für Evangelisation in Deutschland geplant," *idea* 5 (21 July 1975):
2. *idea* is an acronym for Informatsionsdienst der Evangelischen Allianz. For more on the nature of the relationship between the DEA and the
idea-Pressedienst, see Jung, *Was ist Evangelikal?*, 25.

19 For one example, see Evans, *Let Europe Hear*, 28. Recent historical and
sociological scholarship, with the benefit of several decades of hindsight,
has confirmed the assessment of missionaries and German church leaders at the time. For some examples of such work, see McLeod, "Religious
Crisis," 221–8; Chadwick, *Christian Church*, 188–91; Herzog, "Sexual Morality," 377–80; Davie, *Europe*, 5–10; and McLeod, "Crisis of Christianity." For
a study that focuses on Britain but has also made wider application of the
1960s secularization thesis to Western Europe, see Brown, *Death of Christian Britain*.

20 Henley, *Europe at the Crossroads*, 81.

21 "Die Welt verändern," *Ruf* 19 (February 1976): 11; "Come Catch a Vision,"
special issue, *Europe Report – 1974*, newsletter of Campus Crusade for Christ
Europe, Correspondence File, Documents on the History of Campus Crusade – Europe, DCO-CfCE.

22 Lohse, *Erneuern und Bewahren*, 150–1; Roman, "Framework," 322; Anderson, "American Protestants," 114–15; Spindler, "Europe's Neo-Paganism."

23 Jim Morud to Sara Anderson and Kathy Horlacher, 4 September 1980, Memo Re rate of staff growth in Europe, file 2, Documents on the History of Campus Crusade – Europe, DCO-CfCE.

24 Leo Janz, "Rückblick," *Ruf* 22 (February 1979): 9. The original reads: "Die Türen zur Evangelisation sind weit offen. Der Herr schenkt heute noch große Möglichkeiten … Wenn wir die achtziger Jahre noch erleben dürfen, so glauben wir, daß sie die größten Möglichkeiten der Evangelisation für unsere Generation bieten werden. Wir planen jetzt schon die meisten Groß-evangelisationen 2 bis 3 Jaher im voraus."

25 "Auf Feldzug mit Gottes Hammerschlagen," *Südwest Presse*, 9 September 1976, 1; and "Evangelisation im Groß-Zelt," *Darmstädter Tagblatt*, 21 May 1976. Both articles found in Crusade scrapbook binder, "Echo der Veranstaltungen des Janz Teams" (Echo hereafter), JTM, Janz Team Ministries Records Room (JTMRR hereafter), Kandern, Germany. See also "Evangelisations-tage im 'Revier,'" *Ruf* 22 (June 1979): 8–9.

26 Janz turned sixty in 1979 and Graham the year prior.

27 "Die Welt verändern," *Ruf* 19 (February 1976): 11; "History of Campus Crusade for Christ International in Europe," news release for *Student Action Newspaper*, April 1969, Correspondence File, Documents on the History of Campus Crusade – Europe, DCO-CfCE; and McLeod, "Religious Crisis of the 1960s," 224–5.

28 Interview with Cornelius Enns. For more on the history of the pop music genre that became known as Christian contemporary music, see Peacock, *At the Crossroads*; and Baker, *Contemporary Christian Music*. For a British perspective, see Turner, *Cliff Richard*.

29 "Janz Team Singers Tour," *Janz Team Reporter*, January–March 1975, Newsletters Files, Office Records, JTMW; "Gospel-Days '76 in Korbach," *Ruf* 19 (April 1976): 7; and "Gospel Days '75 ein Erfolg," *Neue Osnabrüker Zeitung*, quoted in *Ruf* 18 (July–August 1975): 8.

30 "Auf Feldzug mit Gottes Hammerschlägen," *Südwest Presse*, 9 September 1976, in Echo, JTMRR.

31 "The Early History of Campus Crusade for Christ, Europe," file 2, Documents on the History of Campus Crusade – Europe, DCO-CfCE.

32 For more on the history of Campus Crusade, see Quebedeaux, *I Found It*; and Richardson, *Amazing Faith*; and Turner, *Bill Bright*.

33 "The Early History of Campus Crusade for Christ, Europe," transcript of interview with Dennis Griggs, n.d.; and "Staff Growth Chart, 1987," both in file 2, Documents on the History of Campus for Christ – Europe, DCO-CfCE; and "A Boatload of Boldness," *Heart to Heart*, monthly newsletter of Agape Europe, June 2006, DCO-CfCE.

34 "The Forerunners: More Than Music," *Europe Report* 5 (Summer 1975): 7, Correspondence File, Documents on the History of Campus Crusade – Europe, DCO-CfCE.

35 Jan J. van Capelleveen, "A Missionary Bible and a Missionary Youth," address delivered at the Lausanne Congress on Evangelism, 1974, file 26, box 20, collection 46, Lausanne Committee on World Evangelism, Billy Graham Center Archives, Wheaton, Illinois.

36 Pells, *Not like Us*, 239–41.

37 Janz, *Rebell in Gottes Hand*, 36–7; "Janz Team Singers Tour," *Janz Team Reporter*, January–March 1975, Newsletters Files, Office Records, JTMW.

38 For examples of the conventional literature on contextualization, see Hiebert, "Critical Contextualization"; and Bosch, "Emerging Paradigm." For the challenges of contextualization relating specifically to Western Europe, see Derham, "Evangelical Perspectives," 91–6.

39 Interview with Bob Janz, 17 October 2006, Kandern, Germany, interview notes in personal files of the author.

40 "Brienz: Evangelisation der Janz Team Ambassadors vom 4.–15. Mai 1980 in Kirchengemeindehaus," *Ruf* 23 (July–August 1980): 6–7. See also "Ruf Aktuell," *Ruf* 22 (May 1979): 2; and "Janz Team aktive," *Ruf* 25 (March 1982): 2.

41 For more on the origin and spread of anti-American protests on German university campuses, see Klimke, *The Other Alliance*, 10–107. For a broader historical context of German anti-Americanism during the Cold War period, see Nolan, "Anti-Americanization," 125–35; also Greiner, "Saigon," 51–63; and Markovits, "On Anti-Americanism," 10–15.

42 "Das Persönliche Wort," *Ruf* 18 (July–August 1975): 3. Raymond Aron was known for his critiques of Marxism and of the European intellectual set who championed Marx's ideas. For a summary of Aron's views of Marxism, see Anderson, *Raymond Aron*, 61–121. For Aron's critique of early Cold War European intellectual culture, see Aron, *Opium*.

43 Henley, *Europe at the Crossroads*, 86–7.

44 Rainer Hainisch interview, 6 August 2006, Digital Records (CD copy in possession of the author), DCO-CfCE; and Klimke, *Other Alliance*, 60–80.

45 "European Students Encounter Jesus Christ," *Europe Report*, Spring 1974(?), 1, file 2, Documents on the History of Campus Crusade – Europe, DCO-CfCE.

46 "Evangelisation und Gemeinde" was the German title. See "Kongreß für Evangelisation in Deutschland geplant," *idea* 5 (21 July 1975): 2.

47 Spencer, *Story of German Evangelist Anton Schulte*; and Harding Braatan, "Historical Facts" (unpublished manuscript for Janz Team 50th Anniversary Celebrations, 2004), author's personal copy.

48 "Kongreß für Evangelisation in Deutschland geplant," *idea* 5 (21 July 1975): 2; and "Dokumentation zum Christival," *idea* 6 (11 June 1976), 1–18.

49 "Interview mit Dr. Billy Graham," *idea* 5 (4 August 1975): 6.

50 "973 Deutsche beim Brüsseler EUROFEST," *idea* 5 (4 August 1975): 1.

51 Ulrich Parzany to Billy Graham, n.d., file "Correspondence with Billy Graham," 1970s, Archives of the Deutsche Evangelische Allianz (ADEA), Bad Blankenburg, Germany.

52 Ulrich Parzany to Billy Graham, n.d., file "Correspondence with Billy Graham," 1970s, ADEA.

53 "Zwischen Christus and Marxismus," *idea* 6 (11 June 1976): 13; and "Christival Seminare," *idea* 26 (18 June 1976): 14–15.

54 Ulrich Parzany, "Wir sind Gottes Mitarbeiter"; and "Interview mit Ulrich Parzany," both in *idea* 6 (18 June 1976): 19–20, 11.

55 "Interview with Billy Graham," *idea* 6 (18 June 1976): 6–7; and "Billy Graham's Sermon at Christival," *idea* 26 (18 June 1976): 21–6.

56 Balbier, "Billy Graham in West Germany," 17.

57 Schneider to Graham, 2 November 1978, file "Correspondence with Billy Graham," 1970s, ADEA.

58 "Eurofest für Deutschland," *idea* 6 (30 June 1975): 10.

59 "Ein neuer Impuls zur Weltmission Jugend-Missionskongreß," *idea* 7 (5 January 1976): 1.

60 "Christival '76, Ein kirchengeschichtliches Ereignis," *Ruf* 19 (September 1976): 7.

61 For more on the rise of African churches in Germany and more widely in Western Europe, see Simon, "African Christians," 23–35; ter Haar, "Strangers in the Promised Land"; ter Haar, *Halfway to Paradise*, 98–108. For the mission of African-planted churches in Europe since the end of the Cold War, see Gerloff, "Religion, Culture and Resistance"; and Währisch-Oblau, "From Reverse Mission."

62 Jongeneel, "Mission of Migrant Churches," 32. See also ter Haar, *African Christians*, 166–70; Adogame, "African Christians," 431–48; and Jenkins, *God's Continent*, 87–96.

63 "Select Chronology Listing of Events in the … History of the Billy Graham Evangelistic Association," Billy Graham Center Archives, http://www.wheaton.edu/bgc/archives/bgeachro/bgeachron02.htm. See also "Graham in East Germany," *Decision Magazine* 23 (February 1983): 8–9; "Graham in Moscow: What Did He Really Say?" and "Graham in the Soviet Union," both in *Christianity Today* 28 (18 June 1982): 10–11, 42–3, 48; "Billy Graham Gets a Friendly Reception in Czechoslovakia," *Christianity Today* 26 (17 December 1982): 38–41; Martin, *Prophet with Honor*, 475–529; and Pierard, "Billy Graham and the *Wende*," 6.

64 "Select Chronology Listing of the Events in the … History of the Billy Graham Evangelistic Association."

65 For European Baptist responses to a perceived secular Europe, see Green, *Crossing the Boundaries*, 102.

66 Cauthen and Means, *Advance to Bold Mission Thrust*, 392–3. For a helpful overview of Hughey's role in guiding Southern Baptist missionary strategy in Europe, see Hill, "John David Hughey."

67 "European Strategy Conference Report, July 14–17, 1975," file 21, box 1, Collection – Arr. 711, SBHLA.

68 Ibid.

69 Ibid.

70 "Aktennotiz: deutsch-amerikanisches Gespräch am 20.3 1981 im Bundesmissionshaus Bad Homburg," file 24, box 3, Arr. 711, SBHLA. The original German text reads: "daß es dem deutschen Bund als Minderheitenkirche nicht möglich ist, Deutschland mit eigenen Kräften in ausreichender Weise zu evangelisieren. Aus diesem Grunde können wir gar nichts dagegen haben, daß unsere Glaubensgeschwister aus den USA uns bei der Evangelisierung Deutschlands helfen, zumal sie eine sehr enge Zusammenarbeit mit uns wünschen."

71 "European Strategy Conference Report, July 14–17, 1975."

72 "Aktennotiz: deutsch-amerikanisches Gespräch am 20.3 1981 im Bundesmissionshaus Bad Homburg."

73 "West Germany: Home Churches Away from Home," *Commission* 46 (February–March 1983): 77.

74 Günter Wieske to James Leeper, 3 March 1986, file 41, box 90, Collection – Arr. 551-1, SBHLA.

75 "West Germany: Home Churches Away from Home," 74.

76 J.D. Hughey, "Reflections concerning Cooperation in Europe," paper presented at the European Baptist Convention, 1981, file 11, box 1, Collection – Arr. 711, SBHLA. See also Hughey, *Baptist Partnership in Europe*, 16–17.

77 Escobar, *New Global Mission*, 164–5. The catchphrase did not make it into the lexicon of missions until the publication of Nazir-Ali's *From Everywhere to Everywhere*, but it was reflected in the official document of the Lausanne Congress and reflected the spirit of missionary attitudes thereafter.

78 Shank, "Missionary Approach," 40.

79 "Europe," MCC *Workbook, 1971*, box 6, IX-5-2, Mennonite Central Committee Archives Collection (MCCAC), Archives of the Mennonite Church USA (AMC), Goshen, Indiana.

80 "European Mennonite Bible School Annual Report 1976," file "EMBS 1975–1977," IX-12-6, MCCAC, AMC.

81 For a helpful summary on Mennonite settlements in the USSR, see Klassen, "Mennonites in Russia." For more on *Umsiedler*, see Hildebrandt and von Nissen, "Umsiedler (Aussiedler)," Global Anabaptist Mennonite Encyclopedia Online, 1989, http://www.gameo.org/encyclopedia/contents/U458ME.htm.

82 "Germany," MCC *Workbook, 1975*; and "Germany," MCC *Workbook, 1978*, both in box 7, IX-5-2, MCCAC, AMC.

83 "Germany," *MCC Workbook, 1978*.

84 "Proposed East/West Vision Expanded (1980–1985)," *MCC Workbook, 1980*, box 7, IX-5-2, MCCAC, AMC.

85 "Europe," *MCC Workbook, 1986*, box 9; and "Europe," *MCC Workbook, 1984*, box 8, both in IX-5-2, MCCAC, AMC.

86 "Jahresbericht 1980," Minutes of the Annual Meeting General Council of JTM, November 1980, file "General Council Meetings 1974–1981," Office Records, JTMW.

87 "Minutes of the General Council Annual Meeting, November 1981," file "General Council Minutes 1974–81," Office Records, JTMW.

88 "Minutes of the General Council Annual Meeting, November 1983," file "General Council Minutes 1982–87," Office Records, JTMW.

89 "Report on the European Ministry by Gordon Klenck, Director of European affairs, 1971," file 2 "Documents on the History of Campus Crusade – Europe," DCO-CfCE.

90 "European Staff, Statistical Report 1974," file 2 "Documents on the History of Campus Crusade – Europe," DCO-CfCE.

91 Quebedeaux, *I Found It*, 15–20.

92 Interview transcript from 2006 on the early history of Campus Crusade for Christ, Europe, file 2 "Documents on the History of Campus Crusade – Europe," DCO-CfCE.

93 "European Staff, Statistical Report 1983," file 2 "Documents on the History of Campus Crusade – Europe," DCO-CfCE.

94 *Heart to Heart*, monthly newsletter of Agape Europe (Campus Crusade's new name in Europe), June 2006, DCO-CfCE.

95 Interview with Irmhild Bärend, 19 February 2008, notes in possession of the author.

96 Ibid.

97 Jung, *Die deutsche Evangelikale Bewegung*, 79.

98 Waldorf, "Missionarische Bemühungen, Teil 2," 43; and Jung, *Die deutsche Evangelikale Bewegung*, 83–5.

99 Schneider to Graham, 7 August 1978, file "Correspondence with Billy Graham, 1970s," ADEA.

100 "Report on Rüschlikon to the European Baptist Federation Council 21 September, 1978," file 8, box 7, Arr. 711, SBHLA.

101 Claas to Hughey, 6 April 1978, file 12, box 7, Arr. 711, SBHLA.

102 Das Dozenten-Kollegium des Theologischen Seminars Hamburg to Hughey and Ballinger, 20 April 1978, file 12, box 7, Arr. 711, SBLA.

103 "SBC-FMB Board Meeting Minutes, 27 June 1978," record 812, International Mission Board Archives and Records Services, https://solomon.imb.org/public/ws/oldmin/www2/minutesp/Record?parenttreeid=28743214 & sessiondepth=2&parenttreeid=28743214&sessiondepth=2&w=NATIVE%

28%27MIN_DATE+%3D+%27%27June+27%2C+1978%27%27%27%29&
upp=0&order=native%28%27MIN_DATE%2FDescend%27%29&rpp=
10&r=1&m=1.

104 "Minutes of the Foreign Mission Board, 10–12 October 1988," cited in Keith Parks, "C. Penrose St Amant: President of Rüschlikon," *Perspectives in Religious Studies* 16 (Winter 1989): 54.

105 Merritt, *Betrayal*, 52.

106 Green, *Crossing the Boundaries*, 190–1.

107 For more on those events, see ibid., 185–95; Merritt, *Betrayal*, 57–84; Wagner, "Der Fall Rüschlikon"; and Jones, "International Baptist Theological Seminary."

108 "Switzerland," MCC *Workbook 1975*, box 7, IX-5-2, MCCAC, AMC.

109 "Western Europe Program," MCC *Workbook 1990*, box 9, IX-5-2, MCCAC, AMC.

110 "Germany," MCC *Workbook 1978*, box 7; and "Europe" MCC *Workbook 1984*, box 8, both in IX-5-2, MCCAC, AMC.

111 "Germany," MCC *Workbook 1978*.

112 In the area of pop music, see Ellsworth, *Christian Music*, 120–82; and Baker, *Contemporary Christian Music*, 53–141.

113 The use of the term *post-Christian* by an American missionary to describe Europe comes as early as 1954; see Shank, "Missionary Approach," 40.

114 For an example, see Gilcher-Holtey, *Die 68er Bewegung*.

115 This is supported in Graham's case by the coverage by both religious and secular news media of his visits behind the Iron Curtain. See "Graham in the Soviet Union," and "Graham in Moscow: What Did He Really Say?," both *Christianity Today* 26 (18 June 1982): 42–4, 10–12; and "News Watch, Thomas Griffith: Defaming with Questions," *Time* 59 (24 September 1982): 1–3.

116 Stanley, "Lausanne 1974," 536–7, 551.

117 Holthaus, *Die Evangelikalen*, 20–5.

118 Jung, *Was ist Evangelikal?*, 85.

Conclusion

1 Kreider, "West Europe in Missional Perspective," 214.

2 Robert, "First Globalization"; and Wright, *World Mission*, 170–7.

3 Carpenter, "Propagating the Faith Once Delivered," 92–8.

4 Patterson, "The Loss of a Protestant Missionary Consensus," 73–91.

5 Carpenter, "Propagating the Faith Once Delivered," 94–7.

6 For an example, see Anderson, "American Protestants in Pursuit of Mission," 108–11.

7 "Church World Service Minutes, Committee on Cooperation with the Churches in Europe 22 April 1949," file "Europe 1943–49," box 90, RG 8, Papers of the National Council of Churches and files of the Church World

Service, Presbyterian Historical Society (NCC-CWS, PHS hereafter), Philadelphia.

8 Solberg, *Between Brothers*, 190–1.

9 Mackie, "Inter-Church Aid in Europe," 186–7.

10 "Graham at the Gate," *Christian Century* (CC) 76 (19 October 1960): 1208. For more on *Brot für die Welt* and its creation as a response of gratitude and goodwill by Germans to postwar ecumenical aid, see Berg, "Brot für die Welt," 160, 166–7.

11 Carl E. Schneider, "Fading Ecumenical Mood," CC 66 (15 February 1950): 205–6.

12 For more on the theological discussion that fuelled this new direction, see Hutchison, "Americans in World Mission," 159–60; and Detzler, *Changing Church in Europe*, 25–39.

13 Railton, "German Free Churches," 93–9; and Voigt, *Die Evangelische Allianz*, 25, 39.

14 Railton, "German Free Churches," 99.

15 Geldbach, *Freikirchen: Erbe*, 33–7, 43–4.

16 I am indebted to Brian Stanley's helpful insights for pointing me in this direction.

17 Geldbach, "'*Evangelisch*,' '*Evangelikal*' and Pietism," 157–8.

18 Dibelius, "Komm wieder," *Entscheidung*, March–April 1970, 4.

19 For examples, see *Pfarrer* Jakob Kurz, "Der Herr hat Großes an uns getan, des sind wir fröhlich," *Der Menschenfischer* 3 (September 1959): 4–5; *Pfarrer* K.E. Lohmann, "Gemeinsam ein Ziel," *Ruf* 18 (July–August 1975): 6; and *Prediger* Wolfgang Kegel, "Die Korbacher wußten Beschied," *Ruf* 14 (January 1970): 8.

20 For example, see Beyreuther, *Der Weg der Evangelischen Allianz*, 113–41; also Jung, *Die deutsche Evangelikale Bewegung,* 23, 65–71; and Waldorf, "Missionarische Bemühungen," 10–15.

21 Railton, *No North Sea*, xxi.

22 Balbier, "Billy Graham in West Germany," 17.

23 Noll, *New Shape of World Christianity*, 110–21. In contrasting the American pluralist voluntaristic Christianity specifically to German models, see Lehmann, "Christianization of America," 12.

24 Jung, *Was ist Evangelikal?*, 18–30.

25 Jung, *Die deutsche Evangelikale Bewegung*, 60–1, 77–8.

26 Lützenberger, *... aber Gottes Wort ist nicht gebunden*, 18–45. See also Marquardt, *Meine Geschichte*; on Trans World Radio, see Freed, *Trans World Radio*.

27 Holthaus, *Die Evangelikalen*, 25.

28 For examples, see "Evangelikaler in Deutschland: Um Gottes willen!," http://www.taz.de/Evangelikale-in-Deutschland/!5169874/; "Evangelikale

Christen: konservative bis radikal," http://www.planet-wissen.de/kultur/
religion/jenseits_der_traditionellen_kirchen/pwieevangelikalechristen
konservativbisradikal100.html. See also "Scholz unterstützt Kongress
radikaler Christen," http://www.ndr.de/nachrichten/investigation/
Scholz-unterstuetzt-Kongress-radikaler-Christen,fuehrungskraefte
kongress100.html.

29 "Eine ungeheure Verdrehung der Debatte," 31 March 2009,
http://www.deutschlandradiokultur.de/eine-ungeheure-verdrehung-der-
debatte.954.de.html?dram:article_id=144149.

30 For example, see Gary, *None Dare Call It Conspiracy*; and Roy, *Communism and the Churches*.

31 An example from popular missionary literature is Brother Andrew, *God's Smuggler*.

32 See Cox, *British Missionary Enterprise*; Porter, *Religion versus Empire?*; Stanley, *The Bible and the Flag*; and Stanley, *Missions, Nationalism and the End of Empire*.

33 Reed, *Missionary Mind*; and Preston, "Reviving Religion," 25–54.

34 Balbier, "Billy Graham in West Germany," 14–15.

35 For more on the development of Negro spiritual music in American culture, see Jones, *Wade in the Water*.

36 Kraska, *Es begann mit Musik*, 4.

37 Ibid., 42, 46; and Janz, *Rebell in Gottes Hand*, 36–8.

38 See Lützenbürger, … *aber Gottes Wort*, 41–2.

39 Iain Wilson, "German Churches Fail Youth," CC 65 (30 March 1949): 397–8; and E. Theodore Bachmann, "Self-help in German Churches," CC 64 (31 December 1948): 1609–10.

40 Fehrenbach, "Persistent Myths of Americanization"; Poiger, "American Music"; and Goedde, *GIs and Germans*.

41 For examples, see Stephan, "A Special German Case"; Nolan, "Anti-Americanism"; Pells, "Double Crossings"; and Gienow-Hecht, "Always Blame the Americans."

42 For more on the contours and history of World Christianity, see Sanneh, *Whose Religion Is Christianity?*; and Jenkins, *Next Christendom*.

43 Stafford, "Historian Ahead of His Time."

44 See McLeod, "The Crisis of Christianity in the West."

45 Jenkins, *God's Continent*, 87–102; Jongeneel, "Mission of Migrant Churches," 31–2; and Währisch-Oblau, "From Reverse Mission," 468–71, 475–7.

46 See chapter 8 of ter Haar, *Halfway to Paradise*; and Währisch-Oblau, "From Reverse Mission," 475–6.

47 Barstow to the Council Committee on Germany, 13 November 1945, file –"Europe Committee," box 91, Record Group (RG) 8, NCC-CWS, PHS.

48 "Protestant World Relief," CC 64 (14 May 1947): 614.

49 Bachmann, "Self-help in German Churches."
50 Carl E. Schneider, "Fading Ecumenical Mood," CC 66 (15 February 1950): 205–6.
51 This consensus is reflected in several historical accounts: Bachman, *Together in Hope*, 29, 40; Egan and Reiss, *Transfigured Night*, 130, 160, 164, 169; Conway, "How Shall the Nations Repent?," 619–20.
52 "Germany," *European Relief Notes*, December 1947, 4, Information Services, Periodicals and Newsletters, IX-40-2, Mennonite Central Committee Archives Collection (MCCAC), Archives of the Mennonite Church, USA (AMC), Goshen, Indiana.
53 Jessie Franks, "Our Seven Years," file 3, box 251, Arr. 551-1, Southern Baptist Convention – Foreign Mission Board, Mission Minutes and Reports 1849–1990, Southern Baptist Historical Library and Archives (SBHLA), Nashville, Tennessee.
54 David A. Shank, "Review of Political, Social and Religious Developments in Europe over the Last Decade That Have Had an Effect on Our Mission," paper presented at Mennonite Europe Study Conference, Bienenberg, 18–20 July 1976, file 47, IX-12-4, MCCAC, AMC; and Hughey, *Europe: A Mission Field?*, 10–11.
55 For examples from Southern Baptist publications, see "Cultured Europeans Require Educated Ministry," *Commission* 21 (July 1958): 19; and "A Unifying Force for Europe's Baptists," *Commission* 23 (April 1960): 6. For examples from MCC publications, see "Bienenberg Says Thanks," MCC News Service, 18 October 1968, file "EMBS 1965–1974," IX-12-6, MCCAC, AMC; and Peter J. Dyck, open letter to Mennonite churches in North America – Bienenberg Choir Tour, 23 April 1974, file "EMBS 1965–1974," IX-12-6, MCCAC, AMC.
56 Cauthen and Means, *Advance to Bold Mission Thrust*, 223–7; and J.H. Yoder, "Historical Perspective and Current Issues," European Study Conference 18–21 July 1967, Bienenberg, file 47, IX-12-4; and "Annual Report," MCC *Workbook 1967*, IX-5-2, both in MCCAC, AMC.
57 Balbier, "Billy Graham in West Germany," 13–15.
58 For examples from Janz Team Ministries, see "Liebe Freunde," *Ruf* 15 (September 1971): 3; Prediger Wolfgang Kegel, "Die Korbacher wußten Beschied," *Ruf* 14 (January 1970): 8. For examples from Billy Graham's work, see Brauer, *Europas goldene Stunde*, 82; "Grossevangelisation in Deutschland," *Entscheidung*, Fall 1963, 8–9; and "Deutschlandhalle, 16 Oktober: Dr. Billy Graham in Berlin," *Evangelisches Allianzblatt*, November 1966, 218.
59 I am indebted to Brian Stanley for suggesting this framework for a concluding critique.

REFERENCES

Archival Collections and Institutional Records

American Friends Service Committee Archives, Philadelphia, Pennsylvania
Baptist Historical Society Archives, Valley Forge, Pennsylvania (since moved to Mercer University, Atlanta, Georgia)
Baptist World Alliance records, Angus Library, Regents Park College, Oxford, UK
Billy Graham Center Archives, Wheaton College, Wheaton, Illinois
Billy Graham Evangelistic Association – Germany, Offices of Geschenke der Hoffnung, Berlin, Germany
Campus for Christ – Europe, Records of the Director of Communications office, Kandern, Germany
Deutsche Evangelische Allianz historical records, Bad Blankenburg, Germany
Janz Team e.V. Office records, Kandern, Germany
Janz Team Ministries (since renamed TeachBeyond), office records, Winnipeg, Manitoba
Mennonite Central Committee records, Mennonite Church–USA archives, Goshen, Indiana
Records of the Religion and Educational Affairs Branch of the Occupational Military Government United States (OMGUS) in Germany, National Archives, College Park, Maryland
Southern Baptist Historical Library and Archives, Nashville, Tennessee
World Council of Churches library and archives, Geneva, Switzerland
Yale Divinity School Archives, New Haven, Connecticut

Interviews and Unpublished Personal Papers

Braatan, Harding. "JTM: Historical Facts." Unpublished manuscript for Janz Team 50th Anniversary Celebrations, 2004. Author's personal copy.
Claas, Gerhard. "Oral Memoirs, 26 November 1984–12 October 1987," digital transcript, no. b2500136x, Texas collection, Baylor University Library, Waco, Texas.

Newspapers and Periodicals (Selected issues 1945–1985)

Baptist Quarterly Review (Nashville)
Canadian Churchman (Toronto)
Christian Century (Chicago)
Christianity and Crisis (New York)
Christianity Today (Carol Stream, IL)
Commission (Southern Baptist Convention)
Decision Magazine, Canadian edition (Calgary)
Der Menschenfischer (Lörrach, Germany)
Entscheidung (Frankfurt, Berlin)
Evangelical Christian (Toronto)
Evangelikaler Missiologie (Stuttgart)
Evangelisches Allianzblatt/Evangelischer Allianz Brief (Berlin)
Heart to Heart (Kandern, Germany, Campus Crusade for Christ International)
His Magazine (Intervarsity Christian Fellowship, Chicago)
Home Life Magazine (Southern Baptist)
Home Missions Magazine (Southern Baptist)
idea: Informationsdienst der Evangelischen Allianz (Wetzlar)
Licht und Leben (Elberfeld, Germany)
Missions (American Baptist Foreign Mission Society)
Moody Monthly (Chicago)
Newsweek Magazine (New York)
Other Side (Savannah, OH)
Peoples Magazine (Toronto)
Perspectives in Religious Studies
Reformed Journal (Grand Rapids, MI)
Ruf zur Entscheidung (Lörrach, Germany)
Sonntagsblatt (München)
Stern Magazin (Hamburg)
Sunday School Times (Philadelphia)
Time Magazine (New York)
United Church Observer (Toronto)
United Evangelical Action (Wheaton, IL)
Watchman Examiner (Worcester, NY)
Youth for Christ Magazine (Chicago)

Published Sources and Academic Papers

Adogame, Afe. "African Christians in a Secularizing Europe." *Religion Compass*, 3 July 2009, 431–48.

Airhart, Phyllis. *The Church with the Soul of a Nation: Making and Remaking the United Church of Canada.* Montreal and Kingston: McGill-Queen's University Press, 2014.

Albaugh, Dana M. *Who Shall Separate Us?* Chicago: Judson, 1962.

Anderson, Brian. *Raymond Aron: The Recovery of the Political.* Boston: Rowman and Littlefield, 1997.

Anderson, Gerald H. "American Protestants in Pursuit of Mission: 1886–1986." *International Bulletin of Missionary Research* 12 (July 1988): 98–118.

Andrew, Brother. *God's Smuggler: An Account of a Courageous Man across the Borders of the Iron Curtain.* Westwood, NJ: Revell, 1968.

Aron, Raymond. *The Opium of the Intellectuals.* London: Secker and Warburg, 1957.

Bachman, John W. *Together in Hope: 50 Years of Lutheran World Relief.* New York: Lutheran World Relief, 1995.

Baker, Paul. *Contemporary Christian Music: Where It Came From, What It Is, Where It's Going.* Westchester, IL: Crossway Books, 1985.

Balbier, Uta Andrea. "Billy Graham in West Germany: German Protestantism between Americanization and Rechristianization, 1954–70." *Zeithistorische Forschungen* 7, no. 3 (2010): 2–24.

Balders, Günter. *Theuer Bruder Oncken.* Kassel: Oncken Verlag, 1978.

Barnett, Victoria. *For the Soul of the People: Protestant Protest against Hitler.* Oxford: Oxford University Press, 1992.

Barnhart, Joe E. *The Billy Graham Religion.* Philadelphia: United Church Press, 1972.

Bayley, C.A., Sven Beckert, Matthew Connelly, Isabel Hofmeyr, Wedny Kozol, and Patricia Seed. "AHR Conversation: On Transnational History," *American Historical Review* 111 (December 2006): 1441–64.

Beale, David. *In Pursuit of Purity: American Fundamentalism since 1850.* Greenville, SC: BJU, 1986.

Bebbington, David W. *Evangelicalism in Modern Britain: A History from the 1730s to the 1980s.* Grand Rapids, MI: Baker Book House, 1989.

Bell, Edwin A. *Europe's Jericho Roads.* New York: American Baptist Foreign Mission Society, 1944.

Bender, Harold S. "New Life through the Sunday School," In *The Mennonite Church in America,* edited by J.C. Wenger, 144–81. Scottdale, PA: Herald, 1966.

Bentley, James. *Martin Niemöller.* Oxford: Oxford University Press, 1984.

Berg, Christian. "Brot für die Welt. Bemerkungen zur Entstehung und Bedeutung einer ökumenischen Aktion der evangelischen Christenheit in Deutschland." In *Gemeinde Gottes in dieser Welt: Festgabe für Friedrich-Wilhelm Krummacher zum sechzigsten Geburtstag*, edited by Friederich Bartsch and Werner Rautenberg, 159–70. Berlin: Evangelische Verlagsanstalt, 1961.

Bergen, Doris. *Twisted Cross: The German Christian Movement in the Third Reich.* Chapel Hill, NC: University of North Carolina Press, 1996.

Berman, Russell A. "Anti-Americanism and Americanization." In *Americanization and Anti-Americanism: The German Encounter with American Culture after 1945,* edited by Alexander Stephan, 12–24. New York: Berghahn Books, 2005.

Besier, Gerhard. "Protestantismus, Kommunismus und Ökumene in den Vereinigten Staaten von Amerika." In *Nationaler Protestantismus und Ökumenische Bewegung: Kirchliches Handeln im Kalten Krieg, 1945–1990,* edited by Gerhard Beiser, Armin Boyens, and Gerhard Lindemann, 323–652. Berlin: Duncker and Humbolt, 1999.

Besier, Gerhard, and Gerhard Sauter. *Wie Christen ihre Schuld bekennen. Die Stuttgarter Erklärung 1945.* Göttingen: Vandenhoeck & Ruprecht, 1985.

Beyreuther, Erich. *Der Weg der Evangelischen Allianz in Deutschland.* Wuppertal: Theologischer Verlag Rolf Brockhaus, 1969.

– *Kirche in Bewegung: Geschichte der Evangelisation und Volksmission.* Berlin: CZV Verlag, 1968.

Bjork, David. "A Model for Analysis of Incarnational Ministry in Post-Christian Lands." *Missiology: An International Review* 25 (July 1997): 279–91.

Bodenstein, Walter. *Ist nur der Besiegte schuldig? Die EKD und das Stuttgarter Schuldbekenntnis von 1945.* Berlin: Ullstein, 1986.

Bosch, David J. "An Emerging Paradigm for Mission." *Missiology: An International Review* 11 (October 1983): 485–510.

Boyens, Armen. "Das Stuttgarter Schuldbekenntnis vom 19 Oktober 1945. Entstehung und Bedeutung." *Vierteljahrhefte für Zeitgeschichte* 29 (1971): 374–97.

– "Die Kirchenpolitik der amerikanischen Besatzungsmacht in Deutschland von 1944 bis 1946." In *Kirchen in der Nachkriegszeit,* 7–97. Göttingen: Vandenhoeck & Ruprecht, 1979.

Boyer, Paul S. *By the Bomb's Early Light: American Thought and Culture at the Dawn of the Atomic Age.* New York: Pantheon Books, 1985.

– *When Time Shall Be No More: Prophecy Belief in Modern American Culture.* Cambridge, MA: Harvard University Press, 1992.

Brauer, Wilhelm, ed. *Europas goldene Stunde.* Wuppertal: R. Brockhaus Verlag, 1955.

Brereton, Virginia Lieson. *Training God's Army: The American Bible School, 1880–1940.* Bloomington, IN: University of Indiana Press, 1990.

Briggs, John. "Theology Meets History." In *European Baptists and the Third Reich,* edited by Bernard Green, 235–51. Didcot, UK: Baptist Historical Society, 2009.

Browder, Dewey A. *Americans in Post–World War II Germany: Teachers, Tinkers, Neighbors and Nuisances.* Lewiston, NY: Edwin Mellen, 1998.

Brown, Callum. *The Death of Christian Britain: Understanding Secularisation 1800–2000.* London: Routledge, 2001.

– *Religion and Society in Twentieth-Century Britain.* New York: Pearson Longman, 2006.

Bruce, Steve. *God Is Dead.* Oxford: Wiley-Blackwell, 2002.

Bruns, Hans. *Jakob Vetter.* Giessen: Brunnen Verlag, 1954.

Buscher, Frank. "The Great Fear: The Catholic Church and the Anticipated Radicalization of Expellees and Refugees in Post-war Germany." *German History* 21 (May 2003): 204–24.

Callaway, Timothy Wray, "Training Disciplined Soldiers for Christ: The Influence of American Fundamentalisms on Prairie Bible Institute during the L.E. Maxwell Era – 1922–1980." PhD diss., University of South Africa, Pretoria, 2010.

Campbell, Robert J. *Light for the Night in Europe: Reflections on a Lifetime of Ministry.* USA: Robert Campbell, 1999.

Carpenter, Joel A. "From Fundamentalism to the New Evangelical Coalition." In *Evangelicalism in Modern America,* edited by George Marsden, 3–16. Grand Rapids, MI: William B. Eerdmans, 1984.

– "Introduction." In *The Youth for Christ Movement and Its Pioneers,* edited by Joel A. Carpenter, 1–9. New York: Taylor and Francis, 1988.

– "Propagating the Faith Once Delivered: The Fundamentalist Missionary Enterprise, 1920–1945." In *Earthen Vessels: American Evangelicals and Foreign Missions, 1880–1980,* edited by Joel A. Carpenter and Wilbert R. Shenk, 92–132. Grand Rapids, MI: William B. Eerdmans, 1990.

– *Revive Us Again: The Reawakening of American Fundamentalism.* New York: Oxford University Press, 1997.

Carver, W.O. *The Course of Christian Missions.* New York: Revell, 1939.

Caudil, R. Paul. *The Romance of Relief.* Np: American Baptist Foreign Mission Society, 1950.

Cauthen, Baker J., and Frank K. Means. *Advance to Bold Mission Thrust: A History of the Southern Baptist Foreign Missions, 1845–1980.* Np: Foreign Mission Board, Southern Baptist Convention, 1981.

Cavert, Samuel McCrea. *The American Churches in the Ecumenical Movement, 1900–1968.* New York: Association, 1968.

Chadwick, Owen. *The Christian Church in the Cold War.* London: Penguin, 1992.

Clark, Francis E., and Harriet A. Clark. *Gospel in Latin Lands: Outline Studies of Protestant Work in the Latin Countries of Europe and America.* New York: Macmillan, 1909.

Clay, Lucius D. *Decision in Germany.* New York: Doubleday, 1950.

Coffman, Elesha. "A Long Ride on the Mainline." *Books and Culture* 14 (November/December 2008): 20–3.

Conway, John S. "How Shall the Nations Repent? The Stuttgart Declaration of Guilt, October, 1945." *Journal of Ecclesiastical History* 38 (October 1987): 596–622.

– *The Nazi Persecution of the Churches, 1933–1945.* New York: Basic Books, 1968.

Costa, Ruy O., ed. *One Faith, Many Cultures: Inculturation, Indigenization and Contextualization.* Mary Knoll, NY: Orbis Books, 1988.

Cox, Jeffrey. *The British Missionary Enterprise since 1700.* New York: Routledge, 2008.

– "Master Narratives of Religious Change." In *The Decline of Christendom in Western Europe, 1750–2000,* edited by Hugh McLeod and Werner Ustorf, 201–17. Cambridge: Cambridge University Press, 2003.

Crawley, Winston. *Global Mission: A Story to Tell.* Nashville: Broadman, 1985.

Davidson, Eugene. *The Death and Life of Germany: An Account of the American Occupation.* Columbia, MO: University of Missouri Press, 1959.

Davie, Grace. *Europe: The Exceptional Case – Parameters of Faith in the Modern World.* London: Darton Longman and Todd, 2002.

– *Religion in Britain since 1945.* Oxford: Blackwell, 1994.

Derham, A. Morgan. "Evangelical Perspectives in Western Europe." In *Serving Our Generation: Evangelical Strategies for the Eighties,* edited by Waldron Scott, 87–96. Colorado Springs, CO: World Evangelical Fellowship, 1980.

Detzler, Wayne A. *The Changing Church in Europe.* Grand Rapids, MI: Zondervan, 1980.

Dibelius, Otto. *In the Service of the Lord.* Translated by Mary Ilford. London: Faber and Faber, 1965.

– "Komm wieder." *Entscheidung,* March–April 1970, 4.

Doering-Manteuffel, Anselm. *Wie westlich sind did Deutschen?: Amerikanisierung und Westernisierung im 20. Jahrhundert.* Göttingen: Vandenhoeck & Ruprecht, 1999.

Donat, Rudolf. *Wie das Werk begann. Entstehung der deutschen Baptistengemeinden.* Kassel: Oncken Verlag, 1958.

Douglas, J.D., ed. *Let the Earth Hear His Voice: Official Papers and Responses/International Congress on World Evangelization, Lausanne, Switzerland.* Minneapolis: International Congress on World Evangelization, 1975.

Dulles, Eleanor Lansing. *One Germany or Two: The Struggle at the Heart of Europe.* Stanford: Hoover Institution, 1970.

Dulles, John Foster. *War or Peace.* New York: MacMillan, 1957.

Durnbaugh, Donald F. *The Believers' Church: The History and Character of Radical Protestantism.* New York: MacMillan, 1968.

– *Fruit of the Vine: A History of the Brethren, 1705–1995.* Elgin, IL: Brethren, 1997.

– "John Howard Yoder's Role in 'The Lordship of Christ over Church and State' Conferences." *Mennonite Quarterly Review* 77 (July 2003): 371–86.

Dutschke, Gretchen. *Rudi Dutschke: wir hatten ein barbarisches, schönes Leben.* Cologne: Kiepenheuer und Witsch, 2006.

Dyck, Cornelius J., Robert S. Kreider, and John A. Lapp, eds. *The Mennonite Central Committee Story.* Vol. 2, *Documents: Responding to Worldwide Needs.* Scottdale, PA: Herald, 1980.

Dyck, Peter, and Elfrieda Dyck. *Up from the Rubble.* Waterloo, ON: Herald, 1991.

Effa, Allan. "The Legacy of Paul and Clara Gebauer." *International Bulletin of Missionary Research* 30 (April 2006): 92–6.

Egan, Eileen, and Elizabeth Clark Reiss. *Transfigured Night: The CRALOG Experience.* Philadelphia: Livingston Publishing, 1964.

Eissler, Johannes, ed. *60 Jahre Deutsche Evangelistenkonferenz.* Wetzlar: Deutsche Evangelistenkonferenz, 2009.

Ellsworth, Donald P. *Christian Music in Contemporary Witness: Historical Antecedents and Contemporary Practices.* Grand Rapids, MI: Baker Book House, 1979.

Enns, James. "Every Christian a Missionary: Fundamentalist Education at Prairie Bible Institute, 1922–1947." MA thesis, University of Calgary, 2000.

– "Sustaining the Faithful and Proclaiming the Gospel in a Time of Crisis: The Voice of Popular Evangelical Periodicals during the Second World War." In *Historical Papers 2004, Canadian Society of Church History Annual Conference, University of Manitoba, 3–4 June 2004,* edited by Bruce Gunther, 113–32. Canada: Canadian Society of Church History, 2004.

Ermarth, Michael. "Counter-Americanism and Critical Currents in West German Reconstruction, 1945–1960." In *Americanization and Anti-Americanism: The German Encounter with American Culture after 1945,* edited by Alexander Stephan, 25–50. New York: Berghahn Books, 2005.

Escobar, Samuel. *The New Global Mission: The Gospel from Everywhere to Everyone.* Downers Grove, IL: IVP Academic, 2003.

Estep, William R. *Whole Gospel, Whole World: The Foreign Mission Board of the Southern Baptist Convention, 1845–1995.* Nashville: Broadman and Holman, 1994.

Europe: Where American Baptists Cooperate. New York: American Baptist Foreign Mission Society, 1955.

Evans, Robert, P. *Let Europe Hear: The Spiritual Plight of Europe.* Chicago: Moody, 1963.

Faber, Lynn, and Connie Jost. *Family Matters: Discovering the Mennonite Brethren.* Winnipeg, MB: Kindred Productions, 2002.

Fehr, James Jacob, and Diether Götz Lichdi. "Mennonites in Germany." In *Testing Faith and Tradition: Global Mennonite History Series: Europe,* edited by John A. Lapp and C. Arnold Snyder, 97–152. Kitchener, ON: Pandora, 2006.

Fehrenbach, Heide. "Persistent Myths of Americanization: Germany Reconstruction and the Renationalization of Postwar Cinema, 1945–1965." In *Transactions, Transgressions and Transformations: American Culture in Western Europe and Japan,* edited by Heide Fehrenbach and Uta G. Poiger, 81–108. New York: Berghahn Books, 2000.

Felken, Detlef. *Dulles und Deutschland: Die amerikanishe Deustchlandpolitik 1953–1959.* Bonn: Bouvier, 1993.

Fiedler, Klaus. *The Story of Faith Missions from Hudson Taylor to Present Day Africa.* Oxford: Regnum Books, 1994.

Forbes, Forrest. *God Hath Chosen*. Grand Rapids, MI: Zondervan, 1948.

Foschepoth, Joseph. "German Reaction to Defeat and Occupation." In *West Germany under Construction: Politics, Society, and Culture in the Adenauer Era,* edited by Robert G. Moeller, 73–89. Ann Arbor: University of Michigan Press, 1997.

Foster, David. *Euro 70 Acht Tage Verkündigung der christlichen Botschaft mit den Mitteln moderner Technik in Europa.* Frankfurt/M: np, 1971.

Frady, Marshall. *Billy Graham: A Parable of American Righteousness.* London: Hodder and Stoughton, 1979.

Freed, Paul. *Trans World Radio: Towers to Eternity.* Nashville: Thomas Nelson Publishers, 1979.

Frum, David. *How We Got Here: The '70s.* New York: Basic Books, 2000.

Gabriel, Karl. "Post-war Generations and Institutional Religion in Germany." In *The Post-war Generation and Establishment Religions: Cross-cultural Perspectives,* edited by Wade Clark Roof, Jackson W. Caroll, and David A. Roozen, 113–30. Boulder, CO: Westview, 1995.

Gaines, David P. *The World Council of Churches: A Study of Its Background and History.* Peterborough, NH: R.R. Smith, 1966.

Gary, Allen. *None Dare Call It Conspiracy.* Rossmoor, CA: Concord, 1971.

Gassert, Philipp. "With America against America: Anti-Americanism in West Germany." In *The United States and Germany in the Era of the Cold War, 1945–1990.* Vol. 1, edited by Detlef Junker, Philipp Gassert, and Wilfried Mausbach, 501–9. Cambridge: Cambridge University Press, 2004.

Geldbach, Erich. "'Evangelisch,' 'Evangelikal' and Pietism: Some Remarks on Early Evangelicalism and Globalization from a German Perspective." In *A Global Faith: Essays on Evangelicalism and Globalization,* edited by Mark Hutchinson and Ogbu Kalu, 156–80. Sydney: Centre for the Study of Australian Christianity, 1998.

– *Freikirchen: Erbe, Gestalt und Wirkung.* Göttingen: Vandenhoeck & Ruprecht, 1989.

Genizi, Haim. *American Apathy: The Plight of Christian Refugees from Nazism.* Jerusalem: Bar-Ilan University Press, 1983.

– *America's Fair Share: The Admission and Resettlement of Displaced Persons, 1945–1952.* Detroit: Wayne State University Press, 1993.

– "Problems of Protestant Cooperation: The Church World Service, the World Council of Churches and Post-war Relief in Germany." In *Holocaust and Church Struggle: Religion, Power and the Politics of Resistance,* Studies in the Shoah, vol. 16, edited by Marcia Sachs Littell and Hubert G. Locke, 163–96. Lanham, MD: University Press of America, 1996.

Gerlach, Wolfgang. *And the Witnesses Were Silent: The Confessing Church and the Persecution of the Jews.* Translated by Victoria J. Barnett. Lincoln: University of Nebraska Press, 2000.

Gerloff, Roswith. "Religion, Culture and Resistance: The Significance of African Christian Communities in Europe." *Exchange* 30 (July 2001): 276–88.

Gibbs, Nancy, and Michael Duffy. *The Preacher and the Presidents: Billy Graham in the White House*. New York: Center Street, 2007.

Gienow-Hecht, Jessica C.E. "Always Blame the Americans: Anti-Americanism in Europe in the Twentieth Century." *American Historical Review* 111 (October 2006): 1067–91.

Gilcher-Holtey, Ingrid. *Die 68er Bewegung: Deutschland, Westeuropa, USA*. Munich: Beck, 2001.

Gimbel, John. *The American Occupation of Germany: Politics and the Military, 1945–1949*. Stanford: Stanford University Press, 1968.

– *A German Community under American Occupation: Marburg, 1945–52*. Stanford: Stanford University Press, 1961.

Goedde, Petra. *GIs and Germans: Culture, Gender, and Foreign Relations, 1945–1949*. New Haven, CT: Yale University Press, 2003.

Goodall, Norman, ed. *The Uppsala Report 1968: Official Report of the Fourth Assembly of the World Council of Churches, July 2–20, 1968*. Geneva: World Council of Churches, 1968.

Graham, Billy. *Just as I Am*. New York: Harper Collins, 1997.

Gravel, Mike, ed. *The Pentagon Papers*. Vol. 1. Boston: Beacon, 1971.

Green, Bernard. *A Biography of James Henry Rushbrooke: Tomorrow's Man*. Didcot, UK: Baptist Historical Society, 1997.

– *Crossing the Boundaries: A History of the European Baptist Federation*. Didcot, UK: Baptist Historical Society, 1999.

– *European Baptists and the Third Reich*. Didcot, UK: Baptist Historical Society, 2009.

Greiner, Bernd. "Saigon, Nuremburg, and the West." In *Americanization and Anti-Americanism: The German Encounter with American Culture after 1945*, edited by Alexander Stephan, 51–63. New York: Berghahn Books, 2005.

Hefley, James. *God Goes to High School*. Waco, TX: Word Books, 1970.

Helmreich, Ernst Christian. *The German Churches under Hitler: Background, Struggle and Epilogue*. Detroit: Wayne State University Press, 1979.

Henley, Wallace. *Europe at the Crossroads: A Reporter Looks at Europe's Spiritual Crisis*. Westchester, IL: Good News Publishers, 1978.

Henry, Carl F.H. *The Uneasy Conscience of Modern Fundamentalism*. Grand Rapids, MI: William B. Eerdmans, 1947.

Henry, Carl F.H., and Stanley Mooneyham, eds. *One Race, One Gospel, One Task: World Congress on Evangelism, Berlin 1966*. 2 vols. Minneapolis: World Wide Publications, 1967.

Herman, Stewart. *It's Your Souls We Want*. London: Hodder and Stoughton, 1943.

– *The Rebirth of the German Church*. London: SCM, 1946.

Hermand, Jost. "Resisting Boogie-woogie Culture, Abstract Expressionism, and Pop Art: German Highbrow Objections to the Import of 'American' Forms of

Culture, 1945–1965." In *Americanization and Anti-Americanism: The German Encounter with American Culture after 1945*, edited by Alexander Stephan, 67–77. New York: Berghahn Books, 2005.

Herr, Stephen R., and Matthew L. Riegel. "Stewart W. Herman Jr, from Nazi Berlin to International Envoy." 2001. Accessed 23 July 2009, http://www.ltsg.edu/resources/herman-stewart.pdf.

Herschberger, Guy Franklin. *The Mennonite Church in the Second World War.* Scottdale, PA: Mennonite Publishing House, 1951.

Herzog, Dagmar. "Sexual Morality in the 1960s West Germany." *German History* 23 (August 2005): 371–84.

Herzog, Jonathan P. *The Spiritual-Industrial Complex: America's Religious Battle against Communism in the Early Cold War.* Oxford: Oxford University Press, 2011.

Hiebert, Paul H. "Critical Contextualization." *Missiology: An International Review* 12 (July 1984): 287–96.

Hill, Thomas W. "John David Hughey, Jr: Apostle of Partnership Missions." *Baptist History and Heritage* 23 (January 1988): 42–50.

Hockenos, Matthew, D. *A Church Divided: German Protestants Confront the Nazi Past.* Bloomington, IN: Indiana University Press, 2004.

Hölscher, Lucien. "Semantic Structures of Religious Change in Modern Germany." In *The Decline of Christendom in Western Europe, 1750–2000*, edited by Hugh McLeod and Werner Ustorf, 184–200. Cambridge: Cambridge University Press, 2003.

Holthaus, Stephan. *Die Evangelikalen, Fakten und Perspektiven.* Lahr: Verlag der St-Johannes-Druckerei, 2007.

– *Fundamentalismus in Deutschland: der Kampf um die Bibel in Protestantismus des 19. und 20 Jahrhunderts.* Bonn: Verlag für Kultur und Wissenschaft, 1993.

Honeycutt, Dwight. "Contextualization: A Valuable Missiological Concept." *Theological Educator* 36 (Fall 1987): 9–15.

Hönicke, Michaela. "'Know Your Enemy': American Wartime Images of Germany, 1942–1943." In *Enemy Images in American History*, edited by Tagnihild Fiebig-von Hase and Ursula Lehmkuhl, 231–80. Oxford: Berghan Books, 1997.

Hughey, J.H. *Baptist Partnership in Europe.* Nashville, TN: Broadman, 1982.

– "The Baptist Theological Seminary of Rüschlikon: Retrospect and Prospect." *[Baptist] Quarterly Review* 24 (April–June 1963): 1–11.

– *Europe: A Missionfield?* Nashville, TN: Convention, 1972.

Hühne, Werner. *A Man to Be Reckoned With: The Story of Reinold von Thadden Tiegriff.* London: SCM, 1962.

Hutchison, William R. "Americans in World Mission: Revision and Realignment." In *Altered Landscapes: Christianity in America, 1935–1985*, edited by David W. Lotz, Donald Shriver Jr, and John F. Wilson, 155–70. Grand Rapids, MI: William B. Eerdmans, 1989.

- *Errand to the World: American Protestant Thought and Foreign Missions*. Chicago: University of Chicago Press, 1987.
- *The Modernist Impulse in American Protestantism*. Cambridge, MA: Harvard University Press, 1976.
- "Protestantism as Establishment." In *Between the Times: The Travail of the Protestant Establishment in America, 1900–1960*, edited by William R. Hutchison, 3–20. New York: Cambridge University Press, 1989.

Inboden, William. *Religion and American Foreign Policy, 1945–1960: The Soul of Containment*. Cambridge: Cambridge University Press, 2008.

Iriye, Akira. "Culture and Power: International Relations as Intercultural Relations." *Diplomatic History* 3 (April 1979): 115–28.
- "The Transnational Turn." *Diplomatic History* 31 (June 2007): 373–6.

Iriye, Akira, and Pierrre-Yves Saunier, eds. *The Palgrave Dictionary of Transnational History*. New York: Palgrave MacMillan, 2009.

Janz, Ken. *Rebell in gottes Hand*. Winterthur, Switzerland: Schliefe Verlag, 2003.

Janz, Leo. *The Janz Team Story*. Beaver Lodge, AB: Horizon Books, 1977.

Jarausch, Konrad H. *After Hitler: Recivilizing Germans, 1945–1995*. Translated by Brandon Hunziker. Oxford: Oxford University Press, 2006.

Jenkins, Philip. *God's Continent: Christianity, Islam and Europe's Religious Crisis*. New York: Oxford University Press, 2007.
- *The Next Christendom: The Coming of Global Christianity*. New York: Oxford University Press, 2003.

Jewett, Robert, and John Shelton Lawrence. *Captain America and the Crusade against Evil: The Dilemma of Zealous Nationalism*. Grand Rapids, MI: William B. Eerdmans, 2003.

Johnson, Torrey, and Robert Cook. *Reaching Youth for Christ*. Chicago: Moody, 1944.

Jones, Arthur C. *Wade in the Water: The Wisdom of the Spirituals*. Maryknoll, NY: Orbis Books, 1993.

Jones, Keith G. "The International Baptist Theological Seminary of the European Baptist Federation." *American Baptist Quarterly* 18 (June 1999): 191–200.

Jongeneel, Jan A.B. "The Mission of Migrant Churches in Europe." *Missiology: An International Review* 31 (January 2003): 29–33.

Jung, Friedhelm. "American Evangelicals in Germany: Their Contribution to Church Planting and Theological Education." *Southwestern Journal of Theology* 47 (Fall 2004): 13–24.
- *Die deutsche Evangelikale Bewegung: Grundlinien ihrer Geschichte und Theologie*. Frankfurt a.R.: Peter Lang, 1992.
- *Was ist Evangelikal?* Dillenburg: Christliche Verlagsgesellschaft, 2007.

Kauffman J. Howard, and Leo Driedger. *The Mennonite Mosaic*. Scottdale, PA: Herald, 1991.

Keller, Adolf. *Christian Europe Today*. London: Epworth, 1942.
- *Religion and the European Mind*. London: Lutterworth, 1933.

Keller, Philip W. *Expendable*. Three Hills, AB: Prairie, 1966.

Kennedy, Robert L. "Best Intentions: Contacts between German Pietists and Anglo-American Evangelicals, 1945–1954." PhD diss., University of Aberdeen, 1990.

Kerkofs, Jan. "How Religious Is Europe?" In *The New Europe: A Challenge for Christians*, edited by Norbert Greinacher and Norbert Mette, 75–84. London: SCM, 1992.

Klassen, John. "Mennonites in Russia and Their Migrations." In *Testing Faith and Tradition: A Global Mennonite History – Europe*, edited by John A. Lapp and C. Arnold Snyder, 181–232. Kitchener, ON: Pandora, 2006.

Klimke, Martin. *The Other Alliance: Student Protest in West Germany and the United States in the Global Sixties*. Princeton: Princeton University Press, 2010.

Knappen, Marshall. *And Call It Peace*. Chicago: University of Chicago Press, 1947.

Koop, Allen V. *American Evangelical Missionaries in France, 1945–1975*. Lanham, MD: University Press of America, 1986.

Kraska, Eckhard. "Es begann mit Musik, die Geschichte des Janz Teams 1954–2004," *50 Jahre Janz Team, Janz Team Jubiläums CD, 2004*. Kandern, Germany: Janz Team, 2004.

Krass, Alfred C. *Evangelizing Neopagan North America*. Scottdale, PA: Herald, 1982.

Kreider, Alan. "West Europe in Missional Perspective: Themes from Mennonite Mission 1950–2004." In *Evangelical, Ecumenical and Anabaptist Missiologies in Conversation: Essays in Honor of Wilbert R. Shenk*, edited by James R. Krabill, Walter Sawatsky, and Charles Van Engen, 206–15. New York: Orbis Books, 2006.

Kreider, Robert S. *Looking Backwards into the Future*. Newton, KS: Mennonite, 1998.

– *My Early Years: An Autobiography*. Kitchener, ON: Pandora, 2002.

Kreider, Robert S., and Rachel Waltner Goossen. *Hungry, Thirsty, a Stranger: The MCC Experience*. Scottsdale, PA: Herald, 1988.

Kurlansky, Mark. *1968: The Year That Rocked the World*. New York: Random House, 2005.

Kuzmic, Peter. "Europe." In *Toward the Twenty-First Century in Christian Mission: Essays in Honor of Gerald H. Anderson*, edited by James M. Phillips and Robert T. Coote, 148–63. Grand Rapids, MI: William B. Eerdmans, 1993.

Lammersdorf, Raimund. "The Question of Guilt, 1945–47: German and American Answers." Paper presented at the German Historical Institute Conference, Washington, DC, 25–7 March 1999.

Lapp, John A. "The Peace Mission of the Mennonite Central Committee." *Mennonite Quarterly Review* 44 (July 1970): 281–97.

Larson, Mel. *Youth for Christ: Twentieth-Century Wonder*. Grand Rapids, MI: Zondervan, 1947.

Laubach, Fritz. *Aufbruch der Evangelikalen*. Wuppertal: Brockhaus Verlag, 1972.

"Lausanne Covenant: International Congress on World Evangelization, Lausanne, 1974." In *The Ecumenical Movement: An Anthology of Key Texts and Voices*, edited by Michael Kinnamon and Brian E. Cope, 358–63. Geneva: World Council of Churches, 1997.

Lehmann, Hartmut. "The Christianization of America and the Dechristianization of Europe in the 19th and 20th Centuries." *Kirchliche Zeitgeschichte* 11 (1998): 8–20.

Lewis, Walter O. "The Importance of Europe in the World Picture." In *Eighth Baptist World Congress, Cleveland, Ohio, July 22–27, 1950, Official Report*, 106–14. Philadelphia: Baptist World Alliance, 1950.

Lilje, Hans. *Christianity in a Divided Europe ... The Burge Memorial Lecture Delivered at Westminster House, 1961*. London: np, 1962.

– *In the Valley of the Shadow*. Translated by Olive Wyon. London: SCM, 1950.

Lindsell, Harold. *Park Street Prophet: A Life of Harold John Ockenga*. Wheaton, IL, 1951.

Lissner, Jørgen. *The Politics of Altruism: A Study of the Political Behavior of Voluntary Development Agencies*. Geneva: Lutheran World Federation, 1977.

Lohse, Eduard. *Erneuern und Bewahren: Evangelische Kirche 1970–1990*. Göttingen: Vandenhoeck & Ruprecht, 1993.

Lützenbürger, Hanni. *... aber Gottes Wort ist nicht gebunden: Evangeliums-Rundfunk Auftrag und Dienst*. Wetzlar: ERF Verlag, 1977.

Maase, Kaspar. "From Nightmare to Model?" In *Americanization and Anti-Americanism: The German Encounter with American Culture after 1945*, edited by Alexander Stephan, 78–106. New York: Berghahn Books, 2005.

Mackie, Robert C. "Inter-Church Aid in Europe: End or Beginning?" *Ecumenical Review* 2 (June 1950): 183–7.

Mai, Gunther. "Germany and the Integration of Europe." In *American Policy and the Reconstruction of West Germany, 1945–1955*, edited by Jeffry M. Diefendorf, John Frohn, and Hermann-Josef Rupieper, 85–109. Cambridge: Cambridge University Press, 1993.

Markovits, Andrei S. "On Anti-Americanism in West Germany." *New German Critique* 34 (Winter 1985): 3–27.

– *Uncouth Nation: Why Europe Dislikes America*. Princeton: Princeton University Press, 2007.

Markovits, Andrei S., and Lars Rensman. "Anti-Americanism in Germany." In *Anti-Americanism: History, Causes, Themes*, edited by Brendon O' Connor, 155–72. Oxford: Greenwood World Publishing, 2007.

Marquardt, Horst. *Meine Geschichte mit dem Evangeliums-Rundfunk: Warten-Wunder-Wellen*. Holzgerlingen: Hänssler Verlag, 2002.

Marrus, Michael. *The Unwanted: European Refugees in the Twentieth Century*. New York: Oxford University Press, 1985.

Marsden, George M. "The Evangelical Denomination." In *Evangelicalism in Modern America*, edited by George Marsden, vii–xix. Grand Rapids, MI: William B. Eerdmans, 1984.

– "From Fundamentalism to Evangelicalism: A Historical analysis." In *The Evangelicals: What They Believe, Who They Are, Where They Are Changing*, rev. ed., edited by David F. Wells and John D. Woodbridge, 142–62. Grand Rapids, MI: Baker House, 1977.

– *Fundamentalism and American Culture: The Shaping of Twentieth-Century Evangelicalism 1870–1925*. New York: Oxford University Press, 1980.

– *Reforming Fundamentalism: Fuller Seminary and the New Evangelicalism*. Grand Rapids, MI: William B. Eerdmans, 1987.

– *Understanding Fundamentalism and Evangelicalism*. Grand Rapids, MI: William B. Eerdmans, 1991.

Martin, David. *On Secularization: Towards a Revised General Theory*. Aldershot, UK: Ashgate Publishing, 2005.

Martin, William. *A Prophet with Honor: The Billy Graham Story*. New York: William Morrow, 1991.

Marty, Martin E. "Peace and Pluralism: *The Century* 1946–1952." In *A Century of the Century*, edited by Linda-Marie Delloff, Martin E. Marty, Dean Peerman, and James M. Wall, 73–85. Grand Rapids, MI: William B. Eerdmans, 1984.

– *Righteous Empire*. New York: Dial, 1970.

McAlister, Jack. *Europe: The Heart of the World*. Np: World Literature Crusade, 1961.

McBeth, H. Leon. *The Baptist Heritage: Four Centuries of Baptist Witness*. Nashville, TN: Broadman and Holman, 1987.

McClaskey, Beryl R. *The History of US Policy and Program in the Field of Religious Affairs under the Office of the U. High Commissioner for Germany*. Np: Historical Division, Office of the Executive Secretary, Office of the US High Commissioner for Germany, 1951.

McDougall, Walter A. *Promised Land, Crusader State: The American Encounter with the World since 1776*. Boston: Houghton Mifflin, 1997.

McLeod, Hugh. "The Crisis of Christianity in the West." In *The Cambridge History of Christianity*. Vol. 9, *World Christianities c. 1914–c. 2000*, edited by Hugh McLeod, 323–47. Cambridge: Cambridge University Press, 2006.

– *Religion and the People of Western Europe, 1789–1989*. Oxford: Oxford University Press, 1997.

– "The Religious Crisis of the 1960s." *Journal of Modern European History* 3 (September 2005): 205–29.

– *The Religious Crisis of the 1960s*. Oxford: Oxford University Press, 2007.

McSweeney, Edward O.P. *Amerikanische Wohlfartshilfe für Deutschland*. Freiburg: Caritasverlag, 1950.

Mead, Walter Russell. *Special Providence: American Foreign Policy and How It Changed the World*. New York: A. Knopf, 2002.

Merrill, Karen R. *The Oil Crisis of 1973–1974: A Brief History with Documents*. New York: Bedford St Martins, 2007.

Merritt, John W. *Betrayal: The Hostile Takeover of the Southern Baptist Convention and a Missionary's Fight for Freedom in Christ.* Asheville, NC: R. Brent, 2005.

Miller, Lawrence McK. *Witness for Humanity: A Biography of Clarence E. Pickett.* Wallingford, PA: Pendle Hill Publications, 1999.

Moennich, Martha L. *Europe behind the Iron Curtain.* Grand Rapids, MI: Zondervan, 1948.

Mooneyham, W. Stanley. "Introduction." In *One Race, One Gospel, One Task,* ed. Carl F.H. Henry and W. Stanley Mooneyham, 3–4. Minneapolis, MN: Word Books, 1967.

Murray, Geoffrey. "Joint Service as an Instrument of Renewal." In *The Ecumenical Advance: A History of the Ecumenical Movement.* Vol. 2, *1948–1968,* edited by Harold E. Fey, 199–232. London: SPCK, 1970.

Nation, Mark Thiessen. *John Howard Yoder: Mennonite Patience, Evangelical Witness, Catholic Convictions.* Grand Rapids, MI: William B. Eerdmans, 2006.

Nazir-Ali, Michael. *From Everywhere to Everywhere: A Worldview of Christian Mission.* New York: Harper Collins, 1990.

Newbigin, Lesslie. "Mission in the 1980s." *Occasional Bulletin of Missionary Research* 4 (October 1980): 154.

– "Mission to Six Continents." In *The Ecumenical Advance: A History of the Ecumenical Movement.* Vol. 2, *1948–1968,* edited by Harold E. Fey, 171–98. London: SPCK, 1970.

The New Delhi Report: The Third Assembly of the World Council of Churches 1961. New York: Association, 1961.

Newman, Bernard. *The Three Germanies.* London: Robert Hale, 1957.

Ninkovich, Frank. *Germany and the United States: The Transformation of the German Question since 1945.* Boston: Twayne Publishers, 1988.

Nolan, Mary. "Anti-Americanism and Americanization in Germany." *Politics and Society* 23 (March 2005): 88–122.

– "Anti-Americanization in Germany. " In *Anti-Americanism,* edited by Andrew Ross and Kristin Ross, 125–43. New York: New York University Press, 2004.

Noll, Mark A. *The New Shape of World Christianity: How American Experience Reflects Global Faith.* Downers Grove, IL: InterVarsity Press, 2009.

– *The Rise of Evangelicalism: The Age of Edwards, Whitefield and the Wesleys.* Downers Grove, IL: InterVarsity Press, 2003.

Ohlemacher, Jörg. "Gemeinschaftschristentum in Deutschland im 19. und 20. Jahrhundert." In *Der Pietismus im neunzehnten und zwanzigsten Jahrhundert, Band 3,* edited by Ulrich Gäbler, 371–92. Göttingen: Vandenhoeck & Ruprecht, 2000.

Padilla, Rene. "The Contextualization of the Gospel." In *Readings in Dynamic Indigeneity,* edited by Charles H. Kraft and Tom N. Wisley, 286–312. Pasadena, CA: William Carey Library, 1979.

Palm, Dirk. *"Wir sind doch Brüder!" Der evangelische Kirchentag und die deutsche Frage.* Göttingen: Vandenhoeck & Ruprecht, 2002.

Pannabecker, Samuel Floyd. *Open Doors: A History of the General Conference Mennonite Church.* Newton, KS: Faith and Life, 1975.

Parzany, Ulrich. *Im Einsatz für Jesus. Programm und Praxis des Pfarrers Wilhelm Busch.* Neukirchen: Aussaat Verlag, 2001.

Patterson, James Alan. "The Loss of a Protestant Missionary Consensus: Foreign Missions and the Fundamentalist Modernist Conflict." In *American Evangelicals and Foreign Missions, 1880–1980,* edited by Joel A. Carpenter and Wilbert R. Shenk, 73–91. Grand Rapids, MI: William B. Eerdmans, 1990.

Patterson, W. Morgan, and Richard V. Pierard. "Recovery from the War and Advance to Maturity." In *Baptists Together in Christ 1905–2005: A Hundred-Year History of the Baptist World Alliance,* edited by Richard V. Pierard, 100–29. Falls Church, VA: Baptist World Alliance, 2005.

Peacock, Charlie. *At the Crossroads: Inside the Past, Present and Future of Contemporary Christian Music.* Colorado Springs, CO: Shaw Books, 2004.

Pells, Richard. "Double Crossings: The Reciprocal Relationship between American and European Culture in the Twentieth Century." In *Americanization and Anti-Americanism: The German Encounter with American Culture after 1945,* edited by Alexander Stephan, 189–201. New York: Berghahn Books, 2005.

– *Not Like Us: How Europeans Have Loved, Hated, and Transformed American Culture since World War II.* New York: Basic Books, 1997.

Perrett, Geoffrey. *A Dream of Greatness: The American People 1945–1963.* New York: Coward, McCann and Geoghegan, 1979.

Pickett, Clarence E. *For More Than Bread: An Autobiographical Account of Twenty-Two Years' Work with the American Friends Service Committee.* Boston: Little, Brown, 1953.

Pierard, Richard. "The Baptist World Alliance: An Overview of Its History." *Review and Expositor* 103 (Fall 2006): 707–32.

– "Baptist World Alliance Relief Efforts in Post–Second World War Europe." *Baptist History and Heritage* 36 (Winter–Spring 2001): 1–25.

– "Billy Graham and the *Wende.*" *Reformed Journal* 40 (April 1990): 5–6.

– "Billy Graham and Vietnam: From Cold Warrior to Peacemaker." *Christian Scholar's Review* 10 (January 1980): 37–51.

– "From Evangelical Exclusivism to Ecumenical Openness: Billy Graham and Sociopolitical Issues." *Journal of Ecumenical Studies* 20 (Summer 1983): 425–46.

– "Pax Americana and the Evangelical Missionary Advance." In *American Evangelicals and Foreign Missions, 1880–1980,* edited by Joel A. Carpenter and Wilbert R. Shenk, 155–88. Grand Rapids, MI: William B. Eerdmans, 1990.

Poiger, Uta G. "American Music, Cold War Liberalism, and German Identities." In *Transactions, Transgressions and Transformations: American Culture in Western Europe and Japan,* edited by Heide Fehrenbach and Uta G. Poiger, 127–47. New York: Berghahn Books, 2000.

– *Jazz, Rock, and Rebels: Cold War Politics and American Culture in a Divided Germany.* Berkeley, CA: University of California Press, 2000.

Pollock, John. *Billy Graham: Evangelist to the New World*. New York: Harper and Row, 1979.

– *Billy Graham: The Authorized Biography*. London: Hodder and Stoughton, 1966.

– *Crusades: 20 Years with Billy Graham*. Minneapolis, MN: World Wide Publications, 1966.

Porter, Andrew. *Religion versus Empire? British Protestant Missionaries and Overseas Expansion, 1700–1914*. Manchester: Manchester University Press, 2004.

Preston, Andrew. "The Death of a Peculiar Special Relationship: Myron Taylor and the Religious Roots of America's Cold War." In *America's "Special Relationships": Foreign and Domestic Aspects of the Politics of Alliance*, edited by John Dumbrell and Axel R. Schäfer, 208–22. Oxford: Routledge, 2009.

– "Reviving Religion in the History of American Foreign Relations." In *God and the Global Order: The Power of Religion in American Foreign Policy*, edited by Jonathan Chaplin and Robert Joustra, 25–54. Waco, TX: Baylor University Press, 2010.

– *Sword of the Spirit, Shield of Faith: Religion in American War and Diplomacy*. New York: Alfred A. Knopf, 2012.

Prolingheuer, Hans. *Der ungekämpfte Kirchenkampf, 1933–1945: Das politische Versagen der Bekennenden Kirche*. Cologne: Pahl-Rugenstein, 1983.

Proudfoot, Malcolm J. *European Refugees: 1939–52: A Study in Forced Population Movement*. Evanston, IL: Northwestern University Press, 1956.

Quebedeaux, Richard. *I Found It: The Story of Bill Bright and Campus Crusade*. London: Hodder and Stoughton, 1980.

Railton, Nicholas M. "German Free Churches and the Nazi Regime." *Journal of Ecclesiastical History* 49 (January 1998): 85–139.

– *No North Sea: The Anglo-German Evangelical Network in the Middle of the Nineteenth Century*. Leiden: Brill, 2000.

Ramet, Sabrina P., and Gordana Cmkovic, eds. *Kazzm! Splat! Ploof!: The American Impact on European Popular Culture since 1945*. Oxford: Rowman and Littlefield, 2003.

Redekop, Calvin W. *The Pax Story: Service in the Name of Christ 1951–1976*. Telford, PA: Pandora, 2001.

Reed, James. *The Missionary Mind and American East Asia Policy, 1911–1915*. Cambridge, MA: Harvard University Asia Center, 1983.

Reiss, Elizabeth Clark. *The American Council of Voluntary Agencies for Foreign Service, ACVAFS: Four Monographs*. New York: American Council of Voluntary Agencies for Foreign Service, 1985.

Revival in Our Time: The Story of the Billy Graham Evangelistic Campaigns. Wheaton, IL: Van Kampen, 1950.

Richardson, Michael. *Amazing Faith: The Authorized Biography of Bill Bright*. Colorado Springs, CO: Waterbrook, 2000.

Robert, Dana L. "'The Crisis of Missions': Premillennial Mission Theory and the Origins of Independent Evangelical Missions." In *American Evangelicals and Foreign Missions, 1880–1980,* edited by Joel A. Carpenter and Wilbert R. Shenk, 29–46. Grand Rapids, MI: William B. Eerdmans, 1990.

– "The First Globalization: The Internationalization of the Protestant Missionary Movement between the World Wars." *International Bulletin of Missionary Research* 26 (April 2002): 50–66.

Roman, Edward. "A Framework for the Analysis of Nominal Christianity: A West German Case Study." In *Reflection and Projection: Missiology at the Threshold of 2001,* edited by Hans Kasdorf and Klaus Müller, 322–37. Bad Liebenzel: Verlag der Liebenzeller Mission, 1988.

Rosell, Garth M. *The Surprising Work of God: Harold Ockenga, Billy Graham and the Rebirth of Evangelicalism.* Grand Rapids, MI: Baker Academic, 2008.

Roy, Ralph Lord. *Communism and the Churches.* New York: Harcourt, Brace and World, 1960.

Ruh, Ulrich. *Religion und Kirche in der Bundesrepublik Deutschland.* Munich: Iudicium Verlag, 1990.

Rupieper, Hermann-Josef. "American Policy toward German Unification." In *American Policy and the Reconstruction of West Germany, 1945–1955,* edited by Jeffry M. Diefendorf, John Frohn, and Hermann-Josef Rupieper, 45–68. Washington, DC: German Historical Institute, 1993.

Sandford, Elias Benjamin. *Origin and History of the Federal Council of Churches of Christ in America* [microform]. Ann Arbor, MI: Microfilms International, 1916.

Sanneh, Lamin. *Disciples of All Nations: Pillars of World Christianity.* Oxford: Oxford University Press: 2008.

– *Whose Religion Is Christianity? The Gospel beyond the West.* Grand Rapids, MI: William B. Eerdmans, 2003.

Schäfer, Axel, R. "'What Marx, Lenin and Stalin Needed Was … to Be Born Again': Evangelicals and the Special Relationship between Church and State in US Cold War Foreign Policy." In *America's "Special Relationships": Foreign and Domestic Aspects of the Politics of Alliance,* edited by John Dumbrell and Axel R. Schäfer, 223–41. Oxford: Routledge, 2009.

Scharpff, Paulus. *Geschichte der Evangelisation: dreihundert Jahre Evangelisation in Deutschland, Großbritannien und USA.* Giessen: Brunnen-Verlag, 1964.

Scheerer, Reinhard. *Bekennende Christen in den evangelischen Kirchen Deutschlands 1966–1991, Geschichte und Gestalt eines konservative-evangelikalen Aufbruchs.* Frankfurt-am-Main: Haad und Herchen, 1997.

– *Kirchen für den Kalten Krieg, Grundzüge und Hintergründe der US-amerikanischen Religions und Kirchenpolitik in Nachkriegsdeutschland.* Cologne: Pahl-Rugenstein Verlag, 1986.

Schmidt, William J. *Architect of Unity: A Biography of Samuel McCrea Cavert.* New York: Friendship, 1975.

Schneider, Robert J. "Voice of Many Waters: Church Federation in the Twentieth Century." In *Between the Times: The Travail of the Protestant Establishment in America, 1900–1960*, edited by William R. Hutchison, 95–121. New York: Cambridge University Press, 1989.

Schroeter, Harald. *Kirchentag als vor-läufige der Kirche: der Kirchentag als eine besondere Gestalt des Christseins zwischen Kirche und Welt.* Stuttgart: W. Kohlhammer, 1993.

Schwarz, Fred. *You Can Trust the Communists (to Do Exactly as They Say).* Eaglewood Cliffs, NJ: Prentice Hall, 1960.

Schwartz, Thomas Alan. *America's Germany: John J. McCloy and the Federal Republic of Germany.* Cambridge, MA: Harvard University Press, 1981.

Seigel, Micol. "Beyond Compare: Comparative Method after the Transnational Turn." *Radical History Review* 91 (Winter 2005): 62–90.

Shank, David A. "A Missionary Approach to a Dechristianized Society." *Mennonite Quarterly Review* 27 (January 1954): 39–45.

Siegmund, Johann Jürgen. *Bischof Johannes Lilje, Ab zu Locum.* Göttingen: Vandenhoeck & Ruprecht, 2003.

Silk, Mark. *Spiritual Politics: Religion and America since World War II.* New York: Simon and Schuster, 1988.

Simon, Benjamin. "African Christians in the German-Speaking Diaspora of Europe." *Exchange* 31 (January 2002): 23–35.

Solberg, Richard W. *As between Brothers: The Story of Lutheran Response to World Need.* Minneapolis: Augsburg Publishing House, 1957.

– *Open Doors: The Story of Lutherans Resettling Refugees.* St Louis: Concordia Publishing House, 1992.

Sommer, Karl-Ludwig. *Humanitäre Auslandshilfe als Brücke zu atlantischer Partnerschaft: CARE, CRALOG und die Entwicklung der deutsch-amerikanischen Beziehungen nach Ende des Zweiten Weltkriegs.* Bremen: Selbstverlag des Staatsarchives Bremen, 1999.

Spalding, Elizabeth Edwards. *The First Cold Warrior: Harry Truman, Containment, and the Remaking of Liberal Internationalism.* Lexington: University of Kentucky Press, 2006.

Speier, Hans. *From the Ashes of Disgrace.* Amherst, MA: University of Massachusetts Press, 1981.

Spencer, Bill. *The Story of the German Evangelist Anton Schulte.* Bristol: Evangelism Today, 1979.

Spindler, Marc. "Europe's Neo-Paganism: A Perverse Inculturation." *International Bulletin of Missionary Research* 12 (July 1988): 8–11.

Spotts, Frederic. *The Churches and Politics in Germany.* Middletown, CT: Wesleyan University Press, 1973.

Stafford, Tim. "Historian Ahead of His Time." *Christianity Today* 51 (February 2007): 87–9.

Standifer, Leon. *Binding Up the Wounds: An American Soldier in Occupied Germany, 1945–1946*. Baton Rouge: Louisiana State University Press, 1997.

Stanley, Brian. *The Bible and the Flag: Protestant Missions and British Imperialism in the Nineteenth and Twentieth Centuries*. Leicester: Apollos, 1990.

– "The Future in the Past: Eschatological Vision in British and American Protestant Missionary History." *Tyndale Bulletin* 51 (2000): 101–20.

– "Lausanne 1974: The Challenge from the Majority World to Northern-Hemisphere Evangelicalism." *Journal of Ecclesiastical History* 64 (July 2013): 533–51.

– ed. *Missions, Nationalism and the End of Empire*. Grand Rapids, MI: William B. Eerdmans, 2003.

– *The World Missionary Conference, Edinburgh 1910*. Grand Rapids, MI: Eerdmans, 2009.

Stephan, Alexander, ed. *Americanization and Anti-Americanism: The German Encounter with American Culture after 1945*. New York: Berghahn Books, 2005.

– ed. *The Americanization of Europe: Culture, Diplomacy and Anti-Americanism after 1945*. New York: Berghahn Books, 2006.

– "A Special German Case of Cultural Americanization." In *The Americanization of Europe: Culture, Diplomacy and Anti-Americanism after 1945*, edited by Alexander Stephan, 69–88. New York: Berghahn Books, 2006.

Stolper, Gustav, *German Realities*. New York: Reynal and Hitchcock, 1948.

Strübind, Andrea. *Die unfreie Freikirche: Der Bund der Baptistengemeinden im "Dritten Reich."* Neukirchen-Vulyn: Neukirchener, 1991.

– "German Baptists and National Socialism." *Journal of European Baptist Studies* 8 (May 2008): 5–20.

Stüber, Gabrielle. *Der Kampf gegen den Hunger 1945–1950: Die Erhnärungslage in der britischen Zone Deutschlands, insbesondere in Schleswig-Holstein und Hamburg*. Neumünster: Karl Wachholtz Verlag, 1984.

– "Kanadische Deutschlandhilfe in den ersten Jahren nach dem Zweiten Weltkrieg." *Zeitschrift für Kanada-Studien* 6 (1986): 39–61.

Stupperich, Robert. *Otto Dibelius, Ein evangelischer Bischof im Umbruch der Zeiten*. Göttingen: Vandenhoeck & Ruprecht, 1989.

Symanowski, Horst. *The Christian Witness in an Industrial Society*. Translated by George H. Helm. Philadelphia: Westminster, 1964.

– "The Missionary Responsibility of the Church in Germany." *Ecumenical Review* 1 (Summer 1949): 417–23.

Taber, Charles R. "Contextualization." *Religious Studies Review* 13 (January 1987): 33–6.

Tent, James F. *Mission on the Rhine: Reeducation and Denazification in American-Occupied Germany*. Chicago: University of Chicago Press, 1982.

ter Haar, Gerrie. *African Christians in Europe*. Nairobi: Acton Publishers, 2001.

– *Halfway to Paradise: African Christians in Europe*. Cardiff: Cardiff Academic, 1998.

– "Strangers in the Promised Land: African Christians in Europe." *Exchange* 24 (February 1995): 1–31.

Thiesen, John Caldwell. *A Survey of World Missions*, rev. ed. Chicago: Moody, 1961.

Thimme, Hans. "A Receiving Church Becomes a Giving Church." In *Hope in the Desert: The Churches' United Response to Human Need, 1944–1984*, edited by Kenneth Slack, 12–29. Geneva: World Council of Churches, 1986.

Tizon, Al. *Transformation after Lausanne: Radical Evangelical Mission in Global-Local Perspective*. Oxford: Regnum Books, 2008.

Toews, John A. *A History of the Mennonite Brethren Church: Pilgrims and Pioneers*. Edited by A.J. Klassen. Fresno, CA: Board of Christian Literature, 1975.

Toews, John B. *A Pilgrimage of Faith: The Mennonite Brethren Church 1860–1990*. Winnipeg: Kindred, 1993.

Toews, Paul. *Mennonites in American Society, 1930–1970: Modernity and the Persistence of Religious Community*. Scottdale, PA: Herald, 1997.

Toulouse, Mark G. *The Transformation of John Foster Dulles: From Prophet of Realism to Priest of Nationalism*. Macon, GA: Mercer University Press, 1985.

Turner, John G. *Bill Bright and Campus Crusade for Christ: The Renewal of Evangelicalism in Postwar America*. Chapel Hill, NC: University of North Carolina Press, 2008.

Turner, Steve. *Cliff Richard: The Biography*. Oxford: Lion Hudson, 2005.

Tyrrell, Ian. "American Exceptionalism in an Age of International History." *American Historical Review* 96 (October 1991): 1031–55.

Unruh, John D. *In the Name of Christ*. Scottdale, PA: Herald, 1952.

Van Engen, Charles E. "A Broadening Vision: Forty Years of Evangelical Theology of Mission, 1946–1986." In *American Evangelicals and Foreign Missions, 1880–1980*, edited by Joel A. Carpenter and Wilbert R. Shenk, 203–34. Grand Rapids, MI: William B. Eerdmans, 1990.

Visser 't Hooft, W.A. "Evangelism among Europe's Neopagans." *International Review of Mission* 66 (October 1977): 349–60.

– ed. *The First Assembly of the World Council of Churches held at Amsterdam, August 22nd to September 4th, 1948*. London: SCM, 1949.

– *Memoirs*. London: SCM, 1973.

– *The Ten Formative Years, 1938–1948: Report on the Activities of the World Council of Churches during Its Period of Formation*. Geneva: World Council of Churches, 1948.

Voigt, Karl Heinz. *Die Evangelische Allianz als ökumenische Bewegung*. Stuttgart: Christliches Verlagshaus, 1990.

– *Freikirchen in Deutschland (19. und 20. Jahrhundert)*. Vol. III/6 in Kirchengeschichte in Einzeldarstellungen. Leipzig: Evangelische Verlagsanstalt, 2004.

von Borries, Achim. *Quiet Helpers: Quaker Service in Postwar Germany*. Philadelphia: American Friends Service Committee, 2000.

Wacker, Grant. "A Plural World: The Protestant Awakening to World Religions." In *Between the Times: The Travail of the Protestant Establishment in America,*

1900–1960, edited by William R. Hutchison, 253–77. Cambridge: Cambridge University Press, 1989.

Wagner, William Lyle. "Der Fall Rüschlikon: Hintergründe zur Kontroverse zwischen den Südlichen Baptisten und Teilen des europäischen Baptismus." *Bibel und Gemeinde* 105 (April–June 2005): 55–71.

– *North American Protestant Missionaries in Western Europe: A Critical Appraisal.* Bonn: Verlag für Kultur and Wissenschaft, 1993.

Wagnleitner, Reinhold. *Coca-colonisation und Kalter Krieg: Die Kulturemission der USA in Österreich nach dem Zweiten Weltkrieg.* Wein: Verlag für Gesellschaftskritik, 1991.

Währisch-Oblau, Claudia. "From Reverse Mission to Common Mission ... We Hope." *International Review of Mission* 86 (July 2000): 467–83.

Waldorf, Friedmann. "Missionarische Bemühungen in Kontext gesellschaftlicher Veränderungen in Deutschland von 1945 bis 2000. Teil 1: Unkehr und Neubeginn (1945–1968)." *Evangelikale Missiologie* 23 (1 Quartal 2007): 2–15.

– "Missionarische Bemühungen in Kontext gesellschaftlicher Veränderungen in Deutschland von 1945 bis 2000. Teil 2: Von der 68er Revolution bis zum vereinten Deutschland." *Evangelikale Missiologie* 23 (2 Quartal 2007): 38–53.

Walls, Andrew F. "The Domestic Importance of the Nineteenth-Century Medical Missionary." In *The Missionary Movement in Christian History*, edited by Andrew F. Walls, 211–20. Maryknoll, NY: Orbis Books, 1996.

– "The Missionary Dimension in the History of the Missionary Movement." In *American Evangelicals and Foreign Missions, 1880–1980*, edited by Joel A. Carpenter and Wilbert R. Shenk, 1–25. Grand Rapids, MI: William B. Eerdmans, 1990.

Ward, W.R. *The Protestant Evangelical Awakening.* Cambridge: Cambridge University Press, 1992.

Warren, Heather A. *Theologians of a New World Order: Reinhold Niebuhr and the Christian Realists, 1920–1948.* New York: Oxford University Press, 1997.

Weber, Timothy P. *Living in the Shadow of the Second Coming: American Premillennialism, 1875–1982.* Grand Rapids, MI: Academie Books, 1983.

Weckerling, Rudolf. "Germany: A Mission Field." *World Dominion* 27 (November–December 1949): 325–30.

Welty, Joel Carl. *The Hunger Year in the French Zone of Divided Germany, 1946–1947.* Beloit, WI: Beloit College, 1993.

Willet, Ralph. *The Americanization of Germany, 1945–1949.* New York: Routledge, 1989.

Wilson, Bryan. "American Religious Sects in Europe." In *Superculture: American Popular Culture and Europe*, edited by C.W.E. Bigsby, 107–22. London: Paul Elek, 1975.

Wilson, Roger W. *Quaker Relief: An Account of the Relief Work of the Society of Friends, 1940–1948.* London: George-Allen and Unwin, 1952.

Wirt, Sherwood Eliot. *Billy: A Personal Look at Billy Graham, the World's Best-Loved Evangelist*. Wheaton, IL: Crossway Books, 1997.

Wischnath, Johannes Michael. *Kirche in Aktion: das Evangelische Hilfswerk 1945–1957 und sein Verhältnis zu Kirche und Innere Mission*. Göttingen: Vandenhoeck & Ruprecht, 1986.

Wolf-Phillips, Leslie. "Why 'Third World'?: Origin, Definition and Usage." *Third World Quarterly* 9 (October 1987): 1311–27.

Woodbridge, George. *UNRAA: The History of the United Nations Relief and Rehabilitation Administration*. New York: Columbia University Press, 1950.

Woodfin, Carol Gale. "Rüschlikon: The Establishment and Early Development of an International Baptist Theological Seminary in the Heart of Post-war Europe." MA thesis, Wake Forest University, 1987.

Wright, Robert. *A World Mission: Canadian Protestantism and the Quest for a New International Order, 1918–1939*. Montreal and Kingston: McGill-Queen's University Press, 1991.

Yoder, John Howard. *Discipleship as Political Responsibility*, rev. ed. Translated by Timothy J. Geddert. Scottdale, PA: Herald, 2003.

– *The Politics of Jesus: Vicit agnus noster*. Grand Rapids, MI: William B. Eerdmans, 1972.

– "The Theological Basis of the Christian Witness to the State." In *Peace on Earth*, edited by Donald F. Durnbaugh, 136–45. Elgin, IL: Brethren, 1978.

Zehrer, Karl. *Evangelische Freikirchen und das "Dritte Reich."* Göttingen: Vandenhoeck & Ruprecht, 1986.

Ziemke, Earl F. "The Formulation and Initial Implementation of US Occupation Policy in Germany." In *US Occupation in Europe after World War II*, edited by Hans A. Schmitt, 27–44. Lawrence, KS: Regents, 1978.

Zink, Harold. *The United States in Germany, 1944–1954*. New York: Van Nostrand, 1957.

INDEX

Crawford, Percy, 107
crusades: Billy Graham's, 134, 141,
143–5, 149, 155, 163–4, 166–8, 170,
174, 209, 230n62, 257n13, 259n48,
263n128; Janz Team Ministries,
104–5, 123, 126–7, 131, 133–6, 138, 167,
182, 209–10, 215, 230n60, 253n106.
See also Feldzüge
Czechoslovakia, 93

Das Missionarisches Jahr, 196
decartelization, 37–8
Decision Magazine, 169, 195. *See also*
Entscheidung
demilitarization, 37–8
democracy, 4, 10–11, 22, 24, 33–4,
36–41, 44–6, 58, 61, 88, 90–4,
97–102, 104–6, 111, 114–15, 118–19,
122, 140, 142–3, 187, 213–15, 221,
226n30, 239n7
democratization, 38, 110
denazification, 33, 37–8
Department of Reconstruction and
Inter-Church Aid, 33, 35, 53, 56,
205–6, 221
Der Menschenfischer, 133, 136, 138. *See*
also Ruf
Deutsche Evangelishe Allianz (DEA),
16, 24, 128, 130–3, 142, 144–6, 153–4,
156–7, 159, 163–9, 171–3, 175, 181, 186,
188, 196, 209, 211, 248n2, 257n22,
262n98, 266n18
Deutsche Evangelistenkonferenz
(DEk), 127–8, 144, 154, 163–5, 253n91
Dibelius, Bishop Otto, 48, 57, 155, 162,
167, 171, 173–4, 209–10, 222, 262n111
Diezel, Willie, 115–16, 122
displaced persons (DPs), 29, 37, 80,
232n31, 241n51, 244n103
Dortmund, 145–6
Dulles, John Foster, 11, 154, 234n66
Düsseldorf, 87, 144–5, 155
Dyck, Cornelius (Cornie), 68, 219

East Germany, 93, 99, 156, 158, 189,
205, 241n51, 261n79
East Zone, 154–5, 157, 161. *See also*
Russian Zone
Educational and Religious Affairs
Branch, 7, 35, 232n28
EIRENE, 192, 199
Empie, Paul, 59
Enns, Cornie, 123–4, 127, 136
Entscheidung, 169–70, 195, 263n127. *See*
also Decision Magazine
Epp, Theodore, 138
Essen, 130–1, 133–4, 136, 145, 165, 167,
186
Eurofest, 186–7
Europe: Communist, 12, 135, 179;
democratic, 11; Eastern, 7, 28, 37, 62,
77, 81, 98, 100, 126, 160, 178, 180–1,
192; German-speaking, 17, 21, 71,
93, 105, 123, 131–2, 134, 198; postwar,
3–5, 20, 32, 84, 143; Western, 7, 9–11,
17, 64, 84, 71, 92–3, 100–2, 109, 111,
131, 126, 135, 170, 176, 177–8, 180–1,
183, 186, 189, 191–2, 214, 217, 266n13,
268n38, 269n61
European Baptist Congress, 84
European Baptist Unions, 85–6
European Mennonite Bible School
(EMBS), 72–4, 93, 198. *See also*
Bienenberg
Euro 70, 146–7, 151, 160, 171–2, 211
evangelical(s). *See* conservative
evangelical
evangelicalism, 16, 104, 134, 138, 153,
172, 177, 248n3
Evangelikaler, 13, 15–16, 24, 134, 138–40,
142, 144, 163, 171–3, 175, 181, 185–8,
193, 195–6, 201–2, 209–12
Evangelische Kirche Deutschland
(EKD), 13–16, 21–2, 33, 39–40, 42–3,
45, 48–52, 57, 61–2, 64, 78, 82, 89, 94,
99, 120, 142, 146, 149–50, 158, 161–2,
164–8, 171, 173, 176, 180, 207, 219,